T0323514

# STRATEGIC SOCIAL MEDIA AS ACTIVISM

Drawing on a range of theoretical and empirical perspectives, this volume examines the roles strategic communications play in creating social media messaging campaigns designed to engage in digital activism.

As social activism and engagement continue to rise, individuals have an opportunity to use their agency as creators and consumers to explore issues of identity, diversity, justice, and action through digital activism. This edited volume situates activism and social justice historically and draws parallels to the work of activists in today's social movements such as modern-day feminism, Black Lives Matter, #MeToo, Missing Murdered Indigenous Women, and We Are All Khaled Said. Each chapter adds an additional filter of nuance, building a complete account of mounting issues through social media movements and at the same time scaffolding the complicated nature of digital collective action.

The book will be a useful supplement to courses in public relations, journalism, social media, sociology, political science, diversity, digital activism, and mass communication at both the undergraduate and graduate level.

**Adrienne A. Wallace** is Associate Professor of Advertising and Public Relations in the School of Communications at Grand Valley State University, USA.

**Regina Luttrell** is Associate Professor of Public Relations and the Associate Dean for Research & Creative Activity in the S.I. Newhouse School of Public Communications at Syracuse University, USA.

# STRATEGIC SOCIAL MEDIA AS ACTIVISM

## Repression, Resistance, Rebellion, Reform

*Edited by*
*Adrienne A. Wallace and Regina Luttrell*

Routledge
Taylor & Francis Group

NEW YORK AND LONDON

Designed cover image: Cover art by Rafael "RC" Concepción generated with assistance from AI.

First published 2024
by Routledge
605 Third Avenue, New York, NY 10158

and by Routledge
4 Park Square, Milton Park, Abingdon, Oxon, OX14 4RN

*Routledge is an imprint of the Taylor & Francis Group, an informa business*

© 2024 selection and editorial matter, Adrienne A. Wallace and Regina Luttrell; individual chapters, the contributors

*Library of Congress Cataloging-in-Publication Data*
Library of Congress Cataloging-in-Publication Data
Names: Wallace, Adrienne A., 1976-editor. | Luttrell, Regina, 1975-editor.
Title: Strategic social media as activism: repression, resistance, rebellion, reform/edited by Adrienne A. Wallace, Regina Luttrell.
Description: New York, NY: Routledge, 2024. | Includes bibliographical references and index.
Identifiers: LCCN 2023011105 (print) | LCCN 2023011106 (ebook) | ISBN 9781032272191 (hardback) | ISBN 9781032272184 (paperback) | ISBN 9781003291855 (ebook)
Subjects: LCSH: Social media–Political aspects. | Political participation. | Social action. | Social movements.
Classification: LCC HM742 .S874 2024 (print) | LCC HM742 (ebook) | DDC 302.23/1–dc23/eng/20230413
LC record available at https://lccn.loc.gov/2023011105
LC ebook record available at https://lccn.loc.gov/2023011106

ISBN: 978-1-032-27219-1 (hbk)
ISBN: 978-1-032-27218-4 (pbk)
ISBN: 978-1-003-29185-5 (ebk)

DOI: 10.4324/9781003291855

Typeset in Sabon
by Deanta Global Publishing Services, Chennai, India

# CONTENTS

# ACKNOWLEDGMENTS

It takes so many people to make a project like this successful; to these individuals we owe the greatest appreciation.

For this book to become a reality, our editor, Felisa Salvago-Keyes, had to believe in our underlying vision. We are deeply grateful that she saw the book through to its publication at Routledge. Sean Daly, our editorial assistant, we are grateful for all of your expertise, insights, and support throughout the project.

We set out to recruit the "dream team" of advocacy, and we think we did it. This book would not have come to life without our contributors. Your expertise, insights, and hard work have been invaluable in helping to make the book a success. Your passion and dedication to the subject matter have shone through in your writing, and we have no doubt that your contributions will be of great and lasting value to readers.

We would like to express our sincere appreciation to Rafael "RC" Concepción for creating the image you see on the cover of this book. We are eternally thankful to you for the time and effort you put into this project. We are most grateful for your creative talent. The finished product is simply stunning. We couldn't have asked for a better illustration of the contents held within the pages of this book.

A very special shout out to Ellizabeth Wilson, Allison Schuster, Claire Zoller, Mia Angioletti, Jacob Laros, Allison DeYoung, and Phoebe Bogdanoff – we are deeply grateful for your contributions to this book. This project should be a permanent reminder that you never know how something is going to turn out. We go down one path, yet life throws us a curveball. Your essays became something even bigger, leaving an everlasting impact.

To Adrienne from Gina: we've worked on countless projects together. This book was special, though. It is a testament to our partnership, an enduring legacy of our work together, and the embodiment of our friendship. You are an inspiration to me, and I am honored each time you agree to collaborate with me on one of my many ideas.

To Gina from Adrienne: when I transitioned from 20+ years of firm life to the academy, the silence in the solitary research work was deafening. I'm a classic collaborator and I'm so glad that we formed this "accidental" partnership which has borne much fruit and fun. You're a great mentor, advocate, and friend who works hard to lift up others to make sure we all succeed together.

# THE EDITOR TEAM

**Adrienne A. Wallace** is Associate Professor of Advertising and Public Relations in the School of Communications at Grand Valley State University (GVSU), Allendale, Michigan, USA. Adrienne has a passion for student-to-professional development, and as such, she advises the award-winning student-run PR firm GrandPR and the Public Relations Student Society of America chapter at GVSU.

Adrienne is an award-winning author and prolific conference presenter. She co-authored *Digital Strategies: Data-Driven Public Relations, Marketing and Advertising* and *Social Media & Society: An Introduction to the Mass Media Landscape.* You can find her articles in *Journalism & Mass Communication Educator, Teaching Journalism & Mass Communication,* the *Journal of Public Relations Education, Communication Center Journal, Communication Teacher,* as well as chapters in books like *Democracy in the Disinformation Age, Social Media Influencers and the Changing Landscape of Brand Communication, The Routledge Companion for Public Relations, The Emerging Media Handbook: Theoretical and Applied Trends in Social Media and CMC,* and *Cases in Public Relations Strategy,* among others.

Adrienne received her Ph.D. in Public Administration with a focus on Public Affairs and Public Policy from Western Michigan University, Kalamazoo, USA, where she focused on the intersection of public relations, participation, and lobbying on the creation/implementation of public policy in the United States.

**Regina Luttrell** is Associate Dean, Research & Creative Activity and Associate Professor of Public Relations at the S.I. Newhouse School of Public Communications at Syracuse University, New York State. Recognized as an innovative educator, Regina is a distinguished scholar and an experienced academic leader with a track record of supporting cross-departmental and interdisciplinary collaboration, leading complex research projects, and advocating for faculty in multiple capacities. In addition to her successes in securing external funding for research initiatives, Regina has also contributed broadly within her area of scholarship, authoring more than a dozen books, publishing in academic and professional journals, and presenting at domestic and international conferences. Researching and teaching through a feminist pedagogical lens, Regina's work focuses on public relations, artificial intelligence, mis/disinformation, a multi-generational workforce, social and digital activism, and the intersection of social media with society.

Some of her most recent books include: *Wonder Woman: Warrior, Disrupter, Feminist Icon, GenZ: The Superhero Generation, Social Media & Society: An Introduction to Mass the Mass Media Landscape, Social Media: How to Engage, Share, and Connect, Digital Strategies: Data-Driven Public Relations, Marketing and Advertising, The Millennial Mindset: Unraveling Fact from Fiction, Public Relations Campaigns: An Integrated Approach, Democracy in the Disinformation Age: Influence and Activism in American Politics,* and *The Emerald Handbook of Computer-Mediated Communication and Social Media.*

# CONTRIBUTORS

**Yewande O. Addie, Ph.D.** received her Ph.D. in Mass Communications from the College of Journalism and Communications at the University of Florida (UF) in Gainesville in 2022, her master's in Public Health from UF's College of Public Health and Health Professions in 2019, and a master's degree in Liberal Studies History from Clayton State University, Morrow, Georgia. Yewande is a proud Historically Black College and University graduate of Florida A&M University in Tallahassee and a two-time Fulbright scholar. Her research interests revolve around identity and culture in health messaging, arts and health, narrative storytelling interventions, and mediated representations of Africa and the Black diaspora.

**Mia Angioletti** is a recent graduate of the S.I. Newhouse School of Public Communications at Syracuse University, New York State, where she completed her B.Sc. in Public Relations with a minor in Psychology. Her interest in public relations and psychology stems from a goal of understanding and communicating with different audiences. She plans to move to New York City to work in the public relations space.

**Phoebe L. Bogdanoff,** a New Jersey native, is a recent graduate of Syracuse University, New York State, USA with a B.S. in Public Relations and Ethics and a minor in Native American and Indigenous Studies. Selected as a Newhouse Scholar, Phoebe's dedication to excellence allowed her to graduate summa cum laude and to secure competitive internships at an entertainment PR firm, The Oriel Co., and Good Morning America/ABC News during her college career. Phoebe works to feature and uplift the voices of activists and historically oppressed communities by prioritizing diversity, equity, and inclusion efforts within the entertainment industry.

**Daniel Bunson** attended Davidson College, North Carolina, USA, where he was a Communication Studies major and Data Science minor. At Davidson, he combined his interest in sports with his passion for social change in his thesis on athlete activism. After graduating, he attended Columbia University, New York, USA, completing a master's degree in Sports Management. Daniel currently resides in New York City.

**Li Chen** explored research methods from qualitative to quantitative to computational data analytics while completing her doctoral degree in Mass Communications at Syracuse University, New York State, USA within the S.I. Newhouse School of Public Communications. Her dissertation employed social network analysis and social media research methods to investigate the associations between celebrity culture, networked media, and social movements. Her teaching and research interests include social media data analytics, media and diversity, and popular communication. She is an Assistant Professor of Social Media and Data Analytics at Weber State University, Ogden, Utah, USA.

**Mariana Crespo** is a self-proclaimed third culture kid, having moved all over Latin America. Mariana currently works at the firm Anomaly in New York as an Associate Strategist. Prior to Anomaly, she was at Davidson College, North Carolina, USA, where she studied Sociology and Gender and Sexuality and focused her honors thesis on the intersections of brand activism and social movements. Fascinated by social structures, Mariana is passionate about advertising's role in uplifting consumers and contributing to social good.

**Allison De Young** is a recent graduate from Syracuse University, New York State, USA, who majored in Public Relations in the S.I. Newhouse School of Public Communications and Sociology in the Maxwell School of Citizenship and Public Affairs. After having the absolute pleasure of experiencing Syracuse winters for four years, Allison hopes to someday move back close to where she grew up in sunny Long Beach, California, USA. Upon graduating, Allison plans on working professionally in the public relations industry in an agency setting.

**LaShonda L. Eaddy** is a crisis history expert investigating its impacts on current crises and exploring historical and contemporary crisis parallels at Pennsylvania State University, University Park, Texas, USA. A self-proclaimed "practitioner scholar," she has zeal for research and practice and is accredited in public relations; formerly practicing in healthcare. She was a Dallas Public Relations Society of America 40 Under 40 2021 Honoree.

**Candice L. Edrington** is a scholar-activist. As a mixed-methods scholar, she explores the intersections of social movements, strategic communication, and social media through a public relations lens in both her research and teaching. A passion for social justice and change fuels Candice's desire to uncover both visual and textual messaging strategies that promote action and build effective relationships. She is an assistant professor at the University of South Carolina in Columbia, USA.

**Ashley L. Fromenthal** is a Psychology master's graduate student at the University of Louisiana at Lafayette currently conducting thesis research on a combination of social and developmental psychology. Her main research interests are the subjective and perceptual factors that dictate life satisfaction for older adults, older adult caretaker resilience, sense of belonging, and mental health disorders in older adults. She plans to obtain a Ph.D. in Clinical Psychology with a specialization in geropsychology to apply her research in clinical practice with older adult clients.

**Britney Gulledge** is a doctoral candidate in the Communication, Culture and Media Studies program at Howard University, Washington, DC, USA with a focus on health communication, storytelling, and narratives.

**Leandra H. Hernandez** is an Assistant Professor in the Department of Communication at the University of Utah, Salt Lake City, USA. She enjoys teaching health communication, media studies, and gender studies topics. She utilizes qualitative and Chicana feminist lenses to explore topics such as reproductive justice and gender violence in Latina/o/x communities.

**Jacob Laros** is a graduate of Syracuse University, New York State, USA, majoring in Public Relations at the S.I. Newhouse School of Public Communications. As an emerging PR professional, Jacob has worked in both the healthcare and nonprofit industries.

**Victoria Ann Ledford** is an Assistant Professor in the School of Communication and Journalism at Auburn University, Alabama, USA. Her research focuses on stigma, health, and persuasive messages, and has been published in various outlets, including *Health Communication*,

*Communication Education*, and *The International Encyclopedia of Media Psychology*.

**Manyu Li** is an Assistant Professor in Psychology and a Jack & Gladys Theall/Board of Regents Support Fund Professor in Liberal Arts at the University of Louisiana at Lafayette, USA, conducting social and community psychology research. Manyu's main research area lies in the study of the sense of belonging and intragroup processes across various settings, such as social media activism groups, classroom climate/education, immigrants, and local communities. Manyu studies these topics using various methods from computational social science, as well as traditional qualitative and quantitative methods.

**Amanda R. Martinez** is Associate Professor of Communication Studies and Sociology and Affiliate Faculty Member in Gender & Sexuality Studies and Film & Media Studies at Davidson College, North Carolina, USA. She is the Chair of the Communication Studies department, Director of the Speaking Center in the Center for Teaching & Learning, and the founder of the Davidson Microaggressions Project at Davidson College. She studies media effects and health communication with a focus on underrepresented and minority populations, identity, intersectionality, media stereotyping, entertainment comedy, humorous communication, and inter-group communication dynamics. She is especially interested in how diverse audiences interpret and respond to stereotypes beyond media effects and how those message perceptions might impact real-world interactions.

**Ajia I. Meux** is a fourth-year doctoral candidate in the Gaylord College of Journalism and Mass Communication at the University of Oklahoma in Norman, USA, where she focuses on critical scholarship, exploring the relationship between power, communication, and race. Before transitioning into communications, Ajia worked as a trauma clinician in the Washington, DC area and with the Department of Defense. She is originally from Oakland, California, USA.

**Stevie M. Munz** is Assistant Professor at Utah Valley University in Orem, Utah, USA. As a scholar, she is invested in a line of inquiry that engages questions about how human beings understand and communicate their relational, political, and social identity experiences. Through critical ethnographic and narrative methods, her published research reflects a commitment to understanding and archiving the stories from women, LGBTQ+ students and teachers, and historically minoritized voices. Her research has been published in journals such as *Women & Language, Departures,*

*Communication Education, Basic Communication Course Annual,* and *The Western Journal of Communication,* among others.

**Candace Parrish** is Assistant Professor of Public Relations at Pennsylvania State University at University Park, USA. Candace spearheaded development of the first VR-enhanced Strategic Communication & Public Relations Online Master's Program at Sacred Heart University in Fairfield, Connecticut, USA. Additionally, she has gained national and international recognition for her research regarding visuals used in public relations and health communication.

**Chelsea Peterson-Salahuddin** is University of Michigan President's Postdoctoral Fellow/Incoming Assistant Professor at the University of Michigan School of Information in Ann Arbor, USA. Chelsea's research focuses on the culturally specific ways racially marginalized communities, most often Black women, femmes, and queer folks, engage with mass and digital communications technologies to seek information, produce knowledge, and build community, as well as ways the infrastructure of these technologies helps these communities to overcome or continue to replicate systemic barriers to equity. Chelsea received her MA and Ph.D. in Media, Technology, and Society from Northwestern University in Evanston, Illinois, USA, and her BA in Political Science and Media Studies from Vassar College in Poughkeepsie, New York, USA.

**Monica L. Ponder** is Assistant Professor of Health Communication at Howard University, Washington, DC, USA. Her scholarship offers crisis communication recommendations for public health and healthcare organizations seeking to understand, reach, and engage historically marginalized and underrepresented groups during public health emergencies. As a scholar-activist, Monica has led many successful community initiatives. In her teaching, she leverages her 14+-year career in health communication at the Centers for Disease Control and Prevention. Monica holds B.Sc. and M.Sc. degrees in Chemistry from Clark Atlanta University, Georgia, USA, an M.Sc. in Public Health in Epidemiology from Emory University in Atlanta, Georgia, USA, and a Ph.D. in Communication from Georgia State University in Atlanta, Georgia, USA.

**Arien Rozelle** is Assistant Professor at St. John College in Rochester, New York State, USA. She is interested in the intersection of communication and social change, which has led her to develop innovative courses like Public Relations and Social Movements, and Music, Persuasion and Social Change. She is the proud winner of several teaching awards from both the

Association for Education in Journalism and Mass Communication and the Public Relations Society of America Educators Academy. You can find her work in the *Journal of Public Relations Education* and *The Seneca Falls Dialogues Journal.*

**Brianna L. Sadighian** is a master's student and Graduate Research Assistant in the Psychology department at the University of Louisiana at Lafayette. She is also the Graduate Student Representative for the Southwestern Psychological Association. Brianna is interested in researching the impacts of intersectionality and individual differences on mental health in minority groups, and the effects of mindfulness interventions on negative experiences such as oppression. Currently, she is conducting her thesis research on generational differences in treatment-seeking attitudes in Asian-Americans and the moderation effects of values adherence and stigma toward others.

**Matthew Salzano** is Inclusion, Diversity, Equity, and Anti-Racism Fellow in the School of Communication and Journalism and the Program in Writing and Rhetoric at Stony Brook University, New York State, USA. His research and teaching are at the intersection(s) of rhetorical theory, digital studies, and social movements. His scholarship has appeared in *Critical Studies in Media Communication, Women's Studies in Communication,* and *Communication Teacher.*

**Allison Schuster** is a graduate from the S.I. Newhouse School of Public Communications at Syracuse University, New York State, USA, where she is pursuing a B.S. in Public Relations with a minor in English and Textual Studies. Allison has a special affinity for the nonprofit sector of public relations and aspires to use communications to benefit underprivileged and marginalized groups. Upon graduation, she intends to pursue a career with a nonprofit assisting critically and terminally ill children and their families.

**Anthony Spencer** is a graduate of the journalism program at the University of Texas in Austin, USA, and worked as a local television journalist for a decade reporting from the US and Latin America. In addition to field reporting, he also produced and anchored local newscasts and helped launch early news streaming services for stations in Texas, Oklahoma, and Alabama. Anthony received the Oklahoma Association of Broadcasters' Award for producing/anchoring the best newscast in a small market. He earned a master's degree in Media Studies from the University of North Texas in Denton, Texas, USA, and a Ph.D. in Intercultural/International Communication from the University of Oklahoma in Norman, Oklahoma, USA. Anthony is an Assistant Professor of Communication Studies in the

School of Communication at Grand Valley State University, Allendale, Michigan, USA, where he researches in the areas of journalism, social media, conflict, migration, and international communication.

**Natalie T.J. Tindall** is Isabella Cunningham Chair of Advertising and Director of the Stan Richards School of Advertising & Public Relations at the University of Texas at Austin, Texas, USA. Her research focuses on diversity in organizations, specifically the public relations function, and the situational theory of publics and intersectionality. She has authored book chapters and online publications along with peer-reviewed journal articles published in the *Journal of Public Relations Research*, *Public Relations Review*, *Public Relations Journal*, *Howard Journal of Communications*, *PRism*, and the *International Journal of Strategic Communication*.

**Elizabeth Wilson** is a graduate of the S.I. Newhouse School of Public Communications at Syracuse University, New York State, USA with a double major in Public Relations and Political Science. She has a strong interest in activism and social justice. She is originally from Bexley, Ohio, USA.

**Claire Zoller** is a graduate of the S.I. Newhouse School of Public Communications at Syracuse University, New York State, USA, where she studied Public Relations. Throughout her time in school, she was on the Dean's list consecutively and earned the Invest in Student Success Scholarship. Outside of school, she served on the executive board of the Public Relations Student Society of America, where she worked with freshmen and sophomores on the basics of PR writing. In the future, she's excited to move to New York City, USA to achieve her goal of working for a public relations agency.

# EDITORS' INTRODUCTION

**This Revolution *Shall* Be Retweeted!**

Adrienne A. Wallace and Regina Luttrell

In a world that is constantly changing, it can be easy to feel like our voices are not heard or even matter. However, history has shown us time and time again that the collective voice of the people can bring about tremendous change. *Strategic Social Media as Activism: Repression, Resistance, Rebellion, Reform* brings to light activist movements that made a difference and played a vital role in bringing about change.

Undeniably there have been movements that have defined our nation. From the Suffrage Movement to modern-day feminism, the Abolitionists to the Civil Rights, Black Lives Matter, and #MeToo movements, the role of the public has been vital to activist work and social change for centuries. Today's movements rely upon the speed and connectivity of social media. Through collective action and participatory media, people mobilize quickly, resulting in impactful action and messages that reverberate throughout the social sphere. As social activism and engagement among youth continues to rise, individuals have an opportunity to use their agency as creators and consumers to explore issues of identity, diversity, justice, and action through digital activism.

News headlines alone in the past year have shown there are many determining factors to both success and failure of social media advocacy.

As this continues to unfold in real time, some of the goals of this book are to offer faculty, students, and researchers a means to have these critical conversations in the classroom. We introduce complex issues such as:

- How exactly and why did social media become a powerful factor in social movements?
- Do social media networks have an obligation to aid in collective action?
- Does social media help or hurt advocacy efforts?
- What role does online activism play in today's misinformation war?
- Is social media activism effective?

The social and political tensions stemming from global issues such as the 2016 U.S. presidential election and then the widely debated 2020 U.S. presidential race outcome, the United Kingdom's withdrawal from the European Union, Hong Kong's pro-democracy protests, the 2018 Armenian Revolution (#MerzhirSerzhin), and the civil unrest in Belarus that began in 2020 following the presidential election have renewed interest in activism around the world. As nonprofits and activist groups work to create messaging campaigns designed to push progressive causes, the outpouring of social and digital activism has arguably never been greater. In fact, the power of social media in today's activist movements relies on strategies that promote change. A fundamental aspect of social change is the mobilization of people. This edited volume historically situates activism and social justice by drawing parallels to the work of activists in today's social movements around the globe.

## Organization of the Text

*Strategic Social Media as Activism: Repression, Resistance, Rebellion, Reform* analyzes the impact of social media and its effect on society. Citing a range of perspectives and empirical research, this comprehensive volume celebrates the many disruptions and implications social media has had on our nation. Chapters build upon one another, each adding an additional filter of nuance to the full work to build a complete look at mounting issues through various social media movements and at the same time scaffolding the complicated nature of digital collective action. To that end, this book is divided into four, and each chapter critically examines social media activism through these four distinct parts:

- **Part I: Repression**
- **Part II: Resistance**
- **Part III: Rebellion**
- **Part IV: Reform**

Repression causes rebellion. Rebellions ignite revolutions, and revolutions can transform society and the way that it functions. If resistance is daily acts of opposition to oppression and injustice, rebellion is something more extraordinary: It is embodied in specific events, protests, and moments that upset the order of daily life. One part history, one part demonstration of collective action, this book aids civil conversations in the classroom by providing critical analysis and a glimpse at the future of movements across a spectrum of values via social media. Readers need a book that illustrates the strength and determination of today's social movements fueled by digital and social media, particularly in this highly volatile and hotly charged political environment worldwide.

In addition, throughout the book we have interspersed the chapters with a series of short profiles called "Advocates for Action" that highlight the stories and accomplishments of real-life women who have made an impact on the world. These profiles showcase the diversity and strength of women from various backgrounds and movements. They serve as a source of inspiration for our readers, each having made significant contributions to society through their work, activism, and leadership. By sharing their stories and highlighting their achievements, we hope to recognize their important contributions and to encourage our readers to be inspired by their example.

The research found within the pages of this text unequivocally articulates the intimate connection between theories presented in communication and the impact of social media on digital activism. Drawing on a range of theoretical and empirical perspectives, this collection examines the multiple transformations, and the various implications social media has for social movements.

## Chapter Summaries

### Part I: Repression

#### Advocates for Action: We'wha
Mia Angioletti

#### Chapter 1: Historical Roots and Modern Movements: A Framework for Activism

#### Regina Luttrell
Activist movements have played a significant role in shaping history and pushing for social and political change. These movements have often

emerged in response to perceived injustices or inequalities and have sought to bring about change through a variety of means, including protests, civil disobedience, and grassroots organizing. The history of activist movements is long and varied and includes examples from many different countries and cultures. Some of the key themes that have emerged over time include the struggle for civil rights and social justice, the fight against oppression and discrimination, and the push for greater democracy and political representation. Many of these movements have used a variety of tactics and strategies to achieve their goals, including using the media to raise awareness of their issues and mobilize support, organizing protests and demonstrations, and engaging in acts of civil disobedience. This chapter presents the history of activist movements and the structure of collective action prior to the internet and the social sphere.

**Advocates for Action: Ida B. Wells-Barnett**
Allison Schuster

### Chapter 2: A Refusal to Accept: Oppression around the World

**Adrienne A. Wallace**
Social movements are born out of years of oppression which is sustained over a lengthy period of time. Scholars view social movements through the lens of "collective action" and/or "collective behavior" – a form of action or common or shared interest among two or more individuals. Key tactics have been applied, refined, and shared across social movements for years, including boycotts, hunger strikes, protests, riots, and marches. This chapter systematically provides the structure of collective action grounded in social change and collective behavior.

**Advocates for Action: Mary E. Britton**
Allison Schuster

### Chapter 3: Controlling, Constraining, or Preventing Protest: Social Movement Interference in the Digital Age

**Li Chen**
The repression of social activism is common, yet the ways that power is constrained are often not clearly conceptualized. Individuals, groups, or government entities such as militaries, national police, and local police attempt to control, constrain, or prevent protests. Constraints placed on social movements increasingly limit activist power. Researchers have shown three main structural constraints that limit activist movements: (1)

laws, rules, and norms that restrict activists, (2) notions of political inflation, and (3) the progressive pattern of increasing institutional thickening. This chapter investigates these three constraints which are observable across time, and together suggest growing constraints social movements.

## Part II: Resistance

**Advocates for Action: María Jesús Alvarado Rivera**
Claire Zoller and Allison Schuster

### Chapter 4: Building Momentum: Creating Change

**Arien Rozelle**

Social movements are shaped by the technology available at the time of the collective action, and thus tailor their goals, strategy, tactics, and rhetoric to the media of their time. The potential for discourse contributes to the framing of narratives and building of momentum in order to create change. Sharing of personal stories and use of photo and video contribute to building momentum and allowing broader audiences to take part in the action. Performances that are mediated via online tools can create group solidarity through engagement in risk, thereby contributing to the formation of group identities and creating change.

**Advocates for Action: Wilhelmina Kekelaokalaninui Widemann Dowsett**
Phoebe L. Bogdanoff

### Chapter 5: Early Digital Social Movements: Events, Protests, Moments

**Anthony Spencer**

The first social movements occurred through acts of civil disobedience such as protests. However, the rise of the internet ushered in abundant digital social movements. Online communities such as Facebook groups have connected people worldwide to develop a base and gain awareness of issues. Since then, digital social movements gained momentum and are now one of the most prevalent forms of social activism. This chapter examines some of the earliest movements and investigates best practices.

**Advocates for Action: Sophie Scholl**
Elizabeth Wilson

### Chapter 6: Advocacy and Action: Persuasive Strategies for Digital Activism and Influence

**Matthew Salzano and Victoria Ann Ledford**

Digital media has provided a platform for the masses to amplify their voices, and, in turn, how everyday citizens work together to carry forth the message of a movement. Drawing on a wide variety of philosophical and methodological approaches in communication (e.g., communication science, rhetoric), this chapter offers practical understandings of online strategies used to promote advocacy and outreach for social change. The chapter presents research and case studies that outline how digital activists engage in resistance across participatory social media platforms like Instagram, TikTok, and Twitter. Offering research-driven insight complemented with examples from activist practice, the chapter offers a guide for advocacy in digital spaces.

### Part III: Rebellion

**Advocates for Action: Ani Pachen**
Allison De Young and Jacob Laros

### Chapter 7: Amplified Effort: Networked Social Change, Use, Participation, Algorithms

**Manyu Li, Ashley L. Fromenthal, and Brianna L. Sadighian**

A number of political events, such as the Arab Spring in 2010 and then the protests against abortion restrictions in Texas 11 years later in 2021, illustrate how online platforms help organize large crowds. This chapter explores the terms "networked politics" and "networked social movements" which have become significant in the study of political protests and collective action in the digital age.

**Advocates for Action: Zitkála-Šá (Gertrude Simmons Bonnin)**
Allison De Young

### Chapter 8: Any Time, Any Cause, Anywhere: Hyperlocal Protests Secure Global Support and the Case of #EndSars

**Chelsea Peterson-Salahuddin**

You have seen it before. Thousands of people gather in one part of the world, yet alliance groups protest in solidarity hundreds or thousands of miles away. Mashable reported that a group of protestors in Ferguson, Missouri held up signs written in Chinese to express solidarity with fellow demonstrators overseas working toward greater democracy. The rebellion will not only be retweeted, but thousands of your closest political allies in other countries are here to help your hyperlocal protest secure global support, thus amplifying the message and the (social) media. Despite a "Facebook Reckoning" on the way, this chapter will demonstrate how social media has flattened the world so global citizens can support activism with allies worldwide.

**Advocates for Action: Aki Kurose**
Elizabeth Wilson and Allison De Young

### Chapter 9: Leaderless Rebellions: An Analysis of Digital Feminist Anti-Violence Activism

**Leandra H. Hernandez and Stevie M. Munz**
Mass protests that have broken out in the last few years in Asia, Europe, Africa, Latin America and the Middle East share many connecting characteristics, but among the most dynamic is that they have all been leaderless rebellions, without mission statements, websites, or committee meetings, but instead hatched over WhatsApp, SMS, and hashtags, not charismatic party leaders, shiny public relations campaigns, nor catchy advertising slogans. Revolutions started by mobile devices set to mobilize rallying members cannot be initiated, nor sustained, without social media. Leaderless rebellions use Facebook groups, text messages, and Twitter among the tactics that allow protests to source ideas from the base which typically derive from grievances aired via social media. The biggest risk of leaderless activism? Failure. In this chapter, the will of the people expressed through social media in leaderless rebellions will be discussed. Questions addressed range from is it possible to use digital activism to maintain a strong agenda without a leader to what happens when things become less nebulous and more formalized/organized, and do the activists follow or scatter?

### Part IV: Reform

**Advocates for Action: Marsha P. Johnson**
Elizabeth Wilson and Allison Schuster

### Chapter 10: Grounded in Community: Sustainability and Collective Actions

**Amanda R. Martinez, Daniel Bunson, and Mariana Crespo**
As more of the world becomes connected online, revolutionaries across the globe are empowered to take political action. The use of digital media

becomes more critical in developing, sustaining, and executing modern social movements. This chapter examines the role social media plays in social movement organization and formation through collective action, with a special focus on sustainability factors to demonstrate success or lack thereof in these popular social movements. This chapter offers understanding of grounded community collective action as it serves as the impetus for policy change.

**Advocates for Action: Patsy Takemoto Mink**
Phoebe L. Bogdanoff

### Chapter 11: Does Online Activism Impact Offline Impact? A Cultural Examination of Slacktivism, "Popcorn Activism," Power, and Fragility

**Monica L. Ponder, Yewande O. Addie, Ajia I. Meux, Natalie T.J. Tindall, and Britney Gulledge**

"Raising awareness" is a critical part of social activism, but does it translate to real change? Mobilizing millions via a viral hashtag might not mean what we think it does in terms of bigger picture change. Activists and activist-types can feel like they are creating action, but solidarity doesn't equal policy change in most cases. This chapter examines power dynamics of online activism and the fragility of movements when people *feel* invested, but in reality, have had little impact.

**Advocates for Action: Corazon Aquino**
Allison De Young and Elizabeth Wilson

### Chapter 12: Reclaiming Wholeness: The Future and Hope of Digital and Social Activism

**Candace Parrish, Candice L. Edrington, and LaShonda L. Eaddy**

Clues for the answers of tomorrow's hope and equality can be found in the past. This chapter examines what's next in digital and social activism including mobile and application-based activism while also examining the influence and progression of activism from historical movements in history. By providing an overview of various historical movements that preceded the internet the authors discuss how a foundation for solidarity was created that carries over into digital spaces. The chapter closes with best practices for the field as we continue to grow into digital spaces and a reflection for readers to examine their own perceptions of wholeness in activism and how they perceive the future of social and digital activism.

**Advocates for Action: Wilma Pearl Mankiller**
Allison Schuster, Claire Zoller, and Allison De Young

# PART I

# Repression

# ADVOCATES FOR ACTION

## We'wha

1849–1896
Hometown: New Mexico, USA
Movements: Indigenous people's rights
Organizations: Pueblo of Zuni

*Mia Angioletti*

We'wha was a Zuni Native American from New Mexico known for spreading national awareness of their community's rich culture. Throughout We'wha's life, they used both female and male pronouns, therefore this description will use they/them pronouns to respect both identities. Today they would be considered "two-spirit."[1]

We'wha was orphaned at a young age as their parents are thought to have been exposed to smallpox.[2] We'wha was a member of the *lhamana*, a third gender role within the Zuni community that was traditionally responsible for tasks such as pottery-making and weaving. In Zuni culture, *lhamana* identifies a male-bodied person who takes on and performs female social roles and ceremonial tasks.[3] Throughout their life, We'wha took on more masculine roles such as weaving, but was also part of more traditionally female tasks such as grinding and preparing corn meal.[4] We'wha later befriended anthropologist Matilda Coxe Stevenson, who would publish a significant amount of material on We'wha and the Zuni way of life.[5]

Through their relationship with Stevenson, We'wha began to assume responsibilities as a Zuni ambassador and met with various groups.[6]

DOI: 10.4324/9781003291855-2

Through this ambassadorship, We'wha spread knowledge about the art and culture of Native Americans, and Zuni culture specifically. They traveled to Washington, DC in 1886 as part of the Zuni delegation and met President Grover Cleveland to spread information and knowledge of their culture.[7] Newspapers in DC took interest in We'wha during their visit and often referred to them as an "Indian princess."[8] We'wha may have hoped through this visit to ensure government assistance against poachers of their lands. However, this did not come to fruition, and the relationship between Native American tribes and the US government began to falter even more.[9]

Shortly after returning from DC, We'wha was arrested along with other Zuni leaders and spent a month in jail.[10] We'wha later passed away due to heart disease in 1896 at the age of 49.[11] They left behind an incredible legacy of bravery and creativity through the spread of national awareness of the rich Zuni culture.

## Notes

1  Robinson, Margaret. "Two-spirit identity in a time of gender fluidity." *Journal of Homosexuality* (2019).
2  Brandman, Mariana. n.d. "We'wha." National Women's History Museum. Accessed November 29, 2022. https://www.womenshistory.org/education-resources/biographies/wewha.
3  Tsinhnahjinnie, Hulleah J. "We'wha, the Beloved." *Settler Colonial Studies* 2, no. 2 (2012): 165–166.
4  Ibid.
5  Armitage, Shelley. "Matilda Coxe Stevenson: Pioneering Anthropologist." (2009): 517–518.
6  Roscoe, Will. 1991. *The Zuni Man-Woman*. Albuquerque, NM: University of New Mexico Press.
7  Ibid.
8  Brandman, "We'wha."
9  Isaac, Gwyneira. "We'wha goes to Washington." *Reassembling the Collection: Ethnographic Museums and Indigenous Agency* (2013): 143–170.
10  Swan, Samuel W. 2018. "5 Two-spirit heroes who paved the way for today's native LGBTQ+ community." KQED. Accessed November 29, 2022. https://www.kqed.org/arts/13845330/5-two-spirit-heroes-who-paved-the-way-for-todays-native-lgbtq-community.
11  Brandman, "We'wha."

# 1

# HISTORICAL ROOTS AND MODERN MOVEMENTS

## A Framework for Activism

*Regina Luttrell*

## Introduction

Oppression, inequality, revolution, and protest have shaped world history for thousands of years. Countless uprisings have impacted the geopolitical landscape – with almost too many to name – Spartacus' uprising, the Protestant Reformation, the American, French, Russian, Hungarian, Haitian, and Cuban Revolutions, the Boston Tea Party, the Storming of the Bastille, Nat Turner's Rebellion, Gandhi's Salt March, Women's Suffrage, the Stonewall Riots, Vietnam War protests, Tiananmen Square, anti-Apartheid – the list goes on.[1] Each represented the desire of humankind to be free from subjugation – the need to have a voice.

Instances of each movement often emerged in response to issues of inequality, injustice, or oppression, and sought to bring about social, political, and economic change. We refer to this as **collective action**, meaning all activity of common or shared interest among two or more individuals; this distinguishes social movements from political parties and advocacy groups.[2] There are many factors that can contribute to such a transition in status. These might include change in social and political conditions, the emergence of new leaders or organizers, the presence of a critical mass of people who support the collective goals, or a particular event/issue that galvanizes people to act. A latent movement for civil rights might become active if there is a significant increase in public support for equal rights, or if a high-profile incident of discrimination occurs that inspires people to speak out and act.

DOI: 10.4324/9781003291855-3

A recent example includes the 2022 Iranian protests which were triggered by the death of Mahsa Amini, a 22-year-old woman, when she was arrested by the morality police for "improper attire." During the nationwide protests, women removed the mandatory hijab and set their headscarves on fire in the streets as a sign of protest. After months of demonstrations and more than 185 people killed,[3] Iran's Attorney General Mohammad Jafar Montazeri announced that the Islamic Republic had disbanded the "morality police."[4] These protests have reinvigorated the feminist movement in Iran.

To promote change, it is often necessary to build momentum and gain support from a broad base of supporters. This can take time, and may require a sustained effort in organizing and mobilizing individuals around a common cause. Collective action signifies the process by which a group work together to achieve a common goal or objective.[5] This can involve coordinating their efforts and resources, setting and working toward shared targets, and making decisions together. Collective action can take many forms, including social movements, protests, strikes, or other organized activity – and can be motivated by a variety of factors, such as a desire to bring about social or political change,[6] to address a common problem/issue, or to advocate for a particular cause.[7] It can also be driven by a sense of shared identity and common purpose among group members. Effective collective action requires successful communication and organization, as well as the ability to mobilize resources and support. It can be challenging to coordinate and sustain collective action, particularly if group members have conflicting goals or interests. However, when organized appropriately, collective action can lead to significant social and political change and become a powerful tool for addressing issues and achieving goals.

The structure of collective action can vary widely depending on the specific requirements and tactics of the movement in question. Some movements may be more hierarchical, with clear leaders and decision-making processes, while others may be more decentralized, and consensus-based. Some may be more militant, leveraging methodologies like violence and sabotage, while others may be more peaceful and focused on nonviolent resistance.

Additionally, the reach of the internet and social media have significantly impacted the way social movements operate and mobilize. These platforms provide new channels for communication and organization, allowing activists to connect and mobilize more easily and rapidly than ever before. However, the use of social media has also raised concerns about the potential for online harassment and the spread of misinformation. **Activism** today is often associated with civil rights, LGBTQ+ rights and equality, animal rights, disability rights, gun control, and women's rights, among many other movements. But it can be challenging to understand the depths of activism, especially due to the broadness of application. Activists often seek "to influence political outcomes by mobilizing citizens who were not political insiders to take actions that generate widespread or well-targeted public attention around specific issues."[8]

Some forms of activism involve nonviolent resistance (such as demonstrations), while others prefer persuasive or disruptive forms (such as sit-ins) to bring about justice from mainstream society. The Civil Rights movement, for example, involved various strategies and approaches, including legal action, nonviolent civil disobedience, and Black militancy.[9] It is often the case that activism seeks to create a cyclical event. The initial action draws attention, which in turn leads to further participation. This activity continues and gains more attention until the movement reaches the tipping point and another cycle begins. A pertinent example of this is the Black Lives Matter movement, whose objective is to build power to bring justice, healing, and freedom to Black people across the globe.

The very essence of activism promotes a desire to galvanize individuals toward action. The term "activism" is used to describe the activities of individuals or groups who campaign or work to achieve a political or social goal.[10] Advocacy can take many forms, such as protests, letter writing, or meetings, and can include more creative methods such as art, music, film, and craftivism (e.g., Pussyhats which were made as a protest against vulgar comments Donald Trump made about the freedom he felt to grab women's genitals, these hats designed to look like pussycat ears, were created to "take back" the word "pussy" and transform it into a wearable empowerment statement accessory in relationship to Women's marches post 2017). Throughout history, activists have always been challenged to develop and foster their own methods, tools, and practices.[11] While approaches may change over time, the goal remains the same: to influence outcomes – often political – by mobilizing citizens who are not political insiders to take actions that generate widespread or well-targeted public attention around specific issues.[12] Author Brian Martin asserts that "activism is action on behalf of a cause, action that goes beyond what is conventional or routine."[13] What he describes here happens best in a democratic society.

## Social Activism in a Democratic Society

We can trace activism and **democracy** as far back as ancient Greece. Citizens would gather in the streets to demand change from their government. Because of one simple premise – democracy – they were able to rise up and express their displeasure. An integral component of democracy is that *the people have a voice* – a value which will be revisited throughout this book. In more recent times, individuals continue to use their voices and bodies to stand up against injustice. One well-known example of an **activist** crusade is the Civil Rights movement that took place in the United States.

As a result of the internet and social media, today's activism looks different than it did in the past. Researcher Tim Jordan notes that "activism is generating the future of societies."[14] With this proclamation, London School of Economics professor and researchers Bart Cammaerts and Nico Carpentier maintain that activism represents the practice of struggling for change which is powered by reactionary tendencies and aims.[15] In *Reclaiming the Media: Communication Rights and Democratic Media Roles*, they write:

> Activism is a relatively new term, introduced in the mid-70s and referring to the ability to act and make or change history. "It reminds us that the world not only is, but is made," as Todd Gitlin wrote [in] *Letters to Young Activist*.[16] However, what is implied here is theorized at the level of social change theory, social movement theory, or notions such as resistance, advocacy, or protest. In any case, agency and the makeability of society is central to any tentative definition of activism … Activism, from this perspective, represents the practice of struggling for change and can be fueled by reactionary tendencies and aims, as well as progressive.[17]

Effective activism often requires persistence, creativity, and a willingness to take calculated risks.

Activism and **social movements** are part of the institutionalization of specific struggles or revolutions meant to change the status quo. Participants often represent those impacted by the issues and political agendas to which they are opposed.[18] Efforts for reform include concrete outcomes such as influencing change to/creating new laws, and can also apply to shifts in behavior or attitudes that ultimately affect social change. Social movements, on the other hand, as defined by Charles Tilly in 1999, are "a sustained challenge to power holders in the name of a population living under the jurisdiction of those power holders by means of repeated public displays of that population's worthiness, unity, numbers, and commitment."[19] An entity's power is determined by the connection between the goals of a movement and its relation to policies and practices within that entity.[20]

With the belief that activism is a key driving force in gaining momentum for many progressive causes, it is not always easy to identify the specific role that activism plays in shifting public attention or influencing specific outcomes. However, data show that well-designed and executed activism can often play an important role in accomplishing these objectives:[21]

- Strategic framing to shape public opinion
- Pressuring those in authority to adopt or abandon certain policies or positions
- Catalyzing dialogue, critical thinking, and creativity among citizens

In order to support the potential for positive results, democracy must allow for accountability, transparency, and inclusiveness. Though distinctive, these aims share a complementary goal – to change political outcomes by influencing the way voters think and ultimately act in the voting booth. Accountability provides the basis for understanding how well public officials or policies work over a specific period of time. Transparency offers citizens and stakeholders the opportunity to see what is happening in our democratically accountable institutions, even if they lack control. Lastly, inclusivity promotes equality and diversity, often by finding ways to broaden engagement beyond privileged populations. What separates deliberative democracies from other models of democracy is merely a triad of principles at its core. Deep democratic legitimacy comes not simply by voting, but because of reasoned debate.

## VIVE LA RÉSISTANCE!

For centuries, citizens have revolted against oppressive regimes, laws, or leadership. Some of the more well-known revolts include the French, Russian, and Iranian Revolutions:

- The French Revolution, often cited as the first modern political uprising, began with the Storming of the Bastille on July 14, 1789, marking the beginning of the end for the monarchy of King Louis XVI.[22] Over the next decade, the revolutionaries carried out a number of significant reforms, including the abolition of feudalism, the Declaration of the Rights of Man and of the Citizen, and the establishment of a constitutional monarchy.[23] However, the revolution was also marked by violent conflict and repression, as different factions fought for control and the government struggled to maintain order. Ultimately, the French Revolution led to the rise of Napoleon Bonaparte, who became Emperor of the French, and the establishment of a dictatorship.[24]

- Similarly, the Russian Revolution was a significant event in world history that had far-reaching consequences. It was complex and multifaceted, involving many different social, political, and economic factors. The Russian Revolution began in February 1917, when a series of protests and strikes in Petrograd (now St. Petersburg) led to the toppling of the Tsarist regime.[25] This was followed by the October Revolution, in which the Bolshevik Party, led by Vladimir Lenin, seized power, paving the way for the formation of a communist government.[26] The revolution brought about significant changes in Russia, including the abolition of the monarchy, the establishment of a single-party communist state, and the introduction of a planned economy.[27] It also had a major impact on the global political landscape, as it marked the first successful communist revolution and the beginning of the Cold War between the Soviet Union and the Western powers.[28]

- The Iranian Revolution of 1979 was a significant event in modern Iranian history. It marked the end of the Pahlavi dynasty, having ruled Iran since 1925, and the beginning of an Islamic Republic under the leadership of Ayatollah Ruhollah Khomeini.[29] The revolution was the result of a broad-based popular movement that had been building for many years. The Shah, Mohammad Reza Pahlavi, had faced widespread discontent due to his policies, which included modernizing the country and suppressing dissent.[30] Many Iranians felt that the Shah was out of touch with their needs and values, and that he was imposing Western ideals and ways of life on them.[31] The revolution began in 1978, with widespread protests and strikes.[32] The protesters called for the Shah to be removed and for an end to his rule – and were met with violence by the Shah's security forces, further fueling their anger. In 1979, Ayatollah Khomeini returned to Iran from exile, and his leadership played a crucial role in the success of the revolution.[33] Khomeini, who was a prominent Shia cleric, had been exiled by the Shah in 1964. He returned to a hero's welcome and quickly became the leader of the revolution. However, the revolution was not without its challenges. There was a significant amount of infighting among various factions, and the country faced economic problems and international isolation.[34] The revolutionary outcome ultimately resulted in the establishment of an Islamic Republic, which continues to be the dominant political system in Iran to this day.[35]

## Activism in Action

To gain a better understanding of how activism operates, a systematic literature review was conducted, allowing for a broad overview of common threads running through most activist activities. Unsurprisingly, a critical finding was that movements need structure to be successful. At their base foundational components, activists must be organized in order to galvanize others. The most common structure applied to social movements is the theory of change concept, which outlines the beliefs and assumptions about how a desired change happens and goals are realized.[36]

### *The Concept of Theory of Change*

The **theory of change** is a concept originating in organizational development. This model has also been referred to as the theory of action, theory of influence, pathway of change, strategy, blueprint for change, engine of change, road map, and logic model.[37] This chapter focuses on exploring theories of change for efforts that require multiple areas of action, often seeking to alter underlying conditions, such as systems, social structures, or policies, that are most likely connected to social activism movements that support broader changes for populations and places.[38] Over time:

> this framework has become a fundamental component of many large scale social change efforts because it helps to strengthen strategies and maximize results by identifying the work to be undertaken, the expected signals of progress and the presumed or possible pathways to achieving desired goals that reflect beliefs, hypotheses, and working **assumptions**.[39]

Organizational assumptions can often hinder progress, so it is important to identify both implicit and explicit assumptions as part of the process for implementing theory of change.[40] Since assumptions are based on norms, values, and ideological perspectives about how they world works, they often underpin an organization or even an individual's ideas about how change occurs.[41]

The theory of change is both a conceptual model and a tangible tool that chronicles how to develop a plan that centers on making change happen. Best practices indicate that a theory of change plan should clearly articulate the actions to be undertaken, the change to be achieved, and answer the following questions:

- What actions should be assumed?
- By taking said actions, what can be possible?

- By identifying short-term and long-term goals, what changes or new conditions are expected to occur as a result of those actions?
- Ultimately, who benefits from these actions and/or changes?[42]

This concept proposes that there are specific outcomes that an organization seeks to achieve and offers a series of steps that must be taken to allow for success. This methodology provides a structured way of taking action to achieve intended **outcomes** and **outputs**. The process consists of multiple actions and planned goals, for which there are various solutions. Individuals or organizations can develop a strategic plan using the theory of change model which outlines the changes that need to occur and defines the structured actions that will lead to the intended change.

It is important for organizations to be specific about the type of change they are seeking and how/when they want to achieve it when pursuing broad, ambitious social shifts. Many organizations have benefited from embracing these principles. A variety of templates can be used to map a theory of change. In doing so, organizations begin to clarify priorities by defining goals and creating a path toward success, understand alignment in thinking on how change happens, address power differences that may exist, understand roles and expectations from contributors, and clearly outline where to invest time and resources – all while creating and measuring their strategies.[43] Figure 1.1 shows one example of mapping a theory of change. This illustration follows the broad formula of inputs + outputs = actions, which expresses the overall structure of the theory of change.[44] It includes a clear statement of the desired outcome or goal, as well as a description of the intermediate steps or intermediate outcomes that are believed to lead to the ultimate goal. Mapping out an organization's theory of change provides a blueprint of the building blocks needed to achieve specified outputs/outcomes.

By using this or similar tools, organizations can develop a plan for what they hope to accomplish, when they need to start planning, and who will be instrumental in helping the organization achieve its goals.[45] While theory of change models are developed with the specific needs of individual organizations in mind, framing, coalition-building, campaign-building, and directed action are the four most common areas included among those being mapped out.

### Framing

In social science, **framing** is the theory of how people make sense of information, suggesting that it aids in the process by which people develop a particular conceptualization of an issue or reorient their thinking about

## Theory of Change

| Assumptions | Identify noted assumptions.<br>Explicit assumptions are those that have been identified.<br>Implicit assumptions influence thinking and behaviors without being aware of them. | | | | |
|---|---|---|---|---|---|

| Problem Statement | What is the problem that needs solving? | | | | |
|---|---|---|---|---|---|

| Inputs | Actions | Short-Term Outcomes | Mid-Term Outcomes | Long-Term Outcomes | Outputs |
|---|---|---|---|---|---|
| Resources needed to conduct your activities efficiently. | Actions needed to reach your outcomes. | Outcomes expected of your intervention(s). | Outcomes desired withing the intended timeframe. | Outcomes you hope to observe beyond your intervention timeframe. | Tangible results you produce through your activities. |
| Such as:<br>• People power<br>• HR<br>• Space/Facilities<br>• Technology<br>• Materials<br>• Curriculum<br>• Funding | Such as:<br>• Workshops<br>• Trainings<br>• Marches<br>• Services<br>• Policy advocacy | Such as:<br>• Learning<br>• Awareness<br>• Knowledge<br>• Change in attitude<br>• Opinions<br>• Aspirations<br>• Motivations | Such as:<br>• Actions<br>• Behaviors<br>• Practices<br>• Decisions<br>• Policies<br>• Social actions | Such as:<br>• Conditions<br>• Social contexts<br>• Environmental characteristics | Such As:<br>• Enactment of legislation<br>• Public awareness<br>• Shifts in public opinion<br>• Issue becomes a priority for politicians |

| Impact | What is the desired impact the organization wishes to achieve? | | | | |
|---|---|---|---|---|---|

**FIGURE 1.1** An outline of one model or template for a theory of change which provides a framework for the logical sequence of events that is expected to lead to the desired impact

an issue.[46] In other words, it helps us understand how people interpret and make decisions based on what they see and hear. The theory suggests that how a specific topic is presented to the audience – referred to as "the frame" – influences the choices people make about how to process the information. Often, it is a tool used to analyze and understand how the media presents information to the public.[47] Within this chapter the concept of framing is applied to the interaction between social movements and activists.

From a communication perspective, framing is a strategy that involves presenting information in a way that highlights specific aspects of an issue or message in order to shape public opinion and influence the way people think about the topic. One common framing technique is to use language that evokes emotions or values that are important to the audience.[48] For example, a politician might use language that emphasizes the importance of family values to appeal to a conservative audience or emphasize social justice and equality to appeal to a liberal audience. An alternate framing approach is to present information in a way that accentuates potential consequences of a particular action or policy.[49] For example, a politician might argue that a certain policy is necessary to protect the environment or national security.

Historically speaking, the notion of framing (also referred to as "frames") was first introduced by sociologist Erving Goffman, who argued that we all interpret the world around us based on our own individual perspectives.[50] For Goffman, frames denoted "schemata of interpretation" that enable individuals "to locate, perceive, identify, and label" occurrences within their life space and the world at large. Frames often overlap and work in tandem with other frames, but they can also conflict with one another.[51] The key factor of a frame is that it reveals part of the person who's developing it. Goffman says, "each frame is the partial seeing of one such organized whole, and in this sense each frame subdivides the world."[52] These perspectives are shaped by our culture, values, and experiences; however, we also tend to filter out information that does not fit with our existing beliefs. Framing theory has been extensively used in media studies to analyze how the news media covers controversial issues such as abortion, immigration, and climate change. Scholars have argued that the way these issues are framed can have a significant impact on public opinion.[53]

For instance, research has shown that frames which focus on the costs of immigration are more likely to mobilize support for restrictive policies, while frames focusing on the benefits of immigration are more likely to mobilize support for liberal policies.[54] Additionally, frames emphasizing the risks of climate change are more likely to lead to public support for mitigation measures, while frames that dismiss climate change often use arguments related to economic costs of mitigation to undermine public support for climate action.[55]

Regarding the issue of abortion, there are two dominant frames that are commonly discussed: pro-life and pro-choice. Both the National Organization for Women (NOW) and Concerned Women for America (CWA) have used specific frames to articulate their message during critical moments of the broader abortion debate. Each organization presents itself as an advocate for public policy on women's issues and actively lobbies for policies that support its ideological position. Researcher and author Deana Rohlinger, in her article "Framing the Abortion Debate: Organizational Resources, Media Strategies, and Movement-Countermovement Dynamics," said:

> NOW frames the issue in terms of "rights," arguing that women have a constitutional right to an abortion and that policy regulating first-trimester abortions infringes on women's rights to privacy. CWA frames

the abortion debate in terms of "morality," positing that citizens are obligated to up Christian values, such as the sanctity of human life, and that abortion violates these values.[56]

Generally speaking, pro-lifers tend to see abortion as taking a human life, and therefore it is morally wrong. On the other hand, pro-choice individuals recognize abortion as a woman's right to control her own body, allowing her a choice. The differing views are supported and informed by their respective frames, with personal values guiding how individuals perceive and act on the larger issue of abortion. As a result, and in the aftermath of the 2022 US Supreme Court ruling that overturned the 1973 *Roe v. Wade* decision, both Republicans and Democrats targeted voters with vastly different messages in many of the same states leading up to the November 2022 elections. For example, according to The 19th*, an independent nonprofit newsroom reporting at the intersection of gender, politics, and policy, for seats in key statehouses, Democrats framed the abortion issue as follows:

- The Democratic Legislative Campaign Committee [DLCC] has a campaign focusing on Arizona, Pennsylvania, Michigan, Minnesota and New Hampshire in an attempt to flip chambers or make long-term inroads.
- The group also wants to protect existing political power in Colorado, New Mexico, Maine, Minnesota and Nevada.
- The DLCC announced this month that it raised a record $6.75 million during the second quarter of the year, a total that the group says is tied in part to the Roe Decision.[57]

Republicans targeted many of the same states, framing the issue with a focus on the economy:

- The Republican State Leadership Committee [RSLC] announced this month that it and an affiliated group had raised $9.8 million for the quarter.
- The RSLC has also pointed to internal polling to argue that the voters are more focused on the economic effects of rising inflation and high gas prices than abortion rights.
- Republicans say they have set their sights on flipping statehouses in Colorado, Maine, Nevada, Oregon and Washington. They also want to flip the Minnesota House chamber.[58]

When we think about social movements, it's important to remember the role that framing plays in shaping and directing. Without a clear frame, it can be difficult for people to understand what a movement stands for and why a particular audience should care. In revisiting its basic principle, framing creates a shared understanding of an issue or problem. It involves defining the problem, identifying who is affected by it, and articulating what needs to be achieved to address the issue. A good frame can be incredibly powerful in motivating people to act. Additionally, there are many ways to frame an issue, and no one frame is necessarily better than another. The key is to develop a frame that resonates with the intended audience and helps them see the issue in a new light. Overall, framing is a powerful tool. It is important to be aware of how information is being framed, and to critically evaluate the information being presented in order to make informed decisions. By understanding how framing theory works, activists can more effectively communicate their message and achieve their goals. This theory is integral in understanding how the media can impact public opinion – which, in turn, has also contributed to the evolution of social movements and activism.

### Coalition-Building

Beyond framing, **coalition-building** is another central component of most activist movements.[59] There is no single formula for building coalitions; however, in the context of activist organizations, strong coalitions are absolutely necessary for success. Important elements contributing to a successful activist organization relate to its diversity and ability to resonate in a meaningful way. Organizations rely on coalitions to reach the greatest number and widest range of supporters possible. This "strength in numbers" approach is critical, especially when it comes to combating larger opponents with deep financial pockets.[60]

There are countless ways movements mobilize their coalitions – requesting donations, get out the vote initiatives, voter registration information, donating money, supplies, distributing information such as pamphlets or bumper stickers, and volunteering at events or protests in a supporting role. As an example, the feminist movement is historically considered one of the largest aside from the Civil Rights movement, and would not be nearly as successful without different factions coming together – each contributing their respective piece toward the end goal.

At its most basic level, coalition-building is the process by which individuals and organizations work together to achieve a common goal or objective. It is a key component of activist movements because it allows multiple organizations to leverage the resources, skills, and expertise to amplify a message and/or increase impact. It is important to recognize that there are several steps involved in building a successful coalition, each clearly defined by common principles:[61]

- Identify common goals: The first step in building a coalition is to define the specific issue(s) or goal(s). This involves determining shared values and priorities among the member organizations.
- Gather support: Once the goals of the coalition have been identified, the next step is to gather support from other organizations/individuals who share these views. This likely involves corresponding with potential allies using social media, email, or other forms of communication.
- Establish ground rules: It is important to institute clear ground rules for how the coalition will operate, including decision-making processes, conflict resolution, and resource allocation.
- Develop a plan of action: The coalition should outline the specific steps that will be taken to achieve the shared goals. This may include lobbying, organizing protests or other public demonstrations, and raising awareness through media campaigns.
- Execute the plan: Once the plan of action has been developed, the coalition should work together to execute it – involving the appropriate coordination of activities and resources and mobilizing supporters to act.

Coalition-building is fundamentally important in allowing activists to work together toward a common goal. It can also be an effective way to create lasting change.

### Campaign-Building

**Campaign-building** is another necessity for achieving significant change within a social movement. As has been previously highlighted, social change can be accomplished through marches, rallies, strikes, petition drives, or sit-ins. As such, participants have multiple methods available to them to promote change. By developing the infrastructure needed to sustain a movement, and taking into consideration the importance of strategic framing, organizations can begin to promote their agendas, personalize communications to further engage support, maintain effective public messaging, and reach out to new groups or potential partners. These activities can be achieved using a structured, coordinated approach, allowing room for the movement to grow while simultaneously remaining organized and strategically focused.

*Focused Action*

The tactics used within movements seeking to achieve revolutionary change are part of what is deemed **focused action**. For instance, protests or marches can help spread awareness, but are typically not enough to enact major change as a stand-alone approach. Historically, the common image of focused action in activism includes public protest – such as a rally, march, or public meeting.[62] However, letters to the editor, sending postcards to politicians, toolkits with step-by-by step instructions outlining how to lobby or key messages to reinforce, activating local chapters, and signing petitions are all tactics used to advocate for a cause.[63] Each of these focused actions is highly effective in amplifying messaging and producing impact – which can lead to change.

When developing a theory of change for social movements, it is important to recognize that various tactics can be implemented based on the interests and expertise of each stakeholder group involved. In their step-by-step guide, *Developing a Theory of Change: Practical Guidance*, experts Anne Gienapp and Cameron Hostetter state that "the process values the principle of inclusion which attempts to ensure that everyone's thinking is visible and clearly represented, and that the group articulates and examines assumptions."[64]

## Before the Internet: Early Activism in America

Today, with a simple click of a mouse, an organization can mobilize thousands of people to act. Specific to the United States, early activism focused on movements related to abolition, women's rights, and civil rights. Early activists leveraged a variety of methodologies to promote their messages, including writing and distributing persuasive essays or organizing public speeches.

Historians have often considered social movements that occurred from the 1800s to the advent of the internet (late 20th century) to be much different from those that are experienced today. With low literacy rates and a general lack of a centralized electricity during the early years of America, it was more difficult to organize gatherings and/or sharing ideas on a broad scale – so activists had to get creative. As a result, many of the following tactics were implemented during those times in order to get the word out and build support for a particular cause.

*Storytelling*

Often overlooked and undervalued, storytelling is fundamental to successful social movements. Stories can be powerful weapons in the arsenal of activist movements. After all, stories are how we make sense of the world and connect with one another – building community through narratives. A good story educates and inspires; a great story motivates people to act. Whether they are used to raise awareness about an issue, rally to a cause, or simply inspire hope and compassion, stories have the power to move us in a way that other tactical elements alone cannot.

It has been reported that as one of the most prolific orators of her time, abolitionist and suffragist Lucy Stone was so captivating that she would draw massive crowds to a given event. Originally hired by the Massachusetts Anti-Slavery Society to lecture against slavery, she eventually combined her work to also include the plight of women during the suffragist movement.[65] She understood the importance of connecting with an audience through shared experiences.

## Meetings

In the 19th century, the spectacle of listening to public speakers was generally considered a town event. It is likely that early activists used organized meetings to assemble crowds so they could spread their messages. Meetings, or lectures as they were sometimes called, often gathered in churches, doubling as a town community hall during the evenings.

Today, we take for granted the fact that we can openly express our opinions and meet with like-minded individuals to discuss important issues – but it wasn't always this way. In America's early years, holding meetings to discuss controversial topics was often done in secret, for fear of retribution from the authorities. Despite the risks, many brave individuals spoke out against injustice and fought for change. These meetings were important not only as an outlet for emotions and opinions, but also to help build solidarity and momentum for the cause. As communities continue the fight for equality and justice across the globe, this continued sense of community still exists wherein we are able to share our stories, promoting change through common understanding.

## Letter Writing

Unsurprisingly, the most popular form of early activism involved writing letters. This long-accepted form of communication afforded individuals the opportunity to communicate updates with one another, organize meetings or activities, and also provided a mechanism for providing feedback/disagreement to their elected officials as a way of promoting change. From national issues like tax policy and abortion rights, letter writing has always been an important part of written activism.

According to Sara Finn, author of *Writing for Social Action*, the written word could "move an audience to attend a rally, contact a politician, inform an audience of its legal rights, foster interest in and action towards an issue, create allies and coalitions, or even outline a plan of activist action."[66] If you're an activist working for change, letter writing can be a powerful tool to help promote your cause. Whether advocating for social justice, environmental protection, or any other issue, a well-written letter can be a great way to get people aligned with the cause.

## Pamphlets

Pamphlets were another important form of early activism in America. In a historical sense, pamphlets were commonly used to communicate a message to a wide audience and rally to a cause. Pamphlets were often distributed by hand, and they could be found in public places like churches, town squares, and taverns. Pamphleteers argued for or against various issues, spread news and information, and allowed ordinary citizens to have a voice in the political debates of the day. The first great age of pamphleteering was inspired by the religious controversies of the early 16th century; however, the pamphlet continued to have a powerful influence throughout the 18th century, particularly in North America, and pre-Revolutionary political agitation stimulated the beginning of extensive pamphleteering.[67] In fact, some have argued that Thomas Paine's publication of the pamphlet *Common Sense* caused such a sensation in early 1776 as it explained the need for freedom – but his series of pamphlets later that year may have inspired a colossal American military victory.[68] He wrote in *The American Crisis*, a new pamphlet that appeared in the *Pennsylvania Journal*:

> These are the times that try men's souls: The summer soldier and the sunshine patriot will, in this crisis, shrink from the service of their country; but he that stands it now, deserves the love and thanks of man and woman. Tyranny, like Hell, is not easily conquered; yet we have this consolation with us, that the harder the conflict, the more glorious the triumph.[69]

Less than a week later, General George Washington had Paine's words read out loud to his troops at McConkey's Ferry on the Delaware River as a motivator to press on to victory. Pamphlets have historically been and continue to be an important tool for mobilizing public opinion – and even shaping the course of history.

## Leaflets and Flyers

Leaflets and flyers have always been an important part of early activist movements, representing one of the most basic and effective tools to get a message out – simply by including it on a piece of paper and handing it out to anyone who would take it. Each was used as a mechanism for spreading the word about a cause and/or rallying people to action.

The Online Archive of California, part of the University of California Libraries, manages a massive collection of social movement pieces. Its series contains materials from the Black Civil Rights movement in the United States, including a 1938 advertisement for an event featuring Duke Ellington, Juanita Hall, Georgia Burke, and others, put on by the Negro Cultural Committee. The collection also includes a poster advocating for the freedom of Black Panther prisoners, like David Hilliard.[70] According to Roz Payne of the Sixties Archive:

> the social movements of the Sixties produced hundreds of leaflets, flyers, broadsides, and reprinted articles. These items were an important part of the movement culture and another important organizing tool for activists and organizations. They were mimeographed and circulated widely at meetings, through the mail and by hand.[71]

Today, both are still used as a tool for activism and can be a powerful way to reach people and get them involved in a cause.

## Protests, Rallies, Marches

Protests, rallies, and marches create a powerful and disruptive stage for challenging and confronting the structures of power. By gathering in public spaces, social movements can quickly and easily call attention to their cause. This visibility can inspire more people to join the movement and amplify its power. Additionally, the physical presence of protesters can block or impede access to important buildings or other areas, forcing those in power to take notice. As an example, recent protests in the United States calling for an end to police brutality have led to some police departments banning the use of chokeholds. By gathering in numbers and using visible displays of dissent, protesters can effect real change on social and political issues.

## Sit-Ins

Sit-ins are a form of protest in which people occupy a public space for a prolonged period of time. The purpose of a sit-in is to draw attention to the protesters' cause and to disrupt the normal function of the space. Sit-ins have been used to successfully protest various issues, such as racial discrimination, economic inequality, and war. One of the most infamous sit-ins occurred in 1960 when four African American students – Ezell Blair Jr., David Richmond, Franklin McCain, and Joseph McNeil – from Greensboro, North Carolina launched a series of sit-ins at a Woolworth's department store to protest the segregation of the store's lunch counter.[72] As a result of this sit-in, a wave of similar protests across the South was ignited. Ultimately, this one peaceful action played a key role in the Civil Rights movement.

## Change Agents: Evolution of Activism in America

During times of unrest, a rebellion against the established norms has been a common occurrence throughout history. In the midst of these charged atmospheres, countless people found their voice and became activists for causes they believed in. Shaping American culture, race relations, gender norms, and politics – activism is critical to a democratic society. From Rosa Parks refusing to give up her seat on a bus to the Stonewall Riots, all the way through the Decision Day: We Won't Go Back March for abortion rights, activism has played a vital role in world development.

### *Early Social Activist Movements*

Like many other nations, the United States has a long and storied history that has been shaped through activism and/or protest. Some of the earliest activists were those who fought against slavery. In the 19th century, abolitionists like Frederick Douglass and Harriet Beecher Stowe spoke out against the institution of slavery and worked tirelessly to end it. In the late 19th and early 20th centuries, suffragettes like Susan B. Anthony fought for a woman's right to vote. These early movements helped to define key elements of American history and set the stage for later generations of activists. The final portion of the chapter will examine social movements and agents of change as we explore poignant moments in history beginning in the mid-1800s.

### *Mid-1800s: Labor Movement*

By 1864, labor discontent had taken hold of the United States. The cost of goods was rising much faster than wages, and worker strikes began to break out in cities across the North. St. Louis was no exception. Factory workers in the city went on strike in May 1864, demanding higher wages and better working conditions. The strike quickly turned violent as police tried to disperse the crowd. However, the workers stood their ground and eventually gained traction with some of their demands. The 1864 strike in St. Louis was just one example of the growing labor movement in the country.

### Late 1800s–1920s: Women's Suffrage

During the late 1800s and early 1900s, women's suffrage organizations not only fought for the right to vote, but they also fought for economic/political equality and social reform. These activists understood that by gaining the right to vote, women would be able to effect change in society. In addition to campaigning for the right to vote, these organizations also worked to improve working conditions for women, fight for fair wages, and promote educational and social welfare programs. While they didn't always succeed in their efforts, their work laid the foundation for the modern women's rights movement.

### Early 1940s: Congress of Racial Equality

According to the African American Civil Rights Movement website:

> The Congress of Racial Equality or CORE is an African American Civil Rights group that played a major role in the Civil Rights Movement of the 1960s. It was founded in Chicago in 1942 by Bayar Rustin, George Houser, Homer Jack, and James Farmer as Committee on Racial Equality. Of the fifty original members twenty-eight were men and twenty-two were women, about one third were black and two thirds white.[73]

CORE agreed that voter registration was important for African-Americans in order to spread the message of real freedom. CORE and other civil rights groups focused their efforts on an outreach campaign called Mississippi Freedom Summer – encouraging as many people as possible to register to vote in Mississippi. The campaign was launched by the Southern Christian Leadership Conference and Student Nonviolent Coordinating Committee, with approximately 700 White and Black students assisting with the cause during 1964–1965.

### Mid-1940s–Late 1950s: Anti-Nuclear Activists and Protest Actions

The anti-nuclear movement in the United States has an interesting history, with roots dating back to the early days of nuclear technology. As the

United States developed its nuclear weapons program during the 1950s and 1960s, opposition to these weapons (including nuclear power) began to grow. One of the earliest and most influential groups in the anti-nuclear movement was the Committee for Nonviolent Action (CNVA), which was formed in 1957.[74] The CNVA was a grassroots organization focusing on nonviolent direct action and civil disobedience as a means of opposing nuclear weapons and promoting peace. The CNVA was involved in a number of high-profile campaigns, including the "Appeal to Cheyenne," which sought to stop the construction of a new missile site at F.E. Warren Air Force Base in Wyoming.

Other groups that played a prominent role in the early anti-nuclear movement included the Women's International League for Peace and Freedom, the Student Peace Union, and the War Resisters League.[75] These groups organized protests, sit-ins, and other acts of civil disobedience to raise awareness about the dangers of nuclear weapons and the need for disarmament. Throughout the 1970s and 1980s, the anti-nuclear movement continued to grow, with major protests and demonstrations taking place across the country. In 1979, more than 100,000 people participated in the "No Nukes" rally in New York City, which was organized by musicians including Jackson Browne, Bonnie Raitt, and Bruce Springsteen. In the 1990s, the anti-nuclear movement focused more attention on issues related to nuclear power, with protests and demonstrations against nuclear power plants and uranium mining. Today, the anti-nuclear movement in the United States remains active, with a wide range of organizations working to raise awareness about the dangers of nuclear technologies. While the movement has faced challenges over the years, it has also had a number of successes, including a campaign to shut down the Shoreham Nuclear Power Plant on Long Island, New York in the 1980s.

### 1955: Civil Rights Movement

In the history of the United States, the Civil Rights movement can be identified as a major turning point within the fabric of American society. It was a time of great social and political change, as people of all races and backgrounds came together to demand equal rights and treatment for all. Influential figures led the movement, including Dr. Martin Luther King Jr., Rosa Parks, and Malcolm X – inspiring citizens to take a stand against racism and discrimination. The 1954 Supreme Court case *Brown v. Board of Education*, which declared segregation in public schools to be unconstitutional, was one of the key events of the Civil Rights movement. This decision paved the way for the "Civil Rights Act of 1964 and the Voting Rights Act of 1965, which prohibited discrimination on the basis of race, color, religion, sex, or national origin and ensured that all citizens had the right to vote."[76] The Civil Rights movement was a long and difficult struggle, and it required the efforts of many brave and dedicated individuals and organizations to bring about change. However, it ultimately led to significant improvements in the lives of Black Americans and laid the foundation for further progress in the fight for social justice.

### 1960s–2022: The Women's Movement

Women's history in the United States is full of inspiring and influential figures who have worked to advance the rights and opportunities of women.[77] The women's suffrage movement, which fought for women's right to vote, is a particularly significant and well-known aspect of women's history in America. The movement began in the late 19th century and ultimately led to the passage of the 19th Amendment to the Constitution in 1920, granting women the right to vote.[78] In the 1960s, a second wave of feminism emerged, focusing on a wide range of issues including reproductive rights, equal pay, and ending discrimination against women. This second movement was fueled by many events, including both the Civil Rights movement and the emergence of the counterculture, and had a significant impact on society and the legal landscape.[79] The outcomes also led to further waves of feministic movements. Third wave feminism is characterized by a focus on intersectionality, or the idea that different forms of oppression, such as racism or homophobia, often intersect and overlap.[80] Third wave feminists attempt to increase representation and visibility for marginalized groups within the broader feminist movement, as well as challenging traditional gender roles and stereotypes.[81] Fast-forward to fourth wave feminism, a reference to the current wave of feminism, which is distinguished by its focus on issues such as sexual harassment, assault, and violence against women, as well as continuing the emphasis on intersectionality and inclusivity.[82] This wave of feminism has been marked by the use of social media and the internet – raising awareness about these issues and to mobilize for change.[83] Experiencing recent wins and subsequent setbacks, such as the United States Supreme Court reversal of *Roe v. Wade*, there is still much work to be done to achieve full equality for women. The fight for women's rights and gender equality remains an important and ongoing effort.

### 1960s–1970s: The US Chicano Movement

The Chicano Movement, also known as El Movimiento, was a broad-based civil rights movement that emerged in the 1960s and gained further momentum through the 1970s.[84] At the time, Mexican-Americans faced discrimination in a variety of forms, including segregation, economic exploitation, and violence. As a result, many felt a strong sense of cultural and social alienation and sought to assert their identity and reclaim their cultural heritage through the Chicano Movement.[85] One of the key goals of the movement was to challenge widespread discrimination and injustice and simultaneously promote greater equality and social justice.[86] The Chicano Movement was comprised of students, workers, artists, and intellectuals. Activists were inspired by the civil rights and anti-war movements of the time, and rebelled through acts of civil disobedience, strikes, and protests. Many of the movement's demands, such as increased access to education and voting rights, were eventually won through legislation and court decisions.[87] The movement also played a key role in bringing attention to the struggles and contributions of Mexican-Americans and other Latinx communities in the United States.

### 1964: Anti-Vietnam War Movement

The anti-war movement during the course of the Vietnam War was a diverse, broad-based social movement that opposed the United States' involvement in the Vietnam War.[88] It included people from all walks of life, including students, government officials, labor unions, church groups, and middle-class families. According to the International Center on Non-Violent Conflict, "over the next decade, hundreds of thousands of young people become radicalized in a largely non-violent, diverse and sometimes inchoate popular culture of war resistance, employing tactics ranging from comical street theatre to industrial sabotage."[89] The anti-war movement gained significant momentum in the late 1960s, when the war was at its peak and the draft was in full effect. As more and more young people were being sent to fight in Vietnam, opposition to the war grew.[90] Protests and demonstrations became more frequent and increasingly diverse, with participants spanning all ages and backgrounds. The movement reached its peak in the spring of 1970, when more than two million people participated in protests against the war.[91] This was the largest anti-war demonstration in American history. The movement's efforts eventually helped to bring an end to US combat operations in Vietnam and the suspension of the draft in 1973.

### 1966–1975: Black Power

Black Power was a movement that sought to empower African-Americans and to promote racial pride and self-determination. It was a response to the Civil Rights movement, which had focused on integrating African-Americans into mainstream society through legislation and nonviolent action.[92] Many African-Americans felt that the Civil Rights movement had not gone far enough in addressing the deep-seated systemic racism and economic inequality they faced. The Black Power movement sought to address these issues through a variety of means, including creation of Black-owned businesses, advocating for economic justice and redistributive policies, and building cultural institutions/organizations that would serve the needs of the Black community.[93] The movement also encouraged the celebration and preservation of African American culture and history and sought to promote a positive self-image among African-Americans. Black Power was not a monolithic movement, and there were many different groups and individuals who were involved. Some proponents of Black Power advocated for more militant and confrontational tactics, while others favored a more peaceful and conciliatory approach. Ultimately, the Black Power movement played a significant role in shaping the direction of the Civil Rights movement and in bringing about lasting social and political change for African-Americans.

### 1968: American Indian Movement

The American Indian Movement (AIM) was a grassroots organization founded in 1968 by Native American activists in Minneapolis, Minnesota.[94] AIM's original goals included improving conditions for Native Americans who had recently migrated to urban areas, as well as seeking full restoration of tribal sovereignty and treaty rights for Native Americans. The organization also sought to restore spiritual ceremonies that had been banned since 1884, and to protect and preserve Native American cultures and traditions. AIM's activism took place during a time of great hardship for Native Americans in the Twin Cities, as many Native Americans who had migrated from reservations under the Indian Relocation Act of 1956 found themselves facing low-wage labor, substandard housing, discrimination, violence, and other challenges.[95] In 1969, AIM activists and other Native Americans occupied Alcatraz Island in San Francisco Bay, which had been abandoned by the federal government. The occupation lasted for 19 months and brought national attention to the demands of Native American activists for self-determination and the return of tribal lands.[96] In 1972, AIM and other Native American activists organized the Trail of Broken Treaties, a cross-country caravan to Washington, DC to protest the federal government's failure to honor its treaty obligations to Indigenous peoples. The caravan ended with a demonstration at the Bureau of Indian Affairs headquarters, during which AIM activists occupied the building and issued a list of 20 demands to the government.[97] Then, in 1973, AIM activists, including Leonard Peltier, occupied the town of Wounded Knee on the Pine Ridge Indian Reservation in South Dakota. Lasting 71 days, the occupation was intended to protest the treatment of Indigenous peoples by the federal government and the corruption of the tribal government on the reservation.[98] Today an annual event, in 1978, AIM and other Native American activists organized the first National Day of Mourning, a protest held on Thanksgiving Day to call attention to the ongoing struggles of Indigenous peoples in the United States.[99] Over the years, AIM advocated for the rights of Native Americans while working to improve upon the issues within the Native American communities and bring about lasting change.

### 1987: AIDS Coalition

The AIDS Coalition to Unleash Power (ACT UP) was established on March 12, 1987, at the Lesbian and Gay Community Services Center in New York City.[100] The organization leveraged a variety of tactics, including direct action, civil disobedience, and media campaigns, to bring attention to the HIV/AIDS crisis and advocate for change. Notable actions realized by ACT UP have included protests at the US Food and Drug Administration, the National Institutes of Health, and pharmaceutical companies, as well as the creation of the HIV/AIDS Treatment Data Network, which provided information on experimental treatments to individuals diagnosed with HIV/AIDS. ACT UP has been successful in bringing about significant changes in HIV/AIDS education, treatment, and policies, including the acceleration of Food and Drug Administration approval for HIV/AIDS drugs and the inclusion of people living with HIV/AIDS in the decision-making process for clinical trials. The organization is still active in advocating for the rights of people living with HIV/AIDS.

### 1994: LGBTQ+ Movement

The Stonewall Riots are considered a turning point in the gay rights movement, as they marked the first time that the LGBTQ+ community pushed back against police harassment and discrimination in a significant and organized way.[101] This event inspired the formation of numerous LGBTQ+ advocacy groups and led to the organization of Pride Parades – held in cities around the world every year to celebrate LGBTQ+ culture and honor the legacy of the Stonewall Riots.[102] In the decades that followed, the gay rights movement made significant progress.[103] In 1973, the American Psychiatric Association removed homosexuality from its list of mental disorders.[104] In the 1980s and 1990s, cities and states began enacting laws that protected LGBTQ+ individuals from discrimination in employment, housing, and public accommodations. However, a setback to the rights of the LGBTQ+ community was experienced in 1996 when the Defense of Marriage Act was signed into law, defining marriage as between a man and a woman and denying federal recognition to same-sex marriages.[105] Consequently, this law was struck down by the Supreme Court in 2013 in the case of *United States v. Windsor*, paving the way for the legalization of same-sex marriage in all 50 states as an outcome of the 2015 landmark case of *Obergefell v. Hodges*. CNN Journalists M.J. Lee, Betsy Klein, and Kevin Liptak reported on December 13, 2022:

> President Joe Biden signed landmark new federal protections for same-sex and interracial couples ... the Respect for Marriage Act before thousands of invited guests on the South Lawn at an event the White House said reflected the importance of the moment. At the event Biden said "Marriage is a simple proposition. Who do you love? And will you be loyal to that person you love?" the president asked from the South Lawn. "It's not more complicated than that."[106]

While there have been many victories for the LGBTQ+ community in the United States, there is still work to be done. Discrimination and prejudice continue to be a problem, and transgender individuals in particular face significant challenges, including a lack of legal protections, high rates of violence and discrimination, and difficulties accessing healthcare. The LGBTQ+ community and its allies continue to advocate for full equality and acceptance for all LGBTQ+ individuals.

### 1990s: American Environmental Justice Movement

The environmental justice movement originated with the passing of the Civil Rights Act of 1964 and of Title VI, which prohibited the use of federal funds to discriminate on the basis of race, color, and national origin.[107] Environmental justice is a movement that aims to address the disproportionate impact of environmental harms and policies on marginalized and disadvantaged communities.[108] These communities are often comprised of diverse and indigenous populations, are lower-income, and have residents who are disproportionately affected by environmental pollution, degradation, and other negative impacts.[109] The movement seeks to ensure that all people, regardless of their race, ethnicity, or socio-economic status, have the right to a clean and healthy environment.[110] The movement gained significant momentum in the 1990s with the publication of Dr. Robert Bullard's book *Dumping in Dixie*, which documented the history of environmental racism and the struggle for environmental justice in the United States.[111] As with most movements, much progress still needs to be accomplished. The environmental justice movement continues to make strides in raising awareness about environmental inequalities and advocating for policies and practices that promote environmental justice.

### 2006: #MeToo

The #MeToo movement, which began in 2006 with Tarana Burke's work to empower survivors of sexual violence, gained widespread attention in 2017 when actor Alyssa Milano encouraged people to use the hashtag on social media to show the widespread prevalence of sexual harassment and assault.[112] The hashtag quickly became a rallying cry for survivors of sexual abuse and their supporters, and it sparked a global conversation about these issues.[113] The movement has led to increased awareness of the pervasiveness of sexual harassment and assault, and has encouraged more people to speak out about their experiences and to demand change.[114] #MeToo sparked calls for greater accountability for those who abuse their power, leading to the outing of powerful men, including NBC TV personality Matt Lauer and movie mogul Harvey Weinstein, both of whom were accused of sexual misconduct. Today, the movement continues to be an important force for social change – encouraging use of the hashtag to share stories and promote lasting change.

### 2011: Occupy Wall Street

The Occupy Wall Street movement was a protest that took place in New York City's financial district from September 17, 2011 to late November 2011. The movement was inspired by the Arab Spring and the Spanish Indignant movement, and was motivated by concerns about income inequality, corporate greed, and the influence of corporate money on politics.[115] The protest was organized by a Canadian anti-consumerist publication called *Adbusters*, and was coordinated through the use of social media, including the use of the hashtag #OccupyWallStreet.[116] The protest initially involved a small group of activists, but it quickly grew in size and attracted widespread media attention. The movement spread to other cities around the world, including London, Paris, Berlin, and Toronto, inspiring similar protests in other countries. While the Occupy Wall Street movement did not achieve any of its specific policy goals, it is still seen as a significant moment in modern activist history.[117] It brought attention to issues of income inequality and corporate influence on politics and inspired many people to get involved in activism and social justice movements.

## 2013: Black Lives Matter

According to the Howard University Law Library, the Black Lives Matter movement originated in 2013 with Alicia Garza, Patrisse Cullors, and Opal Tometi responding to the acquittal of George Zimmerman, who was charged with the shooting death of Trayvon Martin, a young Black man, in Florida.[118] The movement gained widespread attention and support in 2014 after the deaths of Michael Brown in Missouri and Eric Garner in New York, both of whom were killed by police officers.[119] Since its launch, Black Lives Matter has organized and participated in protests, demonstrations, and other actions to raise awareness of and demand change to the systemic racism and violence faced by Black people in the United States and around the world. The movement has also called for reforms to the criminal justice system and for greater accountability for police officers who use excessive force or engage in other forms of misconduct.[120]

## Conclusion

Oppression and inequality are among two of the most prominent reasons driving activism. Inequality has plagued society for centuries. Throughout history, power has most often been concentrated in the hands of those who are wealthy, status quo defenders, and politically connected. Society has come a long way in recent decades, but it is still not perfect. Centuries of abuse and privilege speak to our failure as a society to recognize power as inherently corrupting and that fairness is only achieved when every voice is heard and recognized.

With the rise of social media, people can organize and campaign for causes they care about from anywhere in the world. The social sphere has made it easier for people to share their thoughts and experiences, and to connect with like-minded individuals who may not have been reachable before. Activism can also take many forms beyond social media. As this chapter highlighted, there are a multitude of ways that activism has been used throughout history, such as attending protests, writing letters, or making phone calls, or volunteering with organizations that support causes they care about. And while there are more opportunities than ever to make your voice heard, there are also more ways for governments and corporations to silence dissent. That's why it's important to keep fighting, whether continuing to speak out or gathering for a specific cause. Only by coming together can we hope to create a fairer, more just world for everyone.

Not until we achieve equality for everyone, everywhere, will power cease to corrupt.

## Reflections

- How have oppression, inequality, revolution, and protest played a role in activism and social movements?
- What role does democracy play in social movements?
- What are the components of theory of change, and why are they needed?
- Researchers Marie-Line Germain, Phyllis Robertson, and Sarah Minnis have asserted that "social media and digital communication have created a significant dynamic shift in how social movements are shaped, maintained, and grown through rapid dissemination of information and opinions."[121] How has the digital age impacted activism and social movements? Provide explicit examples.
- Have you taken part in social activism? If yes, in what form? If no, why not?
- What, if any, social movements have most impacted your life, and why?
- Which activist or movement most resonates with you, and why?

## Notes

1 El Abbassi, Miriam. "Social media activism or slacktivism?" Accessed July 18, 2022. https://www.excal.on.ca/features/2019/11/08/social-media-activism-or-slacktivism.
2 Drury, John, Christopher Cocking, Joseph Beale, Charlotte Hanson, and Faye Rapley. "The phenomenology of empowerment in collective action." *British Journal of Social Psychology* 44, no. 3 (2005): 309–328.
3 Schonfeld, Zach. "185 people killed in Iran protests: human rights group." Accessed December 17, 2022. https://thehill.com/policy/international/3679922-185-people-killed-in-iran-protests-human-rights-group/.
4 "Iran official claims end of 'Morality Police', to appease protesters." Accessed December 17, 2022. https://www.iranintl.com/en/202212043012.
5 Olson, Mancur. 1989. "Collective action." In *The Invisible Hand*. London: Palgrave Macmillan.
6 Cammaerts, Bart, and Nico Carpentier. 2007. *Reclaiming the Media: Communication Rights and Democratic Media Roles*. Bristol, UK: Intellect, pp. 217–224.
7 Flanagin, Andrew J., Cynthia Stohl, and Bruce Bimber. "Modeling the structure of collective action." *Communication Monographs* 73, no. 1 (2006): 29–54.
8 Giving Green. "Activism: Giving Green's approach." Accessed July 18, 2022. www.givinggreen.earth/us-policy-change-research/activism%3A-overview.
9 Vinthagen, Stellan. *A Theory of Nonviolent Action: How Civil Resistance Works*. London: Bloomsbury Publishing, 2015.
10 Obar, Jonathan A., Paul Zube, and Clifford Lampe. "Advocacy 2.0: An analysis of how advocacy groups in the United States perceive and use social media as tools for facilitating civic engagement and collective action." *Journal of Information Policy* 2, no. 1 (2012): 1–25.

11 Poshar, Andréa. 2019. "Design and activism – a relationship that needs reflection." *DESIGNABILITIES Design Research Journal for Social, Cultural and Political Discourse, Transformation & Activism* 02. https:// designabilities.wordpress.com/2019/02/07/design-and-activism-a-relation-ship-that-needs-reflection/.

12 Giving Green. "Activism: Giving Green's approach."

13 Brian Martin. 2007. "Activism, social and political." In Gary L. Anderson and Kathryn G. Herr (eds.), *Encyclopedia of Activism and Social Justice*. Thousand Oaks, CA: SAGE, pp. 19–27. Benjamin, Themba. "Social Media Activism: Limitation and Benefits." *INOSR Arts and Management* 4, no. 1 (2018): 30–37.

14 Jordan, Tim. 2002. *Activism! Direct Action, Hacktivism and the Future of Society*. Reaktion Books. Cammaerts and Carpentier, *Reclaiming the Media*.

15 Cammaerts and Carpentier, *Reclaiming the Media*.

16 Gitlin, T. 2003. *Letters to a Young Activist*, New York: Basic Books. Benjamin, "Social Media Activism."

17 Cammaerts and Carpentier, *Reclaiming the Media*.

18 Germain, Marie-Line, Phyllis Robertson, and Sarah Minnis. "Protests, rallies, marches, and social movements as organizational change agents." *Advances in Developing Human Resources* 21, no. 2 (2019): 150–174.

19 Tilly, C. 1999. "Interactions to outcomes in social movements." In M. Giugni, D. McAdam, and C. Tilly (eds.), *How Social Movements Matter*. Minneapolis, MN: University of Minnesota Press, pp. 253–270.

20 Germain, Robertson, and Minnis, "Protests, rallies, marches, and social movements as organizational change agents."

21 Giving Green. "Activism: Giving Green's approach."

22 "List of 10 major events of the French Revolution." Accessed December 17, 2022. https://historylists.org/events/list-of-10-major-events-of-the-french-revolution.html.

23 Hunt, Lynn. 2016. "Politics, culture, and class in the French Revolution." In *Politics, Culture, and Class in the French Revolution*. Oakland, CA: University of California Press.

24 Rothenberg, Gunther E. "The origins, causes, and extension of the wars of the French Revolution and Napoleon." *Journal of Interdisciplinary History* 18, no. 4 (1988): 771–793.

25 Wade, Rex A. "The revolution at one hundred: Issues and trends in the English language historiography of the Russian Revolution of 1917." *Journal of Modern Russian History and Historiography* 9, no. 1 (2016): 9–38.

26 Lane, David. "VI Lenin's theory of socialist revolution." *Critical Sociology* 47, no. 3 (2021): 455–473.

27 McFaul, Michael. 2015. "Russia's unfinished revolution." In *Russia's Unfinished Revolution*. Ithaca, NY: Cornell University Press, pp. 189–227.

28 Chari, Sharad, and Katherine Verdery. "Thinking between the posts: Postcolonialism, postsocialism, and ethnography after the Cold War." *Comparative Studies in Society and History* 51, no. 1 (2009): 6–34. Schlesinger, Arthur. "Origins of the Cold War." *Foreign Affairs* 46, no. 1 (1967): 22–52.

29 Khomeini, Ayatollah Ruhollah. 1989. "The Ashura Uprising." The Ashura Uprising an Example for Free Men. Arif, Muhammad."The Iranian Revolution: The Role and Contribution of Ayatollah Ruhollah Khomeini." *Afghan Journalists Committee*, (2012): 1–35.

30 Karimi-Hakkak, Ahmad. "Revolutionary posturing: Iranian writers and the Iranian revolution of 1979." *International Journal of Middle East Studies* 23, no. 4 (1991): 507–531.

31 Heisey, D. Ray, and J. David Trebing. "Authority and legitimacy: A rhetorical case study of the Iranian revolution." *Communications Monographs* 53, no. 4 (1986): 295–310.

32 Buchan, James. "The Iranian revolution of 1979." *Asian Affairs* 44, no. 3 (2013): 418–426.

33 Akhavi, Shahrough. "The ideology and praxis of Shi'ism in the Iranian revolution." *Comparative Studies in Society and History* 25, no. 2 (1983): 195–221.

34 Rasler, Karen. "Concessions, repression, and political protest in the Iranian revolution." *American Sociological Review* (1996): 132–152.

35 Elwell-Sutton, Laurence Paul. "The Iranian Revolution." *International Journal* 34, no. 3 (1979): 391–407.

36 Annie E. Casey Foundation. 2004. *Theory of Change: A Practical Tool for Action, Results and Learning.* Baltimore, MD: author. https://www.aecf.org /resources/theory-of-change.

37 Ibid.

38 Ibid.

39 Ibid.

40 Beer, T., and J. Coffman. 2021. *Guidance on Developing Assumptions.* Washington, DC: Center for Evaluation Innovation. https://www.evaluationi nnovation.org/wp-content/uploads/2021/11/Assumptions-Guidance-2021 -Suggested-Website-Version-copy.pdf.

41 Van Es, M., I. Guijit, and I. Vogel. 2013. *Theory of Change Thinking in Practice: A Stepwise Approach.* The Hague, the netherlands. Beer and Coffman, *Guidance on Developing Assumptions..*

42 Annie E. Casey Foundation, *Theory of Change.*

43 Ibid.

44 Giving Green. "Activism: Giving Green's approach."

45 Luttrell, Regina.2021. "Outreach and empowerment: Civic engagement, advocacy, and amplification of the women's movement." In *Democracy in the Disinformation Age*, Abingdon, UK: Routledge, pp. 58–76.

46 Ajzen, I., and M. Fishbein. 1980. *Understanding Attitudes and Predicting Social Behavior.* Englewood Cliffs, NJ: Prentice Hall.

47 Pan, Zhongdang, and Gerald M. Kosicki. "Framing analysis: An approach to news discourse." *Political Communication* 10, no. 1 (1993): 55–75. Martin, Deborah G. "'Place-framing' as place-making: Constituting a neighborhood for organizing and activism." *Annals of the Association of American Geographers* 93, no. 3 (2003): 730–750. Chong, Dennis, and James N. Druckman. "Framing theory." *Annual Review of Political Science* 10, no. 1 (2007): 103–126.

48 Charteris-Black, Jonathan. *Analysing Political Speeches: Rhetoric, Discourse and Metaphor.* London: Bloomsbury Publishing, 2018.

49 Rhee, June Woong. "Strategy and issue frames in election campaign coverage: A social cognitive account of framing effects." *Journal of Communication* 47, no. 3 (1997): 26–48.

50 Goffman, Erving. "Footing." *Semiotica* 25, nos. 1–2 (1979): 1–30, accessed May 8, 2023, https://doi.org/10.1515/semi.1979.25.1-2.1; Goffman, Erving. "A reply to Denzin and Keller" *Contemporary Sociology* 10, no. 1 (January 1981): 60–68, accessed May 8, 2023, https://doi.org/10.2307 /2067804.

51 Benford, Robert D., and David A. Snow. "Framing processes and social movements: An overview and assessment." *Annual Review of Sociology* (2000): 611–639.
52 Goffman, Erving. 1974. *Frame Analyses: An Essay on the Organization of Experience.* Cambridge, MA: Harvard University Press. p. 508.
53 Druckman, James N. "The implications of framing effects for citizen competence." *Political Behavior* 23, no. 3 (2001): 225–256.; Hopkins, Daniel J., and Jonathan Mummolo. 2016. "Assessing the breadth of framing effects." https://papers.ssrn.com/sol3/papers.cfm?abstract_id=2863930.
54 Massey, D.S., J. Durand, and K.A. Pren. "Why border enforcement backfired." *American Journal of Sociology* 121, no. (5): 1557–1600. Hainmueller, Jens, and Daniel J. Hopkins. "Public attitudes toward immigration." *Annual Review of Political Science* 17 (2014): 225–249.
55 Stecula, Dominik A., and Eric Merkley. "Framing climate change: Economics, ideology, and uncertainty in American news media content from 1988 to 2014." *Frontiers in Communication* 4 (2019): 6.
56 Rohlinger, Deana A. "Framing the abortion debate: Organizational resources, media strategies, and movement–countermovement dynamics." *Sociological Quarterly* 43, no. 4 (2002): 479–507.
57 Becker, Amanda. "Democrats see a winning midterm message: Vote, or Texas-style abortion laws are 'coming to a state near you.'" *The19th\**. https://19thnews.org/2021/11/democrats-midterms-abortion-texas/.
58 Ibid.
59 Beamish, Thomas D., and Amy J. Luebbers. "Alliance building across social movements: Bridging difference in a peace and justice coalition." *Social Problems* 56, no. 4 (2009): 647–676.
60 Van Dyke, Nella, and Holly J. McCammon. 2010. *Strategic Alliances: Coalition Building and Social Movements.* Minneapolis, MN: University of Minnesota Press.
61 Perlman, Judith. 2021. "Build a coalition and partnerships (strange bedfellows)." In *Citizen's Primer for Conservation Activism.* Austin, TX: University of Texas Press, pp. 69–85. Ackerman-Barger, J. Kupiri, R.E. Cooper, C. Gualtieri, L. Martin, B. Nichols, and G.A. Perez. 2022. *Building Coalitions to Promote Health Equity: A Toolkit for Action.* Washington, DC: AARP Foundation. Merrill, Denise. 2008. "Six simple steps to building a medical and early intervention transitional coalition." *Pediatric Services,* last modified May 13, 2021, accessed May 8, 2023, https://www.pediatricservices.com/prof/prof-23.htm. Guillory, Joan D., Jane M. Everson, and Joy G. Ivester. "Community development: Lessons learned about coalition building and community connections for stakeholders with disabilities." *Community Development* 37, no. 3 (2006): 83–96.
62 Martin, Brian. 2007. "Activism, social and political." In Gary L. Anderson and Kathryn G. Herr (eds.), *Encyclopedia of Activism and Social Justice.* Thousand Oaks, CA: SAGE, pp. 19–27.
63 Luttrell, Regina. 2021. "Outreach and empowerment: Civic engagement, advocacy, and amplification of the women's movement." In *Democracy in the Disinformation Age.* Abingdon, UK: Routledge, pp. 58–76.
64 Gienapp, Anne, and Cameron Hostetter. 2022. "Guidance on developing assumptions." In *Developing a Theory of Change: Practical Guidance.* Baltimore, MD: Annie E. Casey Foundation. https://assets.aecf.org/m/resourcedoc/aecf-theoryofchange-steps-2022.pdf.
65 Robb, Lucinda, and Rebecca Boggs Roberts. 2020. *The Suffragists Playbook: Your Guide to Changing the World.* Somerville, MA: Candlewick Press.

66 Finn, Sarah. 2013. *Writing for Social Action: Affect, Activism, and the Composition Classroom.* Amherst, MA: University of Massachusetts Press.

67 Entry for "pamphlet." *Encyclopedia Britannica*, July 9, 2012. https://www.britannica.com/art/pamphlet.

68 "How Thomas Paine's other pamphlet saved the Revolution." *Constitution Daily.* December 19, 2021. https://constitutioncenter.org/blog/how-thomas-paines-other-pamphlet-saved-the-revolution.

69 Ibid.

70 Online Archive of California, University of California Libraries. Social Movements Collection. https://oac.cdlib.org/findaid/ark:/13030/c8mk6k5h/dsc/.

71 Payne, Roz. Sixties Archive. *Leaflets, Flyers, Broadsides and Article Reprints.* Accessed July 24, 2022 https://rozsixties.unl.edu/collections/show/7.

72 Pratt, Robert A. "February one: The story of the Greensboro Four." *Journal of American History* 92, no. 3 (2005): 1110–1111, https://doi.org/10.2307/3660153.

73 African American Civil Rights Movement website: www.african-american-civil-rights.org/congress-of-racial-equality-core/.

74 Price, Jerome. 1982. *The Anti-Nuclear Movement.* Boston, MA: Twayne Publishers, p. 65. Entry for "Anti-nuclear movement in the United States." *Wikipedia.* https://en.wikipedia.org/wiki/Anti-nuclear_movement_in_the_United_States#cite_note-71.

75 Shawyer, Susanne E. "Radical street theatre and the Yippie legacy: A performance history of the Youth International Party, 1967–1968." Accessed December 16, 2022. https://repositories.lib.utexas.edu/bitstream/handle/2152/17999/shawyers56058.pdf?sequence=2.

76 "Civil Rights Act of 1964." Accessed December 16, 2022. https://www.history.com/topics/black-history/civil-rights-act.

77 Sharone, William, and Wendy Martin. 2016. *The Routledge Introduction to American Women Writers.* Abingdon, UK: Routledge.

78 Pearce, Elizabeth. *Working Outside of the System: Social Movements and Activism.* Accessed December 16, 2022. https://openoregon.pressbooks.pub/families/chapter/working-outside-of-the-system-social-movements-and-activism. "Social movements" is adapted from "Understanding Social Movements" in *Sociology* by anonymous. License: CC BY-NC-SA 4.0. Edited for brevity and clarity. "Introduction: feminist movements" is from "Historical and Contemporary Feminist Social Movements." In Miliann Kang, Donovan Lessard, Laura Heston, and Sonny Nordmarken. 2017. *Introduction to Women, Gender, Sexuality Studies.* License: CC BY 4.0.

79 Thornham, Sue. 2004. "Second wave feminism." In Sarah Gamble (ed.), *The Routledge Companion to Feminism and Postfeminism.* Abingdon, UK: Routledge, pp. 25–35.

80 Snyder, R. Claire. "What is third-wave feminism? A new directions essay." *Signs: Journal of Women in Culture and Society* 34, no. 1 (2008): 175–196.

81 Kinser, Amber E. "Negotiating spaces for/through third-wave feminism." *NWSA Journal* (2004): 124–153.

82 Zimmerman, Tegan. "# Intersectionality: The fourth wave feminist Twitter community." *Atlantis: Critical Studies in Gender, Culture & Social Justice* 38, no. 1 (2017): 54–70.

83 Parry, Diana C., Corey W. Johnson, and Faith-Anne Wagler. 2018. "Fourth wave feminism: Theoretical underpinnings and future directions

for leisure research." In *Feminisms in Leisure Studies*. Abingdon, UK: Routledge, pp. 1–12. Mohajan, Haradhan. "Four waves of feminism: A blessing for global humanity." *Studies in Social Science and Humanities* 1, no. 2 (August 25, 2022): 1–8, accessed May 8, 2023, https://doi.org/10.56397/SSSH.2022.09.01. Taslak, Soner, and Nazli Ersoy. 2022. "A bibliometric analysis of digital feminism research." In *Handbook of Research on Digital Violence and Discrimination Studies*. Hershey, PA: IGI Global, pp. 134–162.

84 Carillo, Karen Juanita. 2020. "How the Chicano movement championed Mexican-American identity and fought for change." https://www.history.com/news/chicano-movement.

85 Montoya, Maceo. 2016. *Chicano Movement for Beginners*. Newburyport, MA: Red Wheel/Weiser.

86 Riddell, Adaljiza Sosa. 1997. "Chicanas and el movimiento." In Alma M. Garcia (ed.), *Chicana Feminist Thought: The Basic Historical Writings*. New York: Routledge, pp. 92–94.

87 Gutiérrez, José Ángel. "The Chicano movement: Paths to power." *The Social Studies* 102, no. 1 (2010): 25–32.

88 Kenlon, Philip. "Quakers and the Anti-War Movement during the Vietnam War (1963–1975)." Accessed December 16, 2022. https://library.guilford.edu/VietnamWar.

89 International Center on Nonviolent Conflict. "The US Anti-Vietnam War Movement (1964–1973)." https://www.nonviolent-conflict.org/us-anti-vietnam-war-movement-1964-1973/.

90 Anastasio, Joseph. *The Vietnam War, 1954–1975*. Accessed December 16, 2022. http://ltsgrady.weebly.com/uploads/1/0/3/8/10389380/8_ch.25_vietnam_war.pdf .

91 Wells, Tom. "The Anti-Vietnam War movement in the United States." *The Vietnam War* 1 (1998): 115–125.

92 National Archives. *African American Heritage: Black Power*. Accessed December 16, 2022. https://growingdemocracyoh.org/wp-content/uploads/2021/04/Indigenous-Activism.pdf.

93 Joseph, Peniel E. "The Black Power movement: A state of the field." *Journal of American History* 96, no. 3 (2009): 751–776.

94 American Indian Movement. https://www.mnopedia.org/group/american-indian-movement-aim#:~:text=The%20American%20Indian%20Movement%20(AIM)%2C%20founded%20by%20grassroots%20activists,tribal%20sovereignty%20and%20treaty%20rights. Murnane, Emily. *Indigenous Activism*. Accessed December 16, 2022. https://growingdemocracyoh.org/wp-content/uploads/2021/04/Indigenous-Activism.pdf.

95 Schuttler, John F. 1991. "The American Indian Movement as a revolutionary organization." Master's thesis, University of Montana, pp. 1–84, accessed May 8, 2023, https://scholarworks.umt.edu/etd/9337.

96 Johnson, Troy. "The occupation of Alcatraz Island: Roots of American Indian activism." *Wicazo Sa Review* (1994): 63–79.

97 Schuttler, "The American Indian Movement as a revolutionary organization."

98 Johansen, Bruce E. 2022. "Police fiction: Native American activists' political murders at or Near Pine Ridge, South Dakota, 1973–1976." In Adebowale Akande (ed.), *Handbook of Racism, Xenophobia, and Populism*. Champaign, IL: Springer, pp. 343–360.

99 Weiss, Jana. "The National Day of Mourning: Thanksgiving, civil religion, and American Indians." *Amerikastudien/American Studies* (2018): 367–388.

100 Zafir, Lindsay. 2019. "Act Up." In Howard Chiang, Anjali Arondekar, Marc Epprecht, and Jennifer Evans (eds.), *Global Encyclopedia of Lesbian, Gay, Bisexual, Transgender, and Queer (LGBTQ) History*, vol. 1. Farmington Hills, MI: Charles Scribner's Sons, pp. 1–8.

101 The History Channel, "Gay Rights," June15, 2022, https://www.history .com/topics/gay-rights/history-of-gay-rights.

102 Bruce, Katherine McFarland. 2016. ""Pride parades." In *Pride Parades*. New York: New York University Press, pp. 97–125.

103 Hubbard, Thomas. "The 1980s: A decade of progress for the Gay Rights Movement." Accessed December 17, 2022. https://www.sdlgbtn.com/the -1980s-a-decade-of-progress-for-the-gay-rights-movement.

104 Hermann, Donald H.J. "Extending the fundamental right of marriage to same-sex couples: The United States Supreme Court decision in Obergefell v. Hodges." *Ind. L. Rev.* 49 (2015): 367.

105 Wardle, Lynn D. "Section Three of the Defense of Marriage Act: Deciding, democracy, and the Constitution." *Drake L. Rev.* 58 (2009): 951. Pearce, Marc W. "The Defense of Marriage Act and equal protection rights." Accessed December 17, 2022.) https://www.apa.org/monitor/2011/07-08/jn.

106 Lee, M.J., Betsy Klein, and Kevin Liptak. "Biden signs into law same-sex marriage bill, 10 years after his famous Sunday show answer on the issue." https://www.cnn.com/2022/12/13/politics/white-house-same-sex-marriage -signing-ceremony/index.html.

107 Sierra Club, Environmental Justice Movement. https://www.sierraclub.org/ environmental-justice/history-environmental-justice.

108 Catholic Campaign for Human Development. "Supporting environmental justice in Portland, OR." Accessed December 17, 2022. https://www.pover-tyusa.org/stories/environmental-justice-portland.

109 Wilson, Sacoby M. "Environmental Justice Movement: a review of history, research, and public health issues." *Journal of Public Management & Social Policy* 16, no. 1 (2010): 19–51.

110 Bullard, Robert D. "Dismantling environmental racism in the USA." *Local Environment* 4, no. 1 (1999): 5–19.

111 Ibid. Barca, Stefania. "On working-class environmentalism: A historical and transnational overview." *Interface: A Journal for and about Social Movements* 4, no. 2 (2012): 61–80. Porter, Jayson Maurice. "Agrochemicals, Environmental Racism, and Environmental Justice in US History." *The Organic Center,* last modified February 2022, accessed May 8, 2023, https:// www.organic-center.org/sites/default/files/agrochemicals_racism_and_jus-tice_in_us_history.pdf.

112 Suk, Jiyoun, Aman Abhishek, Yini Zhang, So Yun Ahn, Teresa Correa, Christine Garlough, and Dhavan V. Shah. "# MeToo, networked acknowl-edgment, and connective action: How 'empowerment through empathy' launched a social movement." *Social Science Computer Review* 39, no. 2 (2021): 276–294.

113 Lee, Bun-Hee. "# Me Too movement: It is time that we all act and participate in transformation." *Psychiatry investigation* 15, no. 5 (2018): 433.

114 Manago, A., N. Santer, Logan L. Barsigian, and A. Walsh. "Social media as tools for cultural change in the transition to adulthood." *Cultural Methods in Psychology: Describing and Transforming Cultures* (2021): 146–173.

115 Calhoun, Craig. "Occupy Wall Street in perspective." *British Journal of Sociology* 64, no. 1 (2013): 26–38.

116 Suh, Chan S., Ion Bogdan Vasi, and Paul Y. Chang. "How social media matter: Repression and the diffusion of the Occupy Wall Street movement." *Social Science Research* 65 (2017): 282–293.
117 Van Gelder, Sarah, ed. 2011. *This Changes Everything: Occupy Wall Street and the 99% Movement.* Oakland, CA: Berrett-Koehler.
118 Howard University Law Library, Black Lives Matter History. https://library .law.howard.edu/civilrightshistory/BLM.
119 Garza, Alicia. "A herstory of the# BlackLivesMatter movement." *The Feminist Wire* (blog), (October 7, 2014), accessed May 8, 2023, https:// thefeministwire.com/2014/10/blacklivesmatter-2/.
120 Trivedi, Somil, and Nicole Gonzalez Van Cleve. "To serve and protect each other: How police-prosecutor codependence enables police misconduct." *BUL Rev.* 100 (2020): 895.
121 Germain, Robertson, and Minnis, "Protests, rallies, marches, and social movements as organizational change agents."

# ADVOCATES FOR ACTION

## Ida B. Wells-Barnett

1862–1931
Hometown: Holly Springs, Mississippi, USA
Movements: Civil and women's rights movements, urban reform
Organizations: National Association of Colored Women's Clubs, National
Association for the Advancement of Colored People

*Allison Schuster*

Born Ida Bell Wells, Wells-Barnett was a notable journalist, activist, suffragist, and researcher, who spent her life fighting against racism and sexism.[1] Her strong writing and communication skills allowed her to bring attention to the treatment of the Black community in the South.

Born in 1862 to house servants in Holly Springs, Mississippi, Wells became a schoolteacher during her teenage years to save money so she could attend Rust College.[2] Despite being expelled from the educational institution for an altercation with the university's president, she persevered. A few years later, Wells moved to Memphis, Tennessee, where she pursued a career as an educator after the death of her parents. During her time in Memphis, she thrived, becoming the center of local literary circles.

Then, in 1884, Wells' life changed. She was famously thrown off a train traveling from Memphis to Nashville, Tennessee. The incident occurred when Wells refused to leave the first-class ladies' car and move to the segregated car for African-Americans, which was known as the "Jim Crow" car.[3] Although she would win the subsequent case in the local court, it

DOI: 10.4324/9781003291855-4

was later overturned in a federal court. Shortly after these legal proceedings, Wells began to focus on White mob violence following the lynching of a friend.[4] This event led her to investigate several cases of the lynching of Black men, the findings of which she published in a pamphlet as well as writing several columns for local newspapers. One of these publications about an 1892 lynching so deeply enraged the community that her press was burned, and she was forced to move to Chicago, Illinois under the threat of death.

In Chicago, Wells met famous Black lawyer Ferdinand Barnett. The couple married in 1895 and would go on to have four children.[5] Wells-Barnett is highly respected for how she balanced motherhood with her demanding career, paving the way for many women.[6]

Wells-Barnett continued to draw attention to lynching of Black Americans by traveling internationally and educating others on the situation within the United States.[7] In her time in different countries, she proudly called attention to White suffragists who ignored lynching, leading her to be publicly ridiculed by women's suffrage organizations in the United States. Undaunted, Wells-Barnett founded the National Association of Colored Women's Clubs to address civil rights and women's suffrage issues.[8] Furthermore, although her name is not included as a founder, Wells-Barnett was present in Niagara Falls, New York State for the creation of the National Association for the Advancement of Colored People.[9]

In the final days of her career, Wells-Barnett focused on urban reform in Chicago. Years after her death in 1931, she is still heralded as a prominent and courageous communicator and activist.

## Notes

1 Norwood, Arlisha R. n.d. "Ida B. Wells-Barnett." National Women's History Museum. Accessed January 1, 2023. https://www.womenshistory.org/education-resources/biographies/ida-b-wells-barnett. Holton, Sandra Stanley. "Segregation, racism and white women reformers: a transnational analysis, 1840–1912." *Women's History Review* 10, no. 1 (2001): 5–26.
2 Tucker, David M. "Miss Ida B. Wells and Memphis lynching." *Phylon* 32, no. 2 (1971): 112–122. Norwood, "Ida B. Wells-Barnett."
3 Mack, Kenneth W. "Law, society, identity, and the making of the Jim Crow South: Travel and segregation on Tennessee railroads, 1875–1905." *Law & Social Inquiry* 24, no. 2 (1999): 377–409.
4 National Park Service. 2020. "Ida B. Wells." https://www.nps.gov/people/idabwells.htm.
5 Plant, Deborah. "DeCosta-Willis, Miriam. Ed. 'The Memphis Diary of Ida B. Wells: An Intimate Portrait of the Activist as a Young Woman'" (book review). *Griot* 16, no. 2 (1997): 54.
6 Bay, Mia. "The Improbable Ida B. Wells." *Reviews in American History* 30, no. 3 (2002): 439–444.

7 Totten, Gary. "Embodying segregation: Ida B. Wells and the cultural work of travel." *African American Review* 42, no. 1 (2008): 47–60.
8 Norwood, "Ida B. Wells-Barnett."
9 Giddings, Paula. "Missing in action: Ida B. wells, the NAACP, and the historical record." *Meridians: Feminism, Race, Transnationalism* 1, no. 2 (2001): 1–17.

# 2

# A REFUSAL TO ACCEPT

## Oppression around the World

*Adrienne A. Wallace*

## Introduction

As more of the world becomes connected online, revolutionaries across the globe are being empowered like never before. Although not all are successful at sustaining the movements, the use of information communication technologies is critical in developing and sustaining modern social movements. Social movements are born out of years of oppression sustained over a lengthy period of time. This chapter systematically provides the structure of collective action grounded in social change and collective behavior and systemic oppression as applied to global world events.

## Collective Action, Collective Challenges

Emeritus professor of political science Sidney Tarrow defined a **social movement** as "collective challenges [to elites, authorities, other groups, or cultural codes] by people with common purposes and solidarity in sustained interactions with elites, opponents and authorities."[1] He specifically distinguishes social movements from political parties and advocacy groups. Social movements and collective action are closely connected, as social movements often rely on collective action to achieve their goals. **Collective action** (CA) can be defined as all activity of common or shared interest among two or more individuals.[2] Olson's classic work sets out to explain and illustrate how collective failure occurs when individuals pursue self-interest.[3] The argument assumes that every person individually

DOI: 10.4324/9781003291855-5

acts rationally, but if everyone chooses not to act – in respect to individual costs and benefits – no CA would occur.[4]

Collective identity and frame alignment were developed from CA theory to demonstrate how individuals communicate to frame or analyze grievances that are part of the collective. While most of these theories and frameworks were developed before the internet era, it is of interest to use them to assess online assembly through social media for illustrating social media's impact on social movements. Information communication technologies are critical in developing and executing modern social movements, but have mixed outcomes with regard to sustainability.

Prolific proponent of the networked society Manuel Castells describes mass media being displaced by mass self-communication[5] in altering the communication model from one-to-one to many-to-many.[6] Social media tends to be decentralized, nonmarket, peer-produced, nonproprietary, open-sourced, commons-based, and provides free or inexpensive access and distribution.[7] In order for a social movement driven by social media to live, or to be an event, the activism must not only be displayed through social media, but also have a presence in the world on public display in plain view. As a result of the change in power dynamics between traditional media and social media (new media) with the emergence of the internet, activist groups advocating social change have strained relationships with traditional mainstream media, yet still social movements still rely on mainstream media for legitimacy of actions.[8]

As outlined in chapter 1, the first **social movements** occurred through acts of civil disobedience such as protests. However, the rise of the internet ushered in abundant digital (online) social movements. Online communities such as Meta (Facebook) groups, Reddit, Twitter, Instagram, and TikTok have connected people worldwide to develop a base and gain awareness of issues. Since then, digital, or online social movements have gained momentum and are now one of the most prevalent forms of social activism. Taking on the "establishment" is not a new concept. Social movements worldwide can be tracked back to the early 1700s. Believe it or not, the Declaration of Independence is an example of an early social movement. More modern examples include the labor movement and the Civil Rights movements in the 1960s which then paved the way for digital movements in the 21st century.

While one might be quick to identify the Arab Spring as the earliest social digital movement, we have to take a step back even further to the 1990s to the beginnings of the internet to recall when software company Lotus and credit bureau Equifax "gained access" to the names, addresses, and emails of millions of Americans. The incident, which occurred in 1990, exposed the personal information of millions of Americans, including Social Security numbers, birth dates, addresses, and driver's license numbers. The company initially stated that the breach had affected approximately 143 million US consumers, but later revealed that it also impacted an additional 2.5 million US consumers, as well as an undisclosed number of consumers in Canada and the United Kingdom. While this breach occurred on CD-ROM format, this registers as one of the earliest online social movements. Organizers used emails, bulletin board systems (BBSs), and chat rooms such as Internet Relay Chat through Direct Client Connection to send messages and files to other users and other message boards.

Now, if you cannot recall having to gain access through a disc, have not heard the wails of the modem connect sound through a phone line, or never had an AOL instant message screen name, you might not be able to fully appreciate the simplicity or impact of the first BBS as a means of instant communication, or likewise the sting of the AIM "away" message. However, if you remember downloading songs (maybe even illegally) from Napster or The Pirate Bay, you likely can recall a time before social media platforms were used to amplify messages. Since the early 2000s, the creation and adoption of early digital systems post-email have led to or creates what we now refer to as digital (online) social movements.

## Theories of Social Movements Examined

Regarding the importance of social movements in general, particularly in a new media society, Tarrow[9] reminds us that, as shown in the daily news cycle, the notion of social movements, are defined as "collective challenges, based on common purposes and social solidarities, in sustained interaction with elites, opponents, and authorities" performing "sequences of contentious politics that are based on underlying social networks and resonant collective action frames, and which develop the capacity to maintain sustained challenges against powerful opponents."[10] Sustaining this activity, however, defines the social movement. Tarrow identified four characteristics, or what he calls prerequisites, of sustainable social movements: (1) political opportunities, (2) diffuse social networks, (3) familiar forms of collective action, and (4) cultural frames that can resonate throughout a population.[11]

A grievance in and of itself cannot create a movement as there are "free riders" who cannot be excluded from obtaining the benefits of a collective good once the good has been produced and have little incentive to be voluntary contributors to attainment of that good.[12] To Tarrow, social movements are "collective challenges, based on common purposes and social solidarities, in sustained interaction with elites, opponents, and authorities."[13] Riots and other flashes in the pan are not a social movement – it isn't a movement unless it is "sustained," and above all is triggered by the ebb and flow of political struggle.[14]

The dynamic of cycles of contention taking aim at the essence of political opportunity is a powerful one, Tarrow discusses the fact that as information spreads about the susceptibility of a polity to challenge, additional activists and also "ordinary people" may "begin to test the limits of social control,"[15] and the success of one movement generates or at least contributes to greater opportunity for other movements. When the resulting "cycles of contention" spread to an extreme, revolution may occur: "The difference between movement cycles and revolutions is that, in the latter, multiple centers of sovereignty are created, turning the conflict between challengers and members of the polity into a struggle for power."[16]

Multifactored models of social movement formation are advanced, resources are emphasized, organization is critical to the movement, and political opportunities must exist in addition to existing or consistent grievances built into social institutions, and movements form because of long-term changes in resources, organization of members, and opportunities present for collective action.[17] While Tarrow builds a stronger case for the "sudden" nature of revolutions and social movements in acquisition of resources,[18] I think the duration of the grievance or the history of the grievance are of lesser significance than the political opportunity for mobilization of actors.

The nature of these episodes, while similar, is not beyond empirical explanation: as identified by Smelser,[19] indeterminacy is not an explanation for collective action. Agitation by a minority against a majority in the name of a generalized belief is the very core of social movements, revolutions, and what Smelser calls norm-oriented movement where actors attempt to affect change with social movement at the epicenter.[20] Norm-oriented movements are precursors for "collective outbursts" (or revolutions) and general social movements, in Smelser's opinion.[21] Tarrow and other authors pull out the complexities of the forms in which these take and sustain.[22]

Tarrow demonstrates that political alliances and processes help shape success and failure of social movements,[23] while Jenkins[24] argues that formal organization is not incompatible in creating a social movement; however, he wouldn't agree that it is the most important scalable variable needed to attain success of a movement, but it bears mentioning that at a minimum it does aid in social movement sustainability. The impact on Tarrow is noted[25] as formal organization is not incompatible in the creation of social movements, and obvious for their impact on collective action[26] wherein rational choice and eyes on greater good are well supported at the heart of most social movements.

Movements are dynamic and hard to control because they are loose associations of individuals. Internally, the movement cannot control its participants. Externally, political opportunities and constraints continue to shift, which impacts the social movement in its life cycle.[27] As most theorists would agree, from early works to current ones, movements are highly unstable, and while subject to mass activism, can also suffer from mass apathy, ending the mobilization of efforts.

In *Power in Movement*, Tarrow illustrates the cyclical history of social movements, in the form of the protest cycle.[28] He also convincingly demonstrates how movements can affect various spheres of life, such as personal lives, policy reforms, and political culture.[29] This concept of grievances must be explained, and a revolution, while seemingly spontaneous, is actually quite systematic, as explored by Kornhauser in *The Politics of Mass Society*;[30] collective behavior explains that remote or abstract experiences or symbols do not create terms of mass behavior; only when that concern is localized or personalized can we speak of mass behavior or activism in society; the change in context brings about the willingness in the society as a collective sparking a revolution or social movement.[31]

Complexity is perhaps the one thing social movement theorists *do* agree on. After that, opinions and reports vary on this topic from one theorist to another. Traditionally, the problem has been explaining individual participation in social movements. Jenkins presents that traditional theories which commonly share the assumptions that movement participation was: relatively rare, discontents were transitory, movement and institutionalized action were sharply distinct, and movement actors were arational if not outright irrational.[32] Social movements are traditionally seen as having roots in personal change and institutional change.[33]

Olson[34] attempted to make the case for an economy based on the actions of an individual (rational choice). In *The Logic of Collective Action: Public Goods and the Theory of Groups*, Olson provides an important analysis of the problems of public good cost based on activity of a single actor and his/her collaboration.[35] The economic theory of collective action is concerned with the provision of public goods (and other collective consumption) through the collaboration of two or more individuals, and the impact of externalities on group behavior. It is more commonly referred to as "public choice," and can be seen as an influence on the study of social movements through resource mobilization theory.

Olson[36] made the highly controversial claim that individual rational choice leads to situations where individuals with more resources will carry a higher burden in the provision of the public good than poorer ones, with poorer individuals left with little choice but to opt for the free rider strategy by attempting to benefit from the public good without contributing to its provision. This may also encourage the under-production (inefficient production) of the public good. Where Olson describes this as a "free rider" scenario (taken negatively), perhaps others would point to collective action (i.e., groups, associations, unions) as a rational choice in the power of the disadvantaged (many) allowing them to participate in democracy by collaboration or pooling or mobilization of resources, not just benefiting from the actions without representation or participation.[37]

To qualify as a social movement mass society, differentiation is present coupling social movements within societies creating social movements. Mass behavior is demonstrated at varying levels in societies based on the enabling or stifling of behavior from above and below the social hierarchy. Smelser discussed the nature of these episodes in *Theory of Collective Behavior*,[38] and they are not as mysterious or spontaneous as they may seem, but rather dependent on the variable combinations present. Similar to Zald's[39] take on the emerging synthesis of social movements and revolutions, one must take into account the range, variety, and diversity of mobilizing structures formal, informal and hybrid in social movement organizations; wherein the level of mobilization and framing are essential to understanding movement.

### Importance of Being Current, in Context

As one movement widens and "information spreads about the susceptibility of a polity to challenge," additional activists and also "ordinary people" may "begin to test the limits of social control."[40] In other words, one movement's success creates greater (perceived) opportunity for other movements. When the resulting "cycles of contention" spread to an extreme, revolution may occur.

Tarrow argues that "The difference between movement cycles and revolutions is that, in the latter, multiple centers of sovereignty are created, turning the conflict between challengers and members of the polity into a struggle for power."[41] He maintains "that contention is more closely related to opportunities for and limited by constraints upon collective action than by the persistent social or economic factors that people experience."[42] Nevertheless, "changing opportunities must be seen alongside more stable structural elements like the strength or weakness of the state and the forms of repression it habitually employs."[43]

### Oppression around the World

Social justice and social movement opportunities are not only static, but they can also exist for brief periods of time then disappear, or the political changes because of the influence of mobilization can lead to demobilization or additional/different opportunities or **oppression**. According to feminist and political theorist Iris Marion Young, there are five "faces" or types of oppression: violence, exploitation, marginalization, powerlessness, and cultural imperialism.[44]

> Oppression [is] the social act of placing severe restrictions on an individual group, or institution. Typically, a government or political organization in power places restrictions formally or covertly on oppressed groups so they may be exploited and less able to compete with other social groups. The oppressed individual or group is devalued, exploited, and deprived of privileges by the individual or group who has more power, resulting in powerlessness.[45]

Its major ideas include devaluation, exploitation, and privilege, all of which are integrally tied to the phenomena of oppression, which permeates all cultures and has done so throughout history. The fight against oppression is not new, but the efforts to systemically eradicate oppression are increasingly amplified in a "flat" or otherwise boundaryless world that is connected through the internet and social media.

### Violence

The most overt and evident form of oppression is likely violence. Some people live with the constant terror of arbitrary, unprovoked attacks on their person or property. These assaults aim to harm, humiliate, or completely destroy the target without necessarily having a reason why. Women, Blacks, Asians, Arabs, and the LGBTQ+ community all face such violence threats in American society. Jews, Puerto Ricans, Chicanos, Latino/Latina, or Latinx, Hispanics, and other Spanish-speaking Americans must also be wary of violence in at least some areas. Hate crimes and all forms of sexual violence are common instances of violent oppression. The majority of violent oppression, if not all of it, is a direct result of **xenophobia**.

### Exploitation

The practice of enlisting another person's work for financial gain without paying them fairly is known as exploitation. For example, sweatshop workers are taken advantage of: despite being compensated for their labor, they do not receive fair pay given how much money they generate for the business. When African miners must hire their mining equipment every day, they are also taken advantage of. These miners are not rewarded for their work if they don't find anything valuable on any given day; instead, they are responsible for paying for equipment rental.

Capitalism uses exploitation to oppress. According to capitalism's economic philosophy, people are free to freely exchange goods. However, whenever this has occurred historically, it has led to the creation of separate social classes,[46] including the rich and the impoverished, and even historically encouraged White supremacy.[47]

## Marginalization

One issue that consistently surfaces in addressing radical oppression dissolution efforts is that movements sometimes prioritize one group above another as an exclusionary or marginalization tactic. The Australian Aboriginal groups are one well-known example, which were driven out of civilization and further and further from their ancestral grounds as cities flourished. Marginalization and the concept of Whiteness are strongly related. The majority of marginalized groups in the United States are racially distinct. However, Blacks and Indians in Latin America, as well as East Indians, Eastern Europeans and North Africans in Europe, also experience racial exclusion.

For instance, although the civil rights campaigns in the United States and Northern Ireland in the 1960s attracted attention to discrimination against and denial of human rights to minority groups on the basis of race and religion, respectively, the denial of women's rights was generally disregarded. The causes that led to freedoms for the groups in question (Blacks and other minority groups) in the United States eventually gave rise to the feminist movement and social movements for women, then these changes extended across the Western world in subsequent decades.

Aside from deliberate action, social behaviors that are influenced by particular beliefs and norms can also result in oppression (disadvantage and injustice). It's significant to note that "oppression may develop not merely because society intentionally wants to disfavor particular groups of individuals, but rather because of the impact of social norms, legal frameworks, and untested assumptions."[48] Both acts of commission and omission can result in oppression. As such, a large group of people are excluded from useful social engagement when they are marginalized. These populations thus experience significant material deprivation (they lack access to essential resources) and possibly even extermination (such as genocide).

Universities have been at the center of Iran's anti-government uprising; however, the cost for students protesting in the Islamic Republic has "never been higher," according to current and former activists.[49]

"They are getting killed, arrested, banned from campus, long prison sentences,"[50] said Nasim Sarabandi, a former student leader of the 2009 Green Movement protests for electoral reform. The price paid by this generation of Iranian students demanding their rights is rising day by day. And as the repression deepens, they are giving up on the fight for reform – for years a rallying cry of student movements.

According to *The Washington Post*, the young men and women who have risked their lives and futures in these demonstrations (related to Mahsa Amini's death) want nothing less than the end of oppressive clerical rule and marginalization,[51] but have been met by "state-sanctioned killing," with executions being used as a fear tactic to stamp out dissent.[52]

## Powerlessness

Marx's theory of socialism has a connection to the notion of powerlessness: some people "have" power while others "have not."[53] The inability to develop one's abilities, the lack of decision-making authority, and being subjected to disrespectful treatment due to diminished status are some of the fundamental injustices associated with being powerless. For example, because they believe they cannot do so or that their participation will not matter, the powerless in the United States refrain from taking part in fundamental democratic processes. This typically takes the form of abstaining from voting or other decision-making. In some cases, the state delivers powerlessness in the form of restricting this fundamental democratic process, like in the United States, where prisoners are not able to vote as a result of their incarceration.

The more subtle types of helplessness, however, are even more pernicious. Paulo Freire, a philosopher of education from Brazil, contends that because it permits individuals to oppress both themselves and others, impotence is the strongest type of oppression.[54]

In January 2023, supporters of far-right former President Jair Bolsonaro stormed Brazil's Congress and presidential offices to protest what they falsely believed was a stolen election. The event was the violent culmination of incessant rhetorical attacks by Bolsonaro and his supporters, called "Bolsonaristas," against the nation's electoral systems.[55]

Thousands of protesters ascended a ramp to the roof of the congressional building in Brasília, the capital, while a smaller group invaded from a lower level, according to witnesses and videos of the scene posted on social media through global news outlets.[56] President Luiz Inácio Lula da Silva, who defeated Bolsonaro in October and took office on January 1, 2023, was in São Paulo, and Congress was not in session. Both the congressional building and the presidential offices were largely empty during the attack. The invasions capped months of protests and powerlessness by Bolsonaro's supporters, who camped outside military bases across the country and called on the armed forces to take control of the government and halt Lula's inauguration.[57]

### Cultural Imperialism

Other acts of oppression occur through **cultural imperialism**, which refers to the process by which a designated group is denigrated, devalued, and stereotyped by the ideals of the dominant culture that are established as what appear to be universal norms or common sense, according to

**FIGURE 2.1**   Two young people hold hands at the Bogota Colombia Pride Parade in June 2019 to support "love is love" Photo credit: used with permission of Dr. Anthony Spencer, Grand Valley State University, Allendale, Michigan, USA.

Northway.[58] According to Young,[59] cultural imperialist groups "present their own ideals, experience, and perspectives as normative and universal." In order to justify denying civil rights to those perceived to be "inferior," for example, the cultural imperialism of colonial racism in South Africa under apartheid shaped certain readings of the Bible and of biology. This ideology served to uphold, defend, and maintain minority White dominance, while the statistical majority were awarded minority status.

Rather than being historically and culturally distinctive, the dominant culture portrays some attitudes about superiority and inferiority as natural and taken for granted. Negative stereotypes are "submerged in" devalued groups.[60] The desire to assert the "normality" and "superiority" of the dominant group is at the heart of cultural imperialism, which is why critics claim that the purpose of showing negative images of disabled people in literature, film, and the media is to affirm how different "they" are from "us" and how admirably normal "we" are as a result.[61]

In Latin America, racial discrimination is only one of the manifestations of racism. While it is the most evident, this regime of power historically affected and continues to affect indigenous and Afro-descendant peoples: "In Latin American societies, racism is so naturalized that the majority of the population tends to limit the use of the concept of racism to explicit acts of racial discrimination."[62]

Oppression that culminates in conflict and persecution can, in extreme situations, result in ethnic cleansing, as in Cyprus, Palestine, Bosnia, or Sudan, or even genocide, as horrifyingly experienced during the Holocaust and more recently in Cambodia and Rwanda. The manufactured "eternal ownership" of the territory by the main ethnic nation and the dubious status of minorities have been the shared denominators. Additionally, the idea of an exclusive homeland has the potential to incite a "chain reaction" and turn minorities against one another, which additionally serves the oppressor.

Attitudes against minority communities have never stayed constant. Many multi-ethnic regimes have progressively enacted accommodation policies in recent years as a result of evidence that consistent mistreatment of minorities generally breeds resistance and the potential for insurgency.[63] Despite this change, other regimes continue to isolate and repress minorities, which keeps ethnic strife at a high level and often leads to conflict globally.

Over time, cultural imperialism has persisted. India now is a good illustration. During the colonization of India, the British Empire replaced indigenous languages and beliefs with British language and beliefs. As a result, modern Indians still speak English and exhibit numerous British traits even after their British domination was abolished.

Sexuality is a frequent illustration of cultural imperialism seen throughout the world. All sexual orientations other than heterosexual are categorized as "others" and seen as inferior or aberrant because heterosexuality is the dominant sexual orientation in society. This concept has a term, **heteronormative**, which propagates the idea that heterosexuality is superior and more normal, and is reinforced by culture and educational systems; therefore, people with various sexual orientations are advised to adopt a heterosexual lifestyle.

Stereotypes mark and make invisible those who are the targets of cultural imperialism. They are limited in what they can be by these stereotypes. In addition, these same assumptions reduce these individuals to a group of "others" who lack distinct identities. Because he has the most authority, the "White guy" can be an individual and have a separate identity.

## Conclusion

Oppression is a pervasive problem that exists around the world in many forms, such as violence, exploitation, marginalization, powerlessness, and cultural imperialism. These forms of oppression have been used to limit the access to resources and rights of minority groups. These groups are often denied basic rights, such as the right to vote, and are subjected to disrespectful treatment due to their diminished status. In order to combat oppression, it is essential to recognize the various forms that it takes and to work towards dismantling systems and ideologies that sustain it.

As such, social movements are an important part of the global landscape, empowering individuals and groups to fight against oppression and injustice. Such movements often take the form of collective challenges to political elites, authorities, other groups, or cultural codes. CA theory is a founding theory used to explain how individuals communicate to frame or analyze grievances that are part of the collective, and how collective identity and frame alignment can help movements gain momentum.

With the emergence of the internet, activist groups advocating social change have had strained relationships with traditional mainstream media, yet still rely on mainstream media to legitimize their actions. Digital or online social movements have been driven by online communities such as Meta (Facebook) groups, Reddit, and Twitter, Instagram, and TikTok, and have become one of the most prevalent forms of social activism. Theories of social movements, such as those of Tarrow, Smelser, and Olson, provide a basis for understanding the complexities of how social movements form, sustain, and ultimately succeed or fail.

It is clear that the success of social movements is dependent on multiple factors, including political opportunities, diffuse social networks, familiar forms of collective action, and cultural frames that can resonate throughout a population. In order for social movements to be successful, it is important to be aware, reflective, and have sustaining measures in place for succession and long-term validity.

## Reflections

- What are the key components of a successful social movement?
- How has the internet impacted the development and activities of modern social movements?
- What are the advantages and disadvantages of online social movements?
- What role do resources, organization, and political opportunity play in social movement formation?
- How have traditional theories of social movements been challenged by the rise of online social movements?
- How do collective identity and frame alignment help explain the success of social movements?
- What is the difference between movement cycles and revolutions?
- How do normative orientations influence both social movements and revolutions?
- What are the implications of Olson's "free rider" scenario for understanding social movements?

## Notes

1 Tarrow, Sidney G. 2011. *Power in Movement: Social Movements and Contentious Politics*, 3rd ed. Cambridge, UK: Cambridge University Press.
2 Ibid.
3 Olson, Mancur. 1971. *The Logic of Collective Action: Public Goods and the Theory of Groups, with a New Preface and Appendix*. London: Harvard University Press.
4 Ibid.
5 Castells, Manuel. 2013. *Communication Power*, 2nd ed. Oxford, UK: Oxford University Press.
6 Deluca, Kevin M., Sean Lawson, and Ye Sun. "Occupy Wall Street on the public screens of social media: The many framings of the birth of a protest movement." *Communication, Culture & Critique* 5, no. 4 (2012): 483–509.
7 Benkler, Yochai. 2007. *The Wealth of Networks: How Social Production Transforms Markets and Freedom*. New Haven, CT: Yale University Press.
8 Gitlin, Todd. 2003. *The Whole World Is Watching: Mass Media in the Making and Unmaking of the New Left with a New Preface*. Berkeley, CA: University of California Press. McChesney, Robert Waterman. 2015. *Rich Media, Poor Democracy: Communication Politics in Dubious Times*. New York: New Press.

9 Tarrow, *Power in Movement.*
10 Ibid.
11 Ibid.
12 Olson, *The Logic of Collective Action.* Ostrom, Elinor. 1990. *Governing the Commons: The Evolution of Institutions for Collective Action.* Cambridge, UK: Cambridge University Press.
13 Tarrow, *Power in Movement.*
14 Ibid.
15 Ibid.
16 Ibid.
17 Jenkins, J. Craig. "Resource mobilization theory and the study of social movements." *Annual Review of Sociology* 9, no. 1 (1983): 527–553.
18 Tarrow, *Power in Movement.*
19 Smelser, Neil J. 1962. *Theory of Collective Behavior.* New York: Free Press.
20 Ibid.
21 Ibid.
22 Tarrow, *Power in Movement.*
23 Ibid.
24 Jenkins, "Resource mobilization theory and the study of social movements."
25 Tarrow, *Power in Movement.*
26 Olson, *The Logic of Collective Action.* Olson, Mancur. 2000. *Harvard Economic Studies: The Logic of Collective Action*, 18th ed. Cambridge, MA: Harvard University Press. Ostrom, *Governing the Commons.*
27 Tarrow, *Power in Movement.*
28 Ibid.
29 Ibid.
30 Kornhauser, William. 1959. *The Politics of Mass Society.* New York: Routledge.
31 Ibid.
32 Jenkins, "Resource mobilization theory and the study of social movements."
33 Ibid.
34 Olson, *The Logic of Collective Action.*
35 Ibid.
36 Ibid.
37 Ibid.
38 Smelser, *Theory of Collective Behavior.*
39 Zald, M.N. "Epilogue: social movements and political sociology in the analysis of organizations and markets." *Administrative Science Quarterly* 53, no. 3 (2008): 568–574.
40 Ibid.
41 Ibid.
42 Ibid.
43 Ibid.
44 Young, Iris Marion. 2009. "Five faces of oppression." In George L. Henderson and Marvin Waterstone (eds.), *Geographic Thought: A Praxis Perspective.* New York: Routledge. pp. 55–71. Young, Iris Marion. 2022. *Justice and the Politics of Difference.* New ed. Princeton, NJ: Princeton University Press.
45 Young, "Five faces of oppression." Barker, R.L. (ed.). *The Social Work Dictionary*, 5th ed. Washington, DC: NASW Press, 2003.
46 Berberoglu, Berch. "Class, race and gender: The triangle of oppression." *Race, Sex & Class* 2, no. 1 (1994): 69–77.

47 Nguyen, Cara. "The Relationship between White supremacy and capitalism: A socioeconomic study on embeddedness in the market and society." *Seattle University Undergraduate Research Journal* 4, no. 6: 7–11.

48 Northway, Ruth. "Disability and oppression: Some implications for nurses and nursing." *Journal of Advanced Nursing* 26, no. 4 (1997): 736–743.

49 Berger, Miriam. 2023. "Students in Iran are risking everything to rise up against the government." *The Washington Post.* Accessed January 21, 2023. https://www.washingtonpost.com/world/2023/01/05/iran-protests-students -mahsa-amini/.

50 Ibid.

51 Ibid.

52 Al Jazeera Media Network. 2023. "Iran executions 'state sanctioned killing': UN rights chief." Accessed January 21, 2023. https://www.aljazeera.com/ news/2023/1/10/iran-executions-amount-to-state-sanctioned-killing-un-says.

53 Fromm, Erich. 1961. *Marx's Concept of Man.* New York: Frederick Ungar Publishing.

54 Freire, Paulo. 2020 *Pedagogy of the Oppressed,* 50th ed. New York: Bloomsbury Academic.

55 Bowman, Emma. 2023. "Security forces regain control after Bolsonaro supporters storm Brazil's Congress." National Public Radio. Accessed January 21, 2023. https://www.npr.org/2023/01/08/1147757260/bolsonaro-support-ers-storm-brazil-congress-lula.

56 Pearson, Samantha, and Luciana Magalhaes. 2023. "Jair Bolsonaro supporters storm Brazil's Congress, High Court." *The Wall Street Journal.* Accessed January 21, 2023. https://www.wsj.com/articles/jair-bolsonaro-supporters -storm-brazils-congress-buildings-11673208386.

57 Ibid.

58 Northway, "Disability and oppression." Lugones, Maria C., and Elizabeth V. Spelman. "Have we got a theory for you! Feminist theory, cultural imperialism, and the demand for the 'woman's voice.'" *Women's Studies International Forum* 6, no. 6 (1983): 573–581.

59 Young, "Five faces of oppression."

60 Barnes, Colin, and Geof Mercer. "Disability, work, and welfare: Challenging the social exclusion of disabled people." *Work, Employment and Society* 19, no. 3 (2005): 527–545.

61 Thompson, David. "Profiling the sexually abusive behaviour of men with intellectual disabilities." *Journal of Applied Research in Intellectual Disabilities* 10, no. 2 (1997): 125–139.

62 Magallanes, Jatziri. 2022. "Discrimination continues to affect indigenous population." *UNESCO* blog. Accessed December 30, 2022. https://www .iesalc.unesco.org/en/2022/03/22/ discrimination-continues-to-affect-indig enous-population-mvs-noticias/.

63 Lange, M., T. Jeong, and E. Amasyali. "The colonial origins of ethnic warfare: Re-examining the impact of communalizing colonial policies in the British and French Empires." *International Journal of Comparative Sociology* 62, no. 2 (2021): 141–165.

# ADVOCATES FOR ACTION

## Mary E. Britton

1855–1925
Hometown: Lexington, Kentucky, USA
Movements: Civil and women's rights movements
Organizations: Lexington Women's Improvement Club, Colored Orphan
  Industrial Home, Kentucky Negro Association

*Allison Schuster*

Mary Ellen Britton was a prominent Black journalist, activist, physician, and educator widely respected for becoming the first Black female doctor in the state of Kentucky, practicing in her hometown of Lexington.[1]

Britton had an affluent upbringing that allowed her to pursue prime education for the times, graduating from Berea College in 1874 with a degree in teaching. Britton continued her education, ultimately graduating with a medical degree from the American Missionary College in Chicago, Illinois.[2] In 1902, she became Lexington's first Black woman licensed to practice medicine. After the implementation of Jim Crow laws, healthcare for Black patients became scarce, so Britton made it her life's work to make healthcare more accessible for the Black community.[3]

In addition to being a physician, Britton was a prominent activist within both the suffragist and Civil Rights movements. She wrote columns for a multitude of publications in which she vehemently opposed Jim Crow laws and advocated for social reform, especially focusing on the Separate Coach Law implemented in 1891.[4] She bravely campaigned against the idea of "separate but equal" train cars.[5]

DOI: 10.4324/9781003291855-6

When she was not busy with her work as a physician and activist, Britton's humanitarian nature lent itself greatly to community improvement. She served as president of the Women's Improvement Club in Lexington, fighting to improve women's social status, living conditions, and economic standing. Additionally, in her work as a member of the Kentucky Negro Association, Britton improved the Black community's living conditions through legislative action.[6] Furthermore, she founded and directed the Colored Orphan Industrial Home, working to help impoverished orphans and homeless elderly women acquire food, clothing, housing, and education.[7]

Two years after her retirement, Mary Ellen Britton passed away at the age of 70. She is widely regarded for her strong communications skills and balancing a wide array of community improvements through all of her different efforts in suffragism and activism.[8]

## Notes

1 Wade-Gayles, Gloria. "Black women journalists in the South, 1880–1905: An approach to the study of Black women's history." *Callaloo* 11/13 (1981): 138–152.

2 Vigil-Fowler, Margaret, and Sukumar Desai. "The community of Black women physicians, 1864–1941: Trends in background, education, and training." *History of Science* 59, no. 4 (2021): 407–433.

3 Bradley, Jaime. 2017. "Britton, Mary E." Hutchins Library, Berea College. https://libraryguides.berea.edu/maryebritton.

4 Hollingsworth, Randolph. "African American women voters in Lexington's school suffrage times, 1895–1902: Race matters in the history of the Kentucky woman suffrage movement." *Ohio Valley History* 20, no. 1 (2020): 30–53.

5 Deno, Ashleigh. 2020. "'Women's suffrage is "nothing less than treasonable': An Analysis of rural women and their group activism in the Women's Suffrage Movement in the Jackson Purchase area, 1838–1940."

6 Zackodnik, Teresa. 2021. "African American women and feminism in the 19th century." In *Oxford Research Encyclopedia of American History*.

7 Byars, Lauretta F. "Lexington's Colored Orphan Industrial Home, 1892–1913." *Register of the Kentucky Historical Society* 89, no. 2 (1991): 147–178.

8 Eblen, T. February 14, 2012. "Mary E. Britton Was A Woman Ahead Of Her Time." *Lexington Herald-Leader*. https://infoweb.newsbank.com/apps/news/document-view?p=AWNB&docref=news/16007CFAE00F0800&f=basic.

# 3

# CONTROLLING, CONSTRAINING, OR PREVENTING PROTEST

## Social Movement Interference in the Digital Age

*Li Chen*

The **repression** of social activism is common: individuals, groups, or government entities attempt to control, constrain, or prevent protests. Scholarship on repression has investigated why and how activist power is increasingly limited by the constraints and regulations placed on social movements.[1] In particular, the pervasiveness of digital/social media calls attention to the various factors that influence digital activism repression.[2] By conducting a literature review of social movement interference in the digital age, this chapter will focus on actors and means of social movement interference and how they are applied and developed in the digital sphere.

Despite a long history of intertwined relationships with various media forms, social movements have utilized social media for a variety of purposes: to create and maintain online communities of solidarity for social causes, to mobilize online participants through strong or weak ties, or to frame possible online discourses for social causes and movements.[3] For example, thoughts on the Arab Spring have celebrated social media's robust power in organizing the movement and publicizing police brutality on protesters.[4] Further, repression by different social agents has expanded and intensified by adopting new technology governance as barriers to social movements.[5] Social media's advantage for activists has become its disadvantage as well: policing authorities track and threaten their social ties, infiltrate their communities to prevent social movements, and launch disinformation campaigns to frame unpreferred online discourses for activists.[6]

To systematically investigate the repression of social media activism, scholars often use the term *digital repression* in recent research.[7] Different

DOI: 10.4324/9781003291855-7

from general internet governance,[8] digital repression targets online voices of dissent. Earl, Maher, and Pan suggest three dimensions included in this concept: online activists suffering from traditional repressive actions; digital tools used to oppress protests in traditional ways; and digital tools used to suppress activists in innovative ways.[9] These delineations highlight two critical elements in digital repression: online activists as the target, and new digital tools as the approach. Following Earl's classification of repressive agents as state or non-state,[10] this chapter seeks to understand how repressive actors employ police contention in a global context, particularly regarding social media activism.

Social movements in contemporary societies are embedded in a hybrid media environment.[11] Many activists express their dissent both online and offline. Therefore, the research questions of this literature review are the following: How do conventional repressive actions extend their policing into digital repression? When activists celebrate social media as a new arena in which to practice activism, does this arena increase or decrease the capacity of the state and private agents to intensify their control of domestic dissent? To examine the current scholarship on the research questions, this chapter first sketches several well-cited typologies of repression scholarship.

## Repression Typology: Actors and Means

Historically, repression has been defined and researched in various academic disciplines, such as sociology, political science, and anthropology.[12] Peterson and Wahlström define repression as "the governance of domestic dissent."[13] As Davenport elaborates, repression has its specific targets, which might be social movements, protests, or activism.[14] Including harassment, surveillance, arrests, bans, torture and murder, the means of repression might be physical or threatened, while the goal is to prevent or stop any activities or beliefs that might challenge or distort the dominant political or economic order of state or private agents. Following Tilly's definition of repression as actions raising the costs of noninstitutional collective action,[15] Earl establishes a typology to classify repression as state or private agents using coercion or channeling approaches to overtly or covertly control protests or activism,[16] which can also be considered as an operationalized concept of repression.

Because of its complexity, researchers have created various typologies to study actors and means of repression. Political contexts are crucial in analyzing repression operators. For example, Tilly classifies four types of political regimes regarding the degree of repression: repressive regimes displaying the highest degree of repression; totalitarian regimes repressing fewer groups than repressive regimes; tolerant regimes showing the acceptance of a wide range of dissident actions while stronger ones are suppressed; weak regimes demonstrating more tolerance and little repression.[17] Although this typology is helpful for scholars to examine repressive regimes at a national level, more detailed research on the variance of repression in different kinds of regimes is expected. For instance, while authoritarian regimes might repress social movement groups to a higher degree when confronting digital activism, democracies are not totally excluded from the same story. Christensen and Groshek examined emerging media as tools for governments in 162 democratic and autocratic counties and found that higher levels of digital media usage are positively correlated with both protests and repression.[18] Furthermore, both autocracies and democracies with more sophisticated usage of emerging media are more likely to suppress dissidents.

Means of repression are also dynamic. Coercive actions such as police confrontations, murders, arrests, and threats, together with other policing forms via executive orders, laws, and courts, are just part of the repertoire of state and local governments.[19] For instance, in the United States, the FBI's usage of the H. Rap Brown Law to isolate the 1973 Wounded Knee occupation site at South Dakota by American Indian Movement activists depicts how the US state deploys laws as its institutional power in containing public space.[20]

Research on means of repression focuses on their characteristics and classifications. For example, Della Porta outlines five dimensions of the features of police power: the repressive/tolerant dimension considering what behaviors are allowed and what are prohibited; the selective/diffuse dimension concerning how many social groups the police are dealing with; the preventive/reactive dimension focusing on when the police started the intervention; the hard/soft dimension addressing how much violence the police employed; the dirty/lawful dimension considering what procedures the police followed.[21] Further, Boykoff emphasizes the repression mechanisms various state actors have used.[22] Based on four mechanisms of repression (resource depletion, stigmatization, divisive disruption, and intimidation), Boykoff suggests ten state action modes: direct violence via beatings and shootings deployed by police or military; public prosecutions and hearings via jailing dissidents and/or threatening protesters with the consequences; employment deprivation via losing jobs because of supporting causes; surveillance and break-ins via CCTV, wiretapping, or mail opening; infiltration of informants and the use of agent provocateurs via the increasing usage of spies or undercover police; use of fabricated documents; harassment and harassment arrests; extraordinary rules and laws; mass media manipulation via story implantation or press censorship; mass media deprecation via negative framing or demonization. All these ten police actions have been extended to the digital space by state authorities.[23] The above typologies elaborate the richness of state authorities' repressive toolkit. However, they seldom touch on the policing operation of non-state actors.

By contrast, Earl's typology contains three dimensions: repressors are classified as state or private entities, while their relations with national governments are also considered; repression is categorized as either coercion or channeling, depending on whether policing involves violence; and repression activities are separated as either observable or unobservable.[24] Peterson and Wahlström also employ this typology, with the additional dimension of repression scope: whether repressive activities occur at the local, national, or transnational level.[25] Following Earl[26] and Peterson and Wahlström,[27] this chapter will focus on both state and non-state actors involved in social movements at different scales. The chapter initially discusses conventional repressive patterns, and then turns its attention to how these repressors are involved in social media activism. Democratic or authoritarian state governments, militaries, state or local police, corporations, and countermovements are examples of these repressors. They have developed sophisticated tactics at all levels to stop, constrain, or prevent the development of social movements. Prominent with the ubiquitous advancement of digital media, this chapter discusses the effect of globalization. On the other hand, repression and social movements have always gone hand in hand. Analyzing specific cases can help explain the relationships among the various actors involved in repressing social movements. For analysis, this chapter uses the Umbrella Movement, among other Hong Kong democracy protests of 2014, to examine overt and covert interference.[28] The next section is a brief introduction to the Umbrella Movement in Hong Kong in 2014. The chapter is then organized by three observed patterns in social media activism: state repression intensified with digital governance, the data-driven power of non-state repressors, and the effect of globalization in the digital age.

### The Umbrella Movement

The Umbrella Movement, also known as the Occupy Movement, in Hong Kong from September 26, 2014 to December 15, 2014 was sparked by an important decision of the Standing Committee of the National People's Congress of the People's Republic of China (NPCSC; China's legislature) on August 31, 2014.[29] This decision unavoidably suggested alterations to the Hong Kong electoral system which would make it become similar to the

Chinese Communist Party's prescreening of candidates for Hong Kong's leadership elections. Hong Kong students, activists, and citizens launched a 79-day sit-in protest and demanded repeal of the NPCSC decision.[30]

The repression of the Umbrella Movement was intimidating and persistent. The activists used yellow umbrellas to combat the pepper spray used by the Hong Kong police.[31] Symbolically, these yellow umbrellas acted as a metaphor for the rejection of the NPCSC's reforms.[32] Hong Kong police used violent tactics on protesters; they were pepper sprayed, tear gassed, and attacked by triad members. Umbrella Movement activists reported harassment from political opponents – and some protesters were jailed for their participation. In this sense, the Umbrella Movement in Hong Kong becomes a suitable case to understand the complexity of repressions from various actors in a complicated political environment with an uncertain future – namely, that of "one country, two systems" when autocracies and democracies display power in one regime at the same time.[33]

## RESISTING THE GASHT-E-ERSHAD

The Gasht-e-Ershad, meaning the guidance patrol, is Iran's morality police. Gasht-e-Ershad officers enforce Islamic dress codes in Iranian society, especially on women, by arresting women who the officers think have violated the codes. The Gasht-e-Ershad detained the 22-year-old Iranian woman Mahsa Amini because of her "improper" Hijab wearing. On September 16, 2022, Mahsa Amini died in custody. Her death instigated a series of offline and online protests. The hashtag #Masha_Amini and its Persian version exceeded 80 million tweets. The Iranian regime adopted severe approaches to suppress protests: arresting and killing protesters on the streets, internet shutdowns, blocking apps like WhatsApp and Instagram, and using bots to manipulate the narrative of #Masha_Amini. All of these suppression strategies have been practiced by the Iranian regime for many years.

### State Repression Intensified with Digital Governance

Earl's typology offers an effective categorization through which to understand state repression in terms of repression characteristics, repression visibility, and repression agents' identity.[34] A social movement may be policed by state authorities using various forms of repression: the use of tear gas or arrest as direct coercion, mainstream media framing as channeling for preferable information diffusion, and surveillance or spying as covert coercive actions. Militaries' or police authorities' involvement in repressive actions may incite significant fear among protesters. In the mean time, contentions can also be policed through legislative or legal approach. The policing of protests may occur on contingency or may have been prepared long beforehand.

Abundant scholarship in political science and sociology focuses on repression at the governmental level. As a key institution related to suppressing contention, state repression includes both national and local state coercive authorities such as militaries and law enforcement and bureaucracies such as tax authorities.[35] It should be noted that as part of exercising state power, the strategies used by each organization may vary across nation states. Police authorities at national or local levels have distinctive institutional logics, particularly in Western countries.[36] How they exercise coercive power may partly depend on connections with and allegiance to national political elites,[37] such as the military position to governmental power.[38] Further, in high-capacity authoritarian nations, state power might be exercised in a consistent or even more extreme way.[39]

Political contexts are vital in the study of state repression of social movements. The relationships between repression and opposition vary between authoritarian regimes and liberal democracies.[40] Police authorities in democratic nations are seen as agents with dual responsibilities in public spaces: protecting the right of free speech, and maintaining law and order. In the United States, researchers have identified trending patterns of policing contention from a traditionally more coercive strategy to a more flexible negotiated coping.[41] Selectively, high-risk protesters may be incapacitated while compliant ones may be offered opportunities for negotiation and conversation.[42]

Researchers across different disciplines such as political science, sociology, ethnography, and communication have extensively studied coercive state repression through case studies and field ethnography studies that display the brutality of various cases across the globe. By contrast, forms of *soft repression* have also been examined, such as municipal bylaws, fines, and administrative sanctions; other tactics, for example personal identity checks, have been used in different countries.[43] Among the actors who exert repression on the Umbrella Movement, the ruling elite is prominent, and contains two types of actors: the nation state power of the Chinese government and the Hong Kong government allied with the country's business sector. The Umbrella Movement experienced both violent and tolerant coping strategies from the local government and central Chinese government, demonstrating the complexity of the political environment in 2014 Hong Kong.[44]

Since the 1990s, the emergence of digital media has provided a new arena in which activists can mobilize and challenge mainstream media framing. However, regarding state repression and political influence, the power of digital media is limited. The growing big data age has empowered state police and security services to track and survey potential protests, allowing them to enact preemptive measures.[45] The case of Edward Snowden is an example of such surveillance.[46] Activists frequently use Twitter or other social media platforms to share information about protests and police brutality,[47] but at the same time police authorities can use the same platform to collect information about activists and protesters.[48] For example, Vkontakte, the local social media platform in far northern Russia, has become both the public sphere for grassroots movements and also the surveilled target of government authorities.[49]

**Digital repression** has intensified state repression from various perspectives. For example, Keremoğlu and Weidmann reviewed dictators' control of the internet in three layers: the infrastructure, the network, and the application layer.[50] Regimes have used digital tools from these three layers comprehensively and systematically to contain possible challenges to the political and economic order. Hintz suggests five arenas in digital communication control,[51] three of which are closely related to state repression in digital communication:

1) Access to information: Governments can easily filter web content and curtail access to information by employing a national filtering system. Advanced technology such as machine learning can improve governments' ability to censor information.
2) Access to infrastructure: Authoritarian regimes can shut down the internet to interfere with online communication when and where social movements are launched. Increasingly, democratic countries have struggled with the issue of network neutrality, which may cause difficulty for movement-related websites in reaching broad audiences.
3) Surveillance: As a traditional repressive activity, surveillance has been dramatically intensified by digital technology. Surveillance of social movements can be considered routine, along with the targeted information collection of protesters and activists. The prevalence of digital media and big data has improved the capacity of the state to gather information on targeted activists and the general population.

In those suggested arenas[52] and layers,[53] both authoritarian and democracy regimes have developed digital repression toolkits that often contain the following: digital surveillance via monitoring protesters' profiles, digital activities, visible relationships, and activist communities; hacking via controlling activists' digital accounts, computers, mobile devices, and emails; digital attacks via online harassment, smearing, and disinformation campaigns against protesters.[54] This toolkit extends the ten actions listed by Boycoff that state repression already adopts into a digital and social space, particularly in the intensification of information surveillance, media manipulation, and deprecation.[55] For example, Pearce analyzes how the Azerbaijan state sponsored online harassment to control its political opposition.[56] An Iranian diasporic journalist forged his home country connections because of the fear of surveillance and threats from Iran police agents.[57] China's online censorship authorities silence social media comments that represent or instigate collective actions.[58]

State governments can use these digital repression tools in various ways. Keremoğlu and Weidmann suggest three interaction possibilities: substitution, wherein digital tools replace conventional modes of repression, which may include less violent forms of repression such as censorship and blocking; reinforcement with digital tools to add multiple layers of repression, which can involve banning activists' names on both legacy media and social media channels; and complementary digital tools and traditional repressive activities, which can include digital monitoring of police arrest activists.[59] All three possibilities can be seen in the scholarship of China's online censorship in the Umbrella Movement case.[60] For example, the Chinese government deleted most of the information regarding the Umbrella Movement on Chinese Weibo.[61] From a governmental perspective, this censorship is effective because social media exposure has proven to be positively connected with support for the Umbrella Movement.[62]

Furthermore, Frantz, Kendall-Taylor, and Wright suggest digital repression as a serious complement to the conventional repressions in authoritarian contexts.[63] Earl, Maher, and Pan applied Earl's typology to information surveillance in digital repression,[64] demonstrating how state authorities have utilized digital/social media as intensified monitoring tools against online/offline protesters. As Deibert explains, social media has provided a painful future for dissidents: it has become a crucial tool for authoritarian control.[65]

## The Data-Driven Power of Non-State Actors

Aside from state repression, Earl's typology also highlights nongovernmental regulators,[66] including private actors like the security industry, business sectors, and private foundations,[67] and civil society actors, such as the countermovement of the anti-feminists in China.[68] Investigating the function of private actors for policing dissent at the interpersonal, organizational, societal, and transnational levels requires further research.[69]

At the interpersonal level, nonviolent repression has been researched for movements related to gender, race, or sexuality. Ferree coined the term "soft repression" to classify ridicule, stigma, and silencing as three common strategies employed by non-state actors to nonviolently repress dissent voices.[70] For example, in the #MeToo movement, women are sometimes stigmatized as liars or money-seekers by repressors who intend to decrease the legitimacy of their challenges to the patriarchy.

Violent repression employed by non-state actors also includes local pro-regime vigilantes attacking activists. In the Umbrella Movement, the thugs involved were documented by local or international media outlets; this can be considered an example of a thug attack.[71] Although publicly visible as simple interpersonal confrontations, these attacks have been explained as state power enforcement at the interpersonal level in high-capacity authoritarian regimes.[72]

Further, cooperation among state and non-state actors is increasing. For example, thugs or other vigilantes may be hired by government bodies. Additionally, the privatized military industry has been burgeoning since the 1990s to exercise government repression.[73] Especially for weaker governmental authorities, the private security sector can boost their coercive power.[74] High-capacity governments may also utilize the privatized security sector for intelligence purposes, such as spying on political dissidents.[75]

Civil society is an important non-state actor in containing disagreement. Countermovements are common during social movements.[76] For example, in the United States, the anti-Civil Rights countermovement during the 1950s reflected the will of civil society to suppress racial contention in the American South.[77] Another example is Reddit, a social media platform which demographically has more male users than females, has become a public arena for anti-feminist and misogynistic users due to its algorithm design.[78] In the Umbrella Movement, the countermovements launched by pro-government groups are considered to have powerfully transformed the narrative of the Umbrella Movement; more importantly, the national government may support and organize them.[79]

Corporations and other business sectors are sometimes the targets of protests,[80] and targeted firms, in response, develop tactical repertoires to respond to and prevent such activities.[81] Balsiger maps corporate strategies directly against challenges to social movements into six responses: avoidance (such as non-reaction or denying responsibility); acquiescence (such as collaboration with activists organizations, compromise, self-regulation, negotiations, compensations, or labels); sidestepping (such as reputation/impression management and collaboration with competing activist organizations); confrontation (such as public relations campaigns, grassroots lobbying, coalition formation, or legal action); and prevention (such as media monitoring, research, and infiltration).[82] In one or more of these ways, businesses respond to protest demands by influencing public opinion and policy making. In the case of the Umbrella Movement, for example, Hong Kong business sectors remained largely silent, although they conducted discussions with the Chinese government to maintain their economic order and privilege. At the time, key executive leaders in the Chinese business sector worried about the unexpected influence of the Umbrella Movement on business regulation and resource redistribution. In this sense, they were closely aligned with the Chinese government, which became a critical factor in determining how to deal with social movements in this territory.[83]

Corporations may also overtly or covertly adopt coercive approaches to confront social movements. As Earl notes, business enterprises overtly have a long history of hiring private security to break strikes; covertly, intelligence agencies and blacklists are often employed by US corporations to detect or prevent activities challenging their economic power.[84] In this sense, business corporations are active agents in constraining social movements.

The role of corporations in the development of digital media grants them increased power to interfere with social movements online. As sad as it can be, the digital/social media business model is rooted in personal data collection.[85] Google, Amazon, Apple, and other technology companies accumulate details about the everyday lives of global users – profile information, relationships, browsing history, purchasing habits, etc. – for maximum profit.[86] These data are used to build up an unavoidable web of surveillance, exploited by those technology companies or other power institutions.[87] In the digital age, non-state actors, especially corporations, are empowered by big data to contain and prevent social activism. For example, attacks on human rights activists have escalated in recent years because of digital tracking, data leaks, and digital surveillance.[88]

Technology firms produce and sell hacking applications to governments and other repressive actors to surveil and control activists.[89] Additionally, tech companies as service providers can deny their services to social activism groups in an effort to prevent access to resources.[90] Further, companies can use intellectual property laws to punish those social groups that may illegally access necessary infrastructure to launch social movements. Moreover, companies in the current age of big data have accumulated significant amounts of consumer data, including demographic and psychographic information. Utilizing automated systems such as artificial intelligence, machine learning, and data mining, companies collaborate with state actors to strengthen civilian surveillance in the online social space.[91]

## The Effect of Globalization in the Digital Age

Under globalization, the scale of repression seems unprecedentedly flexible. As Loader notes in his analysis of plural forms of policing at local, national, and transnational levels:

> policing forms are developing both in transnational settings *above* government, and in security markets functioning *beyond* government, such that historically rooted political institutions find themselves increasingly outflanked by (global) corporate and governmental agents whom they appear unable to steer or regulate.[92]

A state institution may exercise its repression capacity in the context of various levels – as can a transnational private company. A local organization or individual may also exercise their power on a larger scale by using digital or social media. Transnational protests and policing encourage exchanges of information, strategies, intelligence, and regulations across borders. Both empowered and restricted, protesters' international movements face new challenges as a result of globalization.

The effect of globalization has intensified since the September 11 attacks in 2001, when the United States government operationalized its "war on terror" principle through law and policy making. Repressive authorities dramatically emphasized foreign threats caused by domestic dissidents in public discourse framing. Numerous anti-terrorist Acts have been passed across the globe, including the Patriot Act in the United States. Globalization not only provides a promising arena for economic development, but also offers a convenient channel for foreign threats. For example, during the Umbrella Movement in Hong Kong, the interference of foreign countries has been framed by the Chinese government as a direct force bringing threats to national security. Meanwhile, the cooperation among law enforcement, security services, and intelligence agencies across the globe has increased in the post-9/11 period.

International corporations have taken a role in policing dissent in the context of a globalization. Following the policing history of domestic business sectors, international companies often hire security forces to maintain their economic power across various countries.[93] For example, global mining corporations have employed the strength of the corporate security industry to perform effective governance in some African countries like Nigeria.[94]

The omnipresence of digital and social media has also enriched the toolkits of state and non-state actors in transnational contexts. State authorities have displayed their power to silence diaspora activists abroad with coercive tactics such as assassination, spyware, or intimidation, or through channeling tactics like migration regulation and financial limita-tion.[95] For example, the Syrian government strategically monitored and controlled the digital space to contain diasporic activists.[96] Michaelson analyzes various cases of diaspora activists who have been spied on, sur-veilled, and constrained by Syrian, Iran, and Saudi Arab governments, and suggests:

> Digital technologies have given authoritarian governments new tools to control, silence, and punish dissent across borders. They enable regimes to monitor and respond to the activities of political exiles and dias-pora communities with greater scope and speed, reducing the costs of extraterritorial political control. Digital technologies have thus become essential components in the toolkit of transnational repression.[97]

As well as activists employing digital and social media to broaden the scope of their movements and mobilize participants across the world (e.g., the #MeToo movement or the #WomensMarch), repressive actors also uti-lize digital technology to suppress these same transnational efforts. In the Umbrella Movement, the visual symbol of the yellow umbrella dif-fused via digital/social media has attracted transnational attention and mobilization.[98] Diasporic activists in particular rely on digital media for their activism and organization because they have been exiled from their home countries. State authorities monitor diasporic activists' digital traces and connections via social media algorithms to target dissidents and crit-ics abroad. Further, private spyware companies can help state authorities advance digital repression, arming them with the technical capacity to do so. With these new capabilities, tactics such as arrests, murders, and threats to activists' families become easier.[99]

## Closing Thoughts

Repression, especially state repression, has been well studied across disci-plines. Digital repression has been discussed as related to technology, poli-tics, policies, communication, and management. As such, scholars have concluded that repression of social movements should be considered as situated in a hybrid media movement.[100] It is necessary for social move-ment scholars and practitioners to consider how conventional repressive activities have been strengthened in the digital and social media age. This literature review discusses how state and non-state actors operational-ize their repressive toolkits and how these toolkits address digital inter-vention, particularly in a globalized age. As Frantz, Kendall-Taylor, and Wright find, digital repression has not been a substitute for conventional repressive tactics; on the contrary, authoritarian regimes have deployed digital tools as a complement.[101] It is crucial for researchers and activists to analyze beyond the positive attributes of digital and social media's function related to social movements. Emergent calls to action should be recognized regarding using digital tools to protect, not harm, activists' agency and capacity under strengthened surveillance and increased repression globally.

## Reflections

- What are the similarities and differences between state repression and non-state repression?
- What does social media bring to repression at state, non-state, and international levels?
- How can social activists protect themselves when using social media as a toolkit for protesting?

## Notes

1 Della Porta, Donatella, and Mario Diani. 2015. *The Oxford Handbook of Social Movements*. Oxford, UK: Oxford University Press.
2 Earl, Jennifer, T.V. Maher, and J. Pan. "The digital repression of social movements, protest, and activism: A synthetic review." *Science Advances* 8, no. 10 (2022). Feldstein, Steven. 2021. *The Rise of Digital Repression: How Technology Is Reshaping Power, Politics, and Resistance*. Oxford: Oxford University Press. Hintz, Arne. "Challenging the digital gatekeepers: International policy initiatives for free expression." *Journal of Information Policy* 2, no. 1 (2012): 128–150.
3 Caren, Neal, Kenneth T. Andrews, and Todd Lu. "Contemporary social movements in a hybrid media environment." *Annual Review of Sociology* 46, no. 1 (2020): 443–465.
4 Lynch, Marc. "After Egypt: The limits and promise of online challenges to the authoritarian Arab state." *Perspectives on Politics* 9, no. 2 (2011): 301–210.
5 Dencik, Lina, Arne Hintz, and Jonathan Cable. 2018. "Towards data justice: Bridging anti-surveillance and social justice activism." In *Data Politics: Worlds, Subjects, Rights*. United Kingdom: Routledge, pp. 167–186. Hintz, "Challenging the digital gatekeepers."
6 Michaelsen, Marcus. 2020. "The digital transnational repression toolkit, and its silencing effects." In *Perspectives on "Everyday" Transnational Repression in an Age of Globalization*. Washington, DC: Freedom House, pp. 4–8.
7 Earl, Maher, and Pan, "The digital repression of social movements, protest, and activism." Feldstein, *The Rise of Digital Repression*. Frantz, Erica, Andrea Kendall-Taylor, and Joseph Wright. 2020. *Digital Repression in Autocracies*. Gothenberg, Sweden: V-Dem Institute. Michaelsen, "The digital transnational repression toolkit, and its silencing effects."

8 Cath, Corinne. 2019. "Internet governance and human rights: A literature review." In Carl Öhman and David Watson (ed.), *The 2018 Yearbook of the Digital Ethics Lab*, Springer International Publishingpp. 105, accessed May 9, 2023, https://doi.org/10.1007/978-3-030-17152-0_8.

9 Earl, Maher, and Pan, "The digital repression of social movements, protest, and activism."

10 Earl, Jennifer. "Tanks, tear gas, and taxes: Toward a theory of movement repression." *Sociological Theory* 21, no. 1 (2003): 44–68.

11 Caren, Andrews, and Lu, "Contemporary social movements in a hybrid media environment."

12 Davenport, Christian. "State repression and political order." *Annual Review of Political Science* 10 (2007): 1–23. Della Porta and Diani, *The Oxford Handbook of Social Movements*. Roggeband, Conny, and Bert Klandermans. 2017. *Handbook of Social Movements across Disciplines*. New York: Springer.

13 Peterson, Abby, and Mattias Wahlström. 2015. "Repression: The governance of domestic dissent." In Della Porta, Donatella, and Mario Diani (eds.), *The Oxford Handbook of Social Movements*. Oxford, UK: Oxford University Press, p. 634.

14 Davenport, "State repression and political order."

15 Tilly, Charles. 1978. *From Mobilization to Revolution*. Boston, MA: Addison-Wesley.

16 Earl, "Tanks, tear gas, and taxes."

17 Tilly, *From Mobilization to Revolution*.

18 Christensen, Britt, and Jacob Groshek. "Emerging media, political protests, and government repression in autocracies and democracies from 1995 to 2012." *International Communication Gazette* 82, no. 8 (2020): 685–704.

19 Loader, Ian. "Plural policing and democratic governance." *Social & Legal Studies* 9, no. 3 (2000): 323–345.

20 D'Arcus, Bruce. "Protest, scale, and publicity: The FBI and the H Rap Brown Act." *Antipode* 35, no. 4 (2003): 718–741.

21 Della Porta, Donatella. 1996. "Social movements and the state: Thoughts on the policing of protest." In D. McAdam, J.D. McCarthy, and M.N. Zald (eds.), *Comparative Perspectives on Social Movements*. Cambridge, UK: Cambridge University Press, pp. 62–92.

22 Boykoff, Jules. "Limiting dissent: The mechanisms of state repression in the USA." *Social Movement Studies* 6, no. 3 (2007): 281–310.

23 Earl, Maher, and Pan, "The digital repression of social movements, protest, and activism."

24 Earl, "Tanks, tear gas, and taxes."

25 Peterson and Wahlström, "Repression."

26 Earl, "Tanks, tear gas, and taxes."

27 Peterson and Wahlström, "Repression."

28 Chan, Johannes. "Hong Kong's Umbrella Movement." *Round Table* 103, no. 6 (2014): 571–580. Chen, Meilin, and John Flowerdew. "Discriminatory discursive strategies in online comments on YouTube videos on the Hong Kong Umbrella Movement by Mainland and Hong Kong Chinese." *Discourse and Society* 30, no. 6 (2019): 549–572. Ortmann, Stephan. "The Umbrella Movement and Hong Kong's protracted democratization process." *Asian Affairs* 46, no. 1 (2015): 32–50.

29 Chan, "Hong Kong's Umbrella Movement."

30 Tong, Carmen. "A chronology of Hong Kong's Umbrella Movement: January 2013–December 2014." *Educational Philosophy and Theory* 51, no. 2 (2019): 194–199.

31 Lo, W.H. "Citizen camera-witnessing: A case study of the Umbrella Movement." *Contemporary Chinese Political Economy and Strategic Relations* 2, no. 2 (2016): 795–815.

32 Veg, Sebastian. "Creating a textual public space: Slogans and texts from Hong Kong's Umbrella Movement." *Journal of Asian Studies* 75, no. 3 (2016): 673–702.

33 Cheung, C.-Y. "'One country, two systems' after the Umbrella Movement: Problems and prospects." *Asian Education and Development Studies* 6, no. 4 (2017): 385–400. Lee, Francis L.F., and Joseph M. Chan. 2018. *Media and Protest Logics in the Digital Era: The Umbrella Movement in Hong Kong.* Oxford, UK: Oxford University Press. Yuen, Samson. "Hong Kong after the Umbrella Movement: An uncertain future for 'one country two systems.'" *China Perspectives* 1 (2015): 49–53.

34 Earl, "Tanks, tear gas, and taxes."

35 Boykoff, "Limiting dissent." Chenoweth, Erica, Evan Perkoski, and Sooyeon Kang, "State repression and nonviolent resistance." *Journal of Conflict Resolution* 61, no. 9 (2017): 1950–1969. Davenport, "State repression and political order."

36 Boykoff, "Limiting dissent."

37 Earl, "Tanks, tear gas, and taxes."

38 Carey, Sabine C. 2009. *Protest Repression and Political Regimes.* London: Routledge.

39 Johnston, Hank. "State violence and oppositional protest in high-capacity authoritarian regimes." *International Journal of Conflict and Violence* 6, no. 1 (2012): 55–74.

40 Christensen and Groshek, "Emerging media, political protests, and government repression in autocracies and democracies from 1995 to 2012."

41 Anisin, Alexei, and Pelin Ayan Musil. "Protester-police fraternization in the 2013 Gezi Park uprisings." *Social Movement Studies* 21, no.4 (2021): 395–412. Baker, David. "Police and protester dialog: Safeguarding the peace or ritualistic sham?" *International Journal of Comparative and Applied Criminal Justice* 38, no. 1 (2014): 83–104. Della Porta, "Social movements and the state."

42 Balsiger, Philip. 2014. "Managing protest: The political action repertoires of corporations." In Della Porta, Donatella, and Mario Diani (eds.), *The Oxford Handbook of Social Movements.* Oxford, UK: Oxford University Press, pp. 1–11.

43 García, Oscar José Martín. "Soft repression and the current wave of social mobilisations in Spain." *Social Movement Studies* 13, no. 2 (2014): 303–308.

44 Cheng, Edmund W. "Street politics in a hybrid regime: The diffusion of political activism in post-colonial Hong Kong." *China Quarterly* 226 (2016): 383–406. Lee and Chan, *Media and Protest Logics in the Digital Era.*

45 Dencik, Hintz, and Cable, "Towards data justice." Dencik, Lina, Arne Hintz, and Zoe Carey. "Prediction, pre-emption and limits to dissent: Social media and big data uses for policing protests in the United Kingdom." *New Media & Society* 20, no. 4 (2018): 1433–1450.

46 Lyon, David. "Surveillance, Snowden, and Big Data: Capacities, consequences, critique." *Big Data & Society* 1, no. 2 (2014): 2053951714541861.

Verble, Joseph. "The NSA and Edward Snowden: Surveillance in the 21st century." *ACM Sigcas Computers and Society* 44, no. 3 (2014): 14–20.

47 Earl, Jennifer, et al. "This protest will be tweeted: Twitter and protest policing during the Pittsburgh G20." *Information, Communication & Society* 16, no. 4 (2013): 459–478.

48 Gunitsky, Seva. "Corrupting the cyber-commons: Social media as a tool of autocratic stability." *Perspectives on Politics* 13, no. 1 (2015): 42–54.

49 Poupin, Perrine. "Social media and state repression: The case of VKontakte and the anti-garbage protest in Shies, in far northern Russia." *First Monday*26 no. 5 (2021). https://doi.org/10.5210/fm.v26i5.11711.

50 Keremoğlu, Eda, and Nils B. Weidmann. "How dictators control the internet: A review essay." *Comparative Political Studies* 53, nos. 10–11 (2020): 1690–1703.

51 Hintz, "Challenging the digital gatekeepers."

52 Ibid.

53 Keremoğlu and Weidmann, "How dictators control the internet."

54 Dencik, Hintz, and Carey, "Prediction, pre-emption and limits to dissent." Feldstein, *The Rise of Digital Repression.* Frantz, Kendall-Taylor, and Wright, *Digital Repression in Autocracies.* Michaelsen, "The digital transnational repression toolkit, and its silencing effects."

55 Boykoff, "Limiting dissent."

56 Pearce, Katy E. "Democratizing kompromat: The affordances of social media for state-sponsored harassment." *Information, Communication & Society* 18, no. 10 (2015): 1158–1174.

57 Michaelsen, "The digital transnational repression toolkit, and its silencing effects."

58 King, Gary, Jennifer Pan, and Margaret E. Roberts, "How censorship in China allows government criticism but silences collective expression." *American Political Science Review* 107, no. 2 (2013): 326–343.

59 Keremoğlu and Weidmann, "How dictators control the internet."

60 King, Pan, and Roberts, "How censorship in China Allows government criticism but silences collective expression." Xu, Xu. "To repress or to co-opt? Authoritarian control in the age of digital surveillance." *American Journal of Political Science* 65, no. 2 (2021): 309–325.

61 Liu, Jun and Jingyi Zhao. "More than plain text: Censorship deletion in the Chinese social media." *Journal of the Association for Information Science and Technology* 72, no. 3 (2020).

62 Lee, Paul S.N., Clement Y.K. So, and Louis Leung. "Social media and Umbrella Movement: Insurgent public sphere in formation," *Chinese Journal of Communication* 8, no. 4 (2015): 356–375.

63 Frantz, Kendall-Taylor, and Wright, *Digital Repression in Autocracies.*

64 Earl, Maher, and Pan, "The digital repression of social movements, protest, and activism."

65 Deibert, Ronald J. "The road to digital unfreedom: Three painful truths about social media." *Journal of Democracy* 30, no. 1 (2019): 25–39.

66 Earl, "Tanks, tear gas, and taxes."

67 Walker, Edward T., and Christopher M. Rea. "The political mobilization of firms and industries." *Annual Review of Sociology* 40, no. 1 (2014): 281–304.

68 Gan, Nector. 2021. "In China, feminists are being silenced by nationalist trolls. Some are fighting back." https://www.cnn.com/2021/04/19/china/china-feminists-silenced-intl-hnk-dst/index.html.

69 Earl, "Tanks, tear gas, and taxes." Earl, Maher, and Pan, "The digital repression of social movements, protest, and activism."

70 Ferree, Myra Marx. 2004. "Soft repression: Ridicule, stigma, and silencing in gender-based movements." In Daniel J. Myers and Daniel M. Cress (eds.), *Authority in Contention*, vol. 25. Bingley, UK: Emerald Group Publishing, pp. 85–101.

71 Lee and Chan, *Media and Protest Logics in the Digital Era.*

72 Johnston, "State violence and oppositional protest in high-capacity authoritarian regimes." Lee and Chan, *Media and Protest Logics in the Digital Era.*

73 Singer, Peter W. "Corporate warriors: The rise of the privatized military industry and its ramifications for international security." *International Security* 26, no. 3 (2001): 186–220.

74 Musah, Abdel-Fatau, Kayode Fayemi, and J'Kayode Fayemi. 2000. *Mercenaries: An African Security Dilemma.* London: Pluto Press.

75 Michaelsen, "The digital transnational repression toolkit, and its silencing effects."

76 Adams, Alison E., Thomas E. Shriver, and Chris M. Messer, "Movement-countermovement dynamics in a land use controversy." *Human Ecology Review* 21, no. 1 (2015): 3–25. https://doi.org/10.22459/HER.21.01.2015.01. Irons, Jenny. "Who rules the social control of protest? Variability in the state-countermovement relationship." *Mobilization* 11, no. 2 (2006): 165–180. Peckham, Michael. "New dimensions of social movement/countermovement interaction: The case of scientology and its internet critics." *Canadian Journal of Sociology/Cahiers Canadiens de Sociologie* 23, no.4 (1998): 317–347.

77 Luders, Joseph. 2003. "Countermovements, the State, and the Intensity of Racial Contention in the American South." In Jack A. Goldstone (ed.), *States, Parties, and Social Movements.* Cambridge, UK: Cambridge University Press, pp. 25–44.

78 Massanari, Adrienne. "#Gamergate and The Fappening: How Reddit's algorithm, governance, and culture support toxic technocultures." *New Media & Society* 19, no. 3 (2017): 329–346.

79 Yuen, Samson, and Edmund W. Cheng. "Neither repression nor concession? A regime's attrition against mass protests." *Political Studies* 65, no. 3 (2017): 611–630.

80 Walker, Edward T., Andrew W. Martin, and John D. McCarthy. "Confronting the state, the corporation, and the academy: The influence of institutional targets on social movement repertoires." *American Journal of Sociology* 114, no. 1 (2008): 35–76.

81 Walker and Rea, "The political mobilization of firms and industries."

82 Balsiger, "Managing protest: The political action repertoires of corporations."

83 Ortmann, "The Umbrella Movement and Hong Kong's protracted democratization process."

84 Earl, Jennifer. "Controlling protest: New directions for research on the social control of protest." *Research in Social Movements, Conflicts and Change* 25 (2004): 55–83.

85 Deibert, "The road to digital unfreedom."

86 Smyrnaios, Nikos. 2018. *Internet Oligopoly: The Corporate Takeover of Our Digital World.* Bingley, UK: Emerald Group Publishing.

87 Feldstein, *The Rise of Digital Repression.*

88 Hankey, Stephanie, and Daniel Ó Clunaigh. "Rethinking risk and security of human rights defenders in the digital age." *Journal of Human Rights Practice* 5, no. 3 (2013): 535–547.

89 McKune, Sarah, and Ron Deibert. 2017. *Who's Watching Little Brother? A Checklist for Accountability in the Industry behind government hacking.*" https://citizenlab.ca/wp-content/uploads/2017/03/citizenlab_whos-watching -little-brother.pdf.

90 Hintz, "Challenging the digital gatekeepers."

91 Dencik, Hintz, and Carey, "Prediction, pre-emption and limits to dissent." Trottier, Daniel. "Policing social media." *Canadian Review of Sociology/ Revue Canadienne de Sociologie* 49, no. 4 (2012): 411–425. Walsh, James P., and Christopher O'Connor. "Social media and policing: A review of recent research." *Sociology Compass* 13, no. 1 (2019): e12648.

92 Loader, "Plural policing and democratic governance."

93 Singer, "Corporate warriors."

94 Campbell, Bonnie. "Good governance, security and mining in Africa." *Minerals & Energy – Raw Materials Report* 21, no. 1 (2006): 31–44.

95 Moss, Dana M. "Transnational repression, diaspora mobilization, and the case of the Arab Spring." *Social Problems* 63, no. 4 (2016): 480–498.

96 Tenove, Chris. "Networking justice: Digitally-enabled engagement in transitional justice by the Syrian diaspora." *Ethnic and Racial Studies* 42, no. 11 (2019): 1950–1969.

97 Michaelsen, "The digital transnational repression toolkit, and its silencing effects."

98 Patsiaouras, Georgios, Anastasia Veneti, and William Green. "The Hong Kong Umbrella Movement as a non-profit organization: An empirical study on the use of visual branding practices for social change." *Journal of Philanthropy and Marketing* 27, no. 2 (2022): e1717.

99 Michaelsen, "The digital transnational repression toolkit, and its silencing effects."

100 Caren, Andrews, and Lu, "Contemporary social movements in a hybrid media environment." Earl, Maher, and Pan, "The digital repression of social movements, protest, and activism."

101 Frantz, Kendall-Taylor, and Wright, "Digital repression in autocracies."

## Bibliography

Adams, Alison E., Thomas E. Shriver, and Chris M. Messer. "Movement–Countermovement Dynamics in a Land Use Controversy." *Human Ecology Review* 21, no. 1 (2015): 3–25. https://doi.org/10.22459/HER.21.01.2015 .01.

Anisin, Alexei, and Pelin Ayan Musil. "Protester-Police Fraternization in the 2013 Gezi Park Uprisings." *Social Movement Studies* (2021). https://doi.org /10.1080/14742837.2021.1884976.

Baker, David. "Police and Protester Dialog: Safeguarding the Peace or Ritualistic Sham?" *International Journal of Comparative and Applied Criminal Justice* 38, no. 1 (2014): 83–104. https://doi.org/10.1080/01924036.2013.819024.

Balsiger, Philip. "Managing Protest: The Political Action Repertoires of Corporations." In *The Oxford Handbook of Social Movements*, edited by Donatella Della porta and Mario Diani, 1. United Kingdom: Oxford University Press, 2015, accessed May 9, 2023, https://doi.org/10.1093/ oxfordhb/9780199678402.013.60.

Boykoff, Jules. "Limiting Dissent: The Mechanisms of State Repression in the USA." *Social Movement Studies* 6, no. 3 (2007): 281–310.

Campbell, Bonnie. "Good Governance, Security and Mining in Africa." *Minerals & Energy-Raw Materials Report* 21, no. 1 (2006): 31–44.

Caren, Neal, Kenneth T. Andrews, and Todd Lu. "Contemporary Social Movements in a Hybrid Media Environment." *Annual Review of Sociology* 46, no. 1 (2020): 443–65.

Carey, Sabine C. *Protest Repression and Political Regimes.* Protest Repression and Political Regimes, 2008. https://doi.org/10.4324/9780203884980.

Cath, Corinne. "Internet Governance and Human Rights: A Literature Review." In *The 2018 Yearbook of the Digital Ethics Lab*, edited by Carl Öhman and David Watson, 105. Springer International Publishing, 2019, accessed May 9, 2023, https://doi.org/10.1007/978-3-030-17152-0_8.

Chan, Johannes. "Hong Kong's Umbrella Movement." *Round Table* 103, no. 6 (2014): 571–80. https://doi.org/10.1080/00358533.2014.985465.

Chen, Meilin, and John Flowerdew. "Discriminatory Discursive Strategies in Online Comments on YouTube Videos on the Hong Kong Umbrella Movement by Mainland and Hong Kong Chinese." *Discourse and Society* 30, no. 6 (2019): 549–72. https://doi.org/10.1177/0957926519870046.

Cheng, Edmund W. "Street Politics in a Hybrid Regime: The Diffusion of Political Activism in Post-Colonial Hong Kong." *China Quarterly* 226 (2016): 383–406. https://doi.org/10.1017/S0305741016000394.

Chenoweth, Erica, Evan Perkoski, and Sooyeon Kang. "State Repression and Nonviolent Resistance." *Journal of Conflict Resolution* 61, no. 9 (2017): 1950–69. https://doi.org/10.1177/0022002717721390.

Cheung, C.-Y. "'One Country, Two Systems' after the Umbrella Movement: Problems and Prospects." *Asian Education and Development Studies* 6, no. 4 (2017): 385–400. https://doi.org/10.1108/AEDS-10-2015-0055.

Christensen, Britt, and Jacob Groshek. "Emerging Media, Political Protests, and Government Repression in Autocracies and Democracies from 1995 to 2012." *International Communication Gazette* 82, no. 8 (2020): 685–704.

D'Arcus, Bruce. "Protest, Scale, and Publicity: The FBI and the H Rap Brown Act." *Antipode* 35, no. 4 (2003): 718–41.

Davenport, Christian. "State Repression and Political Order." *Annual Review of Political Science* 10 (2007): 1–23. https://doi.org/10.1146/annurev.polisci.10 .101405.143216.

Deibert, Ronald J. "The Road to Digital Unfreedom: Three Painful Truths about Social Media." *Journal of Democracy* 30, no. 1 (2019): 25–39.

Della Porta, Donatella. "Social Movements and the State: Thoughts on the Policing of Protest." In *Comparative Perspectives on Social Movements*, edited by D. McAdam, J. D. McCarthy, and M. N. Zald, 62–92. Cambridge: Cambridge University Press, 1996.

Della Porta, Donatella, and Mario Diani. *The Oxford Handbook of Social Movements.* United Kingdom: Oxford University Press, 2015.

Dencik, Lina, Arne Hintz, and Jonathan Cable. "Towards Data Justice: Bridging Anti-Surveillance and Social Justice Activism." In *Data Politics: Worlds, Subjects, Rights*, edited by Didier Bigo, Engin Isin and Evelyn Ruppert, 167–86. London: Routledge, 2018.

Dencik, Lina, Arne Hintz, and Zoe Carey. "Prediction, Pre-Emption and Limits to Dissent: Social Media and Big Data Uses for Policing Protests in the United Kingdom." *New Media & Society* 20, no. 4 (2018): 1433–50.

Earl, Jennifer. "Controlling Protest: New Directions for Research on the Social Control of Protest." *Research in Social Movements, Conflicts and Change* 25 (2004): 55–83. https://doi.org/10.1016/S0163-786X(04)25003-0.

———. "Tanks, Tear Gas, and Taxes: Toward a Theory of Movement Repression." *Sociological Theory* 21, no. 1 (2003): 44–68. https://doi.org/10.1111/1467-9558.00175.

Earl, Jennifer, T.V. Maher, and J. Pan. "The Digital Repression of Social Movements, Protest, and Activism: A Synthetic Review." *Science Advances* 8, no. 10 (2022). https://doi.org/10.1126/sciadv.abl8198.

Earl, Jennifer, Heather McKee Hurwitz, Analicia Mejia Mesinas, Margaret Tolan, and Ashley Arlotti. "This Protest Will Be Tweeted: Twitter and Protest Policing during the Pittsburgh G20." *Information, Communication & Society* 16, no. 4 (2013): 459–78.

Feldstein, Steven. *The Rise of Digital Repression: How Technology Is Reshaping Power, Politics, and Resistance.* United Kingdom: Oxford University Press, 2021.

Ferree, Myra Marx. "Soft Repression: Ridicule, Stigma, and Silencing in Gender-Based Movements." In *Authority in Contention*, edited by Myers, D.J. and Cress, D.M., 85–101. Bingley: Emerald Group Publishing Limited, 2004.

Frantz, Erica, Andrea Kendall-Taylor, and Joseph Wright. "Digital Repression in Autocracies." V-Dem Institute, 2020. www.v-dem.net.

Gan, Nector. "In China, Feminists Are Being Silenced by Nationalist Trolls. Some Are Fighting Back - CNN," April 19, 2021. https://www.cnn.com/2021/04/19/china/china-feminists-silenced-intl-hnk-dst/index.html.

García, Oscar José Martín. "Soft Repression and the Current Wave of Social Mobilisations in Spain." *Social Movement Studies* 13, no. 2 (2014): 303–8.

Gunitsky, Seva. "Corrupting the Cyber-Commons: Social Media as a Tool of Autocratic Stability." *Perspectives on Politics* 13, no. 1 (2015): 42–54.

Hankey, Stephanie, and Daniel Ó Clunaigh. "Rethinking Risk and Security of Human Rights Defenders in the Digital Age." *Journal of Human Rights Practice* 5, no. 3 (2013): 535–47.

Hintz, Arne. "Challenging the Digital Gatekeepers: International Policy Initiatives for Free Expression." *Journal of Information Policy* 2, no. 1 (2012): 128–50.

Irons, Jenny. "Who Rules the Social Control of Protest? Variability in the State-Countermovement Relationship." *Mobilization* 11, no. 2 (2006): 165–80.

Johnston, Hank. "State Violence and Oppositional Protest in High-Capacity Authoritarian Regimes." *International Journal of Conflict and Violence (IJCV)* 6, no. 1 (2012): 55–74.

Keremoğlu, Eda, and Nils B. Weidmann. "How Dictators Control the Internet: A Review Essay." *Comparative Political Studies* 53, nos. 10–11 (2020): 1690–1703.

King, Gary, Jennifer Pan, and Margaret E. Roberts. "How Censorship in China Allows Government Criticism but Silences Collective Expression." *American Political Science Review* 107, no. 2 (2013): 326–43.

Lee, Francis L.F., and Joseph M. Chan. *Media and Protest Logics in the Digital Era: The Umbrella Movement in Hong Kong.* 2018. https://doi.org/10.1093/oso/9780190856779.001.0001.

Lee, Paul S.N., Clement Y.K. So, and Louis Leung. "Social Media and Umbrella Movement: Insurgent Public Sphere in Formation." *Chinese Journal of Communication* 8, no. 4 (2015): 356–75. https://doi.org/10.1080/17544750 .2015.1088874.

Liu, Jun, and Jingyi Zhao. "More than Plain Text: Censorship Deletion in the Chinese Social Media." *Journal of the Association for Information Science and Technology* (2020). https://doi.org/10.1002/asi.24390.

Lo, W.H. "Citizen Camera-Witnessing: A Case Study of the Umbrella Movement." *Contemporary Chinese Political Economy and Strategic Relations* 2, no. 2 (2016): 795–815.

Loader, Ian. "Plural Policing and Democratic Governance." *Social & Legal Studies* 9, no. 3 (2000): 323–45.

Luders, Joseph. "Countermovements, the State, and the Intensity of Racial Contention in the American South." In *States, Parties, and Social Movements*, 25–44, 2003. https://doi.org/10.1017/CBO9780511625466.003.

Lynch, Marc. "After Egypt: The Limits and Promise of Online Challenges to the Authoritarian Arab State." *Perspectives on Politics* 9, no. 2 (2011): 301–10.

Lyon, David. "Surveillance, Snowden, and Big Data: Capacities, Consequences, Critique." *Big Data & Society* 1, no. 2 (2014): 2053951714541861.

Massanari, Adrienne. "# Gamergate and The Fappening: How Reddit's Algorithm, Governance, and Culture Support Toxic Technocultures." *New Media & Society* 19, no. 3 (2017): 329–46.

McKune, Sarah, and Ron Deibert. "Who's Watching Little Brother? A Checklist for Accountability in the Industry behind Government Hacking." March 2, 2017. https://citizenlab.ca/wp-content/uploads/2017/03/citizenlab_whos -watching-little-brother.pdf.

Michaelsen, Marcus. "The Digital Transnational Repression Toolkit, and Its Silencing Effects." In *Perspectives on "Everyday" Transnational Repression in an Age of Globalization*. Freedom House, 2020, 4–8. https://freedomhouse .org/sites/default/files/2020-07/07092020_Transnational_Repression_ Globalization_Collection_of_Essays_FINAL_.pdf

Moss, Dana M. "Transnational Repression, Diaspora Mobilization, and the Case of the Arab Spring." *Social Problems* 63, no. 4 (2016): 480–98. https://doi.org /10.1093/socpro/spw019.

Musah, Abdel-Fatau, Kayode Fayemi, and J'Kayode Fayemi. *Mercenaries: An African Security Dilemma*. London, UK: Pluto Press, 2000.

Ortmann, Stephan. "The Umbrella Movement and Hong Kong's Protracted Democratization Process." *Asian Affairs* 46, no. 1 (2015): 32–50. https://doi .org/10.1080/03068374.2014.994957.

Patsiaouras, Georgios, Anastasia Veneti, and William Green. "The Hong Kong Umbrella Movement as a Non-Profit Organization: An Empirical Study on the Use of Visual Branding Practices for Social Change." *Journal of Philanthropy and Marketing* 27, no. 2 (2022). https://doi.org/10.1002/nvsm.1717.

Pearce, Katy E. "Democratizing Kompromat: The Affordances of Social Media for State-Sponsored Harassment." *Information, Communication & Society* 18, no. 10 (2015): 1158–74.

Peckham, Michael. "New Dimensions of Social Movement/Countermovement Interaction: The Case of Scientology and Its Internet Critics." *Canadian*

*Journal of Sociology/Cahiers Canadiens de Sociologie* 23, no. 4 (1998): 317–47. https://www.jstor.org/stable/3341804

Peterson, Abby, and Mattias Wahlström. "Repression: The Governance of Domestic Dissent." In *The Oxford Handbook of Social Movements*, edited by Della Porta, Donatella, and Mario Diani, 634–52. Oxford: Oxford University Press, 2015.

Poupin, Perrine. "Social Media and State Repression: The Case of VKontakte and the Anti-Garbage Protest in Shies, in Far Northern Russia." *First Monday* 26, no. 5 (2021). https://doi.org/10.5210/fm.v26i5.11711.

Roggeband, Conny, and Bert Klandermans. *Handbook of Social Movements across Disciplines*. Boston, MA: Springer, 2017.

Singer, Peter W. "Corporate Warriors: The Rise of the Privatized Military Industry and Its Ramifications for International Security." *International Security* 26, no. 3 (2001): 186–220.

Smyrnaios, Nikos. *Internet Oligopoly: The Corporate Takeover of Our Digital World*. Bingley, UK: Emerald Group Publishing, 2018.

Tenove, Chris. "Networking Justice: Digitally-Enabled Engagement in Transitional Justice by the Syrian Diaspora." *Ethnic and Racial Studies* 42, no. 11 (2019): 1950–69.

Tilly, Charles. *From Mobilization to Revolution*. Addison-Wesley Publishing Company, 1978.

Tong, Carmen. "A Chronology of Hong Kong's Umbrella Movement: January 2013–December 2014." *Educational Philosophy and Theory* 51, no. 2 (2019): 194–99. https://doi.org/10.1080/00131857.2017.1310017.

Trottier, Daniel. "Policing Social Media." *Canadian Review of Sociology/Revue Canadienne de Sociologie* 49, no. 4 (2012): 411–25.

Veg, Sebastian. "Creating a Textual Public Space: Slogans and Texts from Hong Kong's Umbrella Movement." *Journal of Asian Studies* 75, no. 3 (2016): 673–702. https://doi.org/10.1017/S0021911816000565.

Verble, Joseph. "The NSA and Edward Snowden: Surveillance in the 21st Century." *ACM Sigcas Computers and Society* 44, no. 3 (2014): 14–20.

Walker, Edward T., Andrew W. Martin, and John D. McCarthy. "Confronting the State, the Corporation, and the Academy: The Influence of Institutional Targets on Social Movement Repertoires." *American Journal of Sociology* 114, no. 1 (2008): 35–76. https://doi.org/10.1086/588737.

Walker, Edward T., and Christopher M. Rea. "The Political Mobilization of Firms and Industries." *Annual Review of Sociology* 40, no. 1 (2014): 281–304.

Walsh, James P., and Christopher O'Connor. "Social Media and Policing: A Review of Recent Research." *Sociology Compass* 13, no. 1 (2019): e12648.

Xu, Xu. "To Repress or to Co-Opt? Authoritarian Control in the Age of Digital Surveillance." *American Journal of Political Science* 65, no. 2 (2021): 309–25.

Yuen, Samson. "Hong Kong after the Umbrella Movement: An Uncertain Future for 'One Country Two Systems." *China Perspectives* 2015, no. 1 (2015): 49–53.

Yuen, Samson, and Edmund W. Cheng. "Neither Repression Nor Concession? A Regime's Attrition against Mass Protests." *Political Studies* 65, no. 3 (2017): 611–30. https://doi.org/10.1177/0032321716674024.

# PART II
# Resistance

# ADVOCATES FOR ACTION

## María Jesús Alvarado Rivera

1878–1971
Hometown: Chincha Alta, Peru
Movements: Women's rights in Peru
Organizations: Founder Evolución Feminina, Escuela Taller Moral y
  Trabajo, and National Council of Women of Peru

*Claire Zoller and Allison Schuster*

María Jesús Alvarado Rivera was a Peruvian rebel who was active during the time of the internal conflict in Peru, which took place from 1980 to 2000. She used her skills as a journalist to speak out on women's rights, and is noted as one of the first advocates of female equality in her country.[1] As a woman growing up in Peru, she attended public primary school and later attended a private high school that was established and run by Elvira García y García, who was a leader of the feminist movement in Peru.[2] Here she became impassioned about women's education and rights and became a schoolteacher. She studied sociology to educate herself on important issues and topics.

At the age of 20, with the assistance of her brother, she also landed a position as a columnist for *El Comercio* and *El Diario*.[3] During her time as a journalist, she spoke at multiple conferences promoting the rights of women in Peru. She also started to write about controversial topics, such as arranged marriage. This gained both positive and negative responses. While many people supported her ideas, many also viewed them as too radical and going against a woman's traditional role within the family.[4] In

DOI: 10.4324/9781003291855-9

1914, she founded the first feminist organization in Peru, called Evolución Feminina, and then in 1915 she founded the Escuela Taller Moral y Trabajo, where, from her home, she taught women essential skills. Finally, in 1923, Alvarado Rivera established the National Council of Women of Peru, which continued advocating for the rights of women in Peru. With a primary focus of advocating for women's rights to education and political freedoms, these organizations attempted to move the women's agenda forward. Due to her continued advocacy for women's rights and her radical thoughts for the time, she was jailed and exiled.[5]

During her exile, she spent 12 years in Argentina, where she taught school and directed dramas that centered around social and moral issues in society. She later returned to Peru, where she continued advocating for women's right to vote. Peruvian women ultimately gained the right to vote in 1955, 16 years before she passed away in 1971 at the age of 92. Across Latin America, her work continues to be appreciated and admired by women and feminists.

## Notes

1 Kautzman, Zachary. "María Jesús Alvarado Rivera." Women's Activism NYC, 2020. https://www.womensactivism.nyc/stories/6869.
2 Chaney, Elsa M. 2021. "Old and New Feminists: Women's Rights in Latin America." In *Supermadre: Women in Politics in Latin America*. New York: University of Texas Press, pp. 67–82.
3 Eschinger, Mia. "María Jesús Alvarado Rivera and evolución feminina." COW Latin America. https://cowlatinamerica.voices.wooster.edu/archive -item/maria-jesus-alvarado-rivera-and-evolucion-feminina/.
4 Iida, Kate. 2019. "'To the workers of the republic': María Jesús Alvarado Rivera, Dora Mayer de Zulen, and the Intersection of Indigenous, Labor, and Feminist Activisms, 1909–1925."
5 Alvarado, Jesús, Jesús Rivera, and Jesús Alvarado. n.d. "María Petronila de Jesús Alvarado Rivera (1878–1971)" FamilySearch. Accessed December 4, 2022. https://ancestors.familysearch.org/en/LY9F-4RV/mar%C3%ADa -petronila-de-jes%C3%BAs-alvarado-rivera-1878-1971.

# 4

# BUILDING MOMENTUM

## Creating Change

*Arien Rozelle*

### Introduction: Social Movements Are Shaped by the Dominant Media of the Day

The social and political uprisings stemming from the 2016 election and beyond have underscored the role of technology and communication in the push for social change. Across traditional and social media, in all corners of the internet and on all social platforms available, words, images, videos, and symbols have been used to raise awareness, motivate, and persuade audiences to support or participate in a wide range of social causes.

But this is nothing new. Activists and social causes have long used a variety of tools to influence **public opinion**. The American Revolution, led by Samuel Adams, is often cited as an early and noteworthy campaign to influence public opinion. From articles to speaking engagements, and staged events to symbols, Adams knew that "public opinion results from the march of events and the way these events are seen by those active in public affairs."[1] Adams also knew how to use symbolism to sway public opinion, and is credited with organizing what *PR Week* has called "the greatest and best-known publicity stunt of all time,"[2] the Boston Tea Party.

Today, it's almost impossible to imagine organizing a movement – or a revolution – at a time before even radio was commonly used. And yet, progressive movements and social causes throughout history have managed to communicate, build momentum, gain support, educate, and agitate long before the advent of the internet.

In the 1960s – an era ripe with social change – Canadian media theorist Marshall McLuhan developed the concepts behind the theory of **media**

DOI: 10.4324/9781003291855-10

ecology, the study of different personal and social environments created by the use of different communication technologies. McLuhan observed that *we shape our tools, and they in turn shape us.* He noted that when we continually use a communication technology, it alters our **symbolic environment** – the socially constructed, sensory world of meanings that shapes our perceptions, experiences, attitudes, and behavior. Whether newspapers, radio, television, or today, social media, society is shaped by the dominant medium of the day. Understanding social and cultural change, according to McLuhan, is impossible without understanding how the media work as environments.[3] It's hard to imagine that McLuhan – who also predicted the internet – developed this theory before social media and the smartphone. It's almost as if he could foresee the rapid changes in technology and media we would soon experience, and knew how they would change us, and our world.

Today, it's impossible to understand recent shifts in society without considering the role of technology, the media, and social media. There's no doubt that the growing availability of technology like the internet and smartphones over the past two decades has allowed social movements to build power, persuade, recruit, and inspire action. Technology and media have impacted the way that social movements emerge, recruit, communicate, and agitate throughout history. Real, expected, or even perceived media presence impacts "virtually every aspect of a challenger's experience – recruitment efforts, organization, strategy, and tactics."[4] Social movements are shaped by the technology available at the time of collective action, and as a result, tailor their goals, strategy, tactics, and rhetoric to the media of their time.

While social movements today rely upon the speed and connectivity of social media for fast communication and mobilization, social movements pre-date the internet. The Suffrage Movement is an example of a social movement that relied upon the dominant media of the time – print – to recruit and mobilize. Today, the ability to share not only text-based communication, but photos and videos in real time has greatly increased the speed of communication and, as such, the ability to mobilize quickly. Social media has allowed social movements like #MeToo and Black Lives Matter (BLM) to craft their narratives using rich media, and to bypass **gatekeepers** in traditional media outlets, allowing information to spread that otherwise never would have made headlines.

This chapter will examine the technology and media available to the Suffrage Movement, Black Lives Matter and #MeToo at the time of collective action, and examine strategies and tactics used to build momentum, form group identities, and create change.

## Building Momentum in the Print Age: The Suffrage Movement

By all accounts, the Woman's Suffrage Movement was one of the longest – and most successful – social movements in history. For nearly 100 years, leaders and supporters of the movement utilized nearly every persuasive strategy and tactic available to them at the time. With extensive publicity efforts that included speeches, parades, banners, buttons, speaking tours, silent protests and much more, the Suffrage Movement captured the attention and eventually galvanized the support of the public in America and beyond. But without access to radio, television, or the modern-day connectivity of social media, how were Suffragists successful in recruiting and building momentum for their cause? They utilized the dominant media of the day: print. And they did so during the golden age of newspapers.

In 1800, prior to the start of the Suffrage Movement, 200 newspapers were published in the United States. At the time, newspapers cost about 6 cents. Beginning in the 1830s, the penny press – cheap, **tabloid**-style newspapers – emerged and began being mass-produced, making the news accessible to middle-class citizens at a reasonable price. Thanks to the invention of the steam-powered rotary print press in 1843 and technological advancements in papermaking, typesetting, and printing, mass production of newspapers exploded. Now, millions of copies of a page could be printed in a single day, and print presses could run at a faster pace. These developments helped pave the way for the growth of metropolitan daily newspapers.

During the 1830s and 1840s, newspapers exploded in popularity, with many new urban newspapers reaching unprecedented circulation numbers. According to one estimate, the total annual circulation of all newspapers between 1828 and 1840 doubled from 68 million to 148 million copies.[5] Some scholars also speculate that in addition to advances in technology and printing, the expansion of the press was due to increased political participation of the working and middle classes, higher rates of literacy, and increased leisure time.[6] By 1860, there were 3,000 newspapers published in the United States.[7] From smaller hometown papers to farm papers to huge metro dailies, as print media gained traction across the country and newspaper circulations grew, so too did their coverage. News was expanded to include human interest stories, court reports, and scandals. Special "feature" sections were added to some papers, including sections for women and children. All of these factors were part of a news revolution of sorts, and one that played a crucial role in the Suffrage Movement's ability to recruit, mobilize, and sway public opinion. But it wasn't always easy – or fast.

Because established media tends to support the **status quo**, social movements are often seen as outsiders in their push for social change. This presents a variety of challenges in communicating about their message in a way that will be covered favorably by the media, particularly during a sustained effort. Negative news coverage of the Suffrage Movement was pervasive, and arguments against women's suffrage were plentiful. Often accompanied by derogatory caricatures demeaning Suffragists, anti-suffrage articles were published frequently in newspapers. To combat both negative coverage of the movement and continue to earn supporters, Suffragists utilized every tactic available at the time, including speeches, letter writing campaigns, spectacles, even plays, songs, and more. By 1868, the **mainstream media** had begun to see the movement as "old news," and it was becoming difficult for Elizabeth Cady Stanton and Susan B. Anthony to make their voices heard. Many social movements turned to **self-publishing** as a way to reach new supporters, communicate with current ones, and keep the momentum of the movement going. Stanton and Anthony established *The Revolution*, a weekly women's rights newspaper, which functioned as the official voice of the National American Woman Suffrage Association. The first issue generated publicity by announcing that Anthony had convinced US President Andrew Johnson to buy a subscription.[8] While the paper's circulation never exceeded 3,000, it was hugely influential in shaping the **narrative** of the movement, publishing articles about a range of women's rights issues like suffrage, as well as politics and finance.

While numerous publicity tactics were used during this time, it's often the dramatic events that are critical to activist success, particularly those that are supported by strong visuals. Anthony was adept at working with the media and knew how to "make news." Taking a cue from Samuel Adams, she knew how symbolism could sway public opinion. On election day, November 5, 1872, when she and 14 other women cast their ballots in the presidential race between Ulysses S. Grant and Horace Greeley, they took advantage of a prime opportunity to influence public opinion, using newspapers – and Anthony's relationships with reporters – to their greatest advantage. Anthony's act of voting, while an act of civil disobedience in support of her cause, was also nothing short of a **publicity stunt**. Anthony was by no means the first woman to attempt to vote. In fact, hundreds of women had attempted to vote. But by this time, she was a nationally known figure with well-established relationships with key **stakeholders** – including reporters. As a result, the press, including the notoriously anti-suffrage *New York Times*, gave it space. And a Rochester, New York State paper printed letters to the editor on both sides of the issue, among other publications. While her act of voting could have remained a local or regional story in the Rochester market, the combination of many other **news values** – and subsequent events like her arrest and trial – helped to propel the story to national news. And although Anthony wasn't the first to vote illegally, her celebrity and connections with reporters helped her to make news. Due in part to the role of print media at the time, Anthony's arrest for voting became a seminal moment in Suffrage history and helped keep the momentum of the movement going.

By 1897, suffragists had already spent ample time – nearly 50 years – using a variety of strategies and tactics to promote recruitment and the legitimacy of their cause. But they still had a long way to go. Knowing the importance of print media to their cause, Anthony, as President of the National American Woman Suffrage Association, along with many other Suffragists, embarked on an innovative plan to establish a National Press Bureau. Anthony wrote:

> the age demands that we shall utilize the press of the country ... We must have a National Press Bureau, with a woman at its head who has not only experience and ability, but the leisure and the disposition to give her whole time to reading the press clippings of the entire country, and putting herself in communication with every editor who says a word for or against our movement.[9]

A National Press Bureau would allow the movement to not only disseminate, but also **frame** its messages consistently nationwide, rather than at a state-by-state level, as they had been. This was an important and innovative strategy at the time as it ensured that a clear message was shared from coast to coast – and beyond. Anthony was unable to secure the money needed to establish the National Press Bureau before her death, but her wish for headquarters in a large city center, "from which news of all kinds was sent to the four quarters of the globe," would come to fruition in 1909 when the National Press Bureau was opened in New York City.[10]

A National Press Bureau in New York City lent prestige and reach to the movement and provided more access to writers and editors of national high-profile publications, as well as international publications. New York City was a news town, and New Yorkers had an insatiable appetite for the news of the day. Over time, the Press Bureau supplied thousands of articles in support of Suffrage to hundreds of newspapers. Content was sent to not only mainstream newspapers, but also to farm newspapers and religious, educational, and other specialized newspapers. Thousands of letters to the editor were sent to various papers. Relationships were built with writers and editors at leading magazines to secure articles on Suffrage. News was shared in the form of not only text, but illustrations, and eventually photographs as well. The movement responded to incoming requests for Suffrage news both nationally and internationally, and employed extensive planning, organizing, relationship-building, media relations strategies, and media monitoring efforts, reviewing national and international media coverage to gauge public **sentiment**.

Nothing was more vital in swaying public opinion than their work with the press. Print media, including mainstream newspapers and self-published ones, as well as magazines, helped Suffragists not only to build, but sustain support for their cause over the course of decades. As Suffragists worked toward a federal amendment to the Constitution, the work of the National Press Bureau continued, escalated by the momentum seen by the movement. It continued to conduct a national campaign of agitation, education, organization, and publicity in support of the amendment. Utilizing the press as the dominant media of the time, the Suffrage Movement eventually achieved its long fought for and hard-won objective. On August 26, 1920, three=quarters of the state legislatures ratified the Nineteenth Amendment and American women won full voting rights.

## Social Media Solidarity: The #MeToo Movement

The media, and now the *social* media, landscape have changed dramatically in the century following the passage of the Nineteenth Amendment. While print media remains, newspapers and magazines have seen dwindling readership. Digital media has expanded not only in terms of traditional media adapting and migrating to digital, but in the ability to self-publish via blogs, vlogs and social media. The internet has provided media and other content producers with the ability to share text, rich photos, videos, graphics, charts, illustrations, and more. There are innumerable ways to communicate and share information and personal experiences. For social movements, this has helped to raise awareness, build empathy and support, and increase solidarity.

The #MeToo movement was begun in 2006 by activist and sexual assault survivor Tarana Burke when she coined the term "Me too" on **Myspace** to raise awareness of sex abuse. In October 2017, following multiple sexual abuse allegations against Hollywood producer Harvey Weinstein, the hashtag #MeToo re-emerged on social media. When, on October 15, actress Alyssa Milano's tweet urged those who had been sexually harassed or assaulted to write "Me Too" in a show of solidarity, high-profile actresses like Gwyneth Paltrow, Ashley Judd, and Jennifer Lawrence responded. Other musicians, actors, and actresses soon followed, and their celebrity helped to generate widespread usage of the hashtag on social media. The public and shareable admissions and accusations of sexual abuse on Twitter led countless others – both public and private figures – to share their own personal stories. By the end of the day, #MeToo had been used more than 200,000 times.[11]

What was it about the hashtag that resonated with so many? Social media, Twitter in particular, provided a platform to share stories of abuse very publicly. The act of merely tweeting "#MeToo" in response, or sharing a personal story of abuse, helped to create group **solidarity**. And social movements rely on a sense of **collective identity**, the shared definition of a group that comes from its members' common interests, experiences, and solidarities. A sense of collective identity ties individuals to the movement's values and beliefs. While the #MeToo movement started as a hashtag and was centered around the use of social media to recruit and mobilize, an important part of the early virality of the hashtag – and later the movement – was the forming of group identities. The ability of #MeToo to form a collective identity was due in part to the inherent way that #MeToo **framed**: to imply that one is not alone; *it happened to me, too.* The hashtag itself created a sense of belonging, and media coverage often reflected that.

Because the internet has broken down barriers of time and place, as momentum for the #MeToo movement grew in the United States, broader audiences began to take part in the movement. The sheer volume of people sharing their personal stories helped to lessen the fear and shame they may have felt. Engagement in risk – of exposing oneself as being a victim, and risk in making public accusations against often high-profile figures – also helped to increase solidarity as #MeToo was shared across Twitter, Facebook, Instagram – and the world.

---

**#METOO GOES GLOBAL**

As survivors of sexual abuse and violence in the United States continued to make their voices heard, the movement spread globally. The hashtag has been used in over 85 countries, including in Europe, Australia, the Middle East, and beyond. France saw #BalanceTonPorc ("#SquealOnYourPig"), and in Spain, Mexico, South America, and beyond, #YoTambien. In Italy, the hashtag was #QuellaVoltaChe ("That Time").

---

Some have been critical of social media's role in activism, noting that merely liking a post, sharing a tweet, or signing an online petition involve little effort or commitment to the social movement itself. The term **slacktivism** has emerged to critically describe this type of online advocacy.

But #MeToo, in both its vulnerability and magnitude, demonstrated how commonplace sexual assault and harassment have become. In fact, the #MeToo hashtag became a viral phenomenon, making its way from social platforms to traditional media, and back again. The movement interrupted the news cycle in 2017, dominating headlines for months, if not years. Twitter became the primary place where those who wanted to speak out came to name names, and the accused responded. It also became the primary source for **newsgathering** for traditional media. As more and more people came forward with their stories of abuse and assault, the media turned to Twitter to source their stories. In this way, social media helped the movement galvanize support and frame the message, while traditional media served to amplify it by bringing it to print and digital news outlets. This is an example of **agenda-setting theory,** which describes the ability of the media to influence the importance of certain topics in the public's agenda.

The #MeToo movement appealed to ideas about equality and justice, right and wrong. It spoke to issues in the workplace, in social settings, in relationships. It touched nearly every industry, from Hollywood to professional sports to higher education to politics. People of every race, gender, class, and ethnicity now cared about #MeToo. As such, the movement had a lot of communicating to do – very quickly – with a wide range of audiences, making information accessibility and speed of communication crucial as activists sought to create change.

While social media platforms provide a way for movements like #MeToo to build community and solidarity, websites also play an increasingly important role in developing the legitimacy and credibility of a movement. Websites can function as a vital resource – a "hub" for movements to highlight facts, specific initiatives, events or important moments. Today, #MeToo's website (https://metoomvmt.org) is abundant with resources for survivors in a section called "Explore Healing," information for activists in the "Take Action" section, and facts for the media and others in the "Learn more" section, among a wealth of other sections and resources available on their content-rich website.

As a social movement emerges and sees heightened interest from traditional media, websites can also become a crucial resource for sharing information with the media. A **digital press room** can be housed on the website with fact sheets, press releases, media alerts, b-roll footage, logos, photos, and other content available for use in the media. This can enable a movement to communicate more effectively with the media, which can help to clarify and solidify its message, especially early on. And as social media continues to suffer from widespread **misinformation** and **disinformation,** websites can be a useful tool for social movements to provide access to accurate information about their cause. They can serve as a place to curate content like white papers, e-books, newsletters, infographics, case studies, FAQs, and more, all of which can also be easily shared via social media. Finally, websites allow movements to develop greater and deeper storytelling across platforms. #MeToo's website features an array of video storytelling in the form of its "Survivor Story Series" via YouTube. Its initiative ActToo (https://acttoo.metoomvmt.org) includes content ranging from videos to blogs to action-oriented content like petitions.

Today, the tools activists use to communicate with a range of audiences have also, in turn, shaped the expectations we have about communication and recruitment strategies. To recruit and maintain support, social movements must clearly identify target audiences, and develop content that appeals to them. This content can be shared on social media and housed on a website. #MeToo's website serves as a content-rich hub to communicate with a variety of stakeholders: those impacted by sexual violence or abuse, those interested in joining/supporting the cause, allies, contributors, and those in the media. The digital tools that social movements have access to enable them to curate and create content quickly, in a way that promotes solidarity and the creation of a collective identity.

## Galvanizing Support: BLM's Mediated Mobilization in Today's Global Village

Today, we live in a "global village," marked by the daily production and consumption of media, images, and content by global audiences at a rapid pace. As social media has become one of the most common ways for social movements to organize and mobilize, it's hard to imagine attempting to do so without access to the internet, our mobile phones, and social media. In fact, some social movements were born out of the connectivity available to them via social media. Take the Black Lives Matter movement, for example. In 2013, Alicia Garza, Patrisse Cullors, and Opal Tometi created the #BlackLivesMatter movement following the death of Trayvon Martin and the subsequent acquittal of his killer, George Zimmerman.

Historically, hashtags were an informal way of highlighting ideas or categorizing text as a way to create a conversation around a topic. While most hashtags developed organically, some groups or organizations intentionally use them to promote a message. When Twitter began hyperlinking and compiling hashtags in 2009, this made them searchable. What began as a hashtag for #BlackLivesMatter quickly became a movement utilizing **mediated mobilization,** turning social media into an indispensable tool in organizing efforts. The range of recruitment, mobilization, and communication strategies and tactics utilized by the movement rely heavily on the use of visuals to tell their story. From cellphone footage of police brutality to webinars about police abolition to livestreamed protests, BLM has harnessed **visual storytelling** via social media on platforms like Twitter, Instagram, and YouTube. While #BlackLivesMatter gained more traction following each high-profile incident of police brutality, it was the speed of communication and information sharing combined with high-impact visuals that helped propel it into a movement. In May 2020, when video footage of George Floyd's murder by four Minneapolis police officers circulated online, local protests quickly began. Just days later, live images of protestors burning Minneapolis' Third Police Precinct filled social feeds. Protests nationally and internationally emerged at an unprecedented speed and scale as more and more images of police brutality told the story.

With a flood of content across the internet and social media, movements may struggle with getting their messages across clearly and effectively to intended audiences due to the decentralized nature of social movements. While other modern movements may have struggled with messaging, BLM has been very clear about its objective to highlight racism and inequality experienced by Black people. This clarity may have been the result of work behind the scenes using digital tools for collaboration, information storage, and communication. Platforms like Google Drive, Slack, and Messenger may have allowed leaders of the movement to work together easily and quickly.[12] Likely due in part to collaborative digital tools, BLM has also been effective in cutting through the **noise**. When #BlackoutTuesday flooded Instagram, it became counterproductive to the movement. Blackout Tuesday was a social protest and display of symbolism on social media, particularly Instagram, in which users shared a black square in solidarity with Black victims of police violence. Many tagged their posts with #BlackLivesMatter and #BLM, which led the black squares to overtake the content of the movement. Black screens washed out vital information about protests, organization donations, and content about police violence. BLM supporters were able to quickly correct course by asking others to remove the BLM hashtags from the #BlackoutTuesday posts.

There are generally five distinct tactical areas used by activists to achieve their goals: informational activities, including media interviews; symbolic activities, including boycotts; organizing activities such as passing out information pieces and holding meetings; legal and legislative activities, and pressuring regulatory and administrative agencies; and civil disobedience, including sit-ins, blocking traffic, and trespassing.[13] BLM has participated in a variety of these tactical areas and has done so with social and traditional media in mind. As previously noted, traditional news media tends to focus coverage of social movements on the spectacle or the violence of protests or specific protestors. While this was *certainly* the case for BLM, it also was able to combat negative coverage by crafting a visual narrative that was sympathetic to its cause: the image frequently depicted across traditional and social media of BLM protestors staring into the eyes of police. Narratives play an important role in shaping social reality. Multimedia narratives, both in social media and in news media in the form of images and videos, can be particularly impactful in the public's perception of an issue. This image has been duplicated various times with different protestors, and depicts a refusal to submit to police intimidation. This image carries symbolic and narrative power, as making eye contact with police has historically posed a threat to Black people.

Other tactics like mass protests and reclaiming a physical site of oppression are heavily visual in nature. For example, the Robert E. Lee Confederate monument in Richmond, Virginia was covered in graffiti in an attempt to remove its power to intimidate. Images of the monument were circulated on social media and made headlines in traditional media. A makeshift basketball court was also set up there, turning it into an unexpected community space against the backdrop of the graffiti-covered statute. Black ballerinas used the monument for a stage while giving Black power fists. The site became a court, a canvas, and a stage for protest, and each time, images of these tactics made their way to social media and made headlines in traditional media, working to support BLM's strategies aiming to change public opinion.

Interestingly, BLM and its supporters have utilized several audio tactics as well, at a time when sound has again become a popular form of media (consider the re-emergence and popularity of podcasts). In protests, chants of "Hands up, don't shoot!" are commonplace, and when shouted collectively, can help to build solidarity. Singing can be a unifying tactic among members, as well as a way to recruit, build momentum, and maintain morale. Rapper Kendrick Lamar's song "Alright" became the unofficial anthem of the movement after youth-led protests were heard chanting the chorus. Another creative audio tactic came from digital activists Anonymous, who, in support of BLM, hacked the Chicago police radio system and played "Fuck the Police" by N.W.A, then circulated recordings of the hack on social media.

Today, all types of content – text, images, video, and audio – move at lightning speed, enabling activists to move quickly from their screens to the streets. The Black Lives Matter Movement relied on the internet and social media to raise awareness, build support, and mobilize quickly, becoming mainstream in ways that would have been unthinkable just a few years ago. Americans have staged BLM demonstrations in all 50 states and the District of Columbia – and beyond. Social media enabled the movement to coalesce, mobilize, and disseminate information with speed and clarity in a truly remarkable and unprecedented manner.

## Conclusion

Social movements must attract new followers and allies in order to increase their power, but they are restricted – and shaped – by the technology available at the time of the collective action. The various forms of media – both traditional and social – are vital in attracting media coverage in support of their point of view. As social movements engage in discourse, they must tailor their strategies and tactics to their intended audiences. The potential for discourse contributes to the framing of narratives and building of momentum in order to create change. Sharing of personal stories and use of photo, video, and audio can contribute to building momentum and allow broader audiences to take part in the action. Performances that are mediated via online tools can create group solidarity through engagement in risk, thereby contributing to the formation of group identities and creating change. Today, social movements turn to social media as the dominant medium to spark a movement to incite change.

## Reflections

- How are the strategies and tactics used by the social movements mentioned in this chapter similar or different?
- Why do you think social movements turn to self-publishing?
- How does solidarity contribute to the formation of a collective identity?
- How do photos and videos impact the narrative of a social movement?
- Why is it important for social movements to tailor their communication strategies and tactics to specific audiences?
- How do you think media and technology will change the way social movements recruit 20 years from now?

## Notes

1 Broom, Glen M. 2013. *Cutlip and Center's Effective Public Relations*. New York: Pearson Education.
2 Shortman, Melanie, and Jonah Bloom. "The greatest campaigns ever?" *PR Week*, 2002. https://www.prweek.com/article/1234145/greatest-campaigns -ever-200-year-old-publicity-stuntthat-changed-course-history-product -recall-becomethe-model-crisis-comms-melanie-shortman-jonah.

3 McLuhan, Marshall, and Quentin Fiore. 1967. *The Medium Is the Massage: Co-ordinated by Jerome Angel.* New York: Bantam Books, p. 26.
4 Gamson, W.A. 1992. "The social psychology of collective action." In J. Goodwin and J.M. Jasper (eds.), *Social Movements.* London: Routledge, pp. 168–187.
5 Schiller, Dan. 1981. *Objectivity and the News: The Public and the Rise of Commercial Journalism.* Philadelphia, PA: University of Pennsylvania Press), p. 12.
6 Schudson, Michael. 1978. *Discovering the News: A Social History of American Newspapers.* New York: Basic Books, pp. 35–39, 43–50. Schiller, *Objectivity and the News*, pp. 15–17.
7 Mott, Frank Luther. 1941. *American Journalism: A History of Newspapers in the United States through 250 Years, 1690–1940.* New York: Macmillan, p. 216.
8 Lana F. Rakow and Cheris Kramarae. (eds.). 2016. *The Revolution in Words: Righting Women, 1868 – 1871.* London: Routledge, p. 22, accessed May 9, 2023, https://doi.org/10.4324/9780203708934.
9 Anthony, Susan B. "Anthony Avery Papers." Rare Books and Special Collections, University of Rochester. Accessed July 1, 2022. http://www.lib.rochester.edu/IN/RBSCP/IMAGES/D16AnthonyAveryPapers/Edited-images/Box2/November-1897/image0000043A.jpg.
10 "The History of Woman Suffrage, Volume V." Project Gutenberg. Accessed July 1, 2022. https://www.gutenberg.org/files/29878/29878-h/29878-h.htm, p. 228.
11 Sini, Rozina. "How 'MeToo' is exposing the scale of sexual abuse." BBC News, October 16, 2017. https://www.bbc.com/news/blogs-trending-41633857.
12 Hu, Jane. "The second act of social-media activism." *The New Yorker*, August 3, 2020. https://www.newyorker.com/culture/cultural-comment/the-second-act-of-social-media-activism.
13 Jackson, P. 1982. "Tactics of confrontation." In J.S. Nagelschmidt (ed.), *The Public Affairs Handbook.* New York: American Management Association, pp. 211–220.

# ADVOCATES FOR ACTION

## Wilhelmina Kekelaokalaninui Widemann Dowsett

1861–1929
Hometown: Lihue, Hawai'i, USA
Movements: Women's Suffrage
Organizations: National Women's Equal Suffrage Association

*Phoebe L. Bogdanoff*

Born in Honolulu, Hawai'i in 1866, Wilhelmine Kekelaokalaninui Widemann Dowsett was a half-German and half-Native Hawaiian suffragist whose connection to Hawai'i and the local people was unmatched as she dedicated her life to advocating for Hawaiian civil rights.[1] Throughout her life she was involved in a number of organizations that worked to promote women's rights, including the National American Woman Suffrage Association and the Hawaiian Suffrage Association. Her access to the political sphere stemmed from her royal lineage and her father's position as a cabinet minister of the last queen of Hawai'i.[2] Together with her husband, John McKibbin Dowsett, a senator in the Hawai'i Territorial Legislature, they sought to make a difference for women.[3]

After the annexation of Hawai'i, prominent mainland suffragists like Susan B. Anthony began advocating for Hawaiian women's right to vote, increasing the movement's appeal and relevance across the territory.[4] Believing that her community would be more successful in their endeavors if they worked with the territorial government, she organized the National Women's Equal Suffrage Association of Hawai'i (WESAH) in 1912 and served as president.[5] In 1913, amidst a meeting with local politicians, Dowsett argued that women were superior to men, stating:

DOI: 10.4324/9781003291855-11

I can speak for my Hawaiian sisters, and I can say that in every way the woman is man's superior. She will not only cast her vote fully as intelligently – she will vote, honestly. There isn't enough money in the world to buy her vote. And on the jury she will decide as intelligently, while there will be no question as to her verdict.[6]

In her fight for equality, she used her class privilege to advocate for historically oppressed groups.[7] The territory legislature formulated by the US government forbade the territory from granting suffrage rights not granted by the federal legislature, but Dowsett's advocacy efforts were successful in getting Congress and President Wilson to allow Hawaiians the ability to make those decisions themselves.[8] When the bill to enfranchise women deadlocked in Hawai'i's congress, Dowsett and WESAH adopted a resolution demanding the right to vote in upcoming elections. When the House allowed this issue to be further delayed, Dowsett utilized community organization tactics to assemble 500 women to storm the House floor.[9] Using this momentum, she also planned a local event featuring various speakers to disseminate WESAH's message among local people and the press. Ultimately, she switched her goal to federal legislation and toured the Hawaiian Islands to help create grassroots campaigns lobbying the federal government through territorial representatives.[10]

Throughout her career, Dowsett created an inclusive environment within the Suffragist Movement, setting an example for future activists to use their privilege to fight for historically oppressed groups, eventually leading to the widespread advocacy of civil rights for all. Her communications skills have had long-term impacts on modern women's ability to vote, especially those of Native Hawaiian and Asian descent.

## Notes

1 Gilbert, Shawn. "Suffragists you need to meet: Wilhelmina Dowsett (1861–1929)." League of Women Voters. Accessed November 29, 2022. https://my.lwv.org/california/diablo-valley/article/suffragists-you-need-meet-wilhelmina-dowsett-1861-1929.
2 Ibid.
3 Entry for "Wilhelmine Kekelaokalaninui Widemann Dowsett." Wikipedia. Accessed November 29, 2022. https://en.wikipedia.org/wiki/Wilhelmine_Kekelaokalaninui_Widemann_Dowsett.
4 "Wilhelmina Kekelaokalaninui Widemann Dowsett." Hawai'i Women's Suffrage Centennial Commemoration. https://wscc.historichawaii.org/profile/profile-post-1/.
5 "Wilhelmina Kekelaokalaninui Widemann Dowsett." National Park Service. Accessed November 29, 2022. https://www.nps.gov/people/wilhelmina-kekelaokalaninui-widemann-dowsett.htm.

6 "Equal suffrage hotly debated." *Honolulu Star-Bulletin*, April 25, 1913, p. 7.

7 McKinzie, Edith Kawelohea. 1986. *Hawaiian Genealogies: Extracted from Hawaiian Language Newspapers*, vol. 2, ed. Ishmael W. Stagner II. Honolulu, Hawai'i: University of Hawai'i Press.

8 "Wilhelmina Kekelaokalaninui Widemann Dowsett," National Park Service. Peterson, Barbara Bennett. 1984. *Notable Women of Hawaii*. Honolulu, Hawai'i: University of Hawai'i Press.

9 Gilbert, "Suffragists you need to meet."

10 "Wilhelmina Kekelaokalaninui Widemann Dowsett," National Park Service.

# 5

# EARLY DIGITAL SOCIAL MOVEMENTS

## Events, Protests, Moments

*Anthony Spencer*

## Introduction

Online activism has become an integral component of the social change agenda. We can just as easily belong to a Facebook group for neighborhood cleanup as we can advocate for social change on the other side of the globe. **Activism** is action which we undertake for a cause or group or that is above the ordinary level of help or effort.[1] While it may seem like digital activism has always been part of the toolkit of media and strategic communication professionals, this is a relatively new[2] area in terms of collective and mass organizing for social movements and mobilizations[3] as technological changes in the 21st century have created spaces for people to become more politically and socially active.

As technology has become cheaper and more portable, a greater number of people can participate in political and social movements. The technological revolution was dramatic for everyone, but particularly for poorer nations in the early 2010s as people who did not previously have landline phones were able to buy cellphones – literally going from no access to global access with a single purchase – and by 2015 an average of 80 % of households in the developing world owned a mobile device.[4] At the turn of the millennium, SMS or text messages led the political digital revolution, allowing people to communicate instantly with one another; one example is how people in the Philippines used cellphones to coordinate and oust President Joseph Estrada in 2001.[5] Text messages soon gave way to social media platforms as Facebook and Twitter developed and cell towers and Wi-Fi hotspots became commonplace. This rapid communication shift

DOI: 10.4324/9781003291855-12

contributed greatly to the connectivity of individuals and their participation in public engagement.[6]

This chapter will take a look back at large-scale social movements on social media, focusing on Facebook, and Twitter (before 2013), examine the role of agenda melding[7] in this activism, and discuss some best practices which we can take from early digital activism. The social movements I will discuss here include the Green Revolution or the Iran Election Protests in 2009, the Arab Spring of 2010–2011, and the Occupy Wall Street Movement in 2011. While these protests were conducted in different languages and in diverse physical spaces, we can draw some commonalities from the movements.

## Social Media in a Post-Pandemic World

Perhaps one of the most important points from which to start is that we view media differently in a post-pandemic world. In January 2020, we entered a global pandemic that impacted our healthcare, governmental institutions, and our social media sphere.[8] During the pandemic, Facebook, Twitter, Instagram, and especially TikTok became unvetted sources of news and information. In many ways, early gains in credibility by content producers have been erased because of disinformation, fake news, and staged videos as the pandemic forced us to reevaluate how we interact with social media platforms. With this post-pandemic perspective, we can revisit early social media social movements to gain new and important insights. I have also made every effort to include a diversity of voices and a variety of perspectives in this chapter because we are all interconnected through social media and social justice efforts.

### Facebook

Facebook has seemingly become so entrenched in our personal and professional lives that we often forget it is not even 20 years old. Facebook launched in 2004, first for Harvard students, next for a few elite universities, and then for college and high school students. For many people, Facebook was the gateway platform to a digital existence that has integrated itself into our daily lives. In 2006, Facebook opened up to the general public,[9] and this changed everything in our social media world: within just a few years this platform would greatly impact our daily lives, including how we understand and conduct activism. We make posts, join groups, and message others to share important information. Facebook allows us to post images, videos, and even documents, which are fundamental tools for spreading information and organizing a movement.

Facebook organizes itself by a system of "friends": we essentially share information with people in our interpersonal circles or those who are mutually connected to people in our world. In a way, this design makes Facebook more intimate, but also limits the potential of a message to spread outside a preexisting network. One of the most important shifts on the platform was the change from "wall" to "timeline" organization which started in Fall 2011.[10] The change is particularly salient because it took place just after/during the time period we are discussing. A more recent change, but also important for a re-reading of early activism, is how credibility has become more dubious for information and even news links which are shared on Facebook.[11]

## Twitter

In contrast to Facebook, Twitter allows users to post in a public forum. The platform has created spaces for dissent as people speak out against oppression and interact with one another to form activist coalitions; it has also created spaces for repression and anti-activism. Twitter began in 2006, but became a mainstream brand in 2007 when it played a pivotal marketing role in the *South By Southwest Festival* in Austin, Texas.[12] In 2008, an American graduate student activist who had been arrested by Egyptian authorities used Twitter to let the world know about his arrest.[13] For a decade, Twitter was a 140-character platform which made important and immediate connections for users worldwide. However, much like Facebook, Twitter has also undergone changes, both in the platform and in its reputation. A 2020 Pew Research Study found that more than half of Americans feel Twitter is an important tool for activism; however, more than 75% think Twitter can distract from important issues.[14]

## Iran Protests

In 2009, when incumbent Iranian leader Mahmoud Ahmadinejad declared victory over challenger Mir Hossein Moussavi, who stated he had won by a wide margin, protests broke out across the country,[15] leading to a movement known as the **Green Movement** or the **2009 Iranian Presidential Election Protests**. Moussavi became a rallying point for Iranians who wanted political and social change. According to a 2010 CNN news article,[16] the very name Moussavi had become a trending hashtag (#Moussavi) on Twitter. Activists started Facebook groups in Moussavi's name and began posting updates on Twitter for the world to see. During the coverage of the protests, *Time* magazine reported on the importance of Twitter in a mediated world that was heavily censored like Iran; Twitter is a free medium, can be read on a variety of devices, and is very portable.[17] Social media posts can fill in the gaps of media coverage, or in the case of the protests in Iran, user-generated content may be the only information available.

In 2018 new protests broke out in the Iranian city of Mashhad. A CBC news article notes how the internet infrastructure had grown in the (almost) decade that had passed since the 2009 protests and the social media outlet of choice had transitioned from Twitter to the secure messaging app Telegram for communication within the country. Twitter was still a fundamental part of the communication strategy as it provided a way to share information outside of Iran, but Telegram was how Iranians themselves preferred to communicate with one another and organize. At the time of the 2009 Iranian protests, fewer than 1 million Iranians even owned a smartphone.[18] A decade later, social media outlets and messaging capabilities had reached half of the country's population, and now even Iranian leaders utilize social media for messaging.[19]

### Arab Spring

In December 2010, a young, unemployed fruit vendor in Tunisia, Mohamed Bouazizi, set himself on fire to illustrate his desperation and frustration with the Tunisian government. According to an Al Jazeera news retrospective,[20] Bouazizi's act started protests in Tunisia that caused Tunisian President Zine El Abidine Ben Ali to flee the country. Mohamed Bouazizi died in early January 2011, but his family told Al Jazeera they know his legacy was real change in the country.[21] The protests would also spread to Egypt, where President Hosni Mubarak was ousted, and to Libya, where months later dictator Muammar al-Qaddafi was forced out of office and later killed. Protests also broke out in Bahrain, where demonstrations were curbed with violence, and Yemen and Syria, where civil wars would later break out.[22] The causes of the **Arab Spring** are complex and deeply interwoven into the political and social systems of the region. The results of the protests have varied by nation, and have elicited personal and emotional reactions for people in the Arab world.

In late 2010, just weeks before its scheduled elections, the Egyptian government cracked down on dissenting media outlets and did not allow election observers into the country:

In January 2011, this paradigm of content-based censorship shifted to include blockage of entire web-based platforms such as Facebook and Twitter. Facebook and Twitter are used widely in Egypt, though the former has a significantly higher penetration rate. As of February 2011, there were 3.5 million Facebook users (a 4.5 percent penetration rate);

12,000 Twitter users (.00015 percent); and 13.5 million Internet users (16.8 percent penetration rate) in Egypt.[23]

Gerbaudo contends that social media outlets Facebook and Twitter were important in both Tunisia and Egypt, but more as a symbolic stance than for mobilizing people to take to the streets, citing the low levels of internet connection in the region at the time.[24] As renowned sociologist Manuel Castells referred to the media activities in the Egyptian Revolution, the content was coordinated according to the advantages each medium offers:

> Thus the activists, as some put it, planned the protests on Facebook, coordinated them through Twitter, spread them by SMSs and webcast them to the world on YouTube. Indeed, videos of security forces treating the protesters brutally were shared via the Internet, exposing the violence of the regime in unedited form.[25]

It is this effective use of social media platforms that allowed for the dissemination of the vivid images which were shared in newspapers and television networks around the world.

Many people today associate the Arab Spring with social media. In a 2021 Al Jazeera opinion piece, Tunisian academic Haythem Guesmi claimed that Facebook, Twitter, and Google branded themselves with the Arab Spring, but the major social media companies are a threat to democracy by allowing disinformation and censorship and actually endanger the lives of activists.[26]

## Occupy Wall Street

In 2008, the US, then later much of the world, entered the greatest economic crisis since the Great Depression of the 1930s. Business experts associate unethical lending practices with high-risk mortgages and an overinflated real estate market which led Americans to buy houses they could not afford and eventually could not pay to keep.[27] People lost their homes, banks closed, jobs were lost, and nearly everyone was impacted. However, it seemed the ultra-wealthy did not suffer as much because of bailouts and other protections most ordinary people did not have.

By 2011, many Americans could not take it anymore, and the movement **Occupy Wall Street** (OWS) – or as they often called themselves, The 99% – took to the streets of New York City to tell the world they were fed up with corporate greed and a system which protected the top 1%. The protests began on September 17, 2011, which Castells explains was a strategic decision, as September 17 was the anniversary of the date the

American Constitution was signed.[28] It was a symbolic moment to take part in civic demonstrations. Over the next two months, protests spread to 28 other US cities and international locations, and possibly 750 OWS locations globally.[29] It was a leader-less movement which built on lessons learned from the Arab Spring and would build the foundations of future movements, *The Guardian* referred to OWS in this way:

> One school of thought views it as a transformative event in contemporary US history, a popular uprising against the power of corporate America that helped shift the Democratic party leftwards, enable Bernie Sanders's presidential campaign and the election of self-proclaimed socialist politicians such as Alexandria Ocasio-Cortez. By this reckoning, it was also the original leaderless social media-organised movement on which #MeToo and Black Lives Matter would be modelled.[30]

Gerbaudo claims the Occupy Wall Street Movement did do well to keep the momentum going once the movement started, but could have used the emotional appeal of social media more effectively: "Paradoxically, in the home country of Twitter, Facebook, and several other social media firms, activists showed little ability for exploiting the emotional power of social media."[31] In a similar vein of emotional appeals, Suh et al. found a connection between local Occupy Facebook/Twitter accounts and the likelihood to protest. These researchers also believe that government repression might stop a movement, or it might backfire and motivate protestors depending on the social media messaging.[32] There is much we can learn from previous organizing and activist work.

## Social Media Lessons Learned

Figure 5.1 shows a protestor at an Occupy Wall Street protest in San Francisco, California holding a placard referring to the Arab Spring, which illustrates not only how activists build on the work of previous movements, but also how protestors are in dialogue with one another in various parts of the world.

An example of such a lesson learned is how the Iranian Protest Movement used less framing of the event on social media, while activists in the Arab Spring movement spent a great deal of time framing the issues.[33] Rane and Salem clarify how Facebook and Twitter facilitated the Arab Spring protests, but did not cause the movement.[34] Access alone does not imply a social media user will become an online activist; direct connections to political events are important.[35] These open connections are not always positive; if social media outlets make it easier for us to

FIGURE 5.1  Protestors at the San Francisco Occupy Wall Street demonstration hold a sign which reads "WE ARE THE 99%," referring to their disdain for the one-percenters who profit from extreme greed Photo credit/used with permission: Dr. Richard Besel, Grand Valley State University, Allendale, Michigan, USA.

see activists or even see each other to connect, then it becomes that much easier for repressive governments to see our political participation.[36] This is particularly true in authoritarian states where all communication is controlled by the state and activists are not tolerated.[37]

By 2012, nearing the end point for what we might call early social media activism, 72% of US adults used a social networking platform.[38] A Pew Research survey found that only 18% of Americans said they were

Twitter users, and this group also skewed young (ages 18–29 reported the highest usage). The interest from scholars, activists, and social media users is intense and global. In a study of existing survey data from the *Latin American Public Opinion Research Project 2012*, Salzman found a relationship between social media use and protest participation for the contiguous Spanish-speaking nations from Mexico to Colombia.[39]

### Agenda Melding

For the last half-century, media researchers have turned to agenda setting[40] to understand and explore how the media agenda interacts with the public agenda and the policy agenda[41,42] since McCombs and Shaw published their seminal study in 1972 on how media outlets impact political elections[43]. Luttrell and Wallace explain how content creators can influence the public agenda in much the same way as traditional media outlets.[44] Funk noted that digital communities can even define their own agendas.[45] These concepts are fundamental for understanding activism in a digital world.

This concept of digital communities leads us to **agenda melding**[46] which takes agenda setting a step further and connects media usage and social communities. Agenda melding builds not only on traditional and second level agenda setting,[47] but also on a wide variety of scholarship including the spiral of silence work of Elisabeth Noelle-Neumann;[48] spiral of silence is particularly important when discussing a controversial political movement in the agenda.[49]

Shaw et al. proposed agenda melding to explore the interconnections of media outlets, social groups, and the internet. Agenda melding assumes that active media consumers will seek information from a variety of media outlets.[50] There are three fundamental concepts to understand in agenda melding: the civic community, personal communities, and our own experiences and beliefs.[51] In this agenda model, less authority is placed on legacy media and increasing importance is afforded to social groups. Agenda melding has proven to be an important way to explore how politically salient issues and our social media groups interact.[52]

Agenda melding is a particularly appropriate theoretical framework to understand social media activism. During the Iran Protests, Mueller and Van Huellen noted that the dominance of English-language content posted during the protests was striking across all social media platforms, explaining how this might have been more of a way to send messages to people outside Iran than communicate with other protestors;[53] however, this strategy did create an agenda-setting effect on Western media outlets which otherwise would not have known what was happening on the ground or might not have covered the protests as extensively.

Khondker,[54]and later Hänska Ahy,[55] both advocated for the need to better explore the intersections of traditional and new media of the Arab Spring and other events in the Arab region. Harb[56] explained that regional powerhouse Al Jazeera played an important role of disseminating user-generated content in the Arab Spring. Not only were social media users learning from each other in real time, but the "Pan-Arab satellite television and social media did create a highly integrated media space,"[57] and these shared mediated spaces become important both from a practical viewpoint of learning about organizing and a theoretical perspective of agenda melding. In a survey conducted by Benrazek[58] in 2020, several years after the Arab Spring and during the Hirak Movement, he found not only that a great many people in Algeria used social media to find information, but the outlets also provided a space to discuss the events and the related political discourse.

In the Occupy Wall Street Movement, the agenda melding affect was seen in much the same way as in Iran and the countries of the Arab Spring: there was a mixing of traditional and new media messaging, and the media spaces became very integrated. However, one other interesting development was the high number of social media users sharing news and other links in their tweets. Gleason[59] conducted a case study on the movement by searching for the #OWS hashtag on Twitter. He found that nearly half of the tweets with hyperlinks came from user-generated content as opposed to corporate media. Not only did protestors tweet their own information, images, and photos, but they were sharing links to content from legacy media just as news outlets were sharing posts from Twitter and Facebook.

### Best Practices

This re-reading of early digital activism provides a fantastic opportunity to think differently about how we view early social movements on social media. As early as 2012, scholars[60] had conceptualized social media as part of a larger media and information literacy practice – a skill which should be taught in schools and will likely be included in the toolbox of many professionals. In this section I will highlight three important practices to remember when creating content.

### Gateway to Activism

Social media sites alone will not inspire offline activism; however, digital platforms can be used to instill activism.[61] Social networks can be an important gateway to organizing for people who otherwise would not have exposure to a cause or movement. CNET writer Shelby Brown explains her first foray into activism was merely adding a frame to her profile picture on Facebook to support Planned Parenthood;[62] however, she did not stop there, and became active in the movement. Brown recommends listening to the stories of the people involved and highlighting information that is relatable to others. Do not be afraid to use the tools to invite people to participate. A simple act such as changing a profile picture or liking a photo, or even joining a Facebook group, can lead to activism.

*Avoid Slacktivism*

If you only are able to convince a social media user to offer low-stakes commitment and the engagement stops there, then you run the risk of the person falling into slacktivism. "Slacker" and "activism" form the term **slacktivism**, which is having awareness without engagement,[63] and according to a 2022 Pew Research Report,[64] is a major concern. If you are looking to mobilize people in offline events, raise money, or otherwise create real engagement, then think of ways that will move the user beyond a like or retweet by creating a connection between the user and the collective.[65] Shared connections and emotional appeals will help create real engagement.

*Understand Global Communication*

Social media outlets are forms of **global communication**. What you post can and will be read by users around the world. It is important to understand how people use technology and social media differently based on who they are and where they come from. There are national and cultural differences in motives for social media usage.[66] Both practitioners and scholars should look outside the English-language and Western bubbles of knowledge. Barranquero[67] criticizes the literature on what he calls "digital resistance" as ignoring the Global South in general and Latin America specifically. Even though English has taken over the global media landscape,[68] remember that not everyone can or even wants to communicate in English. There are many other discourses taking place, and you should at least be aware of those discussions. Even if you do not speak a language other than English, try to translate a few of the key words or terms. Look at the important hashtags to examine what they stand for and who they might impact.

**Conclusion**

As we review early social movements on social media it is essential to remember that future activists will be looking at those events with a post-pandemic lens. While social media users might have believed content that was shared before 2013, current and future users will likely be more wary of the credibility of what they read. The world has changed dramatically in ways we never could have imagined. If these early social movements had taken place post-pandemic, how might they be different, or how might we react to them differently? Those are important questions that future activists will need to address.

It is also important to acknowledge that these early movements involved many people who grew up before the digital age. In 2001, Prensky coined the terms *digital native* to refer to people whose first "language" was technology and *digital immigrant* for those who did not grow up in the age of portable technology and internet connectivity.[69] Prenksy uses the analogy of native speakers of technology versus immigrants who have an "accent" in the digital world. While the terms themselves are problematic, they have caught on with journalists, teachers, and scholars. Though the line may not be precise to separate digital natives and immigrants, there is an important distinction, as native digital activism can and likely will change the structure of messaging in social movements.[70] We must work to envision how social activism will be different when all the participants are digital natives. These mediated spaces are fluid and constantly shifting, and as our media landscape changes, we will look back at early digital activism differently.

## Reflections

- What lessons can you take from early social media activism to apply to your personal online engagement? What lessons can you apply to your professional work?
- Choose a more recent social movement you have seen on Facebook or Twitter. What are the differences/similarities you see between the movement you chose and one of the early movements mentioned in this chapter?
- How can you apply your social media skills to promote engagement over slacktivism? What are some of the challenges you might face?
- Find a social movement in a country different from your own. What are some of the major differences you notice in terms of the posts and related content? Why is it important to explore movements in other regions of the world?

## Notes

1 Anderson, Gary L., and Kathryn G. Herr, eds. 2007. *Encyclopedia of Activism and Social Justice*. Thousand Oaks, CA: SAGE Publications.

2 Polletta, Francesca, and James M. Jasper. "Collective identity and social movements." *Annual Review of Sociology* 27, no. 1 (2001): 283–305.
3 Shirky, Clay. 2008. *Here Comes Everybody: The Power of Organizing without Organizations.* London: Penguin. Segerberg, Alexandra, and W. Lance Bennett. "Social media and the organization of collective action: Using Twitter to explore the ecologies of two climate change protests." *Communication Review* 14, no. 3 (2011): 197–215.
4 Poushter, Jacob, James Bell, and Russ Oates. 2015. "Internet seen as positive influence on education but negative on morality in emerging and developing nations." Pew Research Center. Accessed January 12, 2023. https://www .pewresearch.org/global/2015/03/19/internet-seen-as-positive-influence-on -education-but-negative-influence-on-morality-in-emerging-and-developing -nations/.
5 Shirky, *Here Comes Everybody.*
6 Hwang, Hyesun, and Kee-Ok Kim. "Social media as a tool for social movements: The effect of social media use and social capital on intention to participate in social movements." *International Journal of Consumer Studies* 39, no. 5 (2015): 478–488.
7 Shaw, D.L., et al. "Individuals, groups and agenda melding: A theory of social dissonance." *International Journal of Public Opinion Research* 11, no. 1 (1999): 2–24.
8 Croucher, Stephen M., et al. "A comparative analysis of Covid-19-related prejudice: The United States, Spain, Italy, and New Zealand." *Communication Research Reports* 38, no. 2 (2021): 79–89.
9 Phillips, Sarah. "A brief history of Facebook." *The Guardian*, July 15, 2017. https://www.theguardian.com/technology/2007/jul/25/media.newmedia.
10 Gerlich, R. Nicholas. "Marketing to laggards: Organizational change and diffusion of innovation in the adoption of Facebook timeline." *Journal of Academy of Business and Economics* 12, no. 3 (2012): 91–101.
11 Karlsen, Rune, and Toril Aalberg. "Social media and trust in news: An experimental study of the effect of Facebook on news story credibility." *Digital Journalism*, July 21, 2021, pp. 1–17.
12 Griggs, Brandon, and Heather Kelly. "23 key moments from Twitter history." CNN, September 16, 2013. http://www.cnn.com/2013/09/13/tech/social -media/twitterkey-moments/index.html.
13 Arceneaux, Noah, and Amy Schmitz Weiss. "Seems stupid until you try it: Press coverage of Twitter, 2006–9." *New Media & Society* 12, no. 8 (2010): 1262–1279.
14 Auxier, Brooke, and Colleen McClain. "Americans think social media can help build movements, but can also be a distraction." Pew Research Center, September 14, 2020. https://www.pewresearch.org/fact-tank/2020/09/09/ americans-think-social-media-can-help-build-movements-but-can-also-be-a -distraction/.
15 Worth, Robert, and Nazila Fathi. "Protests flare in Tehran as opposition disputes vote." *New York Times*, June 14, 2009. https://www.nytimes.com/2009 /06/14/world/middleeast/14iran.html.
16 "How the turmoil in Iran is playing out on social media web sites" CNN, January 3, 2010. http://edition.cnn.com/2009/TECH/12/31/iran.protests .social.media/index.html.
17 Grossman, Lev. "Iran protests: Twitter, the medium of the movement. *TIME*, June 17, 2009, https://content.time.com/time/world/article/0,8599,1905125 ,00.html.

18  Keath, Lee. "2009 vs now: How Iran's new protests compare to the past." AP News, January 3, 2018. https://apnews.com/article/ali-khamenei-ap-top-news-elections-international-news-mahmoud-ahmadinejad-ab649e21908 34e19b1f006f76493645f.

19  Rezazadeh, Sam. 2020. "The role of social media platforms in political protests in Iran during 2009 and 2017–9 events." PhD diss., University of Saskatchewan.

20  "What is the Arab Spring, and how did it start?" Al Jazeera, December 17, 2020. https://www.aljazeera.com/news/2020/12/17/what-is-the-arab-spring-and-how-did-it-start.

21  Ryan, Yasmine. "The tragic life of a street vendor." Al Jazeera, January 20, 2011. https://www.aljazeera.com/features/2011/1/20/the-tragic-life-of-a-street-vendor.

22  Entry for "Arab Spring. *Britannica*. https://www.britannica.com/event/Arab-Spring.

23  Dunn, Alexandra. "Unplugging a nation: State media strategy during Egypt's January 25 uprising." *Fletcher Forum of World Affairs* 35 (2011): 15–24.

24  Gerbaudo, Paolo. 2012. *Tweets and the Streets: Social Media and Contemporary Activism*. London: Pluto Press.

25  Castells, Manuel. 2015. *Networks of Outrage and Hope: Social Movements in the Internet Age*. Amsterdam, the Netherlands: Amsterdam University Press.

26  Guesmi, Haythem. "The social media myth about the Arab Spring." Al Jazeera, January 27, 2021. https://www.aljazeera.com/opinions/2021/1/27/the-social-media-myth-about-the-arab-spring.

27  Lewis, Victor, Kay, Kenneth D., Kelso, Chandrika and Larson, James, Was the 2008 Financial Crisis Caused by a Lack of Corporate Ethics? (2010). Global Journal of Business Research, Vol. 4, No. 2, pp. 77-84, 2010, Available at SSRN: https://ssrn.com/abstract=1633638

28  Castells, *Networks of Outrage and Hope*.

29  Anthony, Andrew. "'We showed it was possible to create a movement from almost nothing': Occupy Wall Street 10 years on." *The Guardian*, September 12, 2021. https://www.theguardian.com/us-news/2021/sep/12/occupy-wall-street-10-years-on.

30  Ibid.

31  Gerbaudo, *Tweets and the Streets*.

32  Suh, Chan S., Ion Bogdan Vasi, and Paul Y. Chang. "How social media matter: Repression and the diffusion of the Occupy Wall Street Movement." *Social Science Research* 65 (July 2017): 282–293,

33  Tusa, Felix. "How social media can shape a protest movement: The cases of Egypt in 2011 and Iran in 2009." *Arab Media and Society* 17 (2013): 1–19.

34  Rane, Halim, and Sumra Salem. "Social media, social movements and the diffusion of ideas in the Arab uprisings." *Journal of international communication* 18, no. 1 (2012): 97–111.

35  Baym, Nancy K. 2015. *Personal Connections in the Digital Age*. Hoboken, NJ: John Wiley & Sons.

36  Baym, *Personal Connections in the Digital Age*.

37  Spencer, Anthony. "Hasta la victoria siempre: The ongoing rhetorical revolution in Cuba." *Texas Speech Communication Journal* 31, no. 1 (2007): 16–23.

38  Brenner, Joanna, and Aaron Smith. "72% of online adults are social networking site users." Pew Research Center, May 30, 2020. https://www.pewresearch.org/internet/2013/08/05/72-of-online-adults-are-social-networking-site-users/.

39 Salzman, Ryan. "Exploring social media use and protest participation in Latin America." *Journal of Latin American Communication Research* 5, no. 2 (2016): 72–85,

40 McCombs, Maxwell. "A look at agenda-setting: Past, present and future." *Journalism Studies* 6, no. 4 (2005): 543–557.

41 McCombs, Maxwell E., Donald L. Shaw, and David H. Weaver. "New directions in agenda-setting theory and research." *Mass Communication and Society* 17, no. 6 (2014): 781–802.

42 Perloff, Richard M. "The fifty-year legacy of agenda-setting: Storied past, complex conundrums, future possibilities." *Mass Communication and Society* 25, no. 4 (2022): 469–499.

43 McCombs, Maxwell E., and Donald L. Shaw. "The agenda-setting function of mass media." *Public Opinion Quarterly* 36, no. 2 (1972): 176.

44 Luttrell, Regina, and Adrienne Wallace. 2021. *Social Media and Society: An Introduction to the Mass Media Landscape*. New York: Macmillan.

45 Funk, Marcus. "R/Agenda_rejection," *Fifty Years of Agenda-Setting Research* 2, no. 2 (2018): 145–167.

46 Shaw et al., "Individuals, groups and agenda melding."

47 McCombs, Maxwell, et al. "Candidate images in Spanish Elections: Second-level agenda-setting effects." *Journalism & Mass Communication Quarterly* 74, no. 4 (1997): 703–717.

48 Noelle-Neumann, Elisabeth. "The spiral of silence: A theory of public opinion." *Journal of Communication* 24, no. 2 (1974): 43–51. Noelle-Neumann, Elisabeth. 1993. *The Spiral of Silence: Public Opinion – Our Social Skin*, 2nd ed. Chicago, IL: University of Chicago Press.

49 Spencer, Anthony T., and Stephen M. Croucher. "Basque nationalism and the spiral of silence." *International Communication Gazette* 70, no. 2 (2008): 137–153, SAGE Journals.

50 Shaw, Donald, and Rita Colistra. 2008. "Agenda melding." In *The Encyclopedia of Political Communication*.

51 McCombs, Shaw, and Weaver, "New directions in agenda-setting theory and research."

52 Cruz-González, María Catalina, and Juan David Cárdenas Ruiz. "La migración Venezolana y su construcción en la agenda pública en las conversaciones de Twitter en Suramérica 2014–2019." *Colombia Internacional* 112 (2022): 51–79. Shaw, Donald L., Thomas C. Terry, and Milad Minooie. "Military communication strategies based on how audiences meld media and agendas." *Military Review* 95, no. 6 (2015): 16–28. Spencer, Anthony, and Stephen Croucher. "Social media & agenda melding: Understanding Trump's proposed border wall." *Studies in Media and Communication* 10, no. 2 (2022): 296–304. Woo, Chang Wan, Matthew P. Brigham, and Michael Gulotta. "Twitter talk and Twitter sharing in times of crisis: Exploring rhetorical motive and agenda-setting in the Ray Rice scandal," *Communication Studies* 71, no. 1 (2019): 40–58.

53 Mueller, Philipp S., and Sophie van Huellen. "A revolution in 140 characters? Reflecting on the role of social networking technologies in the 2009 Iranian post-election protests." *Policy & Internet* 4, nos. 3–4 (2012): 184–205.

54 Haque Khondker, Habibul. "Role of the new media in the Arab Spring." *Globalizations* 8, no. 5 (2011): 675–679.

55 Hänska Ahy, Maximillian. "Networked communication and the Arab Spring: Linking broadcast and social media." *New Media & Society* 18, no. 1 (2014): 99–116.

56 Harb, Zahera. "Arab revolutions and the social media effect." *M/C Journal* 14, no. 2 (2011).

57 Lynch, Marc. 2014. "Media, old and new." In Marc Lynch (ed.), *The Arab Uprisings Explained: New Contentious Politics in the Middle East.* New York: Columbia University Press, pp. 93–109.

58 Benrazek, Youcef. "The role of social media as a public sphere in the Algerian protests: An analytical study." *Journal of Intercultural Communication Research* 51, no. 2 (2022): 153–173.

59 Gleason, Benjamin. "#Occupy Wall Street." *American Behavioral Scientist* 57, no. 7 (2013): 966–982.

60 Greenhow, Christine, and Benjamin Gleason. "Twitteracy: Tweeting as a new literacy practice," *Educational Forum* 76, no. 4 (2012): 464–478.

61 Wallace, Adrienne. 2021. "Social media for social good through a public policy lens: What role does social media play in the creation and sustainability of social movements?" In Regina Luttrell, Lu Xiao, and Jon Glass (eds.), *Democracy in the Disinformation Age: Influence and Activism in American Politics.* London: Routledge, 2021, pp. 9–36.

62 Brown, Shelby. "How activists use social media for good -- and you can too." CNET, April 6, 2022, https://www.cnet.com/news/social-media/features/how-activists-use-social-media-for-good-and-you-can-too/.

63 Glenn, Cerise L. "Activism or slacktivism? Digital media and organizing for social change." *Communication Teacher* 29, no. 2 (2, 2015): 81–85.

64 Auxier, Brooke, and Colleen McClain. "Americans think social media can help build movements, but can also be a distraction." Pew Research Center, September 14, 2020. https://www.pewresearch.org/fact-tank/2020/09/09/americans-think-social-media-can-help-build-movements-but-can-also-be-a-distraction/.

65 Cabrera, Nolan L., Cheryl E. Matias, and Roberto Montoya. "Activism or slacktivism? The potential and pitfalls of social media in contemporary student activism." *Journal of Diversity in Higher Education* 10, no. 4 (2017): 400–415.

66 Spencer, Anthony T., Stephen M. Croucher, and Carrisa S. Hoelscher. "Uses and gratifications meets the internet: A cross-cultural comparison of US & Nicaraguan new media usage." *Human Communication* 15, no. 4 (2012): 229–240.

67 Barranquero, Alejandro. 2020. "De-Westernizing alternative media studies: Latin American versus Anglo-Saxon approaches from a comparative communication research perspective." In Jan Servaes (ed.), *Handbook of Communication for Development and Social Change.* Singapore: Springer, pp. 329–340.

68 Spencer, Anthony. 2023. "Pandemic communication: International communication." In Stephen Croucher and Audra Diers-Lawson (eds.), *Pandemic Communication.* New York: Routledge, pp. 215–230.

69 Prensky, Marc. "Digital natives, digital immigrants Part 1." *On the Horizon* 9, no. 5 (2001): 1–6. Prensky, Marc. "Digital natives, digital immigrants Part 2: Do they really think differently?" *On the Horizon* 9, no. 6 (2001): 1–6.

70 Li, Yevgeniya, Jean-Grégoire Bernard, and Markus Luczak-Roesch. "Beyond clicktivism: What makes digitally native activism effective? An exploration of the Sleeping Giants movement." *Social Media + Society* 7, no. 3 (2021): 205630512110353.

# ADVOCATES FOR ACTION

## Sophie Scholl

1921–1943
Hometown: Forchtenberg, Germany
Movements: Nazi resistance
Organizations: The White Rose

*Elizabeth Wilson*

Sophia Magdalena Scholl was a member of the White Rose – a Nazi resistance group run by students at the University of Munich during World War II.[1] The organization distributed leaflets and used graffiti to call out Nazi crimes and express their distaste with the political system and war. Sophie was born in May 1921 to an upper-class Christian family. Although her parents were wary of the Third Reich, when Hitler came to power in the early 1930s, Sophie and her siblings joined the Nazi youth groups along with their peers. She enjoyed how the League of German Girls focused on nature and communal experiences, but there were many ways in which Sophie's liberal leanings clashed with the politics of the Third Reich. When her oldest brother Hans was arrested for his involvement in a similar youth group that had been dissolved for being too alternative to Nazi ideology, Sophie began reflecting on her involvement in the Nazi system.[2] Later, in 1942, while studying at the University of Munich alongside her brother Hans, she discovered that he was involved in the White Rose, and demanded to join.

The White Rose was made up of siblings Hans and Sophie Scholl, three other Munich students, and a professor of philosophy and musicology.

DOI: 10.4324/9781003291855-13

The group published six pamphlets over the course of its existence. It grew from small-scale distribution around campus to reaching thousands of households across Germany. By January 1943, the group felt emboldened by their success. The sixth pamphlet reads:

> Even the most dull-witted German has had his eyes opened by the terrible bloodbath, which, in the name of the freedom and honor of the German nation, they have unleashed upon Europe, and unleash anew each day. The German name will remain forever tarnished unless finally the German youths stand up.

On February 18, while distributing flyers with her brother, Sophie pushed a stack off a railing onto one of the main halls on campus. A janitor spotted Hans and Sophie, and turned them in to the Gestapo. They, along with others in the group, were sentenced to death for treason.[3] She was asked in court if she saw that her actions should be seen as a crime against the community, to which she responded, "I am, now as before, of the opinion that I did the best that I could do for my nation. I therefore do not regret my conduct and will bear the consequences that result from my conduct."[4] She was executed by guillotine on February 22, 1943.

Their deaths were hardly published in German newspapers, but internationally, their student opposition gained recognition. The text of the sixth leaflet was smuggled into the United Kingdom and reprinted and dropped over Germany by Allied planes in July of the same year. Today, the White Rose and Sophie Scholl are celebrated for their resistance.[5] Schools, streets, and awards have been named after the group and its members. Sophie's story is retold in books, films, and plays. Although it was not recognized at the time, the ways in which Sophie was able to disseminate information under such circumstances made her a foremother of the public relations industry we know now.[6]

## Notes

1 Bush, Elizabeth. "*We Will Not Be Silent: The White Rose Student Resistance Movement that defied Adolf Hitler* by Russell Freedman (review)." *Bulletin of the Center for Children's Books* 69, no. 8 (2016): 414–415.

2 Atwood, Kathryn. 2011. *Women Heroes of World War II*. Chicago, IL: Chicago Review Press, p. 16.

3 HISTORY.com Editors. "Nazis arrest White Rose resistance leaders." HISTORY, November 5, 2009, updated February 17, 2021. https://www.history.com/this-day-in-history/nazis-arrest-white-rose-resistance-leaders.

4 Wales, Jillian. "Women's resistance efforts in Nazi Germany 1939-45: HerStory." *ANU Undergraduate Research Journal* (2013): 223–242.
5 McDonough, Frank. 2009. *Sophie Scholl: The Real Story of the Woman Who Defied Hitler.* Cheltenham, UK: History Press.
6 Spitzer, Tanja B. "Sophie Scholl and the White Rose." National WWII Museum, 2020. https://www.nationalww2museum.org/war/articles/sophie -scholl-and-white-rose.

# 6

# ADVOCACY AND ACTION

## Persuasive Strategies for Digital Activism and Influence

*Matthew Salzano and Victoria Ann Ledford*

## Introduction

Twenty-first-century social movements have been incredibly persuasive. In a 2022 interview with *The New York Times Magazine*, feminist political theorist Wendy Brown said:

> #MeToo ... did in two years what previous generations of feminists could not pull off, which was to make sexual harassment totally unacceptable in school and workplaces. Black Lives Matter in a summer pushed America's violent racial history and present into the center of political conversation and transformed the consciousness of a generation.[1]

Witnessing inequality and injustice, social movement activists have turned to participatory media such as social media platforms that prompt movement participation. Activists have used platforms like Twitter, Instagram, and TikTok to disseminate their persuasive messages faster, broader, and quippier than previous media channels allowed. Their use of digital platforms has profoundly shifted political culture by making knowledge about politics and activism accessible to the masses.

Despite examples that demonstrate the power of digital social movements, critics have claimed that these activists are sensitive puritans who cannot handle the messy compromises required of politics. Brown argues that this critique, especially when applied to young people, "ignores their rage at the world they've inherited, and their desperation for a more livable

DOI: 10.4324/9781003291855-14

and just one, and their critique of our complacency."[2] This chapter validates the existing digital practices of social movements by situating them as persuasive demands for change. Especially in a world that often resists the pleas of social movements, we discuss existing social movements to offer examples for future digital activists engaging in efforts for social change.

We focus on three communication harms that can create barriers to persuasive digital social movement communication: demagoguery, bias, and stigma. By examining how each of these harms manifests within digital activist movements, this chapter will (1) explain how each type of communication affects social movements, (2) examine one in-depth case study that demonstrates its applicability, and (3) provide research-driven strategies you can use as a digital social media activist to overcome these barriers. Using insight from interdisciplinary studies of social movements and persuasion paired with digital social movement examples, we offer practical suggestions for how communicators of social movements can ethically participate in digital activism.

## What Are Social Movements, and How Are They Persuasive?

What is **persuasion**? When communication researchers use the word "persuasion," they are often referring to a process in which communication artifacts – such as social media posts, speeches, behaviors between people, etc. – attempt to evoke change among an audience. Communication scholars study persuasive messages through different methods and approaches, and in our experience, these "camps" of persuasive study rarely engage with the other's research or findings. Communication scholars who take a humanities approach (e.g., viewing research as a subjective study, often focused on historical, philosophical, and/or critical insight instead of generating generalizable truths) often study **rhetoric**.

Aristotle famously defined rhetoric as "an ability, in each [particular] case, to see the available means of persuasion."[3] Rhetoric is an art of determining "the characteristics and problems of our times" and "guid[ing] actions for the solution of our problems and the improvement of our circumstances."[4] Scholars who study rhetoric use qualitative methods similar to discourse analysis and close reading to reveal conventions or detailed histories of specific public messages or message sets across various media – oral, visual, print, electronic, digital, and so on. Scholars of rhetoric and social movements have explored how social movements practice rhetoric in particular contexts for various purposes, whether constituting new movements or influencing public conceptions of movement function.[5]

Communication scholars who take a social scientific approach often study persuasion by examining the impact persuasive messages have on an audience. Persuasion from a communication science perspective has roots in the rhetorical tradition, but diverges in its use of the scientific method.[6] Social scientists examine patterns, and communication scientists aim to understand how a piece of communication affects people so as to make predictions about that type of communication in the future. These scholars often use more quantitative methods such as experiments and survey questionnaires to examine the effects messages have on an audience or an audience's current perspectives (e.g., their beliefs or attitudes) about a particular topic.

Communication scientists studying the persuasive nature of digital media further extend their methodology by investigating not only how the messages themselves are persuasive, but often how varying features of the digital platforms affect users' beliefs, attitudes, and behaviors. For example, communication scientists studying digital persuasion might experimentally examine how a particular emotional appeal in a tweet about climate change (e.g., hope versus fear) differentially affects people's beliefs, attitudes, or behaviors about the topic; the researchers may simultaneously examine how including a visual image or a high number of retweets and likes of the tweet influence people's perceptions.

When studying social movements, using these diverse methodological approaches can help us understand how activists leverage persuasion for social good. To advance their aims, digital advocates can dually activate lessons from research in persuasion and digital media. A **social movement** can be loosely defined as a collective coalition that aims to enact some social goal through persuasive efforts such as protests, marches, campaigns, demonstrations, and so on.[7] This chapter offers what we term an inter-sub-disciplinary approach to studying persuasive messages: an approach that integrates scholarship from rhetorical and social scientific approaches in the communication discipline.

Our aim with this inter-sub-disciplinary approach is to heed a recent call from communication scholars Kristina Scharp and Lindsey Thomas to "recognize the value of both humanistic and social scientific approaches as well as transformative work that draws from both scholarly ideologies."[8] Like Scharp and Thomas, we, as one humanist and one social scientist, "strive – and encourage our colleagues – to remember: we were born of rhetorical tradition, of *both* humanistic *and* social scientific inquiry."[9] Rhetorical research reveals ethical dilemmas and political shortcomings of existing discourse, and communication science research reveals how humans respond to messages. Faced with specific examples from social movements, they can align insight about existing communicative practices with the political and persuasive goals of a movement.

## Demagoguery: Information and Argumentation

Social movements make arguments and engage in **argument**. What is argument? At its most basic, an **argument** consists of a claim warranted by some data or evidence. One can also engage *in* argument, where two or more people engage in a "process whereby people reason their way from one set of problematic ideas to the choice of another."[10] Social movements present *problematic* ideas in the sense that they present problems through argument. Communication scholars have studied social movement arguments across various media – pre-digital media, with Malcolm X's debates and ACT UP's bodily protest arguments; with the televised Seattle WTO protests; and with digital media, like Arab Spring, Greenpeace, and the Women's March.[11] Social movements engage in argumentation in attempts to persuade publics to shift policy, behaviors and/or attitudes by "contesting social norms, deconstructing the established naming of the world, and suggesting the possibilities of alternative worlds."[12] Social movement arguments reveal how something seemingly settled about our world is not settled, opening the space for argumentation about what something could or should be.

Contemporary argumentation faces at least two tandem challenges: **demagoguery** and information glut. First, arguers must traverse a growing culture of demagoguery. Demagoguery is typically considered a problem of a single speaker – an unethical and coercive demagogue. But scholars like Patricia Roberts-Miller have begun to theorize that a demagogic culture *precedes* a demagogue. She defines demagogic culture as antithetical to the rhetorical culture needed to sustain democracy:

> Demagoguery is discourse that promises stability, certainty, and escape from the responsibilities of rhetoric by framing public policy in terms of the degree to which and the means by which (not whether) the out-group should be scapegoated for the current problems of the in-group. Public disagreement largely concerns three stases: group identity (who is in the in-group, what signifies out-group membership, and how loyal rhetors are to the in-group), need (the terrible things the out-group is doing to us, and/or their very presence); and what level of punishment to enact against the out group (ranging from the restriction of the out-group's rights to the extermination of the out-group).[13]

Demagoguery, by restricting public discourse to these three stases, makes engaging in arguments presented by social movements challenging. How, for example, can LGBTQ+ rights activists advocate for the humane treatment of trans folks if the dominant, demagogic discourse maintains that trans people are an out-group that should be restricted (if not terminated)?[14] No single argument on social media will change that demagogic culture, especially in an information environment where that argument may not spread and generate force for persuasion. Digital activists need to turn to creative, argumentative tools that can change argumentative environments.

The second and related problem for argumentation today is the circulation of information in the environment of digital, participatory media. Not only is information available, but competing, contradictory, and false information is available with a click and little accountability. This makes traditional argumentation challenging. For example, the overwhelming scientific consensus is that climate change is happening and is man-made. Still, global warming skeptics have created a vast information network that spreads bogus claims denying climate change, as Paliewicz and McHendry have detailed. Despite better arguments being made by climate change experts, the skeptics have built a powerful, unchecked network for spreading skepticism that ultimately makes for a forceful argument.[15] Instead of reason exchange, where the best argument wins out by carefully testing and refuting claims, the argument with the largest amount of networked force wins. Given how social movements are already attempting to summon enough force to disrupt the status quo, networks are designed to target and debunk their arguments with great force that pose an incredible threat. Misinformation co-occurs with information glut, and as the World Economic Forum put it a decade ago:

> Social media allows information to spread around the world at breakneck speed in an open system where norms and rules are starting to emerge but have not yet been defined. While the benefits of our hyperconnected communication systems are undisputed, they could potentially enable the viral spread of information that is either intentionally or unintentionally misleading or provocative.[16]

A decade later, this intentionally (disinformation) and unintentionally (misinformation) misleading information permeates the digital world. Often intersecting issues of health and politics, misinformation and disinformation challenge the progress of social movements. For example, misinformation about transgender health care has led to discriminatory policy proposals that would deny equitable health treatment for transgender individuals, not to mention the social harms of the spread of such falsehoods like this one represented on the 2020 Texas Republican primary ballot:

Texas should ban chemical castration, puberty blockers, cross-sex hormones, and genital mutilation surgery on all minor children for transition purposes, given that Texas children as young as three (3) are being transitioned from their biological sex to the opposite sex.[17]

With little accountability for such unchecked misinformation spread, opponents to social movements create an environment where the currency (accurate information) to participate in deliberative argument is not something that everyone carries.

Digital social movements have to work to make deliberative environments for argument possible. This requires infrastructural tinkering: demagoguery and misinformation are infrastructural, environmental problems. Debunking or advancing "good arguments" is not enough, digital activists have to help facilitate the conditions that allow for it – in other words, digital activists have to work to create cultures, rules, practices, and even policies that change our environments such that reasoned, deliberative arguments can happen. The next section provides an in-depth example of *how* activists can cultivate such change.

### Example: Changing Environments with Twitter Bots

Digital activists have experimented with creative uses of Twitter bots as one way to change environments of misinformation and demagoguery on Twitter. Twitter bots are programmed, to varying degrees of complexity, to post messages without a human pressing "Tweet" every time a message is published. Some bots are generated with artificial intelligence and attempt to imitate humans. Others, like the ones discussed here, are programmed for specific activist purposes with a smaller range of potential tweets usually more determined by a programmer than an algorithm.

Some bots attempt to directly rectify our aforementioned concerns about information. For example, researchers have deployed deliberative social bots "to build bridges between separate, ideologically homogeneous subnetworks; to expose tightly knit clusters of users to alternative viewpoints; or to bring about measurable shifts towards deliberative democracy in online discourse."[18] After building bots that categorized the politics of networks of Twitter users, the bots either linked conservative and liberal networks together by retweeting and following users from both sides (Bridgerbot) or disrupted ideologically homogeneous networks with information from the other side (Popperbot). By creating shared networks, these bots could moderate some of the concerns about arguers not sharing information networks – making environments for argumentation more possible. Creating shared informational networks can help prevent the environment that allows demagoguery to thrive. For example, in 2021, two feminist activists developed the @PayGapApp bot to celebrate International Women's Day (IWD).[19] The callout box below details how the @PayGapApp bot works as a "protest bot," as Mark Sample has coined his similar creations, that "reveals the injustice and inequality of the world and imagines alternatives."[20]

---

**INTERNATIONAL CALLOUT BOX**

**International Women's Day and the @PayGapApp**

Francesca Lawson, co-creator of the Twitter bot @PayGapApp, wrote that she and Ali Fensome created the bot to "put the gender pay gap data back into the spotlight."[21] In the United Kingdom, where Lawson and Fensome are based, the government has required firms employing more than 250 people to report their gender wage gap.[22] These findings are then shared in a publicly accessible and easily searched database.[23] Witnessing performative tweets from organizations about feminist issues, Lawson and Fensome were motivated to call out the hypocrisy. Lawson explains how the Twitter bot @PayGapApp protested Tweets from employers about IWD 2022, when they launched the bot:

> When a company listed on the [United Kingdom] government's gender pay gap service tweeted about International Women's Day, the bot automatically responded with their median hourly pay gap data in a quote tweet. ... Our aim was to highlight how photos of smiling female employees and inspirational quotes conceal what's really going on behind the scenes. Women's median hourly pay was less than men's at 77% of companies in 2020–2021, which shows that the support companies' pledge for International Women's Day is rarely backed up by action.[24]

The @PayGapApp page serves as an argument for the ongoing reality of misogyny, for the existence of the pay gap despite those who deny it. The app promotes information distribution conducive to deliberative environments and challenges these organizations' contribution to information glut.

---

Other bots try to prompt users to take responsibility for a democratic rhetorical culture. Empirical research shows that spambots can be effective at reducing racist harassment. Spambots send automated messages based on some trigger word or phrase. In a 2017 study, Kevin Munger created spambots to reduce anti-Black slurs from White men on Twitter. These bots were triggered when an account used the n-word and responded with a tweet like "Hey man, just remember there are real people who are hurt when you harass them with that kind of language."[25] He found that "subjects who were sanctioned by a high-follower white male significantly reduced their use of a racist slur."[26] The reduction of hate speech after this interaction was significant for about one month, but was less significant in month two.[27] In another example, which has not been subject to empirical research, the @DropTheIBot advocates that users stop writing the term "illegal immigrant." The bot responds to that trigger phrase with the tweet: "People aren't illegal. Try saying 'undocumented immigrant' or 'unauthorized immigrant' instead."[28] The creators of the @DropTheIBot describe it as a "modest effort to help America shed some of its historical baggage ... it's time to stop stigmatizing immigrants through our word choices."[29] By speaking to the linguistic conditions that can stifle deliberation on the platform, these bots work to hinder the spread of demagoguery and make more amenable conditions for argument.

### Argumentative Strategies for Activists

What digital activists can take away from this example is twofold. First, that in the age of digital movement activism, creative, critical programming is just as important as creative, critical messaging. In fact, the two can go hand-in-hand. Second, and more abstractly, tinkering with environments to make argumentation possible is a key part of the process of argument. One could argue that environments of argumentation are not the responsibility of activists and marginalized people, who are often excluded from these spaces, but of platforms and people with power. But when people in power cannot even hear the arguments because of the environment, no matter how creative the messaging, it may fall flat. Working to foster the conditions for deliberation is not the only important role of digital activist work, but it should be a key dimension. Another strategy activists might use to respond to the challenge of misinformation is to anticipate and confront misinformation. Persuasion researchers have begun to study "pre-bunking" – a sister to debunking – that involves presenting individuals with potentially incorrect information they may encounter in the future and giving them information needed to refute that falsehood.[30] Based on persuasion research from inoculation theory, pre-bunking relies on research finding that inoculating people against expected future misinformation can strengthen their confidence in their own beliefs and provide them with future argumentative currency.[31] As evidenced from these strategies, an important takeaway for activists is that while change may be the long game, action can be immediate. Creating a comprehensive digital strategy that uses research-derived lessons can support digital advocates in advancing their mission.

## Bias: Implicit to Systemic

Contemporary social movements are often seen as challenging some **bias** – racial bias, gender bias, class bias, and so on. In her book *The End of Bias*, Jessica Nordell suggests bias is a pressing concept for social justice practice, identifying bias as "a habit that reduces the potential of individuals and undermines the gifts and resources of an entire society":

> Most people do not go into their professions with the goal of hurting others or providing disparate treatment. And for those who intend and value fairness, it is still possible to act in discriminatory ways. That contradiction between values of fairness and the reality of real-world discrimination has come to be called "unconscious bias," "implicit bias," or sometimes "unintentional" or "unexamined bias." It describes the behavior of people who want to act one way but in fact act another.[32]

Put differently, bias describes the interpersonal dimensions of systemic oppression like racism, (cis) sexism, homophobia, ableism, and so on that are usually enacted unconsciously. Philosopher of Education Barbara Applebaum describes how biases can be unconscious "in the sense that they are so deeply engrained in our psyches and normalized in society that the perpetrator is unaware that bias has had an effect on behavior."[33] Social movements that work on behalf of marginalized groups, and aim to see their welfare improved in professional, civic, and interpersonal life, thus work to address bias in some form.

Conversations about addressing implicit bias gained popularity in news media coverage after the racial reckoning of summer 2020, and institutions like universities and corporations have responded to this public recognition of biases with implicit bias training, sometimes prompted by activist/movement action.[34] For example, Activists Kayla Reed and Blake Strode from St. Louis, Missouri, USA demanded implicit bias training as a part of comprehensive police reforms that summer.[35] New England law firm Verrill suggested on their legal blog for HR professionals that implicit bias training was a way "companies can show support for the black lives matter (BLM) movement."[36] Meanwhile, in right-wing anti-Critical Race Theory propaganda, training like this is now being used as evidence of anti-White brainwashing.[37] While this propaganda can be dismissed given the total lack of evidence that bias training is "anti-White," there is still a critique of this implicit bias training from the left.

Left critics argue that endeavors to address bias focus on ignorance instead of on the very frameworks that allow such ignorance. In practice, the aforementioned St. Louis organizers shared this critique: they found those "tepid reforms" – that they initially proposed – "have failed [them] repeatedly. Our vision is now one of defunding police departments and abolishing the carceral system."[38] In this case, the carceral state is the true harm, and the biased officers are but a symptom. Maybe implicit bias training could act as a temporary salve, but without systemic change (abolition), the conditions of equality that make removing bias possible are impossible to wholly enact. This pattern holds true across contexts of inequality and bias. In the university context, for example, Applebaum argues that dominant frameworks of intelligibility must be challenged:

> Implicit bias presumes that social injustice is maintained by ignorance of unconscious bias and the remedy is more knowledge … . To correct for epistemic injustice requires more than correcting implicit biases through awareness but also a willingness to challenge dominant frameworks of intelligibility that distort and dismiss the deep violence that marginalize groups experience on campuses and elsewhere.[39]

In this case, dominant epistemologies that sustain unjust university policies and norms are the harm, and biased moments from individual faculty, staff, and students are symptoms of this system. Applebaum philosophically reasons what Reed and Strode have found via activist practice: that addressing bias may not address the very frameworks that create bias. Reed and Strode focus on frameworks of the state, and Applebaum focuses on epistemological frames, but both see a turn to the framework.

### Example: Challenging Bias by Understanding Frameworks

One dimension making confronting bias challenging in participatory media is that scholars have compellingly shown how digital algorithms exhibit biases encoded from their human engineers. Safiya Noble's *Algorithms of Oppression* showed how Google perpetuated misogynistic and racist stereotypes.[40] Ruha Benjamin's *Race after Technology* theorized a "New Jim Code," describing how "tech fixes often hide, speed up, and even deepen discrimination, while appearing to be neutral or benevolent when compared to the racism of a previous era."[41] Social media platforms, in particular, use the algorithm to cultivate feeds, prioritizing whatever content keeps users engaged.[42] Platforms do this without any – or with very little – regard to the political ramifications of that content, as Zeynep Tufekci has explained in her description of YouTube as the "great radicalizer."[43] In October 2021, watchdog group Media Matters found that the TikTok algorithm led users from transphobic content to Neo-Nazi content within 500 videos.[44] Like implicit bias, algorithmic bias works unconsciously because it is deeply ingrained and made invisible because of its hyper-specialization (everyone's feed is different) and in the interests of capital (platforms don't want to reveal how they engineer their proprietary, addictive, and profitable feeds to potential competitors).

Instagram's algorithm has been productively hacked by activists to make political interventions regarding issues of bias. Prior to summer 2020, Instagram was considered a relatively apolitical platform in comparison to Facebook and Twitter, which had both already amassed reputations for family political debates and social movement organizing. But in summer 2020, this changed, as Black Lives Matter activism surged after the murder of George Floyd and the COVID-19 pandemic made social lives even more online.[45] One mode of activist engagement that became popular was the Instagram slideshow. Taking advantage of Instagram carousel posts, where users can post up to ten images in one post, users compile information into a slide deck.[46] Creators of Instagram slideshows have told reporters that they intentionally design their slides to "subvert Instagram's algorithmic tendency to prioritize photographs by merging images of flowers and nature with informative text."[47] They co-opt the style of content that Instagram's algorithm is biased toward – corporate-sponsored aesthetics or vacation and nature photos, for example – and then use it to make a political point. Here are two examples of how these slideshows balanced individual, personal action steps on bias with collective, political responsibility for biased frameworks.

First, some slideshows further discussed how to use the platform's biases to the advantage of the movement. For example, in a slideshow entitled "Virtual Protesting 101," user @sa.liine says it is "Time to use the algorithm to our advantage."[48] The post details how to protest virtually and "Optimize your posts by using hashtags that are geared towards your desired target audience (the oppressor)," like "bluelinebeasts," "draintheswamp," and "serveandprotect." Racial bias of members of oppressive groups is something this post suggests is upheld by the algorithm, and it proposes a political way to react and change the system. Rather than just suggesting platform changes or personal training, it offers a method for intervening in biased feeds. @sa.liine offers an example of how to straddle the personal and political dimensions of bias by making algorithmic bias into a political problem that can be addressed with personal intervention.

Second, other slideshows showed how solutions to bias required political action that affects personal life. In "How to use my voice," @_nanders visualizes overlapping circles of online publics with varying degrees of bias, from Black Instagram to White supremacists.[49] The posts propose users (re-)share content from "people that know more" by "Passing on information directly from black activists that they might not see[,] reaching out directly to have open and non judgemental [*sic*] conversations[, and] rephrasing knowledge to make it more accessible [and] digestible." In the caption, the author explains their point:

> Like a lot of non-Black people I have been doing a lot of introspection this week about how to use my voice. ... Why should I, as someone who as [*sic*] not finished unlearning white supremacy, offer any insights into a matter I am not an expert in?

> My current thoughts are: I am not my most radical friend. I am not who I would turn to for knowledge about these issues. But – I am some of my friends' most radical friend, and the person in their life they are able to ask for resources. We all have access to the same internet, but everyone is experiencing their own personal internet. Our social groups are overlapping circles, not singular bubbles.[50]

The making, posting, and reposting of slideshows is thus envisioned as one way to participate in a political project of undoing bias. In other slideshows, like "Why is it so hard to stand with Asian Americans?" or "The War on Drugs," users take the opportunity to explain systems of oppression and how they work both systemically and interpersonally.[51] Instead of pathologizing bias, as if it were something to be fixed by the individual, the practice of slideshow participation can offer opportunities for persuasive communication that balances the personal and political.

### Anti-Bias Strategies for Activists

What digital activist strategies are best to address bias? As communicators know well, campaigns for awareness are insufficient for social change efforts.[52] Changing biases means addressing foundations: "Structural forms of injustice demand structural remedies and this entails being willing to change the institutions that shape and reinforce dominant ideologies."[53] We would suggest, building from this research, that activists turn to the systemic, political issues that moments of personal bias ultimately imply. Nordell smartly notes:

> Individual acts of bias are concentrations of a vast, diffuse legacy, like light rays focused through a lens into a single burning point. Any effort to reduce injustice and inequality requires foundational legal and policy solutions, as well. But laws and policies are not supernatural inventions: people support them, write them, pass them, and enforce them.[54]

Bias is not just a personal issue to be therapeutically solved via training and interpersonal interventions. It is a political issue that requires *political* response, which of course includes the personal. The challenge for digital activists is to develop creative messages to find the balance between the foundational and the interpersonal, messages that can help trace the connections between the concentrated, biased act and the vast legacy the moment belies.

## Stigma: Problems Not People

A key element of many social movements is narrative change – persuading people to dispel myths, stereotypes, or negative views toward a group of people: change that often seeks to reduce **stigma**. Colloquially used but rarely clearly defined, stigma refers to the "standardized image of the disgrace of a particular social group" created by the group's possession of what society deems "an attribute that is deeply discrediting."[55] In other words, stigma blames *people* for the *problems* (e.g., in this sense – health conditions, societally created differences) rather than seeing people as complex and whole individuals. This characteristic of blame helps explain how groups that face marginalization frequently – in fact, almost always – also face stigmatization. As Link and Phelan define it, stigma occurs through a series of interrelated components that all hinge upon the existence of systemic inequity. Only through power structures (e.g., social strata, economic status, political power, etc.) does the environment exist for people to enact stigma by defining and labeling differences, connecting people to stereotypes, distinguishing people with stigma attributes into otherized groups, and enacting discrimination.[56] People may be categorized into a stigmatized group in a multitude of ways, whether from the possession of a physical characteristic deemed socially undesirable/unacceptable (e.g., physical disability, larger body size) and/or a perceived moral failing that may be visible to others (e.g., substance use disorder) or require disclosure (e.g., HIV).

Regardless of the stigma attribute, the unfortunate thread uniting stigma experiences is the host of negative effects stigma has on both individuals within and outside of the stigmatized group. For people who are stigmatized, stigma may lead to dampened self-esteem and self-efficacy, stress and depressive symptoms, lower general and health-related quality of life, and discrimination.[57] Stigma's harms also reach outward, negatively affecting people's support for helpful policies that can curb health issues (e.g., rehabilitation support for people with opioid use disorders) in addition to harming people's interpersonal support for those in stigmatized groups.[58] Because stigma works to associate people *with* their stigma attribute (e.g., sentiments like "you are your addiction"), advocates working to decrease stigma have to overcome this association.

Just as stigma is often communicated through media platforms, so have social movements attempted to interweave anti-stigma messaging into their digital presence. Social movements have worked to combat stigma for a variety of issues over the last several decades, including HIV and AIDS, mental illness and mental health, abortion, and disability, to name a few, while on different media platforms over different decades, anti-stigma campaigns have continually sought to change public perception and stigma. For example, anti-stigma messaging during the AIDS crisis in the 1980s included a television advertising campaign called *Rumors* that featured popular celebrities dispelling myths about AIDS, such as the myth that AIDS could be spread through shaking hands.[59] Now, social movements have taken to participatory digital media like Twitter to share their message, including the #ShoutYourAbortion campaign – a Twitter movement within the larger conversation on women's reproductive autonomy that encourages people to share their abortion stories online without stigma.[60]

A central challenge often faced by anti-stigma advocates is the criticism that de-stigmatization will lead to widespread acceptance of negative behaviors. Whether implicit or explicit, this sentiment relies on a faulty and scientifically disproven assumption that stigma motivates people to avoid the characteristics associated with stigma. In other words, by claiming that people are responsible for their stigma attribute (e.g., "take control of your life and lose weight"), stigma messages both (1) reduce people to a single characteristic and (2) assume that such stigma will motivate individuals to change. Conversations about weight and "obesity"[61] exemplify this blame game. In the last several years, Fox News has featured experts and articles discussing the weight stigma controversy, interviewing one "education expert" in 2016 who claimed that "I believe that this new wave of entertainment focusing on those that are overweight will do nothing except showcase human flaws for the sole purpose of profiteering," and asked "do we really want are children accepting obesity? Should any of us be 'comfortable' with obesity?"[62] The contradiction is that this type of messaging is exactly what creates stigma that *harms* health and wellbeing.

*Example: Using Participatory Media to Prompt
More Diverse Narrative Exposure*

Digital advocates have begun to activate the power of social media feeds in shaping, and subsequently changing, the narrative environment surrounding social movements. Part of this recognition has come with an assumed premise: that normalization or exposure can help foster acceptance of people who look different or possess different attributes. Empirical research upholds this assumption, indicating that contact with others and exposure to different groups of people, especially through the sharing of personal narratives, can help lead to more positive attitudes toward members of stigmatized groups and express less stigma.[63] As Johns Hopkins public health experts Emma McGinty and colleagues put it, "narratives help to overcome concerns about the role of individuals in their own misfortune by blending engaging stories about individuals with contextual information about a larger social problem."[64]

Advocates of the body positivity movement have used Instagram and TikTok as sites for this type of narrative change. Rooted in larger, historical movements like the fat rights and acceptance movement, the modern body digital positivity movement gained Instagram traction in the 2010s in an effort to normalize and celebrate bodies of all sizes.[65] Hashtags like #BodyPositivity, #LoveYourBody, #AllBodiesAreBeautiful, #EffYourBeautyStandards, and more have proliferated the platform, as users post liberating photos of their bodies and captions that share stories and thoughts that challenge fatphobia.[66] In recent years, TikTok has similarly become a site of transformation for body positive advocacy, with videos, hashtags, and even explicit informational content about fatphobia, body positivity, and body neutrality.

Strong advocate for body acceptance, singer, business owner, and advocate Lizzo has used her celebrity influence to spread the message that body positivity is no longer enough. In a 2020 interview with *Vogue,* Lizzo noted: "I think it's lazy for me to just say I'm body positive at this point. ... It's easy. I would like to be body-normative. I want to normalize my body." Aligning with activists who have begun arguing body positivity has become commodified to the extent that only "perfectly curvy" bodies are accepted rather than "girls with back fat, girls with bellies that hang, girls with thighs that aren't separated, that overlap. Girls with stretch marks. You know, girls who are in the 18-plus club."[67] Add to that complexity the intersection of race and racism, and you'll find stigmatizing sentiments from those yet to get on board with the movement – like Jillian Michaels, who stated in 2020 about Lizzo: "Why are we celebrating her body? Why does it matter? Why aren't we celebrating her music? ... Cause it isn't going to be awesome if she gets diabetes."[68] Completely missing the point of body positivity and neutrality, Michaels reflects a key symptom at play in stigmatizing conversations – a rationalization of stigma that redirects the conversation to "correct" or moral behavior. This redirect does exactly what stigma communication insidiously aims to do – places blame on the individual in order to create distance between an "us" and a "them." The good news for advocates is that there are strategies to combat such stigma.

### Anti-Stigma Strategies for Activists

Digital activists can integrate anti-stigma messaging into their work through narrative change. While addressing policy barriers (a major harm of stigma) should be a long-term goal for advocates, one route to alleviating the symptoms of these barriers (otherizing communication and stigma rationalization) in the short term and policy barriers in the long term is sharing narratives that challenge existing stigma. Activists can tell their own stories or even feature the stories of individuals on board with their movement. But as storytelling ensues, activists must not forget to provide context about the stigma issue and continue the work to shift responsibility beyond the individual. Stigma is fundamentally otherizing, and this symptom of "us" who are not in the stigmatizing group or responsible for "their issue" versus "them" who are responsible for their circumstances communication is often what we "see" when larger systems of discrimination are at play. Shifting the narrative then requires appealing to broader systems that foster such discrimination so as to redirect attention away from solely the individual level. For example, in the substance use stigma context, messages that appeal to structural barriers to health treatment (e.g., lack of access to healthcare or healthcare insurance) are more likely to foster support for beneficial policies *without* creating stigma.

### Conclusion

Social movements require advocacy, and that advocacy has largely gone digital. As advocates advance their cause, they can integrate lessons from communication research, including rhetorical studies and persuasion, into digital strategy. This chapter identifies three areas of communication research that provide insight for digital social movement activists. For each area, we identified the apparent symptoms of movement resistance that can manifest in discourse surrounding social movements, the underlying harms that these symptoms represent, and strategies activists can use to address such issues. Table 6.1 summarizes these findings. By anticipating communication harms, activists can use digital media to participate in social movements.

TABLE 6.1 Persuasive strategies for digital activism and influence

| Communication Harms/Types | Structural Barriers | Symptoms | Strategies |
|---|---|---|---|
| **Demagoguery** | Demagogic culture | Scapegoating, lack of communication, avoiding responsibilities of deliberation | Invent methods for correcting demagoguery within and outside social movements/activist communities – e.g., provide audiences with scripts they can use to call out demagoguery with a clear alternative rhetorical choice |
| | Information glut and misinformation and disinformation | Uninformed information sharing, coercive/forceful argument | Inform communities of potential misinformation prior to its spread, and provide them with arguments to combat such information; provide easy-to-read source material that can be shared with communities that may not have access to the same information landscape – e.g., include this information within existing events or persuasive materials for other aims to integrate information sharing throughout the movement |
| **Bias** | Algorithmic and/or Infrastructural bias (e.g., racism, (cis) sexism, etc.) | Hurtful, biased interpersonal interactions | Craft responses that straddle personal and political responsibility and address foundations of inequality – e.g., provide action steps where people can take infrastructural action, but *also* where they can take interpersonal action (e.g., using your social media feeds to shift harmful, stereotypical narratives) |
| **Stigma** | Discrimination | Otherizing communication | Create narratives that utilize humanizing language and use positive imagery that counters stigmatizing perceptions – e.g., utilize hashtags and images, and share stories that show people in stigmatized groups as *whole* people rather that solely a member of their stigmatized group |
| | Policy barriers | Rationalization, underlying emphasis on morality or correct behavior | Foster discussions and share information about societal responsibility for action in addition to sharing information about the harms of stigmatizing communication – e.g., discuss larger social and policy problems that inhibit policy change which could help curb stigmatized issues and provide audiences with research about the harms of stigmatizing communication and the importance of community-building |

## Reflections

- Consider a digital platform that hasn't been addressed in this chapter, like Snapchat. How does information flow on this platform? How is or isn't argument made possible by the flows of information on this platform? How could you imagine intervening to make deliberation possible on this platform?
- What are examples of bias in the news today? What harms do these biases stem from, and how are digital activists addressing them? Are they doing so in ways that align with the strategies outlined in this chapter? If so, how?
- Think about a public policy that has been proposed but does not yet have widespread support. What is the problem the public policy is attempting to solve? How, if at all, might stigma be inhibiting the persuasiveness (the passing) of this policy? Finally, what narratives could advocates share to help reduce stigmatizing perceptions and promote policy support?
- How did the humanistic study of rhetoric and the scientific study of persuasion work together to generate insights in this chapter? How could you imagine pairing these two approaches together in future studies or in the practice of social movement communication?

## Notes

1 Marchese, David. "Why critics of angry woke college kids are missing the point." *New York Times*, May 2, 2022. https://www.nytimes.com/interactive /2022/05/02/magazine/wendy-brown-interview.html.
2 Ibid.
3 Aristotle. 2007. *On Rhetoric: A Theory of Civic Discourse*, 2nd ed. Trans. George Alexander Kennedy. New York: Oxford University Press, p. 37.
4 McKeon, Richard. 1971. "The uses of rhetoric in a technological age: Architectonic productive arts." In Lloyd F. Bitzer and Edwin Black (eds.), *The Prospect of Rhetoric: Report of the National Developmental Project, Sponsored by Speech Communication Association*. Prentice Hall Speech Communication Series, National Conference on Rhetoric. Englewood Cliffs, NJ: Prentice Hall, p. 52.
5 Foust, Christina R., Amy Pason, and Kate Zittlow Rogness. 2017. *What Democracy Looks Like: The Rhetoric of Social Movements and Counterpublics*, Tuscaloosa: University of Alabama Press. Kang, Jiyeon. "Internet activism transforming street politics: South Korea's 2008 'Mad Cow' protests and new democratic sensibilities." *Media, Culture & Society* 39, no. 5 (2017): 750–761. Chávez, Karma R. "Counter-public enclaves and understanding the function of rhetoric in social movement coalition-building." *Communication Quarterly* 59, no. 1 (2011): 1–18. Enck-Wanzer, Darrel. "Trashing the system: Social movement, intersectional rhetoric, and collective agency in the Young Lords organization's garbage offensive." *Quarterly Journal of Speech* 92, no. 2 (2006): 174–201.

6 Dillard, James Price. 2010. "Persuasion." In *The Handbook of Communication Science*, 2nd ed. Thousand Oaks, CA: SAGE Publications, pp. 203–218.

7 Edited collections on social movements frequently detail ongoing debates about how to define the term "social movements," especially from a rhetorical perspective – e.g., Crick, Nathan, ed. *The Rhetoric of Social Movements: Networks, Power, and New Media*. New York: Routledge. Foust, Pason, and Rogness, *What Democracy Looks Like*.

8 Scharp, Kristina M., and Lindsey J. Thomas. "Disrupting the humanities and social science binary: framing communication studies as a transformative discipline." *Review of Communication* 19, no. 2 (2019): 150.

9 Ibid.

10 Brockriede, Wayne. "Where is argument?" *Journal of the American Forensic Association* 11, no. 4 (1975): 1.

11 Branham, Robert James. "'I was gone on debating': Malcolm X's prison debates and public confrontations." *Argumentation and Advocacy* 31, no. 3 (1995): 117–137. DeLuca, Kevin Michael. "Unruly arguments: The body rhetoric of Earth First!, Act Up, and Queer Nation." *Argumentation and Advocacy* 36, no. 1 (1999): 9–21. DeLuca, Kevin Michael, and Jennifer Peeples. "From public sphere to public screen: Democracy, activism, and the 'violence' of Seattle." *Critical Studies in Media Communication* 19, no. 2 (2002): 125–151. Lewiński, Marcin, and Dima Mohammed. "Deliberate design or unintended consequences: The argumentative uses of Facebook during the Arab Spring." *Journal of Public Deliberation* 8, no. 1 (2012): 13; Brunner, Elizabeth A., and Kevin Michael DeLuca. "The argumentative force of image networks: Greenpeace's panmediated global detox campaign." *Argumentation and Advocacy* 52, no. 4 (2016): 281–299; Farzad-Phillips, Alyson. "Huddles or hurdles? Spatial barriers to collective gathering in the aftermath of the Women's March." *Women's Studies in Communication* 43, no. 3 (2020): 1–24.

12 DeLuca, "Unruly arguments," 10.

13 Roberts-Miller, Patricia. 2017. *Demagoguery and Democracy*. New York: The Experiment p. 33.

14 See the recent uptick in Republican discourse falsely claiming that LGBTQ people are pedophiles and groomers for an example of this demagoguery: Itkowitz, Colby. "GOP turns to false insinuations of LGBTQ grooming against Democrats." *Washington Post*, April 20, 2022. https://www.washingtonpost.com/politics/2022/04/20/republicans-grooming-democrats/. Rogers, Kaleigh. "Why so many conservatives are talking about 'grooming' all of a sudden," *FiveThirtyEight* (blog), April 13, 2022. https://fivethirtyeight.com/features/why-so-many-conservatives-are-talking-about-grooming-all-of-a-sudden/.

15 Paliewicz, Nicholas S., and George F. (Guy) McHendry Jr. "When good arguments do not work: Post-dialectics, argument assemblages, and the networks of climate skepticism." *Argumentation and Advocacy* 53, no. 4 (2017): 287–309.

16 World Economic Forum. "Executive summary." *Global Risks 2013* (blog). Accessed June 23, 2022. https://www.weforum.org/reports/world-economic-forum-global-risks-2013-eighth-edition/.

17 "2022 Republican primary ballot propositions." *Republican Party of Texas* (blog). Accessed June 23, 2022. https://texasgop.org/republican-primary-ballot-propositions/.

18 Graham, Timothy, and Robert Ackland. 2017. "Do socialbots dream of popping the filter bubble? The role of socialbots in promoting deliberative democracy in social media." In Robert W. Gehl and Maria Bakardjieva (eds.), *Socialbots and Their Friends: Digital Media and the Automation of Sociality.* New York: Routledge, p. 198.

19 Tsjeng, Zing. "Behind the twitter bot posting the gender pay gap of brands celebrating IWD." *Vice* (blog), March 8, 2022. https://www.vice.com/en/article/m7vkpx/who-made-gender-pay-gap-bot-international-womens-day. @PayGapApp. "Gender Pay Gap Bot." Twitter. Accessed June 15, 2022. https://twitter.com/PayGapApp.

20 Sample, Mark. "A protest bot is a bot so specific you can't mistake it for bullshit." *Medium* (blog), May 30, 2014. https://medium.com/@sample-reality/a-protest-bot-is-a-bot-so-specific-you-cant-mistake-it-for-bullshit-90fe10b7fbaa.

21 Lawson, Francesca. "I set up a Twitter bot to expose companies' pay gaps." *Metro* (blog), March 14, 2022. https://metro.co.uk/2022/03/14/i-set-up-a-twitter-bot-to-expose-companies-pay-gaps-16272035/.

22 Topping, Alexandra, and Caelainn Barr. "What you need to know about gender pay gap reporting." *The Guardian*, February 28, 2018. https://www.theguardian.com/news/2018/feb/28/what-you-need-to-know-about-gender-pay-gap-reporting. Iain, comment to Blundell, Jack. "UK gender pay gap reporting: A crude but effective policy?" *LSE Business Review* (blog), March 29, 2021. https://blogs.lse.ac.uk/businessreview/2021/03/29/uk-gender-pay-gap-reporting-a-crude-but-effective-policy/.

23 "Search and compare gender pay gap data." GOV.UK. Accessed June 24, 2022. https://gender-pay-gap.service.gov.uk/.

24 Lawson, "I set up a twitter bot to expose companies' pay gaps," paras. 6 and 8.

25 Munger, Kevin. "Tweetment effects on the tweeted: Experimentally reducing racist harassment." *Political Behavior* 39, no. 3 (2017): 639.

26 Ibid., p. 629.

27 Ibid., p. 643.

28 Judah, Sam and Hannah Ajala. "The Twitter bot that 'corrects' people who say 'illegal immigrant.'" BBC News (blog), August 3, 2015. https://www.bbc.com/news/blogs-trending-33735177.

29 Rivas, Jorge, and Patrick Hogan. "We built a twitter bot that corrects people who say 'illegal immigrant.'" *Splinter News*, July 28, 2015. https://splinternews.com/we-built-a-twitter-bot-that-corrects-people-who-say-ill-1793849536.

30 Lewandowsky, Stephan, and Sander van der Linden. "Countering misinformation and fake news through inoculation and prebunking." *European Review of Social Psychology* 32, no. 2 (2021): 348–384.

31 McGuire, William J. "The effectiveness of supportive and refutational defenses in immunizing and restoring beliefs against persuasion." *Sociometry* 24, no. 2 (1961): 184–197.

32 Nordell, Jessica. 2021. *The End of Bias: How We Change Our Minds.* London: Granta.

33 Applebaum, Barbara. "Remediating campus climate: Implicit bias training is not enough." *Studies in Philosophy and Education* 38, no. 2 (2019): 131.

34 Harmon, Amy. "BIPOC or POC? Equity or equality? The debate over language on the left." *New York Times*, November 1, 2021. https://www.nytimes.com/2021/11/01/us/terminology-language-politics.html.

35 Reed, Kayla, and Blake Strode. "How to turn protest power into political power." *New York Times*, May 22, 2021. https://www.nytimes.com/2021/05/22/opinion/george-floyd-protests-blm-movement.html.

36 Alvarez, Tawny L. "Support for the Black Lives Matter movement: Implicit bias training." Verrill Law, *Taking Care of HR Business* (blog), June 19, 2020. https://www.verrill-law.com/taking-care-of-hr-business/support-for-the-black-lives-matter-movement-implicit-bias-training-part-4-of-12/.

37 Gabriel, Trip, and Dana Goldstein. "Disputing racism's reach, republicans rattle American schools." *New York Times*, June 1, 2021. https://www.nytimes.com/2021/06/01/us/politics/critical-race-theory.html.

38 Reed and Strode, "How to turn protest power into political power," para. 4.

39 Applebaum, "Remediating campus climate," pp. 133 and 138.

40 Noble, Safiya Umoja. 2018. *Algorithms of Oppression: How Search Engines Reinforce Racism*. New York: New York University Press.

41 Benjamin, Ruha. 2019. *Race after Technology: Abolitionist Tools for the New Jim Code*. Medford, MA: Polity Press.

42 Reeves, Joshua. "Temptation and its discontents: Digital rhetoric, flow, and the possible." *Rhetoric Review* 32, no. 3 (2013): 318: "As users access online spaces – whether those spaces are traditional web pages or more interactive sites like Facebook – they are confronted with alluring options that have been carefully constructed by designers and/or generated automatically based upon users' past activity profiles."

43 Tufekci, Zeynep. "YouTube, the great radicalizer." *New York Times*, June 8, 2018. https://www.nytimes.com/2018/03/10/opinion/sunday/youtube-politics-radical.html: "What keeps people glued to YouTube? Its algorithm seems to have concluded that people are drawn to content that is more extreme than what they started with – or to incendiary content in general."

44 Little, Olivia, and Abbie Richards. "TikTok's algorithm leads users from transphobic videos to far-right rabbit holes." *Media Matters*, October 5, 2021. https://www.mediamatters.org/tiktok/tiktoks-algorithm-leads-users-transphobic-videos-far-right-rabbit-holes.

45 Stewart, Emily, and Shirin Ghaffary. "It's not just your feed: Political content has taken over Instagram." *Vox*, June 24, 2020. https://www.vox.com/recode/2020/6/24/21300631/instagram-black-lives-matter-politics-blackout-tuesday.

46 Ledford, Victoria, and Matthew Salzano. "The Instagram activism slideshow: Translating policy argumentation skills to digital civic participation." *Communication Teacher* 36, no.4 (2022): 258–263.

47 Nguyen, Terry. "PowerPoint activism is taking over your friends' Instagram accounts." *Vox*, August 12, 2020. https://www.vox.com/the-goods/21359098/social-justice-slideshows-instagram-activism.

48 @sa.liine. "'Virtual Protesting 101' (May 2020)." Instagram Slideshow Archive, May 29, 2020. https://instagramslideshows.omeka.net/items/show/12.

49 @_nanders. "'How to use my voice' (June 2020)." Instagram Slideshow Archive, June 5, 2020. https://instagramslideshows.omeka.net/items/show/10.

50 Ibid., slide 6.

51 @pattiegonia. "'Why is it so hard to stand with Asian Americans?' (March 2021)." Instagram Slideshow Archive, March 28, 2021. https://instagramslideshows.omeka.net/items/show/14. @so.informed. "'The war on drugs' (April

2022).” Instagram Slideshow Archive, April 20, 2022. https://instagramslide-shows.omeka.net/items/show/15.

52 Christiano, Ann, and Annie Neimand. “Stop raising awareness already.” *Stanford Social Innovation Review* 15, no. 2 (2017): 34–41. https://ssir.org/articles/entry/stop_raising_awareness_already#.

53 Applebaum, “Remediating campus climate,” p. 139.

54 Nordell, *The End of Bias.*

55 Smith, Rachel A. “Language of the lost: An explication of stigma communication.” *Communication Theory* 17, no. 4 (2007): 462–485. Goffman, Erving. 1963. *Stigma: Notes on the Management of Spoiled Identity.* Chicago, IL: Touchstone.

56 Link, Bruce G., and Jo C. Phelan. “Conceptualizing stigma.” *Annual Review of Sociology* 27, no. 1 (2001): 363–385.

57 Corrigan, Patrick W., Jonathon E. Larson, and Nicolas Rüsch. “Self-stigma and the ‘why try’ effect: Impact on life goals and evidence-based practices.” *World Psychiatry: Official Journal of the World Psychiatric Association* 8, no. 2 (2009): 75–81. Durso, Laura E., Janet D. Latner, and Anna C. Ciao. “Weight bias internalization in treatment-seeking overweight adults: Psychometric validation and associations with self-esteem, body image, and mood symptoms.” *Eating Behaviors* 21 (2016): 104–108. Corrigan, Patrick W., and Amy C Watson. “Understanding the impact of stigma on people with mental illness.” *World Psychiatry* 1, no. 1 (2002): 16–20. Nobre, Nuno, et al. “HIV-related self-stigma and health-related quality of life of people living with HIV in Finland.” *Journal of the Association of Nurses in AIDS Care* 29, no. 2 (2018): 254–265.

58 Kennedy-Hendricks, Alene, et al. “Social stigma toward persons with prescription opioid use disorder: associations with public support for punitive and public health-oriented policies.” *Psychiatric Services (Washington, D.C.)* 68, no. 5 (2017): 462–469. Ledford, Victoria, et al. “The influence of stigmatizing messages on danger appraisal: examining the model of stigma communication for opioid-related stigma, policy support, and related outcomes.” *Health Communication* 37, no. 14 (2021): 1765–1777.

59 Henry J. Kaiser Family Foundation. 2006. *Evolution of an Epidemic: 25 Years of HIV/AIDS Media Campaigns.* https://www.kff.org/wp-content/uploads/2013/01/7515.pdf.

60 “Shout Your Abortion – about.” Accessed June 24, 2022. https://shoutyour-abortion.com/about/. Brodeur, Nicole. “How ‘Shout Your Abortion’ grew from a Seattle hashtag into a book.” *Seattle Times,* December 12, 2018. https://www.seattletimes.com/life/how-shout-your-abortion-grew-from-a-seattle-hashtag-into-a-book/.

61 Obesity is referenced in quotations here because we do not agree with the validity of the term - a term based on the outdated measure of body mass index – but recognize that the majority of stigma conversations about weight are referenced in the “obesity” context.

62 McKay, Hollie. “Do shows focusing on overweight characters further obesity problem?” Fox News, April 11, 2016. https://www.foxnews.com/entertainment/do-shows-focusing-on-overweight-characters-further-obesity-problem.

63 Li, Minjie. “Mediated vicarious contact with transgender people: How narrative perspective and interaction depiction influence intergroup attitudes, transportation, and elevation.” *Journal of Public Interest Communications* 3, no.

1 (2019): 141. Heley, Kathryn, et al. "Reducing health-related stigma through narrative messages." *Health Communication* 35, no. 7 (2020): 849–860.

64 McGinty, Emma, et al. "Communication strategies to counter stigma and improve mental illness and substance use disorder policy." *Psychiatric Services* 69, no. 2 (2018): 136–146.

65 "From New York to Instagram: The history of the body positivity movement." *BBC Bitesize.* https://www.bbc.co.uk/bitesize/articles/z2w7dp3. Salam, Maya. "Why 'radical body love' is thriving on Instagram." *New York Times,* June 9, 2017. https://www.nytimes.com/2017/06/09/style/body-positive-instagram.html.

66 Dallessandro, Alysse. "11 empowering body positive hashtags that inspire us to love our bodies and everyone else's too." *Bustle,* April 30, 2015. https://www.bustle.com/articles/79764-11-empowering-body-positive-hashtags-that-inspire-us-to-love-our-bodies-and-everyone-elses-too. See also "From New York to Instagram."

67 Van Paris, Calin. "Lizzo wants to redefine the body-positivity movement." *Vogue,* September 24, 2020. https://www.vogue.com/article/lizzo-october-cover-story-body-positivity-inclusivity.

68 Chiu, Allyson. "Jillian Michaels asked why people are 'celebrating' Lizzo's body: Critics slammed her as 'fatphobic.'" *Washington Post,* January 9, 2020. https://www.washingtonpost.com/nation/2020/01/09/jillian-michaels-lizzo-fat-shaming/.

# PART III
# Rebellion

# ADVOCATES FOR ACTION

## Ani Pachen

1933–2022
Hometown: Gonjo County, Chamdo, Tibet
Movements: Opposition to Chinese occupation of Tibet, Free Tibet
  Movement
Organizations: March for Tibet Independence
*Allison De Young and Jacob Laros*

Ani Pachen, known as the "Warrior Nun" for her religious dedication and fight against the Chinese occupation of Tibet, was the sister of the 14th Dalai Lama and a member of the Tibetan nobility. Born in 1933 as Pachen Dolma in Kham, a province in Gonjo in Eastern Tibet, at 17 years old she ran away to a monastery and became a Buddhist nun after learning that her father, the chief of her clan, was planning on marrying her off to a chieftain of another clan. It was at the monastery that her name changed from Pachen Dolma to Ani Pachen. After her family relented on the marriage plans, she returned home and sat by her father's side when the Chinese invaded Tibet in the 1950s. In 1960, at 25 years old, her home was overrun, and she and her family fled to the mountains, where they fought the Chinese until they were defeated, and she was captured by government officials. Pachen was imprisoned by the Chinese for over 20 years and subjected to severe torture methods as well as starvation, but never gave up hope, citing her Buddhist religion as the key to her survival.[1]

Pachen was eventually released in 1981 and fled to Nepal, where she continued to advocate for a free Tibet by traveling around the world to tell her story and to participate in demonstrations.[2] In 2000, her

DOI: 10.4324/9781003291855-16

autobiography, *Sorrow Mountain: The Remarkable Story of a Tibetan Warrior Nun,* was published and spread greater awareness of her life and the Free Tibet Movement. Her efforts also included participating in the March for Tibet Independence, which is a grassroots campaign that to this day advocates for the independence of Tibet from China. It is organized by supporters of Tibet around the world, and involves a variety of activities, including protests, demonstrations, and educational events. The campaign seeks to raise awareness about the issue of Tibetan independence and to pressure governments around the world to support the Tibetan cause. The campaign is inspired by similar movements for independence and self-determination in other parts of the world and seeks to highlight the human rights abuses and cultural repression that Tibetans have experienced under Chinese rule.[3] During the march, Panchen would stop at various locations and retell her harrowing story of survival and perseverance while continuing to advocate for a free Tibet.[4]

Since her death, the Free Tibet Movement has continued, and she is regularly cited as an influential figure within the movement. Her autobiography serves as her legacy and a reminder that a whole culture is in danger of being washed away.[5]

## Notes

1 Donnelley, Adelaide, and Ani Pachen. 2002. *Sorrow Mountain: The Journey of a Tibetan Warrior Nun.* Tokyo, Japan: Kodansha International.
2 Martin, D. "Ani Pachen, warrior nun in Tibet Jail 21 years, dies." *New York Times,* February 18, 2002. https://www.nytimes.com/2002/02/18/world/ani -pachen-warrior-nun-in-tibet-jail-21-years-dies.html.
3 Norbu, J. "Transcending the confines of traditional male-dominated society in old Tibet." *Tibet Journal* 45, no. 2 (2020): 3–25.
4 Gould, Benina Berger. 2004. "Ritual as resistance: Tibetan women and non-violence." In *Frontline Feminisms.* New York: Routledge, pp. 206–228.
5 Hanson, Gayle. "Ani Pachen, warrior nun of Tibet." *Lion's Roar,* September 1, 2000. https://www.lionsroar.com/ani-pachen-warrior-nun-of-tibet/.

# 7

# AMPLIFIED EFFORT

## Networked Social Change, Use, Participation, and Algorithms

*Manyu Li, Ashley L. Fromenthal, and Brianna L. Sadighian*

The use of social media platforms has become a central part to modern-day social movements.[1] These platforms offer spaces for activists to create networks of communities and collectively spread messages to achieve activism goals.[2] This new form of activism is often termed as online/networked social movement,[3] connective actions,[4] **digital activism**,[5] or **hashtag activism**.[6] The goal of this chapter is to (1) explore what networked social movement is, (2) analyze characteristics of effective networked social movements, and (3) discuss future directions on networked social movement research.

### Networked Politics and Networked Social Movements

Network theory has been applied to understand politics (i.e., networked politics), such as how international relations are formed through collaboration among governments, economic organizations, or societies,[7] or how mass media, along with complex social interactions and conversations among individuals, influences presidential campaigns.[8] The term "networked social movement," a type of networked politics, characterizes the decentered or leaderless organization of various parties in a social movement,[9] such as how activists, humanitarian organizations, and community members work together to coordinate collective actions.[10] In the past decade, the study of networked politics and networked social movements has been extended to understand these networks in the context of

DOI: 10.4324/9781003291855-17

social media.[11] Specifically, in the context of social media, "networked social movement" refers to the engagement of individuals on social media network platforms to mobilize social changes, particularly in the form of informal, leaderless "connective" actions. These individuals are connected through a shared sense of identity,[12] **belonging**,[13] cohesion/solidarity,[14] and in many cases, shared empathy[15] or emotion[16] on the issues. They may identify each other through direct or indirect personal online connections, shared online interest groups, or hashtags.[17] Therefore, the "networked social movement" is also termed hashtag activism[18] or digital activism.

While early research of networks in politics or social movements merely considered the concept of networks as a metaphor or a theoretical argument, later research examined networks through qualitative analysis, such as case studies,[19] content analysis,[20] ethnography, and discourse analysis,, and quantitative/computational analysis, such as text analysis, and social network analysis of social media data. This chapter will first present three cases of networked social movement, then discuss theories and research that are relevant to how people act and react in networked social movements (i.e., networked behaviors), and finally, future research directions.

FIGURE 7.1   In addition to offline activism, people nowadays engage in networked social movements on social media Photo by Duncan Shaffer with Unsplash open license.

### Real-World Cases of Networked Social Movements

#### Case 1: Arab Spring Movement

The Arab Spring began in Tunisia in the early 2010s as a series of anti-government protests and armed rebellions sparked up and spread like wildfire in Egypt and the Arab world.[21] Along with different political, economic, and historical reasons,[22] this uprising was undoubtedly magnified when Tunisian protestors used social media websites such as Twitter and Facebook to topple a 23-year-long regime and bring about lasting political change.[23] What began as a simple argument between a street vendor and a police officer over a produce cart quickly became what is sometimes called the Facebook revolution or the Twitter revolution, as the websites helped spread the message embodied by the street vendor, Mohamed Bouazizi, who set himself on fire and died after the conflict with the police officer.[24] The story of Bouazizi was one of the many from the Arab Spring that were shared and retweeted time and time again, giving political oppression a human face and allowing the younger Tunisian population to question the role they played in their government.[25] His death ignited the fervor of many groups that were dissatisfied with their governing body, and saw the likes of unemployed individuals, human rights activists, labor unionists, students, and others beginning the revolution of the Arab Spring.

The shares and retweets quickly turned into Facebook groups and networks formed by tech-savvy social media users, facilitating communication and interaction among those who wished to protest and make a change in their government.[26] These networks are carefully formed when users on social media mention or reply to one another's posts, creating a link between nodes (individuals or themes).[27] From there, these clusters of individuals and ideas expand via online conversations, reaching more and more people.[28] (Isa and Himelboim 2018). In the case of social media activism, many networks are formed via hashtags, allowing easy access to conversations among like-minded users, further expanding and strengthening the links within the network. Research showed that after controlling for various covariates, social media use significantly predicts the likelihood of someone attending a protest. According to Howard et al.[29] (2011), social media became a critical part of the toolbox for greater freedom in the Arab world at the time, as the rate of tweets directly predicted and preceded major events such as the explosion of tweets about political change in Egypt directly before the resignation of President Hosni Mubarak. In Tunisia, social media uproar about liberty, democracy, and revolution directly preceded the event of mass protests, showing that the more individuals talked about political change, the more likely it was to happen.

The social media presence of those involved in the Arab Spring movement was a force to be reckoned with, as many countries involved tried to shut down internet access to evade the harsh truth of their regimes. This ironically backfired, only making those involved fight back stronger, inciting more public activism and fueling the fire within them. As internet access was cut off for those in Egypt in an attempt to prevent uprisings, the only thing left for activists to do was to make their voices be heard loudly on the streets.

Within the next two years, many areas directly targeted by protestors and activists saw great success in taking down oppressive regimes such as Egypt, Tunisia, Libya, Yemen, and Jordan.[30] Due to the overwhelming social media presence that supporters and protestors had online, the revolutions of the Arab Spring seemed to be very successful in achieving their goal in a nonviolent way.[31] However, this was not a plan perfectly executed, as although there was lasting success for both Egypt and Tunisia, the other regions involved were only temporarily successful and fell back into poor, oppressive conditions shortly after.[32] The regions of Egypt and Tunisia saw great success due to their greater ability to access social media, making it more effective for those areas to mobilize and reach larger groups of people. Despite the discrepancy in the outcomes of the Arab Spring protests, it is still a lesson learned and a reminder of the impact that social media has and that the voices connected to every profile are important enough to move the world and make a change.

### Case 2: #HeForShe

Networked social movements can also be initiated by organizations, rather than individuals. For example, the HeForShe movement was created to push for gender equality by UN Women, a United Nations organization that works to uphold standards to ensure that every woman and girl has the opportunity to succeed.[33] The movement calls for men and boys to eliminate the social obstacles that keep women and girls from reaching their full potential. By doing so, women, men, girls, and boys can positively reshape society and the world together. The Twitter hashtag, #HeForShe, was launched in September of 2014, and since then, hundreds of thousands of people, or champions, have joined the movement and committed to gender equality on platforms such as Facebook and Twitter.[34] This includes leaders from all over the world, such as Justin Trudeau, Prime Minister of Canada, and Nana Addo Dankwa Akufo, President of the Republic of Ghana. Champions who commit to pushing for gender equality implement the framework created by UN Women and HeForShe by using resources such as action kits that are specifically made for corporations or universities.

Before its initial launch, the HeForShe movement sneakily got a head start on its social media popularity when Emma Watson tweeted with #HeForShe at the end of her message.[35] This particular tweet was retweeted over 27,000 times and liked 33.000 times, with lots of curiosity from her followers. But this was just the beginning. The HeForShe movement boomed after a viral speech given by Emma Watson was posted to social media. Within the first two weeks following the launch of the HeForShe campaign, the movement generated 1.1 million tweets from 750.000 users. The activist campaign strategically employed social media to raise awareness in the movement. By utilizing their official social media accounts, HeForShe directly asked for its followers to show their support, and that is exactly what happened. Through #HeForShe, the organization has reached users from around the world, with committed users of its campaign website originating from India, Rwanda, and the Democratic Republic of Congo.[36] Since its start on social media, HeForShe has initiated progress within the real world as well.

In 2021, HeForShe made progress toward gender equality in universities, corporations, and thematics due to the movement's spread on Twitter and other social media platforms. Within the universities that are partnered with HeForShe, the percentage of women in senior leadership positions has increased by 90%, the percentage of female tenured professors has increased by 75%, and the percentages of female graduates and undergraduates have increased by 60% and 75% respectively. Over 40% of corporations partnered with HeForShe and 35% of thematic partners have increased female representation in their overall company, the top 6%, boards, and new hires. These increases in female representation come from the movement's popularity on social media platforms and individuals' public commitment to gender equality.

Social media and its ability to quickly spread information have played a major role in the global expansion of HeForShe. With the representation of UN Women at United Nations meetings and the existence of HeForShe summits, more and more people are able to learn about its message and commitment. The movement only continues to grow with the increase in the use of the hashtag, #HeForShe on Twitter.

### Case 3: BTS Fandom BLM Activism

BTS, a music band originating from South Korea, has an immense following, named ARMY. After the murder of George Floyd in May 2020,

BTS made the decision to show their outward support for the BLM movement and donated US$1 million in June of the same year. Shortly after, ARMY organized an external website, called *One In An ARMY* (OIAA), in an effort to match the US$1 million BTS donated. They are led by the idea that their combined power and efforts can create global good and social change. The fundraising goal was met within a mere 25 hours of the creation of the hashtag.[37] OIAA continues to run and successfully fundraise for other campaigns such as #ARMYForEarth, proving that several small donations can make a major impact and push for social change.

Social media played a role in the development and success of this movement by connecting and creating widespread engagement between fans. Without any push from the musical group BTS, the ARMY fandom took it upon themselves to create the hashtag #MatchAMillion to advocate for the BLM movement. While no specific leader or central coordinating organization are planning their activist projects, the ARMY fandom still manage to be highly successful and mobile in their efforts as they are boundaryless and self-governing.[38] The fandom's collective efforts may also suggest that they are more of a cohesive group or community, rather than a simple network of people. The individuals belonging to the ARMY fandom have stated that their success in activism goes further than shared ideals, and can be attributed to a genuine feeling of trust and safety within the group. The most common phrases reported by the fandom when describing their group and the reason their #MatchAMillion campaign was successful were "community," "family," and "supportive."

The ARMY fandom are also generally well known for their active social media presence and their record of supporting movements relating to social justice.[39] The members of ARMY have often taken over hashtags used for White supremacists to congregate on social media and overwhelmed these hashtags with positive messages and videos of their favorite Korean popular music (K-pop) idols performing, flushing out any hateful rhetoric. The ARMY fandom and other K-pop fan groups have a history of using their tight-knit community and diversity to spread positivity and help out social movements as their fanbase is highly organized. In addition to their BLM activist efforts, the ARMY fandom actively engage in campaigns. In the past, the fandom have initiated and organized more than 600 campaigns, bringing in more than US$2 million. Whether it be a political or non-political cause, charity remains an indispensable activity within the ARMY fandom, fueling movements and campaigns toward social change.

## CONNECTING FROM AROUND THE GLOBE

Networked social movements allow people to connect without geographic limitations. This type of activism allows people from around the globe who share similar values to come together to make social changes. For example, in the 2019 Anti-Extradition Law Amendment Bill Movement, a movement to protect the one country, two system policy and the democracy of the Hong Kong Special Administrative Region of China, people around the globe joined together on Twitter to learn about the protest and help to increase global attention on the issues.[40] The activists also intentionally use English to communicate, to ensure effective global communications.

Language use is important in global networked social movements. In 2022, some Chinese-speaking activists started the Great Translation Movement on Reddit (and later turned to Twitter). The Great Translation Movement was initially an anti-war movement that was launched during the 2022 Russian invasion of Ukraine. Activists translated messages from Chinese state media to English, Japanese, French, Korean, etc. to help others understand the sentiments and views of the Chinese Communist Party and the government toward the Russian invasion. The Great Translation Movement started an official account on Twitter and continued to translate messages that focused on other social issues, such as China's zero-COVID policy.

## Theoretical Perspectives and Research into Networked Social Movements

### Perspectives from Social Psychology: Group Theories

The ways online users interact in networked social movements can be explained using **group theories** in social psychology. Group theories deal with how people feel (affect), act (behavior), and think (cognition) in group settings, and how people are being influenced by each other in social situations.[41] They are broadly divided into intergroup theories[42] and intragroup process theories,[43] addressing topics such as prejudice and stereotypes,[44] social identities,[45] and organizations.[46] This section will discuss theories that are relevant to networked social movements.

*Minority Influence*

**Minority influence** refers to the process by which minority members change the norm of the majority members and introduce a new norm to the group.[47] In group settings, minority members (those smaller in number) are often found to yield to majority norms through conformity.[48] Minority influence theory addresses the opposite process, in which the minority exerts influence and pushes the majority to consider a new (opposing) set of norms through changing first the opinions and then the actions of majority members.[49]

These anti-normative minority members who raise new ideas to the group play a crucial role as agents of social change in societies.[50] Indeed, minority influence is crucial in networked social movements.[51] For example, pro-environment individuals (minority) can influence the majority's private opinions and behaviors when they promote pro-environmental attitudes.[52] Asian-Americans who speak out to raise awareness of inclusion in diversity and equity conversations are crucial in serving as activism role models for fellow Asian-Americans and making their collective voices heard.[53] When considering the case of HeForShe, we can see the influence of the minority, women and girls, on the majority, men and boys. Women who voice their opinions about gender equality and the need for change slowly change norm perspectives and private opinions that men may hold. In turn, those men who are influenced by this may join the movement to help fight for gender equality.

*Group Cohesion*

A key for minority influence or networked social movements to succeed is solidarity,[54] or in group theory terminology, group cohesiveness.[55] **Group cohesion** refers to the solidarity of a group, and can be seen by how closely members are linked to the group as a whole.[56] Group cohesion research has generally shown that cohesiveness positively correlates with stable memberships, coherent identities, and members' motivation to adhere to group standards.[57] Similarly, effective networked social movements require that activists be cohesive, sharing highly similar identities and coherent actions. In turn, these coherent actions further consolidate the group cohesiveness.[58]

In recent years, with the rise of social media activism, the range of effective methods to increase group cohesion in networked social movement groups has expanded past the old ways of everyone holding up posters presenting similar messages in a protest to encompass hashtags, retweets, and repeated mentions of concepts centralized to a social movement's end goal.[59] Through these cohesive themes, members of a social movement are "metaphorically singing with one voice,"[60] reflecting the real-world events that occur with collective action. In other words, the use of social media, such as Twitter, enables greater group cohesion by offering a place for information-gathering and information dissemination to happen in real time with great accessibility.[61] For example, the importance of group cohesion can be seen in the case of #MatchAMillion involving the BTS ARMY fandom. The ARMY fandom worked together collectively to raise over US$1 million in order to support the efforts of the Black Lives Matter movement. In this specific case, individual members of ARMY reportedly felt as though ARMY was something greater than themselves alone, and being a part of ARMY allowed these individuals to feel like they belonged to a community with a cohesive goal.

However, cohesion alone is not sufficient for networked social movements to succeed. Instead, the success of social movements often relies on the dynamics of the group, meaning that conflict, power plays, and factionalism will often compromise the success of the movement.[62] When a group of people let their individual differences destroy their ability to see the end goal, social movements fall apart, and social change cannot happen. One cautionary point, however, is that group cohesion may predict groupthink (i.e., overemphasizing group unity and unanimity) and ineffective decision-making.[63] To prevent groupthink, highly cohesive activist groups need to develop a mechanism so that the group does not end up following only one biased voice or group ideal, such as developing equitable communication means by allowing all members to contribute a voice (including opposing voices) and make decisions. When activist groups foster non-biased group cohesion practices and processes, the group culture improves and boosts the wellbeing of members and the effectiveness of their social movement efforts.

## Community Belonging and Place Attachment

In addition to being closely tied as a group, individual perceptions of a feeling of belonging or identification of oneself as a member of a networked social movement are linked to participation in the movement.[64] *Belonging* is defined as one's attachment to a group, and is a basic human need.[65] For example, in the Occupy Wall Street movement, the longing for community and connection seemed to be a common experience among those who expressed their disdain for economic inequality in New York City.[66] A similar phenomenon was seen during the Black Lives Matter movement and protests after the death of George Floyd, as one cause united hundreds of thousands of individuals and created a community of its own with a common purpose.[67]

Different networked social movement groups endorse different strategies to build up a sense of belonging and shared identity. One way to increase belonging is through increasing perceived safety and security.[68] For example, some feminist movements and queer activist groups' sense of belonging is enhanced through building safe spaces,[69] such as practicing separatism and allowing like-minded people to share their experiences. At the same time, these groups transform their sense of belonging into actions by using safe spaces to develop and exchange ideas that can influence the public in their movements. Another way to increase belonging is to ensure the group is sensitive to the diversity of individual members (i.e., bringing individuals with diverse backgrounds together).[70] This is particularly important as the success of social movements is often determined by whether diverse members and organizations can work together to achieve social change.[71]

In addition to a sense of belonging, individuals' place attachment also plays a role in networked social movements. *Place attachment* or psychological place attachment extends belonging to characterize people's bonding to a place or a community through their ABC: affect (A), behavior (B), and cognition (C).[72] The higher place attachment community members have, the more likely members to share positive emotions toward the place and negative emotions toward problems that destroy the place (affect), value the place's wellbeing (cognition), and take actions to protect the place (behaviors).[73]

Place attachment is often observed in local community activism, such as activism for the environment surrounding one's place.[74] Moreover, when communities experience shared trauma together, their attachment to the place may then transform into actions to voice their common concerns, such as when a disadvantaged local community experiences systemic problems in neighborhood development,[75] shooting incidents (e.g., #NeverAgain),[76] and the lack of energy justice.[77]

In summary, in order for a social movement to be effective, there needs to be a sense of belonging and attachment to a particular cause or common interest. Without a community of like-minded individuals, most social movements will never get media traction, never reach the trending page of Twitter, and never get to make social change.

### Social Media Algorithms

Perhaps one of the main differences between offline and online networked social movements is that social media activists, or "algorithmic activists," have to work with and against **social algorithms** (also known as social media algorithms).[78] Social media platforms have started to use various algorithms to sift through all the content that gets posted every day to decide what posts are publicized and what posts are buried.[79] The ultimate goal of social media algorithms is to make the large amount of complex information accessible and processable,[80] although scholars have also observed that algorithms are often intended to be used to make profits.[81] Social algorithms in different social media platforms are rather complex and cannot be easily explained.[82] The limited availability of data also makes it difficult for researchers to understand how social algorithms influence social media behaviors. However, digital activists learn to work with social media algorithms (or at least with their lay theories of how social algorithms work) so that their messages can be spread and seen by a larger audience.

What are these lay theories people form? In other words, what are some common perceptions of social algorithms by social media users? Through interviews and observations, one study identified three dimensions of networked social movement activists' perceptions of social algorithms. The first one was algorithmic conditioned affordances. Activists in the study reported noticing that the algorithm encouraged them to form connections with other members. Activists tended to see this feature as presenting opportunities (rather than constraints) as it allowed them to collaborate on plans for the movements and helped them increase their network size. The second dimension was algorithmic facilitation – the use of social media's algorithm filtering process to filter out irrelevant posts from users' feeds. The opportunities activists saw were that this feature enabled them to continue to connect with people who shared or paid attention to similar content. It also helped them group together efforts scattered across the social media world. However, some noticed that the filtering and sorting process was unclear. It was difficult for activists to know exactly how they could make sure their messages did not get filtered out. The last dimension was algorithmic distortion. For example, some noticed that social media did not display information they posted or hid some users' content from the feed. On the contrary, social media sites may flood the feed with certain types of messages, further preventing users from seeing other messages. These lay theories people form about social algorithms are termed "algorithmic imaginary," – that is "ways of thinking about what algorithms are, what they should be, and how they function."[83]

How do activists fight against social algorithms? The term researchers have given to behaviors of working around algorithms by social media users is **algorithmic resistance**.[84] Algorithmic resistance refers to media users' intention to resist algorithmic power,[85] – that is, the control behind the algorithm.[86] For example, activists considered the relative *weight* (e.g., in Facebook, the number of likes, comments, and reposts) certain messages have and collectively interacted with their target posts so that the algorithm would be triggered to rank their posts as popular. People also tested different methods to get traction for their posts, such as making attempts to control the algorithms, forming theories on how algorithms filter posts, and following people or organizations that could help increase their traction.[87] On Twitter, activists often explicitly or implicitly agree on certain hashtags and tweet and retweet so that their hashtags are recognized by the algorithm as popular trending hashtags, and thus increase the chances that the messages tied to the hashtags are seen nationally and globally. These activists may communicate outside the platform (such as by using direct messaging tools) and discuss how a hashtag is to be used and how narratives relating to the hashtag should be written.

### Perspectives from Computational Social Science

**Computational social science** is an emerging field that integrates social science theories and research methods with data science/computational methods,[88] such as the use of natural language processing (text analysis), social network analysis, other machine learning methods, etc. The rise of using computational methods in social science has led to an increase in computational research on networked social movements, such as understanding the sentiments of popular messages during a networked social movement, finding out common or leading phrases in activism, and observing changes in online interactions at different time periods during the social movement.

One popular method of analysis is social network analysis, which is used to examine a community of connective actions by investigating the actors (the nodes) and the connections among them (the edges or ties).[89] Using social network analysis, one may identify central nodes (actors) through social network indices (centrality, betweenness, etc.) and examine characteristics of networked communities (i.e., communities of actors highly connected with each other, and less so with outside communities) and interaction among communities (i.e., inter-communities).

For example, social network analyses allow the study and comparison of *homophilous* community structures (i.e., networks of people with highly similar attributes, such as ideologies, social characteristics) and *heterophilous* ones (i.e., networks of people with some dissimilar attributes).[90] There are different ways homophily and heterophily can be interpreted in networked social movements, however. A homophilous community (e.g., indicated by more distinctive, isolated cliques) may be inferred as ideology polarization during a networked social movement, while a heterophilous community (e.g., indicated by more overlapping cliques) may be inferred as having diverse ideologies and accepting of different ideologies[91]. Observations of homophilous versus heterophilous networked communities can also be used to understand *who, if any* are collaborating in social movements.[92]

Computational social science methods also allow systematic comparison between online and offline events, a frequently asked research question in networked social movement research. In one study examining the use of #BoycottNFL on Twitter, the structure of inter-communities was found to change as offline events progressed. For example, after President Trump called out to fire players who kneeled during the national anthem, the communities that contained individuals who were pro-Trump and affiliated with sports became the largest community the next day. Interestingly, companies and brands that sponsored NFL players also started to emerge as an interconnected community. In another study, the cohesiveness of digital activists (measured using network indices such as network density and weighted degree) during the Egyptian revolution (one of the Arab Spring movements) changed as the movement turned from the earlier period (i.e., the resignation of President Mubarak and successful start of the revolution by the protestors) to the late period (i.e., the court ruling to drop all charges against former President Mubarak and the crackdown against protestors). Specifically, the cohesiveness of online networked social movement members was much lower in the late period than in the early period, and group polarization (i.e., homophily) was much more prevalent in the late period than in the early period.

In summary, computational social science research opens up new opportunities for researchers to understand the dynamics of online networked social movements and how the online world develops given offline events. The use of techniques such as natural language processing allows researchers to examine the public's language use, attitudes toward, and perception of various messages, etc., and the use of social network analysis allows researchers to examine the network structure and dynamics.

## Future Directions on Networked Social Movements

### Slacktivism versus Activism? The Study of Progressive Networked Behaviors

Social media has been seen as a helpful tool for increasing public participation on important social issues through digital networked activism, as demonstrated by various correlational findings between social media use and political engagement.[93] However, many are also concerned about the risk of having only awareness but not action in networked social movements, or **slacktivism**.[94] Slacktivism (or some may refer to it as clicktivism) combines the words "slacker" and "activism" to describe individuals who feel good just staying online to like, comment, or share posts, making minimal efforts, rather than making committed efforts to push for real changes to achieve political goals. Examples of slacktivism can include modifying profile pictures to a certain symbol or color to show support for a movement, or sharing a black square to show support for the Black Lives Matter movement, but not performing actions to make changes.

While slacktivism may provide an easy entry point for novice activists to practice civic skills and may help spread awareness of important social issues at the quickest pace,[95] slacktivism raises concerns as it could be potentially dangerous and distract individuals from making more meaningful efforts for the movement. One major difference between traditional activism and slacktivist campaigns, compared to traditional political participation, is the reduction in resources that are needed for political participation on social media. More specifically, if information-seeking is the only resource the campaign provides, then a slacktivist campaign is unlikely to have any substantial impacts. Additionally, traditional activism will require significant amounts of time invested by individuals, but is more likely to create strong bonds (cohesion) between members than online networked activism.

Future research on networked social movements may examine how slacktivism can be turned into actions that promote the success of social movements. One key to examining this is to identify the organizational *process* by which successful online networked activists and activism progress over time. For example, a recent synthesis of past research developed a digital activism version of the three-hierarchy framework of political participation[96]: digital spectator activities, transitional activities, and gladiatorial activities.[97] Specifically, the lowest level of involvement, digital spectator activities, starts with three progressive actions, including liking posts or following groups (clicktivism/slacktivism), participating in retweeting/sharing activist messages (meta-voicing), and creating original statements to support the activism (assertion). The medium level of participation, digital transitional activities, involves behaviors such as e-funding (generating funds for the movement online), purchasing from sellers that align with the supported political ideology, and signing or initiating digital petitions. Finally, digital gladiatorial activities, the highest level of participation from a small group of activists, involve data activism which promotes open data and literacy in data-based facts, exposure of confidential information (e.g., Wikileaks), or hacktivism which aims to disrupt operations or destroy data of the opposite sides (e.g., governments, organizations, individuals). Frameworks like this can help researchers break down digital activism behaviors and analyze antecedents, consequences, and transitions of networked social movement slacktivism and activism systematically.

### Leveraging Computational Social Science to Analyze Big Networked Social Movement Data

Computational social science methods are great toolkits to integrate the knowledge of networked social movements in the analysis and interpretation of big digital data.[98] Computational social science differs from computer science or data science in its goal to not only *predict* certain phenomena or behavioral patterns, but also to *explain* human behaviors and construct theories to understand them.[99] Therefore, future networked social movement research using computational science should aim to answer research questions that can promote theoretical development.[100] Further, computational social science also places an emphasis on research *ethics*, such as the collection and use of digital data. The issue of data security itself is highly tied to networked social movements on digital or data justice, such as anti-surveillance movements.[101] Further, activism work involves highly sensitive data, especially in authoritarian states where certain activists may be persecuted.[102] Identifying networks within activism groups may expose the identities of activists and reduce the effectiveness of their activism in such a setting. Therefore, future research may examine ethical research methods and ways to establish best practices for open yet ethical data analysis in studying networked social movements.

### Conclusion

The last decade has witnessed an uprising of individuals and organizations in their participation and networking of important social movements, which may not have been possible without the existence of the internet and social media platforms. The success of networked social movements is achieved through various group behaviors (e.g., minority influence, solidarity/group cohesion, and developing group belonging and attachment), increased knowledge of social media algorithms, and mutual influences between online networks and offline events. Moving forward, computational social science may offer new ways to understand these networked social movements. These advanced analytic methods, combined with the development of theoretical frameworks and an emphasis on ethical research practices, will bring new knowledge as the world continues to witness social changes brought about by growing networked social movements.

## Reflections

- What are networked social movements? What are some examples of networked social movements?
- How can social psychology theories be used to explain effective networked behaviors in social movements? For example, how can minority voices be successfully communicated?
- What is a social algorithm? How do activists use social algorithms to their advantage?
- How does computational social science contribute to the understanding of networked social movements?
- Do you consider networked social movements to be merely slacktivism? How can future research develop theoretical frameworks to understand different levels of engagements in networked social movements?
- How do you see yourself joining with future researchers to understand networked social movements?

## Notes

1 Shen, Y. "The impact of social media on social activism taking black lives matter on twitter as an example," *Proceedings of the 2021 International Conference on Social Development and Media Communication (SDMC 2021)*, (January 17, 2022): 947–951, accessed May 8, 2023, https://doi.org/10.2991/assehr.k.220105.174.

2 Greijdanus, H., et al. "The psychology of online activism and social movements: Relations between online and offline collective action." *Current Opinion in Psychology* 35 (2020): 49–54. Mirbabaie, M., F. Brünker, M. Wischnewski, and J. Meinert. "The development of connective action during social movements on social media." *ACM Transactions on Social Computing* 4 (2021): 1–21.

3 Fenton, N. 2011. "Multiplicity, autonomy, new media, and the networked politics of new social movements." In *Discourse Theory and Critical Media Politics*. London: Palgrave Macmillan, pp. 78–200. Donovan, J. "After the #keyword: Eliciting, sustaining, and coordinating participation across the Occupy Movement." *Social Media and Society* 4 (2018): 1–12.

4 Bennett, W.L., and A. Segerberg. "The logic of connective actions." *Information, Communication & Society* 15 (2012): 739–768.

5 Mendes, K., and J. Ringrose. 2019. "Digital feminist activism: #MeToo and the everyday experiences of challenging rape culture." In *#MeToo and the Politics of Social Change*. New York: Springer, pp. 37–51.

6 Dadas, C. 2017. "Hashtag activism: The promise and risk of 'attention.'" In *Social Writing/Social Media: Publics, Presentations, and Pedagogies*. Denver, CO: WAC Clearinghouse, University Press of Colorado, pp. 17–36.

7 Kahler, M. 2009. *Networked Politics: Agency, Power, and Governance*. Ithaca, NY: Cornell University Press. Hafner-Burton, E.M., M. Kahler, and A.H. Montgomery. "Network analysis for international relations." *International Organization* 63 (2009): 559–592.

8 Sey, A., and M. Castells. 2004. "From media politics to networked politics: The internet and the political process." in M. Castells (ed.), *The Network Society: A Cross-Cultural Perspective*. Northampton, MA: Edward Elgar, pp. 363–381.

9 Castells, M. 2010. *The Power of Identity*, 2nd ed. Chichester: Wiley-Blackwell, ebook. Lee, F.L.F., and Fong, I.W.Y. "The construction and mobilization of political consumerism through digital media in a networked social movement.," *New Media & Society* 0, no. 0 (October 26, 2021): 1, accessed May 8, 2023, https://doi.org/10.1177/14614448211050885.

10 Lake, D.A., and W. Wong. "The politics of networks: interests, power, and human rights norms," *SSRN Electronic Journal*, (August 1, 2007): 1. https://dx.doi.org/10.2139/ssrn.1004199. Juris, J.S. 2004. "Networked social movements: Global movements for global justice." In M. Castells (ed.), *The Network Society: A Cross-Cultural Perspective*. Northampton, MA: Edward Elgar, pp. 341–362.

11 Castells, M. 2015. *Networks of Outrage and Hope: Social Movements in the Internet Age*. Hoboken, NJ: Wiley.

12 Loader, B.D. "Social movements and new media." *Sociology Compass* 2 (2008): 1920–1933.

13 Shahin, S., and Y.M.M. Ng. "Connective action or collective inertia? Emotion, cognition, and the limits of digitally networked resistance." *Social Movement Studies* 21 (2021): 530–548.

14 Donovan, J. "'Can you hear me now?' Phreaking the party line from operators to occupy." *Information, Communication & Society* 19 (2016): 601–617.

15 Suk, J., et al. "#MeToo, networked acknowledgment, and connective action: How 'empowerment through empathy' launched a social movement." *Social Science Computer Review* 39 (2021): 276–294.

16 Park, S.J., Y.S. Lim, S. Sams, S.M. Nam, and H.W. Park. "Networked politics on cyworld: The text and sentiment of Korean political profiles." *Social Science Computer Review* 29 (2011): 288–299.

17 Wang, R., W. Liu, and S. Gao. "Hashtags and information virality in networked social movement." *Online Information Review* 40 (2016): 850–866.

18 Xiong, Y., M. Cho, and B. Boatwright. "Hashtag activism and message frames among social movement organizations: Semantic network analysis and thematic analysis of Twitter during the #MeToo movement." *Public Relations Review* 45 (2019): 10–23.

19 Friedberg, B., and J. Donovan. "On the internet, nobody knows you're a bot: Pseudoanonymous influence operations and networked social movements," *Journal of Design and Science* 6, (August 7, 2019): 1, accessed May 8, 2023, https://doi.org/10.21428/7808da6b.45957184. Park, S.Y., N.K. Santero, B. Kaneshiro, and J.H. Lee. 2021. "Armed in ARMY: A case study of how BTS fans successfully collaborated to #MatchAMillion for Black Lives Matter." In *Proceedings of the 2021 CHI Conference on Human Factors in Computing Systems*. New York: Association for Computing Machinery, pp. 1–14.

20 Li, M., et al. "Twitter as a tool for social movement: An analysis of feminist activism on social media communities." *Journal of Community Psychology* 49 (2021): 854–868.

21 Saideman, S.M. "When conflict spreads: Arab Spring and the limits of diffusion." *International Interactions* 38 (2012): 713–722.

22 Smidi, A., and S. Shahin. "Social media and social mobilisation in the Middle East: A survey of research on the Arab Spring." *India Quarterly* 73 (2017): 196–209.

23 Wolfsfeld, G., E. Segev, and T. Sheafer. "Social media and the Arab Spring: Politics comes first." *International Journal of Press/Politics* 18 (2013): 115–137. Tufekci, Z., and C. Wilson. "Social media and the decision to participate in political protest: Observations from Tahrir Square." *Journal of Communication* 62 (2012): 363–379.

24 Breuer, A., T. Landman, and D. Farquhar. "Social media and protest mobilization: Evidence from the Tunisian Revolution." *Democratization* 22 (2015): 764–792. Mihailidis, P. "New Civic Voices and the emerging media literacy landscape." *Journal of Media Literacy Education* (2011: 2–3. Kavanaugh, A., et al. "Between a rock and a cell phone." *International Journal of Information Systems for Crisis Response and Management* 5 (2013): 1–21.

25 Howard, P.N., et al. "Opening closed regimes: What was the role of social media during the Arab Spring?" *SSRN Electronic Journal* (2011): 1–30.

26 Mourtada, R., and F. Salem. "Civil movements: The impact of Facebook and Twitter. "*Arab Social Media Report* 1 (2011): 1–30.

27 Isa, D., and I. Himelboim. "A social networks approach to online social movement: Social mediators and mediated content in #FreeAJStaff Twitter network." *Social Media + Society* 4 (2018): 205630511876080.

28 David Isa and Itai Himelboim, "A Social Networks Approach to Online Social Movement: Social Mediators and Mediated Content in #FreeAJStaff Twitter Network," *Social Media & Society*, March 1, 2018, [Page #], accessed May 8, 2023, https://doi.org/10.1177/2056305118760807.

29 Philip N. Howard et al., "Opening Closed Regimes: What Was the Role of Social Media During the Arab Spring?," *SSRN*, April 17, 2015, [Page 1-30], accessed May 8, 2023, https://dx.doi.org/10.2139/ssrn.2595096.

30 Tudoroiu, T. "Social media and revolutionary waves: The case of the Arab Spring." *New Political Science* 36 (2014): 346–365.

31 Chenoweth, E., and K.G. Cunningham. "Understanding nonviolent resistance." *Journal of Peace Research* 50 (2013): 271–276.

32 Haseeb, K.E.-D. "The Arab Spring revisited*." *Contemporary Arab Affairs* 5 (2012): 185–197.

33 Harvey, R. "Twitter reactions to the UN's #HeForShe campaign for gender equality: A corpus-based discourse analysis." *Journal of Corpora and Discourse Studies* 3 (2020): 31.

34 Stabile, B., H. Purohit, and A. Hattery. "Social media campaigns addressing gender-based violence: Policy entrepreneurship and advocacy networks," *Sexuality, Gender and Policy* 3, no. 2 (October 17, 2020): 122, accessed May 8, 2023, https://doi.org/10.1002/sgp2.12021. Stache, L.C. "Advocacy and political potential at the convergence of hashtag activism and commerce," *Feminist Media Studies* 15, no. 1 (November 28, 2014): 162, accessed May 8, 2023, https://doi.org/10.1080/14680777.2015.987429.

35 Omoera, O.S., and H. Ryanga. "Can social media set the agenda in addressing violence against women?," *World Scientific News* 60, (November 21,

2016): 40, accessed May 8, 2023, http://www.worldscientificnews.com/wp -content/uploads/2016/06/WSN-60-2016-40-50.pdf.

36 Miambo-Ngcuka, P. ed., "Proven solutions," *HeForShe*, last modified 2021, accessed May 8, 2023, https://www.heforshe.org/sites/default/files/2021-07/ hfs_proven_solutions.pdf.

37 Bhandari, A. "How the South Korean band's fanbase – known as ARMY – raised over \$1 million for the Black Lives Matter movement, mostly in just one day." *Reuters* (2020).

38 Chang, W., and S.-E. Park. "The fandom of Hallyu, a tribe in the digital network era: The case of ARMY of BTS," *Kritika Kultura* 32, (2019): 260, accessed May 8, 2023, https://doi.org/10.13185/2986.

39 Kanozia, R., and G. Ganghariya. "More than K-pop fans: BTS fandom and activism amid COVID-19 outbreak." *Media Asia* 48 (2021): 338–345.

40 Luqiu, L.R., and S. Lu. "Bounded or boundless: A case study of foreign cor- respondents' use of Twitter during the 2019 Hong Kong Protests." *Social Media and Society* 7 (2021). doi:10.1177/2056305121990637.

41 Cooper, C.L. 1975. *Theories of Group Processes*. Hoboken, NJ: John Wiley.

42 Brewer, M B., and R.M. Kramer. "The psychology of intergroup attitudes and behavior." *Annual Review of Psychology* 36 (1985): 219–243.

43 Hogg, M.A. 1996. "Intragroup processes, group structure and social iden- tity." In W.P. Robinson (ed.), *Social Groups and Identities: Developing the Legacy of Henri Tajfel*. Oxford, UK: Butterworth-Heinemann.

44 Rydell, R.J., K. Hugenberg, D. Ray, and D.M. Mackie. "Implicit theories about groups and stereotyping." *Personality and Social Psychology Bulletin* 33 (2007): 549–558.

45 Abrams, D., and M.A. Hogg.2006. *Social Identifications*. New York: Routledge.

46 Steffens, N.K., K.A. Munt, D. van Knippenberg, M.J. Platow, and S.A. Haslam. "Advancing the social identity theory of leadership: A meta-analytic review of leader group prototypicality." *Organizational Psychology Review* 11 (2021): 35–72.

47 Gardikiotis, A. "Minority influence." *Sociology and Personality Psychology Compass* 5 (2011): 679–693. Maass, A., and R.D. Clark. "Hidden impact of minorities: Fifteen years of minority influence research." *Psychological Bulletin* 95 (1984): 428–450.

48 Bernheim, B.D. "A theory of conformity." *Journal of Political Economy* 102 (1994): 841–877.

49 Jung, J., A. Bramson, and W.D. Crano. "An agent-based model of indi- rect minority influence on social change and diversity." *Social Influence* 13 (2018): 18–38.

50 Moscovici, S. "Toward a theory of conversion behavior." *Advances in Experimental Social Psychology* 13 (1980): 209–239.

51 Gillion, D.Q. 2020. *The Loud Minority*. Princeton, NJ: Princeton University Press.

52 Bolderdijk, J.W., and L. Jans. "Minority influence in climate change mitiga- tion." *Current Opinion in Psychology* 42 (2021): 25–30.

53 Grim, J.K., N.L. Lee, S.D. Museus, V.S. Na, and M.P. Ting. "Asian American college student activism and social justice in Midwest contexts." *New Directions for Higher Education* 186 (2019): 25–36.

54 Thomas, E.F., et al. "When and how social movements mobilize action within and across nations to promote solidarity with refugees." *European Journal of Social Psychology* 49 (2019): 213–229.

55 Munro, L. "United we stand: Fostering cohesion in activist groups." *Interface (Maynooth)* 13 (2021): 129–156.

56 Evans, N.J., and P.A. Jarvis. "Group cohesion." *Small Group Behavior* 11 (1980): 359–370. Forsyth, D.R. "Recent advances in the study of group cohesion." *Group Dynamics: Theory, Research, and Practice* 25 (2021): 213–228.

57 Hogg, M.A. 1992. *The Social Psychology of Group Cohesiveness*. London: Harvester Wheatsheaf. Laursen, B., and R. Veenstra. "Toward understanding the functions of peer influence: A summary and synthesis of recent empirical research." *Journal of Research on Adolescence* 31 (2021): 889–907.

58 Vestergren, S., J. Drury, and E.H. Chiriac. "How collective action produces psychological change and how that change endures over time: A case study of an environmental campaign." *British Journal of Social Psychology* 57 (2018): 855–877. Drury, J., et al. "A social identity model of riot diffusion: From injustice to empowerment in the 2011 London riots." *European Journal of Social Psychology* 50 (2020): 646–661.

59 Chiovaro, M., L.C. Windsor, A. Windsor, and A. Paxton. "Online social cohesion reflects real-world group action in Syria during the Arab Spring." *PLoS ONE* 16 (2021): e0254087.

60 Ibid., p. 2.

61 Harlow, S., and D. Harp. "Collective action on the Web." *Information, Communication & Society* 15 (2012): 196–216.

62 Vannucci, D., and R. Singer. 2010. *Come Hell or High Water: A Handbook on Collective Process Gone Awry*. Chico, CA: AK Press.

63 Mullen, B., T. Anthony, E. Salas, and J.E. Driskell. "Group cohesiveness and quality of decision making." *Small Group Research* 25 (1994): 189–204. Janis, I.L. 1987. "Groupthink." In *Shared Experiences in Human Communication*. New York: Routledge, pp. 259–282.

64 Zlobina, A., M.C. Dávila, and O.V. Mitina. "Am I an activist, a volunteer, both, or neither? A study of role-identity profiles and their correlates among citizens engaged with equality and social justice issues." *Journal of Community and Applied Social Psychology* 31, (2021): 155–170. Simon, B., et al. "Collective identification and social movement participation." *Journal of Personality and Social Psychology* 74 (1998): 646–658.

65 Baumeister, R.F., and M.R. Leary. "The need to belong: Desire for interpersonal attachments as a fundamental human motivation." *Psychological Bulletin* 117 (1995): 497–529.

66 Smucker, J.M. "Can prefigurative politics replace political strategy?" *Berkeley Journal of Sociology* 58 (2014): 74–82.

67 Mills, E. 2022. *365 Days of Belonging, Activism and Change: Examining the Perception of Minorities in the UK in the Wake of the Black Lives Matter Summer*. Thesis, Swansea University, UK.

68 Shalka, T.R., and C. Leal. "Sense of belonging for college students with PTSD: The role of safety, stigma, and campus climate." *Journal of American College Health* 70 (2022): 698–705.

69 Hansson, K., M. Sveningsson, and H. Ganetz. "Organizing safe spaces: #MeToo activism in Sweden." *Computer Supported Cooperative Work* 30 (2021): 651–682.

70 Chenoweth, E., and M.J. Stephan. 2012. *Why Civil Resistance Works: The Strategic Logic of Nonviolent Conflict*. New York: Columbia University Press.

71 Nardini, G., T. Rank-Christman, M.G. Bublitz, S.N.N. Cross, and L.A. Peracchio. "Together we rise: How social movements succeed." *Journal of Consumer Psychology* 31 (2021): 112–145.

72 Scannell, L., and R. Gifford. "Defining place attachment: A tripartite organizing framework." *Journal of Environmental Psychology* 30 (2010): 1–10. Li, M., I.H. Frieze, and J. Cheong. "Stay or go? A path model of highly educated individuals' migration desires." *Journal of Behavioural Sciences* 24 (2014): 1–17.

73 Li, M., and I.H. Frieze. "Developing civic engagement in university education: predicting current and future engagement in community services. *Social Psychology of Education* 19 (2016): 775–792. Mihaylov, N., and D.D. Perkins. 2014. "Community place attachment and its role in social capital development." In L. Manzo and P. Devine-Wright (eds.), *Place Attachment: Advances in Theory, Methods and Applications*. New York: Routledge.

74 Mihaylov, N., and D. Perkins. "Local environmental grassroots activism: Contributions from environmental psychology, sociology and politics." *Behavioral Sciences* 5 (2015): 121–153.

75 Berglund, L. "'We're forgotten': The shaping of place attachment and collective action in Detroit's 48217 neighborhood." *Journal of Urban Affairs* 42 (2020): 390–413.

76 Alperstein, N., and T. Jones. "The online social movement of #NeverAgain: How social networks build a sense of membership, influence, support and emotional connection on Twitter." *Journal of Social Media in Society* 9 (2020): 127–149.

77 Sayan, R.C. "Exploring place-based approaches and energy justice: Ecology, social movements, and hydropower in Turkey." *Energy Research & Social Science* 57 (2019): 101234.

78 Maly, I. "New right metapolitics and the algorithmic activism of Schild & Vrienden." *Social Media + Society* 5 (2019).

79 Tufekci, Z. 2017. *Twitter and Tear Gas: The Power and Fragility of Networked Protest*. New Haven, CT: Yale University Press.

80 Coretti, L., and D. Pica. 2018. "Facebook's communication protocols, algorithmic filters, and protest : A critical socio-technical perspective." In *Social Media Materialities and Protest*. New York: Routledge, pp. 72–85.

81 Etter, M., and O.B. Albu. "Activists in the dark: Social media algorithms and collective action in two social movement organizations." *Organization* 28 (2021): 68–91.

82 Lazer, D.M.J. "The rise of the social algorithm." *Science* 38 (2015): 1090–1091.

83 Bucher, T. "The algorithmic imaginary: Exploring the ordinary affects of Facebook algorithms." *Information, Community & Society* 20 (2017): 30–44, at p. 30.

84 Treré, E. 2018. "From digital activism to algorithmic resistance." In Meikle, Graham (ed.), *The Routledge Companion to Media and Activism*. New York: Routledge, pp. 367–375.

85 Velkova, J., and A. Kaun. "Algorithmic resistance: Media practices and the politics of repair." *Information, Community & Society* 24 (2021): 523–540.

86 Bucher, T. 2018 *If ... Then*, vol. 1. Oxford, UK: Oxford University Press.

87 Min, S.J. "From algorithmic disengagement to algorithmic activism: Charting social media users' responses to news filtering algorithms." *Telematics and Informatics* 43, (2019): 101251.

88 Lazer, D.M.J., et al. "Computational social science." *Science* 323 (2009): 721–723. Lazer, D.M.J. et al. "Computational social science: Obstacles and opportunities." *Science* 369 (2020): 1060–1062.

89 Borgatti, S.P., M.G. Everett, and J.C. Johnson. 2013. *Analyzing Social Networks*. Thousand Oaks, CA: SAGE Publications. Freeman, L.C. 2004.

*The Development of Social Network Analysis: A Study in the Sociology of Science.* New York: Empirical Press.

90 Rogers, E.M., and D.K. Bhowmik. "Homophily-heterophily: Relational concepts for communication research." *Public Opinion Quarterly* 34 (1970): 523. Millward, P., P. Widdop, and M.A. Halpin. "'Different class'? Homophily and heterophily in the social class networks of Britpop." *Cultural Sociology* 11 (2017): 318–336.

91 Abul-Fottouh, D., and T. Fetner. "Solidarity or schism: Ideological congruence and the twitter networks of Egyptian activists." *Mobilization* 23 (2018): 23–44.

92 Chung, T.L. (Doreen), O. Johnson, A. Hall-Phillips, and K. Kim. "The effects of offline events on online connective actions: An examination of #BoycottNFL using social network analysis." *Computers in Human Behavior* 115 (2021): 106623.

93 Kahne, J., and B. Bowyer. "The political significance of social media activity and social networks. *Political Communication* 35 (2018): 470–493. Valenzuela, S. "Unpacking the use of social media for protest behavior." *American Behavioral Scientist* 57 (2013): 920–942. Li, M., H. Lin, and M.N.D. Maer. "Relationship of living historical memories and news source with national identity: A latent class analysis." *Asian Journal of Social Psychology* 24 (2021): 364–377.

94 Glenn, C.L. "Activism or 'Slacktivism?' Digital media and organizing for social change." *Communication Teacher* 29 (2015): 81–85.

95 Vitak, J., et al. "It's complicated: Facebook users' political participation in the 2008 election." *Cyberpsychology, Behavior, and Social Networking* 14 (2011): 107–114. Skoric, M.M. "What is slack about slacktivism?" *Methodological and Conceptual Issues in Cyber Activism Research* 77 (2012): 77–92.

96 Milbrath, L.W. "Political participation." 1981. In *The Handbook of Political Behavior.* New York: Springer, pp. 197–240. Milbrath, L.W., and M.L. Goel. 1977. *Political Participation: How and Why Do People Get Involved in Politics?* Chicago, IL: Rand McNally College Publishing.

97 George, J.J., and D.E. Leidner. "From clicktivism to hacktivism: Understanding digital activism." *Information and Organization* 29 (2019): 100249.

98 Cappella, J.N. "Vectors into the future of mass and interpersonal communication research: Big Data, social media, and computational social science." *Human Communication Research* 43 (2017): 545–558.

99 Wallach, H. "Computational social science ≠ computer science + social data." *Communications of the ACM* 61 (2018): 42–44.

100 Edelmann, A., T. Wolff, D. Montagne, and C.A. Bail. "Computational social science and sociology." *Annual Review of Sociology* 46 (2020): 61–81.

101 Dencik, L., A. Hintz, and J. Cable. "Towards data justice? The ambiguity of anti-surveillance resistance in political activism." *Big Data & Society* 3 (2016): 1–12. Milan, S. 2018. "Data activism as the new frontier of media activism." In V Pickard and G Yang (eds.), *Media Activism in the Digital Age.* New York: Routledge, pp. 151–163.

102 Lonkila, M., L. Shpakovskaya, and P. Torchinsky. 2021. "Digital activism in Russia: The evolution and forms of online participation in an authoritarian state." In D. Gritsenko, M. Wijermars, and M. Kopotev (eds.), *The Palgrave Handbook of Digital Russia Studies.* New York: Palgrave Macmillan, pp. 135–153.

# ADVOCATES FOR ACTION

## Zitkála-Šá (Gertrude Simmons Bonnin)

1876–1938
Hometown: Yankton Indian Reservation, South Dakota, USA
Movements: Suffrage and citizenship for Native Americans
Organizations: Society of American Indians, National Council of
  American Indians

*Allison De Young*

Gertrude Simmons Bonnin, also known by her Sioux name, Zitkála-Šá, meaning "Red Bird," was a Yankton Dakota writer, editor, translator, musician, educator, and political activist.[1] She was born in the Yankton Dakota Indian Reservation in South Dakota, USA in 1876, and was one of the first Native American women to publish a book. She is best known for her work as an editor and translator of Dakota folklore and literature, and for her activism on behalf of Native American rights. Zitkála-Šá was a founding member of the National Council of American Indians, where she worked to promote the rights and well-being of Native American communities.

She is remembered as an important figure in the history of Native American literature and activism, and her work has had a lasting impact on the way that Native American culture is understood and appreciated. Many of her accomplishments and passions stemmed from her personal struggles relating to her cultural identity. She attended the Quaker missionary boarding school White's Manual Labor Institute in Wabash, Indiana. There, she learned to read, write, and play the violin and piano. It was at that boarding school she was also given the name Gertrude Simmons.

DOI: 10.4324/9781003291855-18

Some of Zitkála-Šá's major accomplishments include publishing multiple books on Native American culture, being published in numerous magazines, and writing the first American opera, *The Sun Dance Opera*.[2]

Her most influential work, though, was her political activism. Through these efforts Zitkála-Šá worked to improve the education and healthcare systems for Native Americans, preserve the culture, and gain legal recognition of the community. As part of the Society of American Indians, she was a vocal advocate for Native Americans receiving American citizenship and the right to vote.[3] She criticized assimilationist policies and practices created by the Bureau of Indian Affairs.[4] She later co-founded the National Council of American Indians, which worked to unite tribes across America.[5] She also published a report that was instrumental in encouraging the federal government to investigate the exploitation and defrauding of Native Americans by outsiders for access to oil-rich lands.[6]

Since her death, Zitkála-Šá has been recognized as one of the most influential Native American activists of the 20th century. Her activism led to important changes in education, healthcare and legal standing for Native Americans and also helped preserve Native American culture.[7]

## Notes

1 Capaldi, Gina. 2011, *Red Bird Sings: The Story of Zitkala-Sa, Native American Author, Musician, and Activist*. Minneapolis, MN: Millbrook Press.
2 Hafen, P. Jane. "A Cultural duet Zitkala Ša and the Sun Dance Opera."*Great Plains Quarterly* 18, no. 2 (Spring, 1998): 102–111
3 Sarker, Sonita. 2022. "The unsettling times of Zitkála-Šá and Grazia Deledda." In *The Routledge Handbook of North American Indigenous Modernisms*. New York: Routledge, pp. 87–99.
4 Roberts, Christina Ann, and Earl E. Fitz. 2020. "Indigenous literatures." In W Raussert, GL Anatol, S Thies, SC Berkin, and JC Lozano (eds.), *The Routledge Handbook to the Culture and Media of the Americas*. New York: Routledge, pp. 110–120.
5 "Zitkala-Sa (Red Bird/Gertrude Simmons Bonnin)." n.d. National Park Service. https://www.nps.gov/people/zitkala-sa.htm.
6 Angus, Ian. "The Enclosure Movement." https://dgrnewsservice.org/history/
7 Mathias, Marisa. "Zitkála-Šá." National Women's History Museum. 2022. https://www.womenshistory.org/education-resources/biographies/zitkala-sa

# 8

# ANY TIME, ANY CAUSE, ANYWHERE

## Hyperlocal Protests Secure Global Support and the Case of #EndSARS

*Chelsea Peterson-Salahuddin*

## Introduction

On October 3, 2020, posts on Twitter reported that officers of the Special Anti-Robbery Squad (SARS), a division of the Nigerian Police Force (NPF), shot a boy and left him on the side of the road and drove away in his car in Ughelli Delta State, Nigeria. Reports of the shooting and a video of the incident circulated online, leading to renewed calls across Nigeria for the government to #EndSARS.[1] Starting on October 7, protestors took to the streets demanding an end to police brutality and corruption. On social media, protestors used #EndSARS to share stories of SARS harassment and call on journalists and high-profile individuals to share information about the movement.[2] The protests came to a head on the evening of October 20, when the Nigerian Army opened fire on thousands of reportedly peaceful protestors at Alausa and Lekki Toll Gate in Lagos, a day that later came to be referred to as the Lekki Toll Gate Massacre, reportedly killing 12.[3] As the violence against protestors grew, #EndSARS became a global rallying cry to protect human rights and address systemic police brutality, sparking global protests on and offline.[4] The international support for the #EndSARS movement was arguably due to strategic digital coalition-building.

Four months earlier, 6,345 miles away, a parallel social movement to #EndSARS was on the rise. On May 25, 2022, Minneapolis police officer Derrick Chauvin murdered George Floyd, an unarmed Black man, after Chauvin – who was responding to a call about the use of counterfeit money, a charge that would ordinarily result in a fine – placed his knee

DOI: 10.4324/9781003291855-19

on Floyd's neck for 8 minutes and 46 seconds, cutting off his air supply. A video of the incident, recorded and uploaded to Facebook by bystander Darnella Fraiser, went viral on social media and sparked a resurgence of the Black Lives Matter (BLM) movement, also aimed at addressing police brutality. Following Floyd's murder, protestors took to the streets, first in Minneapolis, but soon in major metropolitan cities across the United States, and to social media, using #BlackLivesMatter or #BLM, to protest repeated instances of police brutality and extrajudicial killings aimed at Black Americans.[5]

This chapter draws on the literature on hashtag activism and social movement theory to discuss how hyperlocal protests secure global support, specifically through the case of the #EndSARS movement in Nigeria and its digital appeals for coalition-building with the BLM movement. Included in the chapter, is outline of how End SARS activists used social media to highlight the common socio-political threats and opportunities facing both movements, construct parallel discourse around the movements' common goals of curbing police brutality, extrajudicial killing, and human rights abuses, and create an informational discursive shared Black diasporic culture to facilitate coalition-building and mobilize BLM's global network of. In this way, the text demonstrates how hashtag activism has allowed for new approaches to social movement coalition-building in ways that both align with and push against traditional social movement theory.

## Social Media, Online Coalitions, and the Formation of Global Social Movements

### Social Media and the Rise of Hashtag Activism

Social media platforms have increasingly become an important locus of online discussion, due largely to the hashtag function's ability to catalogue information around a specific topic. Technologist Chris Messina first proposed using the hashtag function in 2007 to help users follow and contribute to specific topical discussions, and create network publics where conversation could flourish.[6] While not all hashtags develop into larger discussions, the inclusion of a hashtag allows a post to reach users who may be outside of a person's direct follower network, creating distinct hashtag networks.[7] Additionally, hashtags have an indexing function, allowing users on social media to mark and find specific information and topical conversations and connect this information to other topically related discussions across the platform.[8]

The term **hashtag activism** refers to the strategic use of the hashtag function to spread information for a specific social or political movement.[9]

The earliest noted use of the term was in a 2011 article in *The Guardian* discussing the Occupy Wall Street Movement, protesting the corruption of global capitalism, which used #OccupyWallStreet to galvanize and inform supporters.[10] Since then, the term has been applied to several social movements around the world that have used hashtags to spread their message, including #MeToo, which sought to bring awareness to sexual assault and abuse, #HongKongPoliceBrutality, which called attention to police misconduct against protestors in Hong Kong, and #BringBackOurGirls, which aimed to bring international attention to the 276 school girls kidnapped from Government Girls Secondary School Chibok in Nigeria by Islamic Jihadist group, Boko Haram.[11]

## #ELENÃO (#NOTHIM): GLOBAL FEMINIST HASHTAG ACTIVISM

The hashtag EleNão (#NotHim) was started by the group Mulheres Unidas Contra Bolsonaro (Women United Against Bolsonaro) on Facebook in early September 2018 in response to what they claimed were racist and sexist comments made by politician Jair Bolsonaro during his presidential campaign. While the Facebook group and hashtag campaign began with a handful of Brazilian activists, within weeks it sparked a global feminist movement, garnering over 2 million Facebook members and fostering global solidarity with women's movements across the globe, organizing for gender-based equality, bodily autonomy, and against gender-based violence. These online actions resulted in a day of global feminist strikes on September 29, 2018 on five continents and in 181 cities, including New York, London, and Lisbon.[12] In this way, #EleNão was able to mobilize hashtag activism and online coalition-building into actionable, on-the-ground, global protests. The #EleNão campaign was unsuccessful in its efforts to stop the election of Bolsonaro, who was elected President of Brazil one month later on October 28, 2018; however, it did successfully spur support for the election of several women to parliament within Brazil's Socialism and Liberty Party, including the first indigenous woman elected to the country's parliament, Joenia Wapichana.[13]

Hashtag activism is often used by people who don't hold institutional power within society to make their positions, lived experiences, and voices heard within a larger social and political discourse.[14] As Castells notes: "By engaging in the production of mass media messages, and by developing autonomous networks of horizontal communication, citizens of the Information Age become able to invent new programs for their lives."[15] Since movement messages spread through hashtags circulated independently from mass media structures, hashtags allows activists to quickly spread information and maintain more autonomy over the movement's narrative.[16] Thus, hashtag activism is often considered a **counterpublic** or **subaltern counterpublic** – discursive communities consisting of marginalized peoples that develop in parallel to the dominant, hegemonic, public sphere.[17]

## Social Movement Coalitions in the Age of Social Media

Since hashtags facilitate macro-level conversations across social media platforms, the counterpublics created through hashtag activism can transcend a singular geographic location, creating transnational coalitions within and between social movements.[18] **Social movement coalitions** occur when two or more distinct activist organizations work together toward a common goal.[19] Coalitions can be both *within-movement*, meaning activist groups organized around the same issue(s) form a coalition, and *cross-movement*, meaning activist groups organized around different issue(s) form a coalition.[20] Social movement coalitions can also have temporal dimensions; coalitions can be short-lived, taking the form of a singular event, or long-term, resulting in long-term alliances.[21]

Previous research has identified five factors that often facilitate coalition-building between organizations.[22] First, research has found that organizations with a shared culture, identity, ideological orientations, and goals are more likely to form coalitions.[23] Conversely, conflicting ideological orientations can impede coalition-building.[24] Second, organizational characteristics such as scope and structure can help influence the formation of coalitions. Groups with clear organizational structures, leadership, and division of labor can often facilitate coalitions.[25] Additionally, multi-issue organizations with broader goals can often facilitate coalitions by bringing together seemingly disparate social movements.[26] Third, drawing on political opportunity theory, research has shown that political opportunities, such as increased legislation toward an organization's goals, can facilitate coalition-building by spurring high levels of mobilization within movements. To an even greater extent, research has shown that political threats to activists' goals, such as the passing of legislation that impedes an organization's goals, can facilitate coalition-building within and across movements.[27] Fourth, a history of social ties and interactions between movements, in the form of "brokers" or "bridge builders" – individuals with membership in multiple social movements – can help facilitate trust, organizational understanding, and communication between these different movements helping set the conditions for successful coalition-building.[28] Fifth, because organizations often compete for resources, in times of scarcity organizations are often less likely to form coalitions, to conserve resources.[29] Research has found the presence of two or more of these factors, under the right conditions, can lead to "successful" coalitions, which Staggenborg argues can be measured in terms of the coalition getting off the ground, goals, and longevity.[30]

Before the development of the internet and information and communications technologies (ICTs), social movement theorists argued that geographical and spatial isolation often left few opportunities for transnational coalition-building due to the lack of "free space" for organizing and coordination.[31] However, the advent of internet-based technologies have created new digital spaces through which organizations can create channels of communication, recognize common goals, develop shared ties, and pool resources.[32] This has led to the development of what Matsilele et al. term **transnational alternative public spheres**, transnationally mediated counterpublic spaces in which geographically disparate individuals, communities, and organizations come together through similarly aligned goals.[33] These alternative public spheres created through social media may be thought of as existing somewhere on a continuum between traditional social movement coalitions and what Tarrow terms "networks" – loose ties between organizations and movements that allow for the exchange of information with little collaborative action.[34] While Tarrow distinguishes between coalitions and networks, I argue that in the digital age, loose hashtag networks can turn into purposeful online and offline actions.

## Transnational Coalitions and the Case of #EndSARS

In the rest of this chapter, I explore these dynamics of hashtag activism and social movement coalition-building through the specific case of the End SARS movement in Nigeria. The End SARS movement was started on Twitter in 2017 by young Nigerians to publicly document the abuses they faced at the hands of SARS and to bring national and global awareness to the unit's decades of corruption, abuses, and brutality.[35] In the following sections, I look at how supporters of End SARS during its resurgence in 2020 used social media, particularly Twitter, to form coalitions within the BLM movement focused on issues of police brutality, human rights, and racial justice. First, I recount the parallel histories that shaped the BLM movement in the United States and the End SARS movement in Nigeria, leading to similar political threats and opportunities, movement goals, and organizational characteristics. I then analyze tweets that rhetorically linked the End SARS movement and the BLM movement in the 48 hours following the Lekki Toll Gate Massacre to explicate the discursive strategies End SARS supporters used to engage in coalition-building with the BLM movement.

### A Shared Ideological Foundation: Parallel Movements against Police Brutality in the United States and Nigeria

Historically, both the United States and Nigeria established policing institutions that systematically discriminated against and oppressed vulnerable populations within each respective country, targeting these communities through police brutality, defined as undue violence and excessive force towards citizenry by police, and extrajudicial killing, the unlawful killing of citizens by governmental institutions.[36] Thus, despite their different historical and cultural contexts, a parallel political threat of civil and human rights abuses set the stage for a common goal between #EndSARS in Nigeria and the larger #BlackLivesMatter movement in the United States.

### American Chattel Slavery, US Policing, and the Legacy of White Supremacy

In the United States, the development of policing was directly related to racialization and the development of White supremacist ideology. As Brucato argues, despite Eurocentric narratives that suggest US policing began with the importation of the London Metropolitan Police Service model of policing into Boston and other northern cities in the 1800s, within the social and political context of the United States, many early policing forces were created to establish and maintain the subordinate position of Black people as chattel slaves.[37] Brucato points to slave codes enacted in southern states in the mid-17th and early 18th century, such as the 1705 Act in Virginia, which established chattel slaves as specifically *non-White* servants, and gave any White southerners the legal right to burn, mutilate, and dismember chattel slaves as punishment for their crimes, to illustrate the simultaneous legal codification of racialized chattel slavery, White citizenship, and systems of policing. To maintain this system of racialized order, slave patrols were developed in the southern states to help enslavers maintain physical control over their Black chattel slaves, and any White male could be conscripted into these patrols to help suppress slave rebellions.[38] These slave patrols became further defined and regulated through increased legislation, such as the South Carolina Slave Code of 1740, which established official policing patrols (previously patrolmen were drawn from state militia), districts of jurisdiction, and beats – further codifying these slave patrols as official institutions.[39]

Following the Civil War and the legal end of American slavery, increased concern around now formerly enslaved people led to waves of suppression and extrajudicial violence against Black populations.[40] Acts of violence and repression swept Black southern communities through domestic terror groups such as the Ku Klux Klan, who burned down Black homes and businesses and lynched Black people who did not "know their place." Police were often complicit in these acts of terror – knowingly ignoring these instances of violence, participating in these extrajudicial crimes, or releasing Black prisoners into the hands of waiting White mobs.[41] These continued acts of violence against Black citizens by police, even after the end of slavery, illustrate how White supremacy as an ideology continues to be deeply embedded into policing as an institution within the United States. As Texeria notes, these biases are not just the consequences of individual bias, but are systemically institutionalized into US police forces through formal and informal policing policies.[42]

### "Black Witnessing" and the Rise of #BlackLivesMatter

Today, the proliferation of ICTs and smartphones allows citizens to record and share instances of police brutality against Black Americans. As Alissa Richardson notes, these instances of "Black witnessing" allow Black people to engage in sousveillance, recording evidence of police brutality, which can then be spread online to call attention to the way policing institutions in the United States uphold systems of White supremacy. Though recordings of anti-Black police brutality existed before the advent of smartphones, the proliferation of these technologies in conjunction with the non-official media channel of hashtag activism has engendered anti-racist advocates to control the narrative around these incidents.[43] Indeed, two key instances of Black witnessing activated the BLM movement on social media.

The BLM movement was initially founded in 2013 by three Black women, Alicia Garza, Patrice Cullors, and Opal Tometi, in response to the acquittal of George Zimmerman, a neighborhood watch volunteer in Sanford, Florida who fatally shot Trayvon Martin, a then 17-year-old Black boy.[44] Yet it was the police murder of unarmed Black men across the United States, specifically a photo documenting the 2015 shooting of 18-year-old Michael Brown in Ferguson, Missouri, that launched an international movement spurred, in large part, by social media.[45] Images and videos of these killings of unarmed Black people by police sparked protests both on and offline, leading to the rise of an international social movement.

### The NFP and the Enforcement of State Power

The End SARS movement drew upon this history of police abuses and movements for police accountability in the United States to highlight similar conditions in its own country.

The history of policing in Nigeria can similarly be traced back to the protection of state and colonial power. As early as 1861, as the British Army colonized new ethnicities and territories within Nigeria, it would establish police forces in the area to maintain order and prevent crime. These police forces often used violence and oppression as a way of suppressing indigenous populations and helping to seed colonial rule throughout the region. Thus, colonial police forces "behaved as 'army of occupation,' killing and maiming, and looting."[46] Thus, as in the United States, police in Nigeria acted in the protection of the government and colonial interests, not the people.

Following the end of colonial rule in the 1960s, a series of successive constitutions called for the establishment of a Nigerian Police Force. The modern-day NPF was established by the 1999 Constitution, which called for the creation of a centralized federal policing and prison service, funded and managed by the Federal Ministry of Police Affairs, which oversees the country's 36 states.[47] The NFP also acts in accordance with the Police Act, which outlines officers' primary duties, among them: to obey and enforce the law, detect and prevent crime, and protect human lives and property.[48] While these guidelines are meant to create transparency and stop police officers from abusing their power, post-colonial Nigeria's social and political conditions have often hindered these efforts. As Ake notes, despite political independence, "the character of the state remained much as it was in the colonial era," based on centralized state structures aimed at maintaining dominance over indigenous and subordinate populations.[49] As a result, the NFP has remained an institution of control in Nigeria, aiding government officials and elites in maintaining political and economic power.[50] Additionally, due to low pay, poor working conditions, and lack of training, the NFP officers are often ill-equipped to fulfill their duty of protecting the people.[51] These social, political, and economic factors have resulted in NFP officers bribing, harassing, and violently targeting common, everyday people – especially youths and those of a lower socio-economic class – as they are seen as having the least access to legal recourse.[52]

*The Globalization of #EndSARS*

It is within this structural context of the NFP that SARS was created. SARS was established in 1992 in the Nigerian southwestern states to counter armed robbery and kidnapping.[53] The unit has often been charged with engaging in extortion, police brutality, and extrajudicial violence. According to a field report conducted by Amnesty International, from 2017 to 2019, SARS officers have engaged in a pattern of abuses against the citizenry, including the inhumane and violent treatment of those in SARS custody, bribery, extortion, and the targeting of younger citizens (aged 17–30) and journalists. In 2018, in response to the initial wave of End SARS protests in 2017, Nigerian Vice President Yemi Osinbajo called for immediate reform of SARS and directed the National Human Rights Council to set up a judicial panel to investigate allegations of SARS officers' illegal activities. This resulted in a name change from Special Anti-Robbery Squad (SARS) to the new Federal Special Anti-Robbery Squad (FSARS), with the appointment of high-ranking officials to oversee the refurbished police unit. However, research has shown that despite these reforms, SARS officers continued to engage in the torture and extrajudicial killings of those in their custody. Thus, the resurgence of the #EndSARS movement in late 2020 developed in reaction to these continually failed promises to curb violence on the part of SARS.

### Hashtag Coalition-Building from #EndSARS to #BLM

Previous studies show that End SARS protestors drew on their shared socio-political focus and ideological orientation with the BLM movement throughout the protest. Like Black Lives Matter activists, End SARS protestors shared stories, pictures, and videos of police abuses on social media, particularly Twitter, as a form of sousveillance to draw attention to instances of police brutality.[54] In their study of millennial activist posts during the End SARS protests in 2020, Adibade, Olyaoku, and Herro found that social media posts focused on issues of police brutality and the need for police reform, and leveraged diasporic connections across the UK – at times drawing on the rhetoric of #BLM – to garner international support. In this way, the End SARS movement drew on its shared ideology, identity, culture, and goals with the BLM movement to create a broader coalition and networks of support.[55]

In addition to a shared ideological foundation, the End SARS and the BLM movements had similar organizational characteristics. As Nwakanma argues, both movements were informed by Black and Afrofeminist thought, and drew on the intersectional dimensions of police brutality, creating a common political and ideological orientation.[56] Both

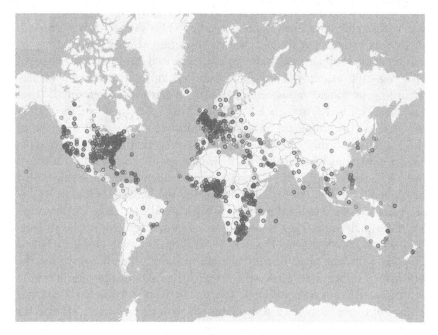

FIGURE 8.1    #EndSARS, #BlackLivesMatter, and #BLM tweet map

movements also relied on decentralized network structures instead of hierarchical or centralized leadership.[57] While classic social movement theory may suggest the decentralized nature of these organizations would impede the facilitation of coalition-building, in this case, I contend that the parallel decentralized structure of these networks fed into a common ideological orientation toward egalitarian, communalist, and Black feminist ideals.

To further explore how the End SARS movement used hashtag activism to achieve this goal, I analyze tweets that aimed to rhetorically link the End SARS movement and the BLM movement in the 48 hours following the Lekki Toll Gate Massacre, by including the hashtags #EndSARS and #BlackLivesMatter or #EndSARS and #BLM. I chose this moment because it was a significant turning point in the movement and represented an important moment of political threat that would potentially prompt End SARS activists to engage in coalition and network-building around their cause. Tweets were collected using the Twitter API. A map of the tweets collected shows that tweets mentioning #EndSARS and #BlackLivesMatter or #EndSARS and #BLM, while mainly sent from the United States and western Africa where these two movements began, also originated from other regions around the world, including Europe, the Middle East and North Africa, South Asia, and Australia, highlighting the global solidarity mobilized around these movements through hashtag activism.[58]

Using the Python programming language, a random sample of tweets (10%) were selected to be coded using qualitative thematic coding. Findings suggest that End SARS supporters on Twitter used four main strategies to build a digital coalition with the BLM movement: (1) calls for reciprocal solidarity, (2) appealing to diasporic support for the protection of Black lives, (3) aligning their shared goal of combating police brutality, and (4) appealing to information opinion leaders.

### Calls for Reciprocal Solidarity

Many of the tweets linking #EndSARS and #BlackLivesMatter or #BLM expressed anger and frustration at the fact that Nigerians had vocally supported the BLM movement earlier in the summer, but did not feel similarly supported in their cause by BLM supporters and activists. Some tweets called out specific international and diplomatic leaders for their lack of support:

FIGURE 8.2   End SARS protest in Nigeria

> Any African Leader who tweeted about #BlackLivesMatter and failed to tweet about #EndSARS is a total hypocrite. #EndSARSImmediately #BuhariResignNow #BabaJideSanwoOluMustGo[59]

However, other tweets generally noted the lack of support for the End SARS movement from BLM protestors and activists, despite previous support they received from Nigerian citizens:

> Surprisingly the world stood by all black Americans during the #BlackLivesMatter protest. But we are barely seeing those people do same to support Nigerians. Even the black Americans themselves. The world is watching. #EndSARS #EndBadGoveranceInNigeria[60]
> Remember how we reacted to #BlackLivesMatter? Can we do the same for #endsars #BuhariResign #EndPoliceBrutality #UnfollowBuhari #OgbomosoProtest #SarsMustGo[61]
> y'all remember when george floyd was murdered the whole became one nd hashtags trended around the whole world #BlackLivesMatter #AllLivesMatter but now nigeria is bleeding no one really bothers that much #EndPoliceBrutalityinNigera #EndSARS we better than ths [sic].[62]
> WHERE ARE ALL YOU #BLM PEOPLE!!! MY COUNTRY NIGERIA IS SUFFERING AND YOUR SILENCE IS NOT COOL #EndSars #wenodoagain[63]

These tweets simultaneously point to the large numbers of people and movements that supported the Black Lives Matter movement after the murder of George Floyd and the corresponding lack of global support for the End SARS movement, which addressed similar issues. In this way, these tweets used a discourse of "reciprocal support" to call upon existing supporters of the BLM movement to lend their voice and support to the End SARS movement in a show of mutual solidarity and recognition of their common cause.

These tweets also call our attention to the fact that for End SARS activists, the success of the BLM movement signified a political opportunity. As End SARS protestor Oko Nya noted, "If some of us didn't see how Black Lives Matter protestors in America forced some local governments to defund their police departments, we wouldn't have believed it is possible for any action to be taken against the police."[64] Thus, by calling for mutual support, these tweets highlighted how the success of the BLM movement could be replicated (or fail to be replicated) through mutual support of the End SARS movement.

In comparison to these tweets expressing frustration and anger, a handful of tweets took the opposite approach, not *calling out*, but *calling in* existing BLM supporters:

This is the wrong time for y'all to be having Africans vs African American debates. WE ARE DYING ALL OVER THE WORLD! COME TOGETHER & EXPOSE THE TRUTH TO BRING JUSTICE & PEACE! Not throw hate at each other!! #EndSARS #FREECONGO #BLM!!!!!![65]

Nigeria is in flames and instead of raising awareness you people started #EndSARS vs #BLM oppression olympics. All while ignoring the fact that BLM is more popular because it has been a movement for years while EndSARS started two weeks ago. Please refocus[66]

Instead of showing frustration with BLM supporters for not being more supportive of the End SARS movement, these tweets called upon BLM supporters to recognize the commonalities between these two social movements. The second tweet, by someone who identified themself as a Nigerian-American in the United States, highlights how rhetorically calling on mutual support from BLM supporters could allow the End SARS movement to access and mobilize its large, pre-existing base of supporters. While the tweet mischaracterizes the End SARS movement as being only two weeks old, it highlights how social media allows disparately located causes to form generative cross-movement coalitions that enable less well-known social movements, such as End SARS, to tap into the larger network and resources of more high-profile movements, such as BLM.

## Diasporic Support for Black Lives

The second-largest contingent of tweets focused on the global dimensions of Black Lives Matter. These tweets highlighted the fact that a statement in affirmation of Black Lives should not only apply to the lives of Black Americans, but is rooted in a diasporic call for the protection of global Black Life:

#BlackLivesMatter is not just a UK or USA matter but is an issue and movement that extends globally. To know more #EndSARS and how you can support visit this website: https://t.co/EyudgDhERy[67]

Nigerians are also black lives !!#BlackLivesMatter #EndBadGoveranceInNigeria #ENDSARS[68]

You can't be #BlackLivesMatter and not be #EndSARS – advocacy for black and brown bodies is not based in geography[69]

Black Lives Matter means ALL BLACK lives matters..IT MIGHT NOT BE YOUR COUNTRY, BUT DON'T BE SILENT..#endsars #blm #PrayForAfrica[70]

These tweets call attention to the diasporic nature of the Black condition under systems of oppression. Despite the divergent way the Nigerian and US governments mobilized policing institutions to uphold systems of power, in both cases, legacies of Western colonization informed the continued, violent suppression of Black people. In one instance, legacies of European colonization led to the continued oppression of vulnerable indigenous Nigerian peoples, and in the other, legacies of colonization and White supremacy led to the internal colonization and violent brutalization of Black Americans. Therefore, in calling attention to these shared histories of Blackness, Twitter users rhetorically unveil how support for the BLM movement should necessitate support for the End SARS movement. In his writing on Black Twitter, an online community composed of a network of Black Twitter users who actively use the platform to discuss, perform, and negotiate collective understandings of "Blackness," communications studies scholar Andre Brock argues that digital Blackness is "not as a virtual identity but as an informational one – an identity powered by discourse, technology, and the phenomenology of embodiment in a white supremacist ideology."[71] Drawing on this argument, I suggest that supporters of the End SARS movement used hashtag activism to mobilize discourse of diasporic Blackness informed by overlapping histories of oppression, in turn creating an informational Black identify that linked the threats faced by Nigerians and Black Americans. Similarly, tweets also expanded this discourse of diasporic Blackness by pairing mentions of #EndSARS and #BlackLivesMatter/#BLM with hashtags that called attention to the violent oppression of people in other African nations, including #CongoleseLivesMatter, #CongoIsBleeding, #ZimbabweanLivesMatter, and ##AnglophoneCrisis, highlighting the ongoing violence against citizens in the Congo, Zimbabwe, and Cameroon. In this way, hashtag activism allowed End SARS supporters to claim a discursive global Black identity.

## Police Brutality

Several tweets also noted the End SARS and BLM movements' shared goal of addressing issues of police brutality and extrajudicial killing. Many of these tweets came from End SARS supporters outside Nigeria, who used their network's existing support for the BLM movement to try to mobilize similar support for the End SARS movement, as can be seen in the following tweets from users in Manchester, New Orleans, and London, respectively:

What is happening in Nigeria hurts my heart 💜 no matter where we are in this world we should be protected by our government and police

not brutally killed for speaking up! #BlackLivesMatter #EndSARS #EndPoliceBrutality #Nigeria #SarsMustGo #SARSMUSTENDNOW[72]
Americans we MUST SHARE #EndSARS like we do #BLM in the states! Police Brutality is a GLOBAL issue! Police Brutality impacts those in the African/Black Diaspora at a higher rate all over the WORLD! Raise awareness! This has to stop![73]
Police Brutality has no colour. #EndSARS #BlackLivesMatter #blackTuesdayNigeria

Additionally, in a less explicit fashion, other tweets highlighted this shared goal by also using hashtags that referenced police brutality:

Stay strong and keep fighting our brothers and sisters NGNGNG 💚😔 we stand together with you in these trying times 💚 #EndSARS #EndPoliceBrutalityinNigeraNOW #LekkiMassacre #LekkitollgateMassacre #BlackLivesMatter #StopKillingNigerianYouth[74] #endsars #endpolicebrutality #blacklivesmatter #period

Additionally, some tweets also invoked the hashtags of other social movements addressing the issue of human rights and police brutality to create an even larger network of cross-movement support:

#EndSARS
#MilkTeaAlliance
#DefundThePolice
#HongKongProtests
#StandWithThailand
#EndPoliceBrutality
#JusticeForCameroon
#ZimbabweanLivesMatter
#BlackLivesMatter 🐾
#PrayForPhilippines
#DeLaMingaAlParo2020[75]

In this way, End SARS supporters used the linking and indexing functions of hashtags to link these movements to the underlying issue of police brutality, to mobilize a broader coalition of social movements with similar motivations.

### Appealing to Information Opinion Leaders

Finally, the last main context in which these hashtags were linked was in tweets appealing to opinion leaders such as celebrities, politicians, and media outlets to help bring increased awareness to the End SARS movement. As previous research on the End SARS movement has shown, a key strategy of youth activists on the ground was tweeting at celebrities or hashtagging their names on Twitter, urging them to tweet about their cause (eg Adibade, Olyaoku and Herro). These tweets were not only directed at Nigerian celebrities, such as the singers Burna Boy, WizKid, and Davido, but also at many Black American and British celebrities who had previously publicly supported the BLM movement:

> @BigSean When BIGGER NATIONS faces Police BRUTALITY, the whole world STANDS UP for them and that caused #blacklivesmatter WORLDWIDE. Today, NIGERIA is in CRISIS and we need our VOICES to be AMPLIFIED more than ever before. We're fighting not just against #endsars but good government[76]
>
> @ManUtd [Manchester United] Pls your fans are dying here in Nigeria. Most of us where unable to watch today's fixture due to the killing of the youth #Lekkitollgate 🖐️🖐️🖐️join us as we plead to #EndSARS and #EndBuhari pls save #BlackLivesMatter @paulpogba @B_Fernandes8 @D_DeGea @ManUtd[77]
>
> @LewisHamilton you've been an active voice for the #BlackLivesMatter We need your voice for the #EndSARS #EndPoliceBrutality movement in Nigeria Now. Speak up. Your voice matters[78]
>
> Beyoncé literally constructed an entire website for the #BLM movement. But all of a sudden she believes speaking up on social media about #endsars is not that important. After profiting off of Nigeria earlier this year … yeahhh her publicist could've stayed silent 😔😔[79]

The mention of Black American rappers Big Sean and Wale, players on the British soccer team Manchester United, Black British race car driver Lewis Hamilton, and Black American singer Beyoncé called on these celebrities of the Black diaspora to spread information and bring greater awareness to the End SARS movement. Again, these tweets drew on calls for reciprocal solidarity, noting how many of these celebrities' previous support for the BLM movement should translate to network-building with the End SARS movement.

Many tweets also used this same strategy to call on political figures in other countries and the larger international community to help strengthen the force of their cause. For example, tweets addressed to former US President Barack Obama, Queen Elizabeth, and governing bodies such as the United Nations Human Rights Watch and the World Health Organization called on these leaders and international governing bodies that had previously been vocal about the BLM movement to aid their cause:

Coming from a former president that endorsed #BuhariHasBeenABadBoy in 2015 and has not said one single thing about #Badgovernment in Nigeria. Same energy you kept for #BLM should transfer @BarackObama #end-sars #FakeNews #WhereIsBuhari[80]

@UNWatch please intervene in the present situation going on in my goddamn country ♥NG♥ so many lives lost today due to the bad governance which the youths are protesting #EndSARS #StopNigeriaGovernment     #BlackTuesday     #BuhariResignNow #BlackLivesMatter[81]

@HQNigerianArmy unarmed Nigeria youths are been shot dead @ lekkitollgate for fighting for their lives and future ... Nigerian army you all disgusting and shameless slaves ... #EndSARS #UnitedNationsHelp #unarmed #UnitedKingdomListing #QueenElizabeth #HumanRights #WYO #WHO #BLM #CNN[82]

These tweets to political and international leaders often urged them to pressure Nigerian President Muhammadu Buhari by calling him out for human rights abuses.

Finally, many tweets directly addressed international news and media outlets, calling them out for their lack of coverage of the End SARS movement, while also providing them with protest information and sousveillance video coverage of Nigerian police and armies killing peaceful protestors, to gain increased coverage of the situation on the ground:

@BBCNews @BBCWorld @BBCBreaking a lot of people are being hurt/ dying in Nigeria and Congo it would be nice if you guys spoke on the situation and make everyone aware #BlackLivesMatter #EndSARS[83]

@SkyNews Peaceful protesters in Nigeria are being brutalized by the Nigeria police and the international community isn't giving it attention like they did to #BlackLivesMatter 🙏 ... 🇳🇬Our lives matter in Nigeria too 🇳🇬#EndSARS[84]

@UN @CNN @AJENews @BBCBreaking #BlackLivesMatter #EndSARS #basedonwhat live shooting at protester at Lekki toll gate[85]

End SARS supporters used the non-institutionalized means of communication offered by social media to both shape the narrative around the movement and to provide information to international media outlets about the situation on the ground. Activists used Twitter to circumvent state and institutionalized media channels that failed to report on or suppressed information about the protests, and used hashtag activism to shape and provide key information about their movement to build transnational coalitions with other organizations supporting human rights and against police brutality.

## Conclusion

In an interview with *Vogue Magazine* published the day before the Lekki Toll Gate Massacre, BLM co-founder Nigerian-American Opal Tometi noted, "The imagery and the rallying cries are so incredibly similar because the issues are connected: poor governance; poverty; injustice in every system, from health care to high unemployment rates to the criminalization of poor people."[86] As Tometi calls our attention to, the parallels between the End SARS movement in Nigeria and the BLM movement in the United States are clear – both movements were spurred by a similar threats of police brutality and extrajudicial killing against a historically socially and politically marginalized population to uphold systems of power rooted in Western colonization. As such, both movements were, in their own historical and cultural context, motivated by the goal of addressing a long history of police brutality and extrajudicial.

In this chapter, I examined how social media discourse rhetorically facilitated these coalition-building efforts by analyzing tweets that mentioned both #EndSARS and #BLM or #BlackLivesMatter in the 48 hours following the Lekki Toll Gate Massacre. Findings suggest that these tweets often used calls for reciprocal solidarity between these movements, discursive constructions of diasporic Blackness, mentions of a shared goal of addressing police brutality, and appeals to media and opinion leaders to galvanize support from BLM movement activists and supporters for the End SARS movement. These strategies reveal how through linking and indexing functions of hashtag activism, End SARS protestors were strategically able to facilitate conditions for coalition-building – allowing them to tap into BLM's global network of activists and supporters and use non-institutionalized media to communicate and bring attention to what they were experiencing, making parallels to other activist movements faced with state-sanctioned violence. Additionally, drawing on the work of Andre Brock, I noted how within the context of hashtag activism, the coalition-building strategy of pulling on a shared culture or identity can take a discursive and informational form. In other words, hashtag activists can use tweets and other media to create a collective identity that draws in other culturally and geographically disparate movements.

Here, it is important to recognize that these two movements had key differences because of their varying cultural contexts. One difference was how these two organizations aimed to confront the issue of systemic police brutality. While in the United States the over-policing and surveillance of Black Americans led to calls to defund policing institutions, in Nigeria, where police brutality stemmed partly from bribery spurred on by poor payment of police, protestors called for better pay for NFP officers.[87] Additionally, in Nigeria and within the context of End SARS, policing institutions were not directly tied to upholding White supremacy; indeed, many tweets pointed to the fact that police brutality by SARS highlighted brutal intra-racial and ethnic violence. However, despite these disparate cultural contexts, recognizing a common goal between these movements was paramount in facilitating coalition-building that extended End SARS from a hyperlocal to a global protest.

Following the Lekki Toll Gate Massacre, the international community, especially Black people of the diaspora, increasingly rallied in response to the call to #EndSARS. In the months following the massacre, international protests in support of the End SARS movement took place internationally in cities such as Atlanta, London, Berlin, New York, and Dublin.[88] In response to calls to show support for the movement, in the hours following the massacre, Black American celebrities such as Beyoncé, singer Rihanna, and actress Gabrielle Union took to social media to post messages of support for protestors.[89] Also, in the months following the incident, high-profile BLM activists and celebrity supporters of the BLM movement, including singer Alicia Keys and actress Kerry Washington, wrote a letter to President Buhari urging him to free jailed protestors and ensure a fair and transparent investigation into the shooting of unarmed protestors.[90] Further, on a diplomatic level, a week after the massacre, during a previously planned US State Department delegation visit to Nigeria, State Department spokesman Morgan Ortagus said that during meetings in the US State Department, Counselor T. Ulrich Brechbühl "expressed the U.S. condemnation of the use of excessive force by military forces who fired on unarmed demonstrators in Lagos."[91] In this way, through intentionally building coalitions and networks with the BLM movement, End SARS activists were able to bring support, resources, and attention to their movement, both on and offline, in actionable and measurable ways.

### Reflections

As researchers and students continue to think about the role of social media in allowing hyperlocal protests to secure global support, it is important to consider:

- How has the advent of hashtag activism changed how we traditionally think about the dichotomy between transnational coalitions and networks?

- What new opportunities for global coalition-building are opened when we consider digital identities and cultures as informational?
- Are digital strategies of hashtag activism conducive to some forms of coalition-building over others (e.g., international versus national, cross-movement versus within-movement, short-term versus long-term)?.

## Notes

1 Abati, Reuben. "#EndSARS: Almost a revolution." *Premium Times*, October, 13, 2020. https://opinion.premiumtimesng.com/2020/10/13/endsars-almost-a-revolution-by-reuben-abati/. "End Sars: How Nigeria's anti-police brutality protests went global." BBC, October 17, 2020. https://www.bbc.com/news/world-africa-54575219.
2 Ibid.
3 "Nigeria: Killing of #EndSars protesters by the military must be investigated." Amnesty International, October, 21, 2020. https://www.amnesty.org/en/latest/news/2020/10/killing-of-endsars-protesters-by-the-military-must-be-investigated/.
4 Jones, Mayeni. "Black Lives Matter: Activists demand #EndSars protesters' release." BBC, December, 10, 2020. https://www.bbc.com/news/world-africa-55258074.
5 Boone, Anna. "One week in Minnesota." *Star Tribune*, June 3, 2020. https://www.startribune.com/george-floyd-death-ignited-protests-far-beyond-minneapolis-police-minnesota/569930771/.
6 Habermas, Jürgen. 1962/1989. *The Structural Transformation of the Public Sphere*. Cambridge, MA: MIT Press. Messina, Chris. "Groups for Twitter; or a proposal for Twitter tag channels." *Factory Joe*, August 25, 2007. https://factoryjoe.com/2007/08/25/groups-for-twitter-or-a-proposal-for-twitter-tag-channels/. Burns, Axel, and Jean Burgess. 2015. "Twitter hashtags from ad hoc to calculated publics," In Nathan Rumbukkana (ed.), *Hashtag Publics and the Power of Political Discursive Networks*, New York: Peter Lang, p. 16.
7 Ibid., p. 19. Burns, Axel, and Hallvard Moe. 2014. "Structural layers of communication on Twitter." In Axel Bruns, Merja Mahrt, Katrin Weller, Jean Burgess, and Cornelius Puschmann (eds.), *Twitter and Society*. New York: Peter Lang, pp. 17–19.
8 Bonilla, Yarimar, and Jonathan Rosa. "#Ferguson: Digital protest, hashtag ethnography, and the racial politics of social media in the United States." *American Ethnologist* 42, no.1 (2015): 4–17.
9 Goswami, Manash P. 2018. "Social media and hashtag activism." In Susmita Bala (ed.), *Liberty, Dignity and Change in Journalism*. New Delhi: Kanishka Publishers, p. 2. Jackson, Sarah, Moya Bailey, and Brooke Foucault Welles. 2020. *Hashtag Activism: Networks of Race and Gender Justice*. Cambridge, MA: MIT Press, p. xxvii.
10 Augenbraun, Eric. "Occupy Wall Street and the limits of spontaneous street protest." *The Guardian*, September, 29, 2011. https://www.theguardian.com/commentisfree/cifamerica/2011/sep/29/occupy-wall-street-protest.
11 Emma, Obiaso Uche. "The hashtag as a channel of international communication: A study of the #BringBackOurGirls hashtag." *Communication Panorama: African and Global Perspectives* 1, no. 1 (2015): 1–13. Dejmanee, Tisha, Zulfia Zaher, Samantha Rouech, and Michael J. Papa. "#MeToo;

#HimToo: Popular feminism and hashtag activism in the Kavanaugh hearings." *International Journal of Communication* 14 (2020): 3947–3948. Wang Rong, and Alvin Zhou. "Hashtag activism and connective action: A case study of #HongKongPoliceBrutality," *Telematics and Informatics* 61 (2021): 101600.

12 Zentgraf, Lea Loretta. "#EleNãoMeRepresenta [#HeDoesNotRepresentMe]: An international feminist strike." *FKW Magazine for Gender Research and Visual Culture* 70 (2022): 69–74.

13 Pinheiro-Machado, Rosana. "The far right won: Feminists, anti-racists and LGBTs too." *The Intercept Brazil*, January, 8, 2019. https://theintercept.com/2019/01/08/extrema-direita-feministas-antirracistas-lgbts/. Mussi, Daniella, and Alvaro Bianchi. "Rise of the radical right: Jair Bolsonaro's win in October's elections signals dark days ahead for the working class, women, Afro-Brazilians, the LGBTI community, and activists in Brazil. Can the left rebuild?" *NACLA Report on the Americas* 50, no. 4 (2018): 351–355.

14 Jackson, Bailey, and Welles, *Hashtag Activism*, p. xxvii.

15 Castells, Manuel. 2015. *Networks of Outrage and Hope: Social Movements in the Internet Age.* Malden, MA: Polity Press, p. 9.

16 Johnson, Hailey. "#NoDAPL: Social media, empowerment, and civic participation at Standing Rock." *Library Trends* 66, no. 2 (2017): 157. Jackson, Bailey, and Welles, *Hashtag Activism*, p. xxix.

17 Fraser, Nancy. "Rethinking the public sphere: A contribution to the critique of actually existing democracy." *Social Text* 25/26 (1990): 67. Warner, Michael. 2002. *Publics and Counterpublics.* Durham, NC: Duke University Press, pp. 56–57.

18 Moe and Burns, "Structural layers of communication on Twitter," pp. 17–18; Castells, *Networks of Outrage and Hope*, p. 6.

19 McCammon, Holly J., and Mingyung Moon. 2015. "Social movement coalitions." In Donatella Della Porta and Mario Diani (eds.), *The Oxford Handbook of Social Movement.* Oxford, UK: Oxford University Press, pp. 326–327. Gamson, William. 1975. *The Strategy of Social Protest.* Homewood, IL: Dors. Steedly, Homer, and John Foley. "The success of protest groups: Multivariate analyses." *Social Science Research* 8 (1979): 10.

20 McCammon and Moon, "Social movement coalitions," p. 327.

21 Levi, Margaret, and Gillian H. Murphy. "Coalitions of contention: The case of the WTO protests in Seattle." *Political Studies* 54, no. 4 (2006): 655.

22 McCammon and Moon, "Social movement coalitions," pp. 328–331. Van Dyke, Nella, and Bryan Amos. "Social movement coalitions: Formation, longevity, and success." *Sociology Compass* 11, no. 7 (2017): 3–8.

23 Bandy, Joe, and Jackie Smith. 2005. *Coalitions across Borders: Transnational Protest and the Neoliberal Order.* (Lanham, MD: Rowman & Littlefield, pp. 7–8; Di Gregorio, Monica. "Networking in environmental movement organisation coalitions: Interest, values or discourse?" *Environmental Politics* 21, no. 1 (2012): 19–20.

24 Lichterman, Paul. "Piecing together multicultural community: Cultural differences in community building among grassroots environmentalists." *Social Problems* 42, no. 4 (1995): 527.

25 Borland, Elizabeth. "Social movement organizations and coalitions: Comparisons from the women's movement in Buenos Aires, Argentina." *Research in Social Movements, Conflicts and Change* 28 (2008): 83–112.

26 Van Dyke, Nella. "Crossing movement boundaries: Factors that facilitate coalition protest by American college students, 1930–1990." *Social Problems* 50, no. 2 (2003): 240–242.

27 Staggenborg, Suzanne. "Coalition work in the pro-choice movement: Organizational and environmental opportunities and obstacles." *Social Problems* 33, no. 5 (1986): 380. McCammon, Holly J., and Karen E. Campbell. "Allies on the road to victory: Coalition formation between the Suffragists and the Woman's Christian Temperance Union." *Mobilization* 7, no. 3 (2002): 241.

28 Obach, Brian K. 2004. *Labor and the Environmental Movement: The Quest for Common Ground.* Cambridge, MA: MIT Press, pp. 5–6. Beamish, Thomas D., and Amy J. Luebbers. "Alliance building across social movements: Bridging difference in a peace and justice coalition." *Social Problems* 56, no. 4 (2009): 666–667.

29 Staggenborg, "Coalition work in the pro-choice movement." p. 386; Van Dyke, "Crossing movement boundaries," p. 242. Diaz-Veizades, Jeanette, and Edward. T Chang. "Building cross-cultural coalitions: A case-study of the Black-Korean alliance and the Latino-Black Roundtable." *Ethnic and Racial Studies* 19, no.3 (1996): 688.

30 Staggenborg, "Coalition work in the pro-choice movement," p. 374. Van Dyke and Amos, "Social movement coalitions," p. 3.

31 Bandy and Smith, *Coalitions across Borders*, p. 8.

32 Van Dyke and Amos, "Social movement coalitions," p. 3. Vicari, Stefania. "Networks of contention: The shape of online transnationalism in early twenty-first century social movement coalitions." *Social Movement Studies* 13, no.1 (2014): 95.

33 Matsilele, Trust, Shepherd Mpofu, Mbongeni Msimanga, and Lungile Tshuma. "Transnational hashtag protest movements and emancipatory politics in Africa: A three country study." *Global Media Journal – German Edition* 11, no. 2 (2022): 4.

34 Tarrow, Sidney. 2005. *The New Transnational Activism.* Cambridge, UK: Cambridge University Press, pp. 163–164.

35 Amnesty International. 2020. *Nigeria: Time to End Impunity Torture and Other Violations by Special Anti-Robbery Squad (SARS).* Ubuja, Nigeria: Amnesty International Nigeria, p. 3. Dambo, Tamar H., Metin Ersoy, Ahmad M. Auwal, Victoria O. Olorunsola, Ayodeji Olonode, Abdulgaffar O. Arikewuyo, and Ayodele Joseph. "Nigeria's #EndSARS movement and its implication on online protests in Africa's most populous country." *Journal of Public Affairs* 22, no. 3 (2020): 2.

36 Osuyi, Edo, and Sagay J. Oritsedere. "The Nigerian Police, extrajudicial killings and the dilemma of human security: A theoretical reflection." *Pakistan Journal of Social Sciences* 9, no. 3 (2012): 133. Nelson, J. 2000. *Police Brutality.* New York: W.W. Norton, pp. 9–11; Amnesty International. n.d. "Police violence." https://www.amnesty.org/en/what-we-do/police-brutality/. Nelson, *Police Brutality*, pp. 13–14. Abiodun, Temitope F., Adedokun O. Oloyede, Owoyemi E. Ademola, Ogechi Abah, and Opeyemi Segun Kehinde. "Unlawful killings of civilians by officers of the Special Anti-Robbery Squad (SARS) unit of the Nigerian Police in Southwest Nigeria: Implications for national security." *African Journal of Law, Political Research and Administration* 3, no. 1 (2020): 52–53.

37 Brucato, Ben. "Policing race and racing police: The origin of US police in slave patrols." *Social Justice* 47, nos. 3–4 (2020): 116–117.

38 Kelley, Robin D.G. 2000. "'Slangin' Rocks … Palestinian Style': Dispatches from the occupied zones of North America." In Jill Nelson (ed.), *Police Brutality*. New York: W.W. Norton, pp. 25–26; Brucato, "Policing race and racing police," pp. 124–129.

39 Ibid, p. 128.

40 Texeira, Mary Thierry. "Policing the internally colonized: Slavery, Rodney King, Mark Fuhrman and beyond." *Western Journal of Black Studies* 19, no. 4, (1995): 237. Kelley, "'Slangin' rocks,'" pp. 26–32.

41 Ibid., pp. 30–32.

42 Texeira, "Policing the internally colonized," p. 239.

43 Richardson, Alissa. 2020. *Bearing Witness: African Americans, Smartphones, and the New Protest #Journalism*. New York: Oxford University Press, pp. xiii–xiv.

44 Black Lives Matter n.d. "About." https://blacklivesmatter.com/about/. Alvarez, Lizette, and Cara Buckley. "Zimmerman is acquitted in Trayvon Martin killing." *New York Times*, July, 13, 2013. https://www.nytimes.com /2013/07/14/us/george-zimmerman-verdict-trayvon-martin.html.

45 Jackson, Bailey, and Welles, *Hashtag Activism*, pp. 124–125.

46 Alemika, Etannibi, and Innocent C. Chukwuma. 2005. *Analysis of Police and Policing in Nigeria*. Lagos, Nigeria: CLEEN Foundation, p. 8.

47 Alemika and Chukwuma, *Analysis of Police and Policing in Nigeria*, p. 9. Abiodun et al., "Unlawful killings of civilians by officers of the Special Anti-Robbery Squad (SARS) unit of the Nigerian Police in Southwest Nigeria," p. 51.

48 Police Act Cap P19 LFN 2004. Abiodun et al., "Unlawful killings of civilians by officers of the Special Anti-Robbery Squad (SARS) unit of the Nigerian Police in Southwest Nigeria," p. 51.

49 Ake, Claude. 1996. *Democracy and Development in Africa*. Washington, DC: Brookings Institute, p. 173. Osuyi and Oritsedere, "The Nigerian Police, extrajudicial killings and the dilemma of human security," p. 135.

50 Ibid.

51 Alemika and Chukwuma, *Analysis of police and policing in Nigeria*, p. 13; Abiodun et al., "Unlawful killings of civilians by officers of the Special Anti-Robbery Squad (SARS) unit of the Nigerian Police in Southwest Nigeria," p. 58.

52 Osuyi and Oritsedere, "The Nigerian police, extrajudicial killings and the dilemma of human security," pp. 136–137.

53 Nnadozie, Emma. "How I founded SARS in the Police–RTD CP Midenda," *Vanguard*, December, 23, 2017. https://www.vanguardngr.com/2017/12/ founded-sars-police-rtd-cp-midenda/.

54 Ekoh, Prince C., and Elizabeth O. George. "The role of digital technology in the EndSars protest in Nigeria during COVID-19 pandemic." *Journal of Human Rights and Social Work* 6, no. 2 (2021): 161–162. Ujene, Godspower, and Agatha Orji-Egwu. "Information Communication technology as a tool for social control: A study of Nigeria's #EndSars." *Journal of Human Capital* 11 (2019): 6–10.

55 Abimbade, Oluwadara, Phillip Olayoku, and Danielle Herro. "Millennial activism within Nigerian Twitterscape: From mobilization to social action of #ENDSARS protest." *Social Sciences & Humanities* 6, no. 1 (2022): 4–5.

56 Specter, Emma. "Opal Tometi on the ongoing fight against police brutality, from Nigeria to the U.S." *Vogue*, October, 19, 2020. https://www.vogue.com /article/opal-tometi-nigeria-protests-video-interview. Nwakanma, Adaugo P. "From Black Lives Matter to EndSARS: Women's socio-political power and

the transnational movement for Black Lives." *Perspectives on Politics* 20, no. 4 (2022): 4–8.

57 Olaoluwa, Azeezat. "End Sars protests: The Nigerian women leading the fight for change." BBC, December 1, 2020. https://www.bbc.com/news/world-africa-55104025. Adibade, Olayoku and Herro, "Millennial activism within Nigerian Twitterscape," p. 6. Nwakanma, "From Black Lives Matter to EndSARS," p. 1.

58 Because Twitter allows user to decide whether to include location data on the tweets, the map in Figure 8.1 only includes tweets by users who turned on their location data at the time of tweeting.

59 Kwabena (@GilbertFofie1). Twitter, October 21, 2020. https://twitter.com/GilbertFofie1/status/1318722609815703553.

60 Frisky U (@iansuzir). Twitter, October 21, 2020. https://twitter.com/iansuzir/status/1318826313021620226.

61 Mellisa.mngomezulu (@CarlMellisa). Twitter, October 21, 2020. https://twitter.com/CarlMellisa/status/1318996866093273090.

62 Shmood bw Ȱ(@orenstama_Bw). Twitter, October 21, 2020. https://twitter.com/orenstama_Bw/status/1318780189858537472.

63 NAIJA BOI (@MANLIKENAIJA). Twitter, October 21, 2020. https://twitter.com/MANLIKENAIJA/status/1318730725848395777.

64 Obaji, Phillip. "Nigeria's #EndSARS protesters draw inspiration from Black Lives Matter movement." *USA Today*, October 26, 2020. https://www.usatoday.com/story/news/world/2020/10/26/nigerias-endsars-protesters-draw-inspiration-black-lives-matter/6044452002/.

65 Ceez (@CeezMaraj). Twitter, October 21, 2020. https://twitter.com/CeezMaraj/status/1318871838563454977.

66 Osaceles Triangle ▲(@ThtNigerianKid). Twitter, October 21, 2020. https://twitter.com/ThtNigerianKid/status/1319012141509246978.

67 Glitch (@GlitchUK_). Twitter, October 21, 2020. https://twitter.com/GlitchUK_/status/1318975181436715010.

68 Princess🏰🦋(@iamborteley). Twitter, October 21, 2020. https://twitter.com/iamborteley/status/1318668426219540480.

69 The Dude Lurch© (@TheDoodleLurch). Twitter, October 21, 2020. https://twitter.com/TheDoodleLurch/status/1319032855541010432

70 … JACKSON (@jacksonakim67_). Twitter, October, 21, 2020. https://twitter.com/jacksonakim67_/status/1318951052142673923.

71 Brock, Andre. 2020. *Distributed Blackness: African American Cybercultures.* New York: New York University Press, p. 37.

72 Cassandra Snowden (@Cassie_Snowden). Twitter, October 21, 2020. https://twitter.com/Cassie_Snowden/status/1318843125381693440.

73 Bre Loc'DBooktician 📖🍱⚜ (@dbooktician). Twitter, October 20, 2020. https://twitter.com/dbooktician/status/1318701115223855110.

74 Just Jess (@Jessie_Mthethwa). Twitter, October 21, 2020. https://twitter.com/gossip_girl_tea/status/1318831055907028992.

75 Mekhla (@MekhlaRai). Twitter, October 21, 2020. https://twitter.com/MekhlaRai/status/1318823776008704001.

76 FAITH (@NigeriaYouthM). Twitter, October 20, 2020. https://twitter.com/NigeriaYouthM/status/1318719154107678720.

77 Ife Jehoshaphat (@ife_jehoshaphat). Twitter, October 20, 2020. https://twitter.com/ife_jehoshaphat/status/1318689072890642438.

78 Tobby (@AlabedeTobi). Twitter, October 21, 2020. https://twitter.com/AlabedeTobi/status/1318841500084699136.

79  Chi Daddy (@Dinmaaa). Twitter, October 20, 2020. https://twitter.com/ Dinmaaa/status/1318757932784361472.
80  Mrs. Velli (@dat_sass). Twitter, October 21, 2020. https://twitter.com/dat _sass/status/1319070903011930112.
81  Ogbablogger (@nigababa18). Twitter, October 20, 2020. https://twitter.com/ nigababa18/status/1318687149596737536.
82  Kimanif@fireboi (@FireVanquisher). Twitter, October 20, 2020. https://twit-ter.com/FireVanquisher/status/1318664018857426945
83  Alpha (@_angxlicca). Twitter, October 21, 2020. https://twitter.com/_angx-licca/status/1318870224205189121.
84  GET YOUR VOTERS CARD #OBIdiently! (@RaphChima). Twitter, October 21, 2020. https://twitter.com/RaphChima/status/1319019060391256065.
85  Odumade Adetayo (@phemmiestrings). Twitter, October 20, 2020. https:// twitter.com/phemmiestrings/status/1318638991139344388.
86  Specter, "Opal Tometi on the ongoing fight against police brutality."
87  Nwakanma, "From Black Lives Matter to EndSARS," p. 8.
88  Lawal, Shola, and Adenike Olanrewaju. "Nigerians demand end to police squad known for brutalizing the young." *New York Times*, October 21, 2020. https://www.nytimes.com/2020/10/12/world/africa/nigeria-protests -police-sars.html. Iwuoha, Victor C., and Ernest T Aniche. "Protests and blood on the streets: Repressive state, police brutality and #EndSARS protest in Nigeria." *Security Journal* 35 (2021): 1102–1124.
89  Ryu, Jenna. "What is the #EndSARS movement in Nigeria? See why Beyoncé, Rihanna and more are speaking up." *USA Today*, October, 21, 2022. https:// www.usatoday.com/story/entertainment/celebrities/2020/10/21/end-sars -celebrities-address-police-brutality-nigeria-beyonce-rihanna/6003436002/.
90  Jones, "Black Lives Matter."
91  US Mission in Nigeria. "Read-out: Counselor Brechbühl's meeting with Nigerian Vice President Osinbajo." U.S. Embassy and Consulate in Nigeria, October, 22, 2020. https://ng.usembassy.gov/read-out-counselor-brechbuhls -meeting-with-nigerian-vice-president-osinbajo/.

# ADVOCATES FOR ACTION

## Aki Kurose

1925–1988
Hometown: Seattle, Washington, USA
Movements: Pacifism
Organizations: American Friends Service Committee, Congress of Racial
  Equality, and young Women's Christian Association
*Elizabeth Wilson and Allison De Young*

Aki Kurose was born Akiko Kato to Japanese immigrant parents in
Seattle, Washington State, USA. Kurose had a happy childhood and
grew up in a diverse neighborhood, making her comfortable around people from different backgrounds. Her parents also made sure to emphasize pacifist teachings and being inclusive in the friendships she made,
and together, she and her family would celebrate holidays from different cultures. Her life changed in 1941 when the Japanese bombed Pearl
Harbor, and like many Japanese-Americans, she was soon faced with
racist abuse from peers and had to move to an internment camp at the
Puyallup Fairgrounds, and later to the Minidoka internment camp in
Idaho.[1] Despite these abuses she faced after the bombing of Pearl Harbor,
Kurose remained dedicated to her pacifist teachings and fighting for
peace through justice.

In the 1960s, Kurose joined the Congress of Racial Equality to help
desegregate schools, housing, and construction unions, and eliminate
employment discrimination. She also helped bring the first Head Start
Program in Washington State, where she discovered her passion for
teaching kids.[2] After earning her bachelor's degree in Sociology in 1972,

DOI: 10.4324/9781003291855-20

Kurose began to teach at elementary schools for the Seattle Public School System. In the mid-1970s, the Seattle Public School System desegregated its schools, and Kurose was moved to a predominantly White elementary school where she faced questioning from parents and other educators about her qualifications to teach.[1] Rather than matching the hostile attitudes, Kurose used her pacifist upbringing to communicate and resolve conflicts. One angry parent said, "You know, the only reason you have this job is because you're a minority ... I don't think you're a good teacher at all."[3] She also recalled an exchange with a fellow teacher, when the person asked:

> "What are you?" And I said, "What do you mean, what am I?" And she says, "Well, who are you?"' And I said, "I'm Aki Kurose." And she said, "Well, what are you?" And I said, "I'm a teacher." And she said, "Where did you come from?" And I said, "From Madrona." And she was getting furious with me, and she said, "No. You know what I mean, where did you come from?" So I said, "Oh, Martin Luther King School." And she said, "I'm asking you where you came from?" So I said, "Are you trying to ask my ethnicity?" I said, "I told you I'm from Madrona, I told you I'm from Martin Luther King School, you know ... and you're still asking me where I came from." And she said, "Oh." And I said, "Are you wondering whether I'm Japanese, or Chinese? Well, I'm Japanese American." And she said, "Oh." And she walked away.[4]

Throughout her years teaching, Kurose won numerous awards and much recognition for "her passion for teaching science and its usefulness for teaching children about the world in a non-sexist, multicultural way."[5] When she retired, the elementary school she worked at and its parents dedicated a peace garden to her, and after she died in 1998, spaces, scholarships, and awards continued to be named after her to honor her work. Today, her legacy is still honored by having a middle school, the Aki Kurose Middle School Academy, named after her, with its mascot being the Peace Cranes.[6]

## Notes

1 Nomura, Gail M. "'Peace empowers': The testimony of Aki Kurose, a woman of color in the Pacific Northwest." *Frontiers: A Journal of Women Studies* 22, no. 3 (2001): 75–92.
2 Macdonald, Moira. "Aki Kurose (1925–1998)." *Seattle Times*, March 5, 2010. https://www.seattletimes.com/life/women-who-ran-seattle-aki-kurose -believed-that-peace-cant-come-without-justice/.

3 Nomura, Gail M. "'Peace empowers': The testimony of Aki Kurose, a woman of color in the Pacific Northwest." *Frontiers: A Journal of Women Studies* 22, no. 3 (2001): 75–92.
4 Ibid, p.82.
5 SEAneighborhoods. "AAPI Heritage Month: Aki Kurose." Front Porch: Seattle Department of Neighborhoods. May 10, 2021. https://frontporch .seattle.gov/2021/05/10/aapi-heritage-month-aki-kurose/.
6 Ott, Jennifer. "Women who ran Seattle: Aki Kurose believed that 'peace can't come without justice.'" HistoryLink, March 10, 2022. https://www .historylink.org/File/9339.

# 9

# LEADERLESS REBELLIONS

## An Analysis of Digital Feminist Anti-Violence Activism

*Leandra Hernández and Stevie M. Munz*

## Introduction

The past several years have witnessed a firestorm of activism and protests in relation to racial violence, gendered violence, and outright cultural and social unrest. Within a racial violence and gendered violence context, transnational and parallel protests have sought to counteract and combat anti-abortion legislation, the murdering of Brown and Black bodies, the incarceration of women in reproductive contexts, and lack of action in response to missing and murdered indigenous women (MMIW) and individuals. For example, around the same time that anti-femicide Ni Una Menos (NUM) protests were occurring across Latin America, abortion rights activists organized in Ireland and Poland, and American activists marched and organized in response to the murder of George Floyd and other Black individuals.

Most recently, at the time of writing of this chapter, reproductive rights activists organized across the United States in reaction to the Supreme Court's overturning of *Roe v. Wade*. Put simply, there has been no shortage of both national and international activism and organizing over the past several years. Historically, organizing methods for protests and activism have evolved, given technological advancements through WhatsApp, SMS text messaging, and social media websites. Such technological modalities have led to the rise of "leaderless rebellions," horizontal networks facilitated by new technologies that are based on the direct engagement of citizens and bottom-up organizing through social media and phone methods, as opposed to the hierarchical model of organizational, bureaucratic

DOI: 10.4324/9781003291855-21

politics. In other words, leaderless rebellions or networks focus on "building relationships and forging solidarity rather than simply providing information."[1] They are not represented by a "longstanding revolutionary figurehead, traditional opposition leader, or charismatic speechmaker to radicalize the public."[2] This chapter focuses on two leaderless rebellions in particular – anti-femicide organizing and MMIW organizing – to explore the ways in which both movements utilize social media channels and other modalities to engage in feminist anti-violence solidarity and to organize across state and country lines.

We selected these two leaderless rebellions because of our own positionalities, research interests, and community outreach efforts. Leandra, for example, is a queer Mexican-American woman who has published widely on anti-femicide activism and organizing in digital and reproductive justice contexts.[3] Moreover, as a reproductive justice activist and outdoor enthusiast, she blends her passions for both contexts by serving as a co-organizer and board member for two local organizations that seek to empower queer communities and communities of color in the outdoors. She also connects students and community members to justice-related organizations. For example, she facilitated a community event for queer climbers and climbers of color that raised funds for the Utah Abortion Fund in the wake of the overturning of *Roe v. Wade*. Together, Leandra and Stevie engage in feminist-guided pedagogy and mentorship. As a feminist activist scholar, Stevie engages in social justice research that examines how folks narrate minorized identity experiences. Her interests in advocacy draw her to connect with students to host and present critical art-based installation events on topics on campus. Thus, through an analysis of anti-femicide organizing and MMIW organizing, this chapter explores the following questions:

1) Is it possible to use digital activism to maintain a strong agenda without a leader?
2) What happens when efforts become less nebulous and more formalized/organized?
3) How do such efforts impact activist organizing outcomes?

## Digital Assemblies, Violence against Women, and Anti-Violence Activism

In what follows, we examine two cases to explore digital feminist anti-violence activism. The first case study, "Ni Una Menos and Anti-Feminicide Organizing," highlights the organizing to address the gendered violence committed against Mexican and Latin American women. Secondly, we present "Missing Murdered Indigenous Women," a social media activist movement that draws attention to the high rates of murdered, missing, and indigenous women across the United States and Canada. Together, both case studies draw attention to the systemic gendered violence (and the motivators) against women internationally.

### Case Study 1: Ni Una Menos and Anti-Feminicide Organizing

The term **femicide** was created in 1976 when Diana Russell, a feminist advocate and sociologist, testified about the mass murdering of and violence against women at the International Tribunal on Crimes Against Women. The term later became more popularized in public discourse in 1992, when Diana Russell and scholar Jill Radford operationalized the term as "the misogynistic killing of women by men."[4] Later, in 2001, Russell and Radford revised the term and defined it as "the killing of females by males because they are females,"[5] thus highlighting the gendered nature of the violence committed against women and the purpose and motives underlying the violent acts. Their reconceptualization of the term and phenomenon is significant because it highlights the uneven power relations and the driving force of male power and domination over women.[6] As Hernández and De Los Santos Upton note, however:

> While Russell's terminological trajectory has indeed inspired decades of research and activism, Latin American feminist scholars have [also utilized] the term feminicide (or feminicidio) to more thoroughly encompass and articulate the relationships between and among sex, gender, and violence in Latin American contexts with an attention to the ways in which feminicidios manifest themselves in different state and nation contexts.[7]

The term **feminicide** – or *feminicidio* – first coined by Mexican feminists Julia Monárrez and Marcela Lagarde centralizes the experiences of Mexican (and also Latin American) women and expands femicide, "a gender-specific word for homicide," to include the killing of women *based on their gender*: "the murder of women because of their sexuality, reproductive features, and social status or success."[8] In other words, according to Fregoso and Bejarano, the term feminicide disrupts "essentialist notions of female identity that equate gender and biological sex and looks instead to the gendered nature of practices and behaviors, along with the performance of gender norms."[9] Moreover, the term thus "shift[s] the analytic focus to how gender norms, inequities, and power relationships increase women's vulnerability to violence."[10] It also strengthens the tie to

"Latin contexts and subjectivities, as feminicide is a direct English translation of the Spanish term *feminicidio*, and as such provides the space for a transborder, transcultural, translocational focus."[11] Thus, drawing upon research by Hernández and De Los Santos Upton, moving forward, we employ the use of the term *feminicidio* as a political transborder concept and as a means to center Latin American and indigenous women as agents who can contribute activism lessons that are both theoretical and material through a praxis, organizing, and activist lens.[12]

With several writers referring to Latin America as the most dangerous place in the world for women,[13] scholarship illustrates that women across Latin America feel they are not treated with respect and dignity.[14] Estimates suggest that almost 5000 women were victims of femicide in 2020 across Latin America, in spite of greater visibility to anti-violence efforts and activism.[15] As English and Godoy describe, "Although notable progress in gender equality has been seen in recent years, this low percentage in relation to the rest of the world reflects how gender inequality and violence against women persist throughout Latin America."[16] A key factor contributing to the rise of feminicides and violence against women is Latin America's macho culture, which "tends to blame women for the violence inflicted on them" and condones it.[17] Ada Beatriz, one of the key members of Ni Una Menos, stated that machismo is a cultural issue:

> The aggressor feels a woman belongs to him and he can do what he wants with her. We're talking about machismo that sees a woman as an object, as inferior and someone who has to obey. If she doesn't, disobedience is punished with beatings and even death.[18]

The movement known as Ni Una Menos grew from the streets of Argentina into an internationally known movement that speaks out against feminicides and the senseless murdering of women throughout Latin America. The collective's name came from a 1995 phrase from the Mexican activist and poet Susana Chávez Castillo, "Ni una muerta más," which refers to the Ciudad Juárez femicides from the 1990s. Chávez Castillo was later assassinated in 2011, and her phrase became "el símbolo de la lucha" moving forward.[19] Its origin story has roots in the 2015 murder of Chiara Páez, a 14-year-old Argentinian girl who was eight weeks pregnant when she was murdered by her boyfriend. She was discovered under the patio of her boyfriend's family home, and reports suggest that he murdered her after discovering she was pregnant. According to news reports, her 16-year-old boyfriend, Manuel Mansilla, was charged with aggravated murder, forced abortion, and femicide after accepting responsibility for murdering her.[20] When her body was found, "investigators also found traces of a drug commonly used in clandestine abortions, fueling speculation that her killing could have been the result of an argument with her boyfriend over her pregnancy."[21] Mansilla's mother and stepfather were also charged in the case, and his conviction was overturned in early 2022. The court found that his jail term was "unconstitutional," given that it "applie[d] to sentencing guidelines for adults convicted of manslaughter or murder."[22]

Páez's murder inspired the first Ni Una Menos (Not One Less/Not One More) march against gender violence, and was a pivotal case influencing the creation of this Latin American grassroots feminist movement, although movement organizers have also noted that the movement's genealogy also includes the Mothers of the Plaza de Mayo, the mothers of victims of the Argentinian dictatorship in the late 1970s. Regarding the genealogy of the movement, it held its first-ever women's mass strike in Argentina in October of 2016 in response to the murder of 16-year-old Lucía Pérez. She was found drugged, raped, and impaled in Mar del Plata, and the ensuing protest utilized the hashtag #MiércolesNegro (Black Wednesday).[23] This strike gained traction both nationally and internationally, with similar demonstrations occurring during the same time frame in Bolivia, Paraguay, El Salvador, Guatemala, Brazil, and Mexico, to name a few.[24] Lucía's case also highlights one of the fundamental distinctions between the terms femicide and feminicide/*feminicidio*. While some American feminists might place violence against women on the femicide end of the spectrum more broadly, the context of violence against women in Latin America, "the systematic and sexual nature of feminicide – painfully reflected in Lucía's case – are closer to an experience of what Italian philosopher Adriana Cavarero has called 'horrorism.'"[25] Drawing upon work by Adriana Cavarero that highlights how horrorism focuses on the suffering and powerlessness of the victims, the angle of horrorism is more akin to the nature of feminicides that occur across Latin America because of the sadistic and sensationalized nature of the violence. Put simply, "Following Cavarero's ideas, we may assert that women's permanent fear of sexual violence, along with the feeling of powerlessness vis-à-vis their rapist, is closer to horror than terror. Rape followed by feminicide is sexual horrorism."[26] Such violence is always linked to what Rita Segato describes as a "pedagogy of cruelty," wherein feminicides and violence against women are the outcome of perpetrators' desires to reinscribe and make visible power relations aimed to "keep women in their place" and prevent them from speaking out or attempting to gain independence.[27] Moreover, within this pedagogy of cruelty, the violence is both spectacle and spectacularized as another aim to impact women both existentially and physically, which has led to the direct formation of the politics of resistance on behalf of Ni Una Menos and the MMIW movement.[28]

Referred to as a "continental alliance of feminist forces," Ni Una Menos has, as some authors have argued, revitalized feminist efforts across Latin America because it has "pushed past old boundaries" in now utilizing an intersectional approach that focuses on labor unions, environmental concerns, and expanded advocacy for sexual, economic, and social rights.[29] The original movement was founded by a collective of journalists, writers, communicators, organizers, and community members with similar interests in anti-violence advocacy and communicating their messages to the masses.[30] Furthermore, the movement has "become a political counterbalance" to political and legislative wars against women both throughout Latin America and worldwide, particularly as it engages in transnational organizing with women's marches and strikes across the world.[31] Additionally, one of the movement's main contributions is its ability to engage multiple subjectivities in one space. As opposed to starting from a preconceived notion of what it means to be a woman, rather, the movement has utilized both technological and physical organizing in diverse spaces and organizations that connect individuals with diverse positionalities to organize around issues related to sexism, violence, and more.[32]

In light of Ni Una Menos' efforts, organizers and activists have spoken out against the tendency for the legal system or the mass media to refer to femicides as isolated incidents or "crimes of passion."[33] Rather, the movement has called attention to the following: "The men who commit gender violence are not psychopaths or isolated cases, nor is the media responsible for the way they behave. There is a whole sociopolitical and economic framework that we need to understand in order to better see how women's bodies are converted into a territory subject to conquest."[34] Referring to the murder of Berta Caceres, Luci Cavallero and Verónica Gago note that one of the contributions of the movement is a reconfiguration of the current terrain with a focus on community power within a movement that features women protagonists as agentic, empowered organizers in the "dispute over territorial control."[35]

From an organizing perspective, the Ni Una Menos movement has created a new "political discourse and practice" by utilizing a combination of physical presence and digital assemblies.[36] Transnationally, the Ni Una Menos movement has resulted in "feminist assemblies, working groups, and conversations [that] proliferate in digital and physical spaces, producing new feminist encounters and creating a sense of solidarity among women and other 'dissident identities.'"[37] Its efforts have utilized multiple organized strategies – marches, protests, strikes, and transnational coalition-building efforts – that have resulted in media attention, policy change, and a fundamental reconceptualization of the relationships among gender violence, capitalism, labor exploitation, and more. Moreover, the effectiveness of the collective's efforts can be attributed to the creation of texts that were complex yet accessible, political yet nonpartisan, and that highlighted both the collective's efforts and the role of the individual in the larger digital and physical sphere.[38]

As Mason-Deese has illustrated, the movement transitioned from a set of hashtags to the coordinated involvement of millions of women through the sharing of personal stories and violence testimonies on social media, the use of SMS technologies to connect across regional lines, the use of technologic alliance-building to coordinate with the mass media, and the ultimate "weaving of webs."[39] In other words:

> what was important about the digital space was not only that it allowed women to express themselves individually, to name their own experiences, but even more importantly, that it allowed them to connect to one another and begin naming their experiences in a collective voice.[40]

The hashtags (#NiUnaMas, #NiUnaMenos, #YoParo, #InternacionalFeminista, #JuntasSomosInfinitas, #NotOneWomanLess, and #NosotrasParamos#) were often decided upon during in-person meetings and assemblies.[41] The use of social media groups, SMS technologies, and hashtags allowed for the publicizing of both micro and macro issues – both personal and structural issues – associated with gendered violence against women, particularly because women could share their experiences anonymously, connect with other women across time and space, disseminate collective and multilingual anti-violence manifestos, and later have the potential to meet and organize in person.[42] Ultimately, Ni Una Menos has gained traction and strength through its intentional combination of symbolic performance, assembly-building, and digital networking, strategies that are both learned and improvised to result in transformative justices.[43]

Building upon research by Mason-Deese that analyzes the "intersection between the material practices of the feminist movement and its forms of knowledge production and digital presence,"[44] Palmeiro highlights several technological strategies that the Ni Una Menos movement has deployed to achieve its organizational aims, such as " using strategies of online agitation and the dissemination of hashtags (keywords) through social media in order to mobilize large numbers of people, and to activate a new political subject – the feminist global tide."[45] As Fuentes describes, hashtags are both technological and performative, in that they have transformative, material effects due to their citational/cataloging nature and their ability to "shape feminist publics, help disseminate counter-pedagogies seeking to debunk patriarchal pedagogies of cruelty, and, ultimately, usher in utopian futures."[46] Furthermore, through the lens of technopolitics,[47] the Ni Una Menos movement technologically, materially, and symbolically united women across the world in the global fight against feminicides. As Fuentes illustrates:

> Hashtags not only allow NUM's supporters to find each other or to find information about NUM's protests. Placed in contiguity, hashtags draw connections among different forms of gendered violence and efforts to discipline women. By pairing up #NiUnaMenos with other hashtags such as #LibertadParaBelen (#FreeBelen) or #AbortoLegal (#LegalAbortion), NUM has shown that femicide is only the tip of the iceberg within a wide range of instances of institutional, cultural, and interpersonal violence.[48]

Through the use of physical coalition-building and the technological construction of digital assemblies, supporters and organizers of Ni Una Menos are able to engage in both dialogue and action about legislation, activism, and outreach. Thus, the "feminist global tide" referred to vis-à-vis the organizing efforts of Ni Una Menos represented a massive tide of feminist bodies across languages, identities, and regional/national borders – a tide that Palmeiro describes accordingly: "Ni Una Menos is a hashtag, the name of a collective, the name of a broader social movement, a claim, a utopia, a keyword, password, a declaration of solidarity, and a collective war cry."[49] Ultimately, the digital space is an "important space of sociality, allowing for possibilities for nonhierarchical and more autonomous organization" that must remain connected to physical, material bodies and concrete organizing practices, as well.[50]

### Case Study 2: Missing and Murdered Indigenous Women

The Missing and Murdered Indigenous Women movement is an activist effort aimed at ending the violence against indigenous women and girls across Turtle Island, an Indigenous phrase for North America (Turtle Island). In 2012, Sheila North Wilson, the former Grand Chief of Manitoba Keewatinowi Okimakanak Inc., coined the hashtag #MMIW.[51] It is important to note that in 2014, #AmINext was created by Holly Jarret to raise awareness about #MMIW.[52] The MMIW movement draws attention to the high rates of murders and disappearances of indigenous women and girls across the United States and Canada. Today, the movement is associated with the color red and symbolized through red handprints across the mouth and red dresses hung from trees. Hashtags such as #MMIW, #MMIWG, #MMIWG2S, and #NoMoreStolenSisters, accompanied with #CallsForJustice, #GoneButNotForgotten, and #Genocide are associated with the movement. Calling for the much-needed work to address MMIW, in 2017 the US Senate resolved for May 5 to be designed National MMIW Day. The MMIW movement is closely associated with the color red. For many First Nations peoples, the color red holds deep meaning and is understood to transcend the physical world, and calls to ancestors in the spirit world for protection or guidance.

The widespread violence against Indigenous women continues without answers or justice. Data on MMIW remain difficult to ascertain due to limited tribal resources, underreporting, racial misclassification, and US federal Indian policies that are outdated and fail to protect Native women.[53] The MMIW movement aims to address the silencing of indigenous women, girls, and two-spirit people as well as repeal, amend and reform the colonial legal systems in the United States and Canada. The alarming violence experienced by Indigenous women and girls begins at childhood and continues onward through life without meaningful responses or advocacy from family, friends, or legal systems.[54] Today, it is estimated that:

- four out of five Indigenous women have experienced violence.
- Indigenous women are twice as likely to experience violence compared to White women.
- Indigenous women are murdered at rates ten times the US national average.
- 34.1% of Native women will be raped in their lifetime.

Currently, there are 5712 missing or murdered Indigenous women in the United States. Only 116 of those women are recorded in the Department of Justice's National Missing and Unidentified Person database.[55] In Canada, across the past three decades there have been as many as 4000 missing and murdered Indigenous women and girls.[56] Simply put, the violence against Indigenous women is an epidemic. The activist effort by MMIW is a grassroots movement aimed at decolonizing the voices of Indigenous women relegated as subjugated **Others** to the margins of society.

To define the MMIW movement, we must understand the long history of violence against Indigenous women. The history of violence against Indigenous women long pre-dates the advent of the Twitter or Instagram social media platforms. In the 1600s, with the arrival of English and French colonialists, Indigenous women and children became victims of violence and were forcibly entered into a hi/story of assault, kidnapping, trafficking, and murder. Many are familiar with the whitewashed story of Pocahontas and John Smith. Popularized by Disney as Pocahontas, Matoaka (aged approximately 11 or 12) was kidnapped, trafficked, and raped and murdered by English colonizers. Matoaka is commonly considered the first MMIW. The fairytale story propagated by Disney failed to highlight the atrocities she and other Indigenous people experienced at the hands of White colonizers. Rather than a love story as presented by Disney, the tragic life of Matoaka reflects the framework of US colonization of Native women – a system of gendered, economic, political, and legal control with (legal) force and (legal) violence.

From the moment Indigenous women were contacted by White colonizers, violence ensued. #MMIW is an activist movement which reveals how colonial policies have created the system and social framework for violence against Indigenous women. Today, the General Crimes Act and the Major Crimes Act of 1885 are the cornerstones of federal Indian law, both laws failing to punish perpetrators of violence against indigenous women. The pattern of minimal prosecutions for domestic violence and sexual assault has created a colonial framework with no protections or safeguards for women. Misinterpretations of federal statutes, Public Law 280, and the 2005 Violence Against Women Act led to decades of Indian Nations failing to prosecute sexual assaults and other crimes because of the understanding that enumerated crimes divested tribes of authority.[57] #MMIW brings awareness to the devastating lack of real protections or justice for indigenous women for the last 500 years. Caught in a system of failed federal government support, broken promises, and ill-conceived policies, missing indigenous women suffer disproportionate gender violence and have fewer resources organized to help or locate them. Instead, Indigenous women, unlike #GabbyPetito, are dependent on a podcast episode, mini-documentary, or a trending social media post for justice.

The MMIW activist movement connects and amplifies the crisis of missing, murdered Indigenous women, girls, and two-spirit people. #MMIW garnered attention from the Canadian government and US policymakers to launch investigations and introduce new legislation. Across North America, University of Minnesota Communication Professor Rachel Presley argues that #MMIW activists face the challenge of elevating their subjugated voices to first world audiences.[58] Earlier efforts of the #MMIW movement focused on public demonstrations like Canada's annual Women's March,[59] or community art/performance installations like Red Dress Project[60] or No More Stolen Sisters.[61]

Today, #MMIW is used to spread news of protests, ceremonies, and exhibits, and share personal stories of missing loved ones through Twitter and Instagram. By doing so, both cold and new cases of MMIW are boosted in the public eye, and according to scholar Zizi Papacharisii, feelings of connectedness or affective publics in the digital age are created.[62] Creating spaces of affective feelings on social media platforms creates an opening for members from broader society to enter and connect with the violence experienced by Indigenous women. Ultimately, the strengths of affective publics are the mobilizing efforts and ability of Indigenous members to transcend state, national, and tribal boundaries.

The #MMIW activist movement is liminal in its organizing and nebulous in its representation as a formal entity. Rather, the #MMIW movement is reflected through the continued grassroots movements to locate and advocate for justice for Indigenous women and girls. Organizations such as the Red Dress Project, Faceless Dolls Project, and Walking with Our Sisters Project are a few of the more organized groups with prominence in the #MMIW movement. Like many Indigenous activist movements, a barrier to organizing is the existing White colonial systems of oppression and violence. The absence of financial resources, uninvested record-keeping by state and national governments, as well as ill-informed laws are barriers #MMIW faces to gain media attention for the crisis facing Indigenous women. The structures have created and re-create perpetual systemic violence, and for Indigenous women their positionality in the system is no different. Today, #MMIW is a growing and maturing as a movement with heightened political support. In 2020, both the Canadian and US governments committed to a National Day of Awareness and willingness to take political action to address the historical and current violence against Indigenous women, girls, and two-spirit people. The efforts of the #MMIW movement are deeply connected with reeducating North Americans about Indigenous history, legal reforms, and the present-day reality for Indigenous people.

### Reflections on Feminist Anti-Violence Technological Organizing

As our analysis has illustrated, Ni Una Menos and the MMIW movement have engaged in digital activism over the past several years by reclaiming the power of technological and digital spaces, areas that have traditionally been constructed as inherently hegemonic and masculinist.[63] As scholars have long highlighted, the development and practice of feminist digital spaces have arisen as countervailing forces to long histories of racism, sexism, violence, and exclusionary practices in digital spaces.[64] In this case specifically, logics of connective action[65] can help us understand how these two leaderless networks utilized various physical and digital means of assemblies to engage in anti-violence activism, movements, and efforts that are undoubtedly gendered and cultural. By exploring the hybrid, technological, physical, and material organizing of both movements, we can trace how activists engage in intersectional organizing that is anti-capitalist, anti-oppressive, and anti-violence. In other words, gender is not the sole axis upon which both movements organize and view their calling. Ni Una Menos, for example, was able to utilize social media and hashtags to organize protests and strikes, share women's stories, and ultimately redefine and re-present violence against women as a civic matter of concern.[66] They collectively combined "online and off-line contagion of emotions, digital and traditional communication, mainstream and alternative media, information with entertainment, and performances," mostly through the use of Twitter.[67] However, both movements face material, political, and economic consequences in fulfilling their calls to action and justice for the victims and survivors of gendered violence, particularly when facing consequences as a result of majority technological assemblies and having leaderless movements.

First, the origins of both movements are nebulous to varying degrees, and the hashtags for both activist movements represent ruptures of border violence in state, regional, national, and international contexts. Materially, both contexts illustrate the reality of political and legal borders within borders (e.g., tribal lands within the United States). When we closely consider the work of both activist movements presented in this chapter, we can see the pervasiveness of gendered violence across North America and how it is largely ignored, underreported, and many argue embedded within the legal systems. For Indigenous women on tribal lands across North America, there is confusion regarding whether tribal or state governments are responsible for supporting victims and investigating and prosecuting perpetrators (especially in cases where the assailant is non-native and White). The lack of commitment by both tribal and state governments to use resources in cases of missing or murdered Indigenous women reveals how colonial policies created the social contexts of gendered violence.

Second, there is a lack of coalition-forming across different racial/ethnic identity groups. For MMIW groups, there is a smaller focus on Latinx/Latin American indigenous women. Transnational and transethnic/transracial coalition-building could address such exclusionary issues, but the issues are bifurcated because of different racial histories and regional/national politics that inform organizing efforts. The whitewashing of history across both contexts contributes to the invisibility of missing or murdered women. Trending hashtags for #MMIW challenge Canadian racial, ethnic, and aboriginal identity politics, and according to scholar Samira Saramo, #MMIW reclaims space to address the gendered violence experienced by Indigenous women.[68] In other words, ethnic, racial, and geopolitical classifications matter (Latina versus Latin American versus indigenous), especially with the entities that govern the locales within which the activist efforts are occurring. Some groups have adopted the colonial politics of their origins. We are left with the question: How do you move outside a colonial system, especially when definitions of indigeneity are concerned?

Ultimately, the hashtag activist movements we have presented in this chapter are case studies of gendered violence across America. As leaderless rebellions, both activist movements find themselves forced to challenge white colonial power structures and systems laced with racism and femicide violence. The injustices experienced by women across Latin America and Indigenous women, girls, and two-spirit people in the United States and Canada reflect a history of gendered violence almost entirely ignored by legal systems. Both movements reflect activist efforts that embrace feminism, intersectional, and gender political frames to create mediated, technological social justice efforts. We hope this chapter serves as a snapshot of the coalition-building of two separate hashtag movements with similar social, legal, and political justice goals.

## Reflections

We offer the following discussion questions to continue analyzing and examining leaderless rebellions, calling attention to digital feminism and anti-violence activism:

- What is the relationship between grassroots leaderless rebellions organizing in physical spaces and then transitioning to digital, discursive spaces?
- What are the impacts of multimodal leaderless rebellions and activist organizing?
- How might digital leaderless rebellions fall short when concerned with achieving justice for victims and survivors?

## Notes

1  Frangonikolopoulos, Christos A., and Ioannis Chapsos. "Explaining the role and the impact of the social media in the Arab Spring." *Global Media Journal: Mediterranean Edition* 7, no. 2 (2012): 11.
2  Howard, Philip N., and Muzammil M. Hussain. "The upheavals in Egypt and Tunisia: The role of digital media." *Journal of Democracy* 22, no. 3 (2011): 37.
3  Hernández, Leandra Hinojosa, and Sarah De Los Santos Upton. 2018. *Challenging Reproductive Control and Gendered Violence in the Américas: Intersectionality, Power, and Struggles for Rights.* Blue Ridge Summit, PA: Lexington Books. Hernández, Leandra Hinojosa, and Sarah De Los Santos

Upton. "Critical health communication methods at the US-Mexico border: Violence against migrant women and the role of health activism." *Frontiers in Communication* 4 (2019): 34. Hernández, Leandra Hinojosa, and Sarah De Los Santos Upton. "Transgender migrant rights, reproductive justice, and the Mexico–US border in the time of COVID-19." *QED: A Journal in GLBTQ Worldmaking* 7, no. 3 (2020): 142–150. Hernández, Leandra Hinojosa, and Sarah De Los Santos Upton. 2021. "Reproductive justice and activism online: Digital feminism and organizational/activist use of social networking sites." In S. Macdonald, B.I. Wiens, M. Macarthur, and M. Radzikowska (eds.), *Networked Feminisms: Activist Assemblies and Digital Practices*. Blue Ridge Summit, PA: Lexington Books.

4 Russell, Dianna. "The origin and importance of the term femicide." 2011. http://www.dianarussell.com/origin_of_femicide.html.

5 Radford, Jill, and Diana Russell. 1992. *Femicide: The Politics of Woman Killing*. Boston, MA: Twayne Publishers, p. 3.

6 Hernández and De Los Santos Upton, *Challenging Reproductive Control and Gendered Violence in the Américas*. Widyono, Monique. 2009. *Strengthening Understanding of Femicide: Using Research to Galvanize Action and Accountability*. Washington, DC: Program for Appropriate Technology in Health, InterCambios, Medical Research Council of South Africa, and World Health Organization.

7 Hernández and De Los Santos Upton, *Challenging Reproductive Control and Gendered Violence in the Américas*, p. 71.

8 Estévez, A. "Latin American women's problem: We keep getting murdered." *The Conversation*, October 26, 2016. Accessed June 1, 2022. https://theconversation.com/latin-american-womens-problem-we-keep-getting-murdered-67351, para. 17.

9 Fregoso, Rosalinda, and Cynthia Bejarano. 2010. "Introduction: A cartography of feminicide in the Américas." In R. Fregoso and C. Bejarano (eds.), *Terrorizing Women: Feminicide in the Américas*. Durham, NC: Duke University Press, pp. 1–42, at p. 3.

10 Ibid., p. 4.

11 Hernández and De Los Santos Upton, *Challenging Reproductive Control and Gendered Violence in the Américas*, p. 71.

12 Ibid.

13 Estévez, "Latin American women's problem."

14 English, Cynthia, and Johanna Godoy. "Respect and dignity for women lacking in Latin America." Gallup, October 14, 2014. Accessed June 1, 2022. https://news.gallup.com/poll/178427/respect-dignity-women-lacking-latin-america.aspx.

15 Economic Commission for Latin America and the Caribbean. 2021. "ECLAC: At least 4,091 women were victims of femicide in 2020 in Latin America and the Caribbean, Despite greater visibility and social condemnation." United Nations. Accessed June 1, 2022. https://www.cepal.org/en/pressreleases/eclac-least-4091-women-were-victims-femicide-2020-latin-america-and-caribbean-despite.

16 English and Godoy, "Respect and dignity for women lacking in Latin America," para. 2.

17 Moloney, Anastasia. "Killing of 14-year-old girl alerts Argentina to femicides-rights group." *Reuters*, May 21, 2015. Accessed May 2, 2022. https://www.reuters.com/article/argentina-womensrights-femicide/killing-of-14-year-old-girl-alerts-argentina-to-femicides-rights-group-idINKBN0O61UK20150521, para. 16.

18 Ibid., para. 17.
19 "#NiUnaMenos: ¿Quién fue la autora de la consigna que une a miles contra la violencia de género?" *Minuto Uno*, June 3, 2015. Accessed June 5, 2022. https://www.minutouno.com/sociedad/niunamenos/quien-fue-la-autora-la-consigna-que-une-miles-contra-la-violencia-genero-n365815, para. 5.
20 Moloney, "Killing of 14-year-old girl alerts Argentina to femicides-rights group."
21 "Court overturns conviction for femicide that prompted 'Ni una menos' movement." *Buenos Aires Times*, February 12, 2022. Accessed May 1, 2022. https://www.batimes.com.ar/news/argentina/court-overturns-conviction-for-femicide-that-prompted-ni-una-menos-movement.phtml.
22 Ibid., para. 5.
23 Goñi, Uki. "Argentina: Hundreds of thousands of women set to protest against violence," *The Guardian*, October 19, 2016. Accessed June 1, 2022. https://www.theguardian.com/world/2016/oct/19/argentina-women-strike-violence-protest.
24 Gordon, Sarah. "NiUnaMenos: How the brutal gang rape and murder of a schoolgirl united the furious women of Latin America." *The Telegraph*, October 21, 2016. Accessed June 1, 2022. https://www.telegraph.co.uk/women/life/niunamenos-how-a-schoolgirls-brutal-gang-rape-and-murder-united/.
25 Estévez, "Latin American women's problem," para. 19
26 Ibid., para. 22.
27 Fuentes, Marcela A. 2019. "#NiUnaMenos (#NotOneWomanLess): Hashtag performativity, memory, and direct action against gender violence in Argentina." In A.G. Altinay, M.J. Contreras, M. Hirsch, J. Howard, B. Karaca, and A. Solomon (eds.), *Women Mobilizing Memory*. New York: Columbia University Press, pp. 172–191.
28 Ibid.
29 Gago, Verónica. "Argentina's life-or-death women's movement," *Jacobin*, March 7, 2017. Accessed May 5, 2022. https://jacobin.com/2017/03/argentina-ni-una-menos-femicides-women-strike.
30 Bedrosian, Alyssa. "How# NiUnaMenos used discourse and digital media to reach the masses in Argentina." *Latin American Research Review* 57, no. 1 (2022): 100–116.
31 Ibid., para. 3.
32 Mason-Deese, Liz. "Not one woman less: From hashtag to strike." *Spheres: Journal for Digital Cultures* 6 (2020): 1–15.
33 Gago, "Argentina's life-or-death women's movement," para. 18.
34 Ibid., para. 17.
35 Ibid., para. 36.
36 Palmeiro, Cecilia. "Ni Una Menos and the politics of translation." *Spheres: Journal for Digital Cultures* 6 (2020): 1.
37 Mason-Deese, "Not one woman less," p. 1.
38 Bedrosian, "How# NiUnaMenos used discourse and digital media to reach the masses in Argentina."
39 Mason-Deese, "Not one woman less," p. 4.
40 Ibid.
41 Ibid.
42 Mason-Deese, "Not one woman less." Palmeiro, "Ni Una Menos and the politics of translation."
43 Fuentes, "#NiUnaMenos (#NotOneWomanLess)."
44 Mason-Deese, "Not one woman less," p. 2.

45 Palmeiro, "Ni Una Menos and the politics of translation," p. 1.
46 Fuentes, "#NiUnaMenos (#NotOneWomanLess)," p. 180.
47 Toret, Javier. "Tecnopolítica: La potencia de las multitudes conectadas. El sistema red 15M, un nuevo paradigma de la política distribuida." *Tecnopolítica*, June 15, 2013. http://tecnopolitica.net/node/72.
48 Ibid, p. 181.
49 Palmeiro, "Ni Una Menos and the politics of translation," p. 2.
50 Mason-Deese, "Not one woman less," p. 3
51 Moeke-Pickering, Taima, Sheila Cote-Meek, and Ann Pegoraro. "Understanding the ways missing and murdered indigenous women are framed and handled by social media users." *Media International Australia* 169 (2018): 54–64.
52 Watson, Kaitlyn. "Missing and Murdered Indigenous Women: The role of grassroots organizations and social media in education." *Canadian Woman Studies* 33, nos. 1–2 (2018–2019). https://cws.journals.yorku.ca/index.php/cws/article/view/37772.
53 Native Hope. n.d. *Missing and Murdered Indigenous Women (MMIW)*. Accessed July 24, 2022. https://www.nativehope.org/missing-and-murdered-indigenous-women-mmiw.
54 Ibid.
55 Ibid.
56 Ellsworth, Barry. "Canada Releases Plan on Missing, Murdered Indigenous Women, Girls. *Anadolu Ajansı*, March 6, 2021. https://www.aa.com.tr/en/americas/canada-releases-plan-on-missing-murdered-indigenous-women-girls/2263305.
57 Native Hope. n.d. *Missing and Murdered Indigenous Women*.
58 Presley, Rachel. "Embodied liminality and gendered state violence: Artivist expressions in the MMIW movement." *Journal of International Women's Studies* 21 (2020): 91.
59 "32nd Annual February 14 Women's Memorial March." *Feb 14th Womens Memorial March*, January 10, 2023. Accessed April 26, 2023. https://womensmemorialmarch.wordpress.com/.
60 Black, Jaime. "The REDress Project." 2020. https://www.jaimeblackartist.com/exhibitions/.
61 Native Hope. n.d. *Missing and Murdered Indigenous Women (MMIW)*. Accessed July 24, 2022. https://www.nativehope.org/missing-and-murdered-indigenous-women-mmiw.
62 Papacharissi, Zizi. "Affective publics and structures of storytelling: Sentiment, events and mediality." *Information, Communication & Society* 19, no. 3 (2020): 307.
63 Banerjee, Sutanuka, and Lipika Kankaria. "Networking voices against violence: Online activism and transnational feminism in local-global contexts." *Journal of International Women's Studies* 24, no. 2 (2022): 1–16.
64 Chenou, Jean-Marie, and Carolina Cepeda-Másmela. "# NiUnaMenos: Data activism from the global south." *Television & New Media* 20, no. 4 (2019): 396–411. McLean, Jessica. 2020. *Changing Digital Geographies: Technologies, Environments and People.* New York: Palgrave MacMillan. Rodino-Colocino, Michelle. "Me Too, # MeToo: Countering cruelty with empathy." *Communication and Critical/Cultural Studies* 15, no. 1 (2018): 96–100.
65 Bennett, Lance W., and Alexandra Segerberg. 2015. "The logic of connective action: Digital media and the personalization of contentious politics." In *Handbook of Digital Politics* Northampton, MA: Edward Elgar, pp. 169–198.

66 Belotti, Francesca, Francesca Comunello, and Consuelo Corradi. "Feminicidio and# NiUna Menos: An analysis of Twitter conversations during the first 3 years of the Argentinean movement." *Violence Against Women* 27, no. 8 (2021): 1035–1063.
67 Ibid, pp. 1057–1058.
68 Saramo, Samira. "Unsettling spaces: Grassroots responses to Canada's Missing and Murdered Indigenous Women during the Harper government years." *Comparative American Studies: An International Journal* 14 (2016): 204.

## References

Banerjee, Sutanuka, and Lipika Kankaria. "Networking Voices against Violence: Online Activism and Transnational Feminism in Local-Global Contexts." *Journal of International Women's Studies* 24, no. 2 (2022): 1–16.

Bedrosian, Alyssa. "How# NiUnaMenos Used Discourse and Digital Media to Reach the Masses in Argentina." *Latin American Research Review* 57, no. 1 (2022): 100–116.

Belotti, Francesca, Francesca Comunello, and Consuelo Corradi. "Feminicidio and# NiUna Menos: An Analysis of Twitter Conversations during the First 3 Years of the Argentinean Movement." *Violence Against Women* 27, no. 8 (2021): 1035–1063.

Bennett, W. Lance, and Alexandra Segerberg. "The Logic of Connective Action: Digital Media and the Personalization of Contentious Politics." In C. Stephen and F. Deen (Eds.), *Handbook of Digital Politics*, pp. 169–198. Edward Elgar Publishing, 2015.

Boler, Megan, Averie Macdonald, Christina Nitsou, and Anne Harris. "Connective Labor and Social Media: Women's Roles in the 'leaderless' Occupy Movement." *Convergence* 20, no. 4 (2014): 438–460.

Canning, Andreae. "Watch the Dateline Episode 'The Secrets of Spirit Lake' Now." *News*. August 6, 2021. https://www.nbcnews.com/dateline/in-the -news/watch-dateline-episode-secrets-spirit-lake-now-n1278074.

Chenou, Jean-Marie, and Carolina Cepeda-Másmela. "# NiUnaMenos: Data Activism from the Global South." *Television & New Media* 20, no. 4 (2019): 396–411.

"Court Overturns Conviction for Femicide that Prompted 'Ni una menos' Movement." *Buenos Aires Times*. February 12, 2022. https://www.batimes .com.ar/news/argentina/court-overturns-conviction-for-femicide-that -prompted-ni-una-menos-movement.phtml (Accessed May 1, 2022).

Economic Commission for Latin America and the Caribbean. "ECLAC: At Least 4,091 Women Were Victims of Femicide in 2020 in Latin America and the Caribbean, Despite Greater Visibility and Social Condemnation." United Nations, 2021. https://www.cepal.org/en/pressreleases/eclac-least-4091 -women-were-victims-femicide-2020-latin-america-and-caribbean-despite (Accessed June 1, 2022).

Ellsworth, Barry. "Canada Releases Plan on Missing, Murdered Indigenous Women, Girls." March 6, 2021. https://www.aa.com.tr/en/americas/canada -releases-plan-on-missing-murdered-indigenous-women-girls/2263305.

English, Cynthia, and Johanna Godoy. "Respect and Dignity for Women Lacking in Latin America." *Gallup*. October 14, 2014. https://news.gallup.com/poll/178427/respect-dignity-women-lacking-latin-america.aspx (accessed June 1, 2022).

Estévez, A. "Latin American Women's Problem: We Keep Getting Murdered." *The Conversation*. October 26, 2016. https://theconversation.com/latin-american-womens-problem-we-keep-getting-murdered-67351 (accessed June 1, 2022).

Frangonikolopoulos, Christos A., and Ioannis Chapsos. "Explaining the Role and the Impact of the Social Media in the Arab Spring." *Global Media Journal: Mediterranean Edition 7*, no. 2 (2012): 10–20.

Fregoso, R., and C. Bejarano. "Introduction: A Cartography of Feminicide in the Américas." In R. Fregoso and C. Bejarano (Eds.), *Terrorizing Women: Feminicide in the Américas*, pp. 1–42. Durham, NC: Duke University Press, 2010.

Fuentes, Marcela A. "#NiUnaMenos (#NotOneWomanLess): Hashtag Performativity, Memory, and Direct Action against Gender Violence in Argentina." In A. G. Altinay, M. J. Contreras, M. Hirsch, J. Howard, B. Karaca, and A. Solomon (Eds.), *Women Mobilizing Memory*, pp. 172–191. Berlin: Columbia University Press, 2019.

Gago, Verónica. "Argentina's Life-or-Death Women's Movement." *Jacobin*. March 7, 2017. https://jacobin.com/2017/03/argentina-ni-una-menos-femicides-women-strike (accessed May 5, 2022).

Goñi, Uki. "Argentina: Hundreds of Thousands of Women Set to Protest Against Violence." *The Guardian*. October 19, 2016. https://www.theguardian.com/world/2016/oct/19/argentina-women-strike-violence-protest (accessed June 1, 2022).

Gordon, Sarah. "NiUnaMenos: How the Brutal Gang Rape and Murder of a Schoolgirl United the Furious Women of Latin America." *The Telegraph*. October 21, 2016. https://www.telegraph.co.uk/women/life/niunamenos-how-a-schoolgirls-brutal-gang-rape-and-murder-united/ (accessed June 1, 2022).

Hernández, Leandra Hinojosa, and Sarah De Los Santos Upton. *Challenging Reproductive Control and Gendered Violence in the Américas: Intersectionality, Power, and Struggles for Rights*. Pennsylvania, USA: Lexington Books, 2018.

Hernández, Leandra H., and Sarah De Los Santos Upton. "Critical Health Communication Methods at the US-Mexico Border: Violence against Migrant Women and the Role of Health Activism." *Frontiers in Communication* 4 (2019): 34.

Hernández, Leandra Hinojosa, and Sarah De Los Santos Upton. "Transgender Migrant Rights, Reproductive Justice, and the Mexico–US Border in the Time of COVID-19." *QED: A Journal in GLBTQ Worldmaking* 7, no. 3 (2020): 142–150.

Hernández, Leandra Hinojosa, and Sarah De Los Santos Upton. "Reproductive Justice and Activism Online: Digital Feminism and Organizational/Activist Use of Social Networking Sites." In S. Macdonald, B. I. Wiens, M. Macarthur, and M. Radzikowska (Eds.), *Networked Feminisms: Activist Assemblies and Digital Practices*. Pennsylvania, USA: Lexington Books, 2021.

Howard, Philip N., and Muzammil M. Hussain. "The Upheavals in Egypt and Tunisia: The Role of Digital Media." *Journal of Democracy* 22, no. 3 (2011): 35–48.

Mason-Deese, Liz. "Not One Woman Less. From Hashtag to Strike." *Spheres: Journal for Digital Cultures* 6 (2020): 1–15.

McLean, Jessica. *Changing Digital Geographies: Technologies, Environments and People*. Camden, UK: Palgrave MacMillan, 2020.

*Missing and Murdered Indigenous Women (MMIW)*. n.d. Retrieved July 24, 2022, from https://www.nativehope.org/missing-and-murdered-indigenous -women-mmiw.

MMIW. n.d. "Native Womens Wilderness." Retrieved July 24, 2022, from https://www.nativewomenswilderness.org/mmiw.

"MMIW: Understanding the Missing and Murdered Indigenous Women Crisis Beyond Individual Acts of Violence." n.d. Accessed July 25, 2022. https://www .niwrc.org/restoration-magazine/june-2020/mmiw-understanding-missing -and-murdered-indigenous-women-crisis.

"MMIW." n.d. Native Womens Wilderness. Accessed July 24, 2022. https://www .nativewomenswilderness.org/mmiw.

Moeke-Pickering, Taima, Sheila Cote-Meek, and Ann Pegoraro. "Understanding the Ways Missing and Murdered Indigenous Women Are Framed and Handled by Social Media Users." *Media International Australia* 169, no. 1 (2018): 54–64. https://doi.org/10.1177/1329878X18803730.

Moloney, Anastasia. "Killing of 14-year-Old Girl Alerts Argentina to Femicides-Rights Group." *Reuters*. May 21, 2015. https://www.reuters.com/article/ argentina-womensrights-femicide/killing-of-14-year-old-girl-alerts-argentina-to -femicides-rights-group-idINKBN0O61UK20150521 (accessed May 2, 2022).

"#NiUnaMenos: ¿Quién fue la autora de la consigna que une a miles contra la violencia de género?" *Minuto Uno*. June 3, 2015. https://www.minutouno .com/sociedad/niunamenos/quien-fue-la-autora-la-consigna-que-une-miles -contra-la-violencia-genero-n365815 (accessed June 5, 2022).

Palmeiro, Cecilia. "Ni Una Menos and the Politics of Translation." *Spheres: Journal for Digital Cultures* 6 (2020): 1–7.

Papacharissi, Zizi. "Affective Publics and Structures of Storytelling: Sentiment, Events and Mediality." *Information, Communication & Society* 19, no. 3 (2016): 307–324. https://doi.org/10.1080/1369118X.2015.1109697.

Parsloe, Sarah M., and Rashaunna C. Campbell. "'Folks Don't Understand What It's Like to Be a Native Woman': Framing Trauma via #MMIW." *Howard Journal of Communications* 32, no. 3 (2021): 197–212. https://doi.org/10 .1080/10646175.2021.1871867.

Presley, Rachel. "Embodied Liminality and Gendered State Violence: Artivist Expressions in the MMIW Movement." *Journal of International Women's Studies* 21, no. 7 (2020): 91–110.

Radford, J., and D. E. H. Russell. *Femicide: The Politics of Woman Killing*. Woodbridge, CT: Twayne, 1992.

Rodino-Colocino, Michelle. "Me too,# MeToo: Countering Cruelty with Empathy." *Communication and Critical/Cultural Studies* 15, no. 1 (2018): 96–100.

Russell, D. E. H. "The Origin and Importance of the Term Femicide." 2011. Retrieved from http://www.dianarussell.com/origin_of_femicide.html.

Saramo, Samira. "Unsettling Spaces: Grassroots Responses to Canada's Missing and Murdered Indigenous Women During the Harper Government Years." *Comparative American Studies An International Journal* 14, nos. 3–4 (2016): 204–220.

Segato, Rita Laura. "Patriarchy from Margin to Center: Discipline, Territoriality, and Cruelty in the Apocalyptic Phase of Capital." *South Atlantic Quarterly* 115, no. 3 (2016): 615–624.

"The REDress Project." 2020. https://www.jaimeblackartist.com/exhibitions/.

Toret, Javier. "Tecnopolitica: La Potcncia de las Multitudes Conectadas. El Sistema Red 15M, un Nuevo Paradigma de la Politica Distribuida." *Temopolitica.* June 15, 2013. http://tecnopolitica.net/node/72.

Watson, Kaitlyn. "Missing and Murdered Indigenous Women : The Role of Grassroots Organizations and Social Media in Education." *Canadian Woman Studies* (2018). https://cws.journals.yorku.ca/index.php/cws/article/view /37772.

Widyono, M. "Strengthening Understanding of Femicide: Using Research to Galvanize Action and Accountability." Washington, DC: Program for Appropriate Technology in Health (PATH), InterCambios, Medical Research Council of South Africa (MRC), and World Health Organization (WHO), 2009.

"Women's Memorial March." 2022. Feb 14th Annual Women's Memorial March. https://womensmemorialmarch.wordpress.com/.

# PART IV
# Reform

# ADVOCATES FOR ACTION

## Marsha P. Johnson

1945–1992
Hometown: Elizabeth, New Jersey, USA
Movements: LGBTQ+ activism and gay and transgender rights
Organizations: STAR, Gay Liberation Front
*Elizabeth Wilson and Allison Schuster*

Marsha P. Johnson was a transgender queer activist, drag queen, performer, and survivor. She famously fought back at the Stonewall Riots – a historical standoff between police and queer youth at the Stonewall Inn in New York City – and marched in the first Pride parade the following year in recognition of Stonewall's anniversary. She additionally co-founded an activist group known as the Gay Liberation Front and created the organization Street Transvestite Action Revolutionaries (STAR) alongside Sylvia Rivera.[1] STAR dedicated itself to sheltering homeless transgender youth, both through activism and organizational action. In addition to her activism, she was a popular figure in New York City's social and art scene, even modeling for Andy Warhol and performing with the drag group Hot Peaches.[2]

Johnson was a successful community organizer who attended and planned protests, marches, and community meetings with a clear mission in mind: LGBTQ+ acceptance. Since she was so connected in New York, she was able to bring together various people and organizations to support her work. Despite being such a cultural icon and influential figure, she, like many transgender women of color, often struggled to gain

DOI: 10.4324/9781003291855-23

acceptance from other LGBTQ+ members even though she fought on behalf of everyone.[3]

As Johnson gained recognition in the queer community as a leader throughout the 1960s and 1970s, she started conducting media interviews to represent the Gay Liberation Front, STAR, and her other activist work. Under pressure to represent her marginalized community, she spoke of transgender people as deserving, everyday individuals.[4] She specifically discussed overlooked issues like youth homelessness and HIV and AIDS.[5]

Sadly, Johnson's body was found in the Hudson River in 1992 when she was just 46.[6] Although initially ruled a suicide, many of her friends and family believe that her death came under suspicious circumstances as many transgender women were subject to violence and murder at the time. Despite the tragedy of her death, Marsha P. Johnson's legacy lives on. Society has slowly become more accepting of the queer community, and people are turning to figures like Johnson to properly respect the revolutionary activist and effective communicator behind the early queer movement.[7]

## Notes

1 Calafell, Bernadette Marie. "Narrative authority, theory in the flesh, and the fight over the death and life of Marsha P. Johnson." *QED: A Journal in GLBTQ Worldmaking* 6, no. 2 (2019): 26–39.

2 Stone, Martha E. "Pop goes the sexual revolution." *Gay & Lesbian Review Worldwide* 23, no. 1 (2016): 50–51.

3 Jackson, Sarah J., Moya Bailey, and Brooke Foucault Welles. "# GirlsLikeUs: Trans advocacy and community building online." *New Media & Society* 20, no. 5 (2018): 1868–1888.

4 Ziegler, Kortney Ryan, and Naim Rasul. 2014. "Race, ethnicity, and culture." In Laura Erickson-Schroth (ed.), *Trans Bodies, Trans Selves: A Resource for the Transgender Community*. Oxford, UK: Oxford University Press, pp. 24–39.

5 Calafell, Bernadette Marie. "Narrative authority, theory in the flesh, and the fight over the death and life of Marsha P. Johnson." *QED: A Journal in GLBTQ Worldmaking* 6, no. 2 (2019): 26–39.

6 De Kosnik, Abigail, Clement Hil Goldberg, Julia Havard, and Paige Morgan Johnson. 2020. "Trans memory as transmedia activism." In *Social Movements, Cultural Memory and Digital Media*. New York: Palgrave Macmillan, pp. 33–57.

7 Rothberg, Emma. n.d. "Marsha P. Johnson." National Women's History Museum. https://www.womenshistory.org/education-resources/biographies/marsha-p-johnson.

# 10

# GROUNDED IN COMMUNITY

## Sustainability and Collective Actions

*Amanda R. Martinez, Daniel Bunson,*
*and Mariana Crespo*

### Mass Media and New Media Convergence

Mass media sets the public's media agenda and serves as a gatekeeper, and new media can complement existing mainstream reporting. As audiences embrace digital devices and news platforms, media organizations have adapted and moved online, too. Media convergence makes content available on several platforms – such as television, websites, and social media – and expands the potential reach of media consumers.[1] The US media environment exists within two simultaneous, concerning trends: (1) mainstream commercial mass media is increasingly concentrated among a small number of multinational media conglomerates, and (2) new media has seemingly democratized access, enabling users to create, distribute, reproduce, and circulate both their original content and existing content in powerful new ways.[2] When new media content holds the power to compete for attention with mass media messaging, the online public has access to multiple interpretations of stories or events.

Media frames schematically guide perceptions by reducing the complexity of information and interpreting and reconstructing reality through layered frames laden with shared significance and meaning.[3] Scholars describe media "liveness" as part of ritualistic usage because media connect our shared, current realities as they are happening,[4] and live reality flourishes as an inherent element across social media in today's digital age. With popularity of new media among multiple generations, social media sites have emerged as popular spaces for users to make and maintain connections, acquire new information, and receive updates about ongoing

DOI: 10.4324/9781003291855-24

movements. Social media describes online interactions that combine both mass and interpersonal communication processes as opinion environments, where users "gauge, form, and express opinions on topics of public interest."[5]

## Social Movements and Social Media Activism

New digital technologies provide individuals with new opportunities to stand up against issues with which they disagree and engage with social movement causes and activism agendas. Social media activism anchors communicative processes among individuals collectively working towards raising awareness and solving problems. Skeptics of digital forms of activism have imagined a tendency for activists to over-rely on technology bordering on determinism, and other critiques have inferred an anti-technology bias or hesitation, while others are simply misinformed about what constitutes activism.[6] Early critics witnessing the rising potential of social media-fueled activism pointed to the uniqueness of elite youth leaders, speculating that new technology would not likely convert people who were not already predisposed to civic engagement, and therefore this form of activism would likely be modestly impactful.[7] Critics felt that serious activism could not happen online, and invented the catchy term, "slacktivism," referring to slackers posing as activists.[8] **Slacktivism** characterizes a social media free rider problem where participants' use of social media for collective action appears poorly committed, with easy action that requires little effort or commitment.[9]

Some scholars reason that social media facilitate "micro-acts of participation,"[10] which includes forms of participation such as updating a status on Facebook, tweeting or retweeting others' content, signing an electronic petition to initiate momentum and dialogue among potential advocacy partners,[11] sharing articles, and donating to support a social movement's cause. These efforts show how a small act can snowball into a movement when millions of people do it, and participants may even "organize without organizations."[12] Participation is best conceptualized as a matter of degree in activeness and passivity: even if people are just listening and watching media produced by others, the potential for contributions to the broader conversations in various spaces is great.[13,14] Through social media, where everyone can take part in a social movement, each individual effort counts. Though some activism may sometimes primarily exist online, it holds effectiveness potential by creating traction for the social movement by (re-)posting about the cause and prompting critical thought through information sharing, thereby providing a strong sense of collective solidarity and support that motivates further momentum. Importantly, the possible repercussions for social media activists depend on the political climate, and no dissent action should be so easily dismissed; for example, tweeting carries danger in repressive political contexts whereas street protests are easier within a democracy.[15] Indeed, those leveraging social media for their activism combined with localized collaboration and sustained efforts open to shifts as movements progress are using any and all media necessary to change the world through personal and collective storytelling.[16]

Asynchronous and synchronous communication via social media simultaneously enable rapid mobilization, information sharing, and attention drawn to issues, causes, grievances, and protests linked to social movements and other community-based collective actions. The power of hashtags and social media in fueling activism emphasizes the fact that the speed of information dispersion within social networks makes social media useful to mobilize protestors because it allows them to quickly inform others about what is happening in the movement.[17] New media fuel top-down organization and activism as well as grassroots organization, persuasion, and mobilization. **Mobilizing** "refers to the process by which inspirational leaders or other persuaders can get a large number of people to join a movement or engage in a particular movement action" **organizing** "entails a more sustained process as people come to deeply understand a movement's goals and their own power to change themselves and the world"; and "**netroots activism**" describes online protestors, and is a clever language play upon the more traditional non-digital grassroots activism.[18] Social movements require all types of activism, such as organizing to form follower bases, leadership concentration, and sustenance through collaborative possibilities.

Digital technology encompasses a set of new protest forms and possibilities for organization and mobilization that we have at our disposal, and the expanse of political impact depends on how imaginatively and effectively these tools are used, by whom, and when.[19] The Internet as a place for both facilitation and action that moves people to both on and offline forms of action has proven skeptics wrong, demonstrating major impact that shows no signs of stopping. Social media sites function as starting places where awareness raising, and information sharing motivate and move people to action through organization, recruitment, and multifaceted modes of participation. Skeptics hesitant to embrace the power of social media activism have pointed out correctly, however, that this new activism benefits a spectrum of political constituents and contexts, including "established democracies, countries in transition, and authoritarian regimes alike."[20] Examples include Egypt's "We Are All Khaled Said" Facebook group, Syrian videos on YouTube, Moroccan resistance to atheist activism online, and social media actions employed by the Syrian Electronic Army.[21] Charlene Caruthers, racial justice activist and founding national director of the Black Youth Project 100, reminds us that "people build movements. Not technology. Not the Internet. Not social media," because the foundation to revolutions is rooted in first connecting, organizing, and mobilizing people.[22]

## Social Media Activism: Expanded Participation Possibilities

The use of social media as a tool in information sharing and quickly mobilizing the masses across time and space began in 2011 with the onset of the Arab Spring and Occupy movements around the world, influencing how those on the margins and at the center make meaning and agitate for sociopolitical shifts in culture, routines, policy, and structures.[23] In fact, in 2011, *Time* magazine dubbed "The Protester" as its "Person of the Year" in reference to the popular and widespread Arab Spring protests where protesters from multiple countries banded together in attempts to end corruption in dictatorial governments.[24] Globally, leveraging social media and Internet communication assumes a centrality unmatched by any other form of media due to its instantaneous speed and vast potential to reach the masses quickly. For many years leading up to the 2011 Egyptian uprisings, research points out that the most successful social movements whose activists employed social media (i.e., Kefaya, April 6th Youth, We Are All Khaled Said) effectively mobilized the masses by expanding networks, encouraging collaborative efforts, and globalizing the reach and resources through opposition leaders who then furthered solidarity and collectivism through unifying symbols, issue framing, and transforming online into offline activism.[25]

The **hashtag** is defined as the "discursive and user-generated" method for the designation of "collective thoughts, ideas, arguments, and experiences that might otherwise stand alone or be quickly subsumed within the fast-paced pastiche of Twitter."[26] **Hashtag activism** describes "the strategic ways counterpublics and their allies on Twitter employ this shortcut to make political contentions about identity politics that advocate for social change, identity redefinition, and political inclusion."[27] Often, the stories that coalesce around hashtags gain traction faster than traditional media, which explains Twitter's rise as one of the major dissemination tools used by laypeople and activists alike.

Among the most hotly contested debates occupying center stage in assessing the vitality and effectiveness of collective action remains what, exactly, constitutes action. A key lesson gleaned from the last decade of scholarly reflection on this topic shows clearly that the definition of action has expanded to include many kinds of online and offline activities, sometimes with blurred boundaries around where the online ends and the offline begins; the reality is that activists typically stay connected online as they participate on the ground because information sharing helps sustain social movement momentum. Additionally, sharing firsthand images, livestreams, or recorded videos intensifies the power afforded by social media to compete with the historically dominant mainstream mass media framing of protest events and related social movement issues. Social media content may inform mass media coverage of protests, adding to intermedia agenda-setting or transmedia activism and mobilization. Traditional offline forms of activism have by no means disappeared, and in fact have increased worldwide amid the rise of social media activism, which not only introduces new mechanisms for participation, but also new ways to accomplish traditional forms of activism, such as contacting decision-making officials with letters urging action.[28] Participatory politics include activities such as circulation of information, dialogue, and feedback among community members, production of original content, mobilization of others to help accomplish goals, and actively investigating issues of public concern. The preceding activities inevitably align with social media activism, including mobilization and sustaining momentum as movements progress.

Often, the online and offline mechanisms of communication intertwine as extensions of one another.[29] In a study comparing two decades' worth of feminist activism by groups in Turkey, scholars have highlight the reality that old, traditional forms of activism and communication especially adapted in the early 2000s to social media for networking, political discussions, and protest organization and the speed and force behind such quick actions resulted in stronger, more powerful women's activism and lobbying efforts.[30] Moving beyond the simple inquiry about whether hashtag feminism effectively supports social movement activism, other research has considered the perspectives of hashtag activists themselves to understand how they negotiate the tactics they use with careful consideration of the sociotechnical constraints they endure.[31] Activists personally situate their politics in posting highly visible agendas to move beyond the individual level of experience and toward bridging the collective with the systemic nature of social injustices, such as #MeToo's emphasis on gendered violence worldwide. When feminist activists identify online risks, they retain a constant self-reflexivity to maintain momentum online and advance solutions for the broader activist agenda.

What counts as political participation and civic engagement has expanded beyond typical and measurable forms (i.e., voting, joining organizations) to include new Internet-based forms of engagement, such

FIGURE 10.1   São Paulo, Brazil, September 11, 2016: a woman with a megaphone shouting slogans during an action against the coup and
calling for new elections and other social agendas for the country

as comments, jokes, parodies, and memes that make a point "about how
the world should look and the best way to get there."[32] Memes, as a popular, succinct mode of communication that typically capitalizes on popular
culture, are a form of persuasion, advocacy, grassroots action, expression,
and public discussion.[33] In 2017 the She Says women's rights nonprofit
in India started the Twitter hashtag #LahukaLagaan ("tax on blood") to
protest a recent government-imposed Goods and Services Tax on sanitary products with the rationale that they are luxury commodities; the
cultural resonance and catchiness of the hashtag alone quickly resulted
in the online protest's popularity among women and men, especially with
the humorous tone in which a well-known Indian feminist comedian in a
parody video compared sanitary pads to a monthly subscription.[34]

Other types of participation have been spawned by social media with
the objectives of facilitating participation, interaction, and collaboration,
including protest artforms, maptivism, culture jamming, meme warfare,
hacking, and sharing firsthand video footage captured on the ground to
skirt mass media's gatekeeping and framing filters.[35] Often, the same content is repurposed as it "spread[s] through Facebook pages and Twitter
postings, talk radio and audio magazines, street art and oratory."[36] A

small percentage of social media content constitutes viral messages that result from the social process of users sharing remarkable content in large numbers to create a collective virality.[37] Going viral is highly desirable because of the fast-moving information flows and high attention, which have implications for individuals, collectives, and institutions. Social media usage as part of social movement activism adheres to the typical participatory political goals of achieving equitable treatment and pushing for policy changes by amplifying many voices to influence decision-making processes and ultimately benefit the collective.[38] Early patterns of cyberactivism embraced in social movements show that advocacy organizations have cautiously embraced some platforms, like Twitter and Facebook, for overall communication speed and the ability to strengthen existing efforts, but have hesitated to embrace others (i.e., Google + and Tumblr) for fear of the possibility they might divert resources from proven strategies.[39] Most recently, because digital activism has infused social movement activism intensely in the last decade, patterns of widening technopolitical frames of interpretation beyond cyberactivism as mere tools to add on to existing efforts have evolved as they aid collective action.[40] Next, we consider the wealth of analyses that examine how social movements leverage social media towards sustaining cause momentum, advocacy and collaboration efforts, and collective actions through various protest waves and stages of movement beyond active protest efforts.

### Mass, Alternative, and Social Media News Connections

Among the most complex relationships with the rise of social media usage in political movement activism are those with existing mainstream mass media outlets. One dilemma that protestors confront is the mass media tendency to cover situations with sensational elements, such as confrontations, violence, or altercations with police on scene,[41] adhering to the yellow journalism adage, "if it bleeds, it leads." Another pattern is for mass media to outright ignore or fail to give attention by way of news coverage to social movement activism efforts with a presence offline and online. For example, protestors used social media to plan and organize the 2012 Occupy Nigeria protests, and though the media chose not to report on the protests due to pressure from the government, the mainstream media ultimately shifted course and focused attention on the student-led protests after pressure from protestors intensified. In a stunning characterization of this pressure's outcome, some scholars even named social media the fifth estate in Nigeria because of its demonstrated power to fuel "interaction, socialisation, collective engagement, and liberation that was not present in the mainstream media."[42] In an analysis of interview data with various actors involved in the 2011 protests in Israel, including activists, campaigners, techies, and journalists, scholars unveiled that each vantage point highlighted different perceptions of the significance and role of mass and social media; Facebook was deemed extremely important to protest success in the early development stages, whereas mainstream media spreads information and awareness about protests and movements among wider audiences, thereby helping lend credibility and legitimacy to their broader agendas.[43] Sustainability for a movement's ongoing messaging beyond protest arcs may motivate the need for reliance upon or the development of new alternative media outlets to centralize information flows. As an outgrowth of activism generally and within-group disagreements on political and organizational logistics, a local branch of Indymedia was established in Belgium to provide a platform where many voices could be heard and democratic debates and idea sharing could ensue about strategies, tactics, and coordination momentum for both social and grassroots movements.[44] Traditional news coverage validates protestors' efforts by giving them national publicity and providing mobilizing information to empower others to join the demonstrations.

## Navigating Risk: Counter-surveillance and Resistance

Perhaps the most powerful accountability purposes of social media usage in social movement activism are the novel tactics activists develop. In nondemocratic contexts, social media oppositional expressions hold potential for great personal risk for activists. In Cambodia, the authoritarian regime exudes a contentious political climate where great danger exists as well as a high likelihood for surveillance and censorship for the youth exhibiting dissent activism; however, digitally active Cambodian youth not only boldly express their political opposition, but they also employ "hidden tactics to exert influence on public issues."[45] Hidden tactics typically function in nonviolent, nondisruptive, and unconventional ways with the goal of evading repression from those in power, yet still gaining momentum among counterpublics by elevating counternarratives. In a similar vein, researchers describe the nonviolent forms of resistance, including distant witnessing via online video streaming and livestreaming, orchestrated by the Sioux tribes of Standing Rock Reservation to protest the controversial construction of the Dakota Access Pipeline (DAPL).[46] Through the Digital Smoke Signals Facebook page, asynchronous videos prompted various connective action with users frequenting the page, so that videos posted online were seen as information to circulate, and livestreamed videos facilitated more dialogue with audiences. These tactics demonstrate the importance and utility of an attentive, reactive public. Leaders of the DAPL resistance movement have directly requested help from their audience with tasks like fact-checking or calls to strengthen organizing that may counter the dominance of mass media framing. This interactivity heightens the value of social media participation, attentiveness, and direct responses between on-the-ground and online activists.

Another function of social media affordances' direct contribution to the transformation of protest power is the counter-surveillance that livestreaming or posting recorded videos lends. In the 2012 Quebec Student Strike, participants strategically integrated livestreamed videos to their resistance movement, and this counter-surveillance of police officers emphasized the subjectivity of activism in the streets as experienced from these multiple livestreamed vantage points.[47] Similarly, in the 2014 neighborhood riots in the Gamonal neighborhood in Burgos, Spain, activists posted video recordings that documented firsthand the violent police interventions and questionable interaction procedures, leveraging counter-surveillance and portraying a testament to the power of the people to function as a sort of alternative journalistic collective.[48]

## Movement Critiques and Challenges:
## Intersectionality, Embodiment, and Leadership

Social media activism requires constant self-reflexivity and social movement awareness because internal dynamics may shift and require new directions of focus to maintain key principles of inclusivity and desirable strategies to achieve collective goals. Hashtags associated with a movement can function as offshoots that highlight tensions. Intersectional tensions within movements are one such example displayed through social media in recent years. Instances of racial justice hashtag activism include #NotYourAsianSideKick and #SolidarityIsForWhiteWomen, which were created to draw attention to the intersectionality and fluidity of race within feminist movement.[49] Further evidence of intersectional tensions in productively raising critical thought through hashtags is the unquestioned ableism within movements. Scholars have focused attention on the #CripTheVote campaign as a prime example of activism that pushes our existing ways of conceptualizing the very embodiment emphasis in social "movement."[50] The hashtag expressly calls out the changes needed to the compulsory able-bodiedness of social movements to address concerns of disabled people through strong awareness on disability issues pertaining to political movements and systems, while also advocating political participation toward change, such as voter advocacy. Others argue that individual forms of visual embodiment representations help to enhance and develop collective identity among people because these forms of participation connect individuals "beyond the constraints of space, time, or even ability" and push:

> the boundaries on what constitutes real social movement engagement. Is it more real to attend a march or rally and post a selfie of being at that march or rally or is it more real to reveal nuanced embodied identity practices online through image and narrative?[51]

Of course, the issue readily presents itself in the very positioning of this logic as an either/or false dichotomy when the answer has historically shown that a both/and perspective is best.

Deeper, more sophisticated ideas about visual stimuli and embodiment on the ground in social movement activism afforded by social media activism enhance inclusive possibilities. The Tunisian uprising's success may be attributed largely to the bridging of geographical and class-based divides with interests and actions converged in both online and offline spaces.[52] Visual evidence dramatically amplifies the intensity of a situation through shareable messages that can transform a local incident into a spectacle that expands framing to resonate more widely within a given population, thereby creating a hybrid network that connects people to act.[53] Similar patterns of success characterize the Right to Information movement in India, whereby social media expanded geographic reach, amplified messaging, and pressured powerful entities such as corporate and government spheres.[54]

Some scholars critique the widespread and pervasive idea that social media activism means that movements have transitioned to an open leaderlessness in their horizontal information workflows. Increasingly evidence for a leadership collective emanates as we now have analyses and reflections on many worldwide social movements utilizing social media to further activist efforts. In an analysis of three regional Canadian cases of grassroots collective action, and with particular attention to the barriers mobilizers faced specifically, researchers have pinpointed the clear need for an enduring, well-organized, tech-savvy, collaborative network to function primarily in relation to facilitating organization and mobilization across time and space.[55] Social media teams have been dubbed "digital vanguards" because they are often composed of small groups of activists who serve in an informal, collective leadership role to direct collective action through social media.[56] Though problematic intricacies and complexities characterize their formation, composition, internal coordination, and control of the social media accounts, leadership and leaders steering the movement's activism are still relevant and necessary, even as

**FIGURE 10.2** Protestors join together on the streets in solidarity

they may endure growing pains of sustaining the common agenda. The importance of shifting, new forms of leadership developing through social media activism should not be underestimated when we consider the concept of "connective leadership" in action which is decentered, emergent, and collectively performed.[57] Many agree that digital activism's future in connection to the political culture of trade unionism must be driven primarily by the horizontal communication and agendas pushed by workers in both the articulation of future changes deemed desirable, and future organization and mobilization; furthermore, the ongoing processes of identifying and building alliances with other communities and social movements remain top priorities to further mutual collaborations to meet various connected ends.[58]

### Collective Identity and Shared Motivation: Activating the Activism

Networked protest and social media activism have contributed to a global digital environment where collective identity formation transcends typical political and social divisions, adding to these networks' persistence as inter-agenda solidarity motivates participation in ongoing global movements.[59]

Compared to social movements in both North America and Europe, protest activity in Chile has proven tremendously successful, resulting in legal and policy changes, many of which gained momentum and widespread participation through Facebook publicity thanks to organizing among young adults.[60] In survey data collected from 18–29-year-old Chilean youths in 2011, results revealed that using Facebook for news consumption and socializing with others was associated with increased participation in protests, demonstrating the power of Facebook as "a resource for creating a collective agency."[61] In a two-year study of the Mexican #YoSoy132 movement, research highlighted how Mexican student activists reclaimed their agency from the powerful PRI (Institutional Revolutionary Party) to reframe and activate fellow would-be activists by using the backstage communication affordances through Facebook and WhatsApp to cultivate collective identity and movement cohesion.[62] These forms of backstage communication prove invaluable for groups' quick, widespread activism activation. Scholars have examined what they refer to as "sub-dynamics" of social media use by ethno-cultural minorities to raise awareness, relay information about issues and situations, and encourage a sense of connectedness to mobilize supporters.[63] The Idle No More movement, an ongoing protest initiative in Canada since 2012 led by indigenous group members, aims to mobilize its own members locally, nationally, and internationally, and inspire non-indigenous allies to join and amplify the cause. The group simultaneously educates by expressing cultural specificities and accompanying struggles, and advocates for tangible policy changes pertaining to socio-economic issues, governance, and the environment. Centering indigenous culture anchored its primary thematic and communicative means of information and mobilization energy.[64]

As part of the recent waves of digital feminist activism associated with the feminist movement across Spain, feminists took collective action by tweeting their outrage at the announcement of abuse convictions for the five accused gang rapists on trial in the case of *La Manada* with frames of collective indignation and criticism that permeated digital platforms. The feminist activism further strengthened street protests nationwide, and accentuated the feminist demands rooted in the broader social implications around gendered violence and the legitimacy the case's outcome gives to the acceptability of violence towards women. Hashtag activism fuels momentum: "hashtags organize the contents, images channel the emotions better and enrich the content and links extend the conversation by directing to other sources."[65] Building on the Spanish feminist movement, Las Periodistas Paramos (a collective of five women journalists on strike due to discrimination) began their protest initiatives by first banding together in a closed Twitter group a week before the International Women's Day strike took place.[66] They amassed support through manifesto signatures and joined local strikes in Madrid, and the feminist agenda eventually rippled across the country. Indeed:

> feminists soon created their own area in the Plaza del Sol campsite, which then attracted younger generations of women who had not previously considered their situation. The capacity for dialogue and debate showed that Spanish feminism could address this demand for intersectionality.[67]

They did this by emphasizing economic marginalization of women in the in-person protests and creating a Twitter hashtag campaign to highlight realities such as the wage gap and glass ceiling.

Various news media had shown interest in and given attention to the feminist movement demands circulated via social media thanks to the increased mobilization of women joining the movement and becoming activists; these masses then engaged networks online and facilitated and participated in protests on the ground. Precisely because of this critical momentum amassed online encouraging participation in the movement through Facebook and Twitter, the internal structure was in prime condition for further collective action, and #LasPeriodistasParamos broadened its goals to leverage the online community to take even more actions, including an expansion of leader "units" for various action purposes, including translation, patrol, territories, materials, video, and photo production and management. The group's ability to organize online, amass interest via social media, then promote concrete participation in the streets and in community spaces where further momentum might take shape, such as mass media attention to create coverage and awareness raising for those impacted but not yet engaged in the movement, demonstrates the power of online mobilization around a common cause.

A political South Korean Twitter community used social media to make specific political demands, including the elimination of a conservative national daily newspaper.[68] Contrary to early popular opinion about social media organizing being purely horizontal communication and leaderless, the group organizer whose primary responsibilities included providing information and coordinating activism helped strengthen the group's sustainability. Furthermore, collective identity reached a sense of salience with massively coordinated retweeting to help frame the group's political concerns with the goal of impacting discourse, along with culture jamming tactics, which are forms of collective action that also provide the added structural benefits of enhancing group solidarity, which broadened the support base and crystallized online and offline political participation.[69] Attention to how social media expands democratic forms of protest and political participation in general has spread to consider non-Western democracies. For example, scholars have attended to variously politicized environments: Taiwan (young liberal democracy), Hong Kong (partial democracy), and China (one-party state) exist as very different political contexts, but the cultural similarities make this three-country comparison worthwhile.[70] Like other studies, the pattern of online political information sharing, and connection-building consistently predicted both offline and online forms of participation, such as expression and activism, across all three countries.

## Sustaining Collaboration and Collective Action

### Identity, Efficacy, and Anger

Shared grievances that lead to community-building are among the most important functions that protest movement activities may inspire, and this new vast network composition could set the stage for long-term activism.[71] The core components known to precede protest participation include identity, efficacy, and anger.[72] Pertaining to the pro-democracy movement in Hong Kong, spurred by an emphasis on structural inequalities in wealth gaps and social issues, those who consumed alternative news online showed greater intention to participate in protests with a sense of identity and a salience of anger fueling this motivation. Furthermore, anger and efficacy motivated those who consumed social media news to participate in protests.[73] Perhaps the collectivizing nature of empowerment to effect change via public demonstrations was best felt through non-mainstream news sources and the inherently participatory nature of social media. Using time-series data patterns in Twitter, Facebook, and onsite protests to assess what motivates people to move into the next stages of action within a movement, some scholars have argued that contentious communication on Twitter and Facebook preceded the Indignados and Occupy protests, but with patterns also showing that protest activity varies according to the roots of political unrest.[74] The video and image content on Twitter associated with the 2018 protests in Iran chronicled users' likelihood to share visual posts depicting protest activity with efficacy-focused elements more than emotionally arousing visuals.[75] When protests are in progress, the imagery communicates volumes about possibilities when the masses are engaged, attentive, and mobilized.

The #BlackLivesMatter hashtag and social movement (co-founded by three Black women in 2013, Patrisse Cullors, Alicia Garza, and Opal Tometi) gained momentum after the 2012 murder of Trayvon Martin in Sanford, Florida, USA which led to awareness raising online and people protesting nationwide. One example is the Million Hoodie March. In fact, a Change.org online petition that over 2 million people signed pressured police to arrest Trayvon Martin's murderer and launch an investigation. Prior to the online momentum, George Zimmerman was briefly detained and then released. In 2014, the #Ferguson, Missouri police execution of unarmed Black teenager Michael Brown was captured by witnesses via social media and protestors flooded the streets, and "then came the police, the National Guard, the national news cameras, the eyes of the world."[76] The US systems of racist oppression, including the police force's disproportionate brutality and use of force when interacting with Black people and the unjust legal system, occupied center stage. Hashtag activism existed as one among many spaces for action, as activists and community organizers mobilized collaborative efforts. Everyday citizens, activists, and journalists formed a cohesive and multifaceted collective on Twitter to provoke critical thought and drive attention and motivation to participate in public debates. These forms of early dissent following Brown's murder helped to mobilize online dissent and frame the developing story more critically.[77]

**FIGURE 10.3**  Demonstrators from different cultures and races protest on the streets for equal rights

In a show of solidarity forged by shared struggles of oppression and resistance efforts, Palestinian activists in Ferguson joined Black Lives Matter protesters to cultivate a "community of feeling," exemplifying the activism as both strategic and affective, leading to the development of a transnational collective identity.[78]

Social media usage has received partial credit for the success of the Black Lives Matter movement. Hashtag activism scholars credit the connectivity and social networking of social media as helping Black Lives Matter protests by "capturing public attention, evasion of censorship, logistics and coordination of protest events."[79] Beyond the #Ferguson hashtag, organizers invited others to join the protests via social media, and WordPress crowdfunding minimized economic barriers. The core organizer group met to collaborate with community organization leaders ahead of time to enable relationship-building toward activity and capacity-building as well as mutual support for local organizations that might be sustained beyond the protest waves.[80] The social media sphere erupted with demands for justice and a collective memory around the deep ills of the US criminal justice system as #BlackLivesMatter went viral then, and endures still now to remind us all that police violence still threatens Black lives.[81]

### Comparative Cases: #BlackLivesMatter, Athlete Activists, and Pepsi versus Nike Activism

We now turn our attention to two original research studies that focus on unique further engagement with #BLM beyond the typical trends of the lay masses uniting to uplift the social movement agenda into the mainstream public sphere. We might initially imagine that the more attention a movement gets, the better, since awareness raising remains an ongoing intention. We examine public reactions to the following two social media activism forms driven by high-profile and known public entities: professional athlete activists on Twitter, and popular brands integrating #BLM activism frames into their product advertisements.

Professional athletes are one particularly noteworthy group of public figures who have leveraged social media to draw attention to social justice issues and movements, calling for action among their follower bases. Because of the attention they receive from the public, high-profile athletes are some of our society's prominent opinion leaders, leveraging social media to draw attention to social justice issues and accompanying movements, and calling their follower bases to action. Credibility for athlete activists as opinion leaders and social media influencers can be enhanced through consistency frames in terms of how beliefs and values align with observed behavior,[82] and when a media frame is consistent with actions and beliefs, believable, supported by evidence, and backed by credible individuals, it is more likely to be perceived as credible, and to be adopted within the social movement.[83]

### Racial Justice Athlete Activists: LeBron James, Colin Kaepernick, and Maya Moore

Most social movement amplifiers in the last decade have focused sustained attention on the #BlackLivesMatter movement, and most demonstrators with big social media presences are Black public figures, including professional athletes.[84] Three important athletes who have demonstrated a commitment to combating racial injustice and whose Twitter presences clearly show their dedication to using their public figure status and platform for being vocal in support of the movement are LeBron James, Colin Kaepernick, and Maya Moore. The mass media has closely covered their actions, as it does with prominent public figures. Each athlete has a large following on Twitter – as of spring 2020, LeBron James had 45.8 million followers, Colin Kaepernick had 2.2 million followers, and Maya Moore had 210800 followers. Tweets between January 1, 2019 and December 31, 2019 were logged and examined. LeBron James produced 49 tweets, Colin Kaepernick produced 47 tweets, and Maya Moore produced 20. Then the top ten comments produced by Twitter's ranking algorithm on each of these posts were further examined to assess the overall public pulse in response to their social media activism.

LeBron James is considered one of the best professional basketball players ever, and he has almost 70 million more social media followers than any other NBA player.[85] Over the last few years, James has publicly spoken out several times about racial injustice, including wearing a hooded sweatshirt in tribute to Trayvon Martin, condemning Los Angeles Clippers owner Donald Sterling after he was caught on video spreading racist remarks, and tweeting after the police shootings of Alton Sterling and Philando Castile.[86] Former professional NFL football player Colin Kaepernick famously made headlines for his protest on the football field when he knelt on one knee during the national anthem to protest police brutality and excessive use of force against Black people after a slew of incidents turned violent, many resulting in the death of unarmed African-American men and women, across the nation. Kaepernick opted out of his contract with the 49ers after the 2016 season, making him a free agent before a likely release from his contract.[87] Kaepernick has continued his activism, appearing in an award-winning Nike campaign and contributing money to organizations dedicated to combating racial inequality.[88] The

WNBA Minnesota Lynx drafted Maya Moore with the first overall pick in 2011. During her eight years with the Minnesota Lynx, Moore won four championships and one Most Valuable Player award, and was selected for five All-Star Games, and her successes throughout her entire playing career led *Sports Illustrated* to deem her the greatest winner in the history of women's basketball.[89] Still in her career prime, Moore announced that she was taking time away from basketball during 2019–2020 to focus on criminal justice reform, concentrating on a particularly striking case of injustice.[90] During a visit to Missouri's Jefferson City Correctional Center in 2007, Moore met an African-American prisoner named Jonathan Irons, who had been serving a 50-year sentence for burglary and assault since 1998. Despite insufficient evidence, an all-White jury tried and convicted 16-year-old Irons as an adult. Moore supported Irons when he appealed his conviction in 2019 and in 2020, and a Missouri judge finally overturned his conviction.[91]

Comparing the Twitter presence of three prominent athlete activists, the athletes' tweets clustered thematically into four categories: (1) supporting another activist, (2) commenting on an injustice, (3) promoting their own activism, and (4) calling for action. Athletes attempt to enact social change through their social media pages by highlighting the work other activists have done to impact the communities around them, thereby elevating the voices of community-level efforts and actions, including lay organizers and leaders. They comment on various injustices in the world, bringing light to social issues that are important to them, and promote instances of their own activism, demonstrating their commitment to various causes and seeking recognition for their work. Finally, they can ask their followers to act, requesting support in their efforts to achieve social justice and change.

Previous sentiment research has pointed to eight common emotions exhibited by humans: anger, anticipation, disgust, fear, joy, sadness, surprise, and trust.[92] Through the lens of these common emotions, analyses of the Twitter activity surrounding social justice issues reveal that Maya Moore received the highest percentage of positive reactions to her posts, with many expressing trust in her character, joy in viewing her content, and anticipation of what comes next. Colin Kaepernick received a lot of positive public feedback from his tweets, and many followers expressed trust in his social justice messages. LeBron James' followers did not engage as positively with his tweets, as he received a higher proportion of comments responding with anger, fear, and sadness than the other two athletes. Users exhibited substantial feelings of trust in each athlete, and the athletes engaged with their followers well overall, demonstrating a positive thematic tone attributed to them as they leverage their prominent platform as Black public figures in support of the #BLM movement, racial justice, and social media activism efforts.

Some received higher quality and greater depth of engagement than others. Of the 137 comments on Moore's posts, 95 directly addressed the cause she promoted, the highest proportion among the three athletes. Kaepernick also received significant engagement with causes that he endorsed, as 284 of the 468 comments left on his tweets related to the issue he promoted. James received the least meaningful engagements, with 242 of the 490 comments on his posts actively engaged with his content. Regardless of the differences between each athlete, these results support previous conclusions about the important function of social media sites as platforms where meaningful discussion about important societal issues can occur.[93] Based on these results, it would be easy to say that Maya Moore's approach is superior and that others should adopt the strategies she uses on Twitter. However, countless other factors may be at play. First, there are many individual differences between the athletes. LeBron James is an active athlete, while Colin Kaepernick and Maya Moore currently do not belong to any sports team or organization, which has implications about credibility and status that influence social media activist agendas. Whether professional athletes as public figures should engage vocally and leverage their platform concerning charged politicized issues arises as part of this conversation, and is a perceptual difference that may influence the public's reaction to athlete activists' communication. There are many factors that can affect an athlete's ability to reach their audience in a meaningful and worthwhile manner, but as previously discussed, using social media to further amplify and draw attention to a social movement's agenda and enact engagement personally lends credibility and funnels further momentum online that may translate to offline movement activity.

### Brand Activism: Pepsi's "Live for Now" and Nike's "Dream Crazy"

Marketing research has investigated brand motives for associating with a cause and audiences' familiarity with the cause.[94] If consumers think that the brand's motives are serving society rather than self-serving, as in solely capitalistic motives, then they react positively to the brand message. Brands reflect the "zeitgeist of the times" by grounding themselves in cultural contexts and often leveraging the social climate to appeal to potential consumers through media. Brands sometimes enact social resistance positioning through brand activist framing by engaging in activism efforts to promote, impede, or direct social reform with the desire to make improvements in society.[95] Brand activism borrows from social movement campaigns, emulating their aesthetics of authenticity, and leads typically to consumers responding by boycotting or buycotting.[96] Pepsi and Nike are two examples of brands that aligned themselves with social movement energies fueled by cultural tensions to resonate with consumers through their respective campaigns: "Live for Now" and "Dream Crazy."

On April 4, 2017, Pepsi released "Live for Now", a short film featuring model Kendall Jenner participating in a fictitious protest in which Jenner hands a police officer a Pepsi, effectively ending the need to protest. The ad was criticized by consumers for co-opting imagery from Black Lives Matter, calling Pepsi out for its tone-deaf ad, saying it appropriated and trivialized resistance movements. The criticism was so overwhelming that Pepsi pulled the ad in less than 24 hours after its release.

On September 3, 2018, Colin Kaepernick teased Twitter fans with a preview of the Nike ad "Dream Crazy" by posting a black-and-white portrait of himself with the quote "Believe in something. Even if it means sacrificing everything" and the hashtag #JustDoIt.[97] "Dream Crazy" was released on September 6, 2018 during the first timeout in the third quarter of the NFL's season opener in celebration of Nike's 30 years of #JustDoIt campaigns. It features Kaepernick narrating stories of 16 athletes with inspirational stories, motivating consumers to follow their dreams. The release of "Dream Crazy" resulted in partisan responses from consumers, partly because of Kaepernick's inclusion.

Using Kaepernick as the protagonist of "Dream Crazy" was a controversial choice because it demonstrated Nike's support for his previous protests. While some saw the ad as an act of treason and "anti-American," others were thankful and empowered by Nike's support for Black Lives Matter.[98] Social media activists such as Shaun King and Charles Robinson commended Nike's marketing team for providing Kaepernick with a platform to accentuate the core values behind his "anthem" protests.[99]

An analysis of the ads' brand activist framing along three dimensions – stylistic features, protagonists and set of frames – reveals that "Live for Now" positions itself in the Black Lives Matter movement through a protest imagery narrative, while "Dream Crazy" does so through Colin Kaepernick's protagonist role. Furthermore, "Live for Now's" stylistic features, protagonist choice, and set of frames were incongruent with schemas of social resistance, while "Dream Crazy's" were congruent. To understand how these campaigns were received and perceived by consumers, sentiment analysis was conducted to tag tweets into eight emotions and two sentiments. The leading emotion for both advertisements was "trust," which referred to the public's perception of the campaign. "Live for Now" had predominantly negative sentiment, while "Dream Crazy" had predominantly positive sentiment. The public's perception of these campaigns and their brand activism efforts differed. Pepsi's

"Live for Now" was criticized for co-opting resistance and appropriating Black Lives Matter, and was called "exploitative brand social activism."[100] Nike's "Dream Crazy" campaign was met with partisan responses because, while Kaepernick's biographical attributes and identity resonate with social resistance making him into a metaphor that encapsulates social resistance, Jenner's evoke an appropriation and trivialization of social resistance. For effective coat-tailing of cultural epicenters, there needs to be cultural resonance between the brand and the movement.

When a brand's positioning in relation to a social movement seems authentic and credible, a brand can be deemed a "cultural producer"; however, if the brand lacks authenticity and credibility, the perception becomes one of a "cultural parasite." Furthermore, relying on the scholarly framing terms of "arrows" and "targets," the "Dream Crazy" ad functioned as an arrow, while "Live for Now" functioned as a target.[101] Nike's pro-Black Lives Matter stance resonates with consumers since Nike predominantly sponsors Black athletes and has ties to the African-American community more broadly, which helped lend authenticity to the ad's message and Nike's ability to skirt the fine line of movement appropriation for sales. Conversely, "Live for Now" embodied negative aspects through the trivialization and sanitization of social resistance. The incongruencies between the narrative, Jenner as protagonist and Black Lives Matter as a serious, enduring racial justice movement caused "Live for Now" to come across as a whitewashed co-option of social resistance. By playing upon Black Lives Matter and referring to police brutality in a playful way by following a White woman model around as she easily and happily interacts with protestors and police, Pepsi's "Live for Now" becomes an insensitive bandwagon ultimately deemed detrimental to social resistance. "Live for Now" borrows from social movements through its flippant use of protest imagery and Jenner, while "Dream Crazy" emulates social movement authenticity through Kaepernick. Lastly, "Live for Now" and "Dream Crazy" evoke several characteristics of brand activism: both campaigns have symbolic character and value, engage a global audience, and have digital roots.[102] The social resistance positioning and brand activist framing of these campaigns differ because while "Dream Crazy" redefines politics and defends Kaepernick's Black Lives Matter protest, "Live for Now" appropriates social resistance. Alignment between brand consumer and cause is crucial for brand activism to be effective. Though it might put social movement issues on the radar of the mass public, it could backfire by provoking incongruencies, and the framing is often heavily contingent upon the leader(s) depicted in driving attention to the cause through advertisements.

### Emotion, Persistence, and Organizational Involvement

Numerous social media activist examples churn support through anger-induced efforts online that then expand into other realms of protest and further mobilization among the masses. Emotional motivation endures beyond the activation that anger seems to ignite and moves people to activism efforts. A common theme throughout much of the research emphasizes the important role emotional displays and themes in social movement posts play. The 2016 "candlelight vigil" in South Korea developed through digital activism for people to express opposition to President Park, and scholars found that linguistic mechanisms connect people around common identities, and that commonality further enhances the intensity of engagement with the activist efforts.[103] Though the vigil itself remained in the realm of affect with a diversity of ideas loosely connecting the networks, scholars have emphasized the fact that "users' temporary voices, when integrated into digital networks, can be resilient enough to create large-scale social movements."[104] Indeed, the social media platforms are the communication catalysts, and the people themselves use them quite strategically toward various aims where the individual and personal stories lend themselves well to cultivate the collective sense of agency propelled forward by emotional backdrops that move people to action. In the #WhyIStayed feminist hashtag tweets that arose in response to the 2014 domestic violence controversy in the NFL, one study found that a set of dramatic elements began with online personal stories, and then moved to collective action online, lending further momentum to the messages.[105] The #MeToo and #HimToo hashtag content that occurred amid the controversial sexual assault history of Supreme Court Justice Brent Kavanaugh in 2018 conveyed some common themes: personal experience, identification and disidentification, calls to action, and discursive appropriation.[106] Importantly, the #HimToo hashtag response demonstrates the relative ease with which misogynistic impulses can eclipse a movement and even compete with the intended framing to cast doubt on the cause's seriousness and impact.

Beyond the online realms of activism in relation to social movements, and especially once activist arcs dissipate, maintaining attention around the issues remains an important ongoing task. Researchers examined data from young people in Hong Kong in 2019 to assess attitudes about the Umbrella Movement after the previous peak of activist mobilization, to better understand in-between periods of time amid protest waves.[107] Evidence demonstrates that social media helps to maintain momentum around the issues and protest potential even when on-the-ground mobilization opportunities are in a lull. Tin-Yuet Ting stressed the importance of the everyday, mundane forms of grassroots and networked activism that followed Hong Kong's Umbrella Movement to highlight the possibilities for ongoing momentum, which we might best describe as habitual activism as a form of persistence.[108] Another way activism mobilization may remain intact is through organizational involvement. Scholars have studied the dialectic tensions between offline/online and permanence/temporality in social movement activism efforts through political bloggers in Singapore, and found that those with membership in offline organizations enjoyed more social influence and collective identity sense with other bloggers; however, those belonging to online-based groups enjoyed strong ties and a longevity to their communication that transcended the time limitations of political campaigns or activist agendas at peak moments.[109] The salience of multiple forms of involvement and investment in social movement activism both online and offline becomes particularly relevant when thinking beyond the immediacy of protest mobilization.

## Conclusion

Social media activism in the last decade of our ability to observe its influence has demonstrated its key importance in spreading information about causes, moving people to action, and sustaining impact through demands and agitation for change. Co-creation and collaboration among various actors and platforms, intense connectivity with on-the-ground groups, partnering with alternative media, and influencing mainstream mass media coverage for amplified attention are all gains that benefit the sheer volume of exposure potential of social movement agendas. People have power in influencing stories and frames, but "mass media holds a privileged voice in the flow of information."[110] It behooves us to abandon an all-or-nothing or either/or approach to examining the utility of social media in activist agendas, because people can and do work together when collectively empowered around a common goal.[111] Counterpublics are alive and well in today's civil society, and social media affords users great potential to push the mainstream public sphere on social justice issues most directly perhaps than ever before.[112] Movements and accompanying activism must maintain capacity for openness to shifts in light of challenges as they arise.[113] Affordances on social media do not automatically lend themselves to equal participation or smooth processes, as collective action is all about constant negotiation and a balance of individual voices, and the will of the group to further fuel the momentum of the various social movement agendas.

## Reflections

- As we have seen over the last decade, social media activism in relation to social movements can reach the masses quickly and move them to a variety of actions. Given the relatively short time social media activism has existed, what future potential do you see with the roles social media plays in social movements around the world? How do technological affordances influence action possibilities? What role do political climate and context play?
- Emotion, anger in particular, ignites attention and efficacy, which often motivate people toward action. What are your thoughts about social media activists leveraging a range of emotions to grab attention and sustain relevance? Discuss any moral or ethical implications of emotional appeals from within movements.

## Notes

1 Jenkins, Henry. 2006. *Convergence Culture: Where Old and New Media Collide.* New York: New York University Press, p. 3.
2 Ibid., pp. 17–18.
3 Scheufele, Dietram A. "Framing as a theory of media effects." *Journal of Communication* 49, no. 1 (1999): 103–122.
4 Couldry, Nick. 2005. *Media Rituals: A Critical Approach.* New York: Routledge, p. 97.
5 Neubaum, German, and Nicole C. Krämer. "Opinion Climates in social media: blending mass and interpersonal communication." *Human Communication Research* 43, no. 4 (2017): 467.
6 Reed, Thomas Vernon. 2018. *Digitized Lives: Culture, Power and Social Change in the Internet Era.* New York: Routledge, pp. 128–129.
7 Palfrey, John, and Urs Gasser. 2011. "Activists." In Mark Bauerlein (ed.), *The Digital Divide: Arguments for and against Facebook, Google, Texting, and the Age of Social Networking.* New York: Penguin, pp. 189–203.
8 Reed, *Digitized Lives*, p. 128.
9 Tufekci, Zeynep. 2017. *Twitter and Tear Gas: The Power and Fragility of Networked Protest.* New Haven, CT: Yale University Press, p. xxvi.
10 Margetts, Helen, Peter John, Scott Hale, and Taha Yasseri. 2015. *Political Turbulence: How Social Media Shape Collective Action* Princeton, NJ: Princeton University Press, p. 46.
11 Strange, Michael. "'Act now and sign our joint statement!' What role do online global group petitions play in transnational movement networks?" *Media, Culture & Society* 33, no. 8 (2011): 1236–1253.
12 Margetts et al., *Political Turbulence*, p. 46.
13 Jenkins, Henry. 2016. "Youth voice, media, and political engagement." In Henry Jenkins, Sangita Shresthova, Liana Gamber-Thompson, Neta Kligler-Vilenchik, and Arely M. Zimmerman (eds.), *By Any Media Necessary: The New Youth Activism.* New York: New York University Press, pp. 41–43.
14 Jenkins, Henry, Sam Ford, and Joshua Green. 2013. *Spreadable Media: Creating Value and Meaning in a Networked Culture.* New York: New York University Press, p. 155.

15 Tufekci, *Twitter and Tear Gas*, p. xxvi.

16 Jenkins, "Youth voice, media, and political engagement," pp. 17–21.

17 LeFebvre, Rebecca Kay, and Crystal Armstrong. "Grievance-based social movement mobilization in the #Ferguson Twitter storm." *New Media & Society* 20, no. 1 (2018): 8–28.

18 Reed, *Digitized Lives*, pp. 128–130.

19 Ibid., p. 125.

20 Palfrey and Gasser, "Activists," p. 191.

21 Youmans, William Lafi, and Jillian C. York. "Social media and the activist toolkit: User agreements, corporate interests, and the information infrastructure of modern social movements." *Journal of Communication* 62, no. 2 (2012): 315–329.

22 McIlwain, Charlton D. 2020. *Black Software: The Internet and Racial Justice, From the Afronet to Black Lives Matter*. New York: Oxford University Press, p. 252.

23 Jackson, Sarah J., Moya Bailey, and Brooke Foucault Welles. 2020. *#HashtagActivism: Networks of Race and Gender Justice*. Cambridge, MA: MIT Press, p. xxvii.

24 Shifman, Limor. 2014. *Memes in Digital Culture*. Cambridge, MA: MIT Press, p. 122.

25 Lim, Merlyna. "Clicks, cabs, and coffee houses: Social media and oppositional movements in Egypt, 2004–2011." *Journal of Communication* 62, no. 2 (2012): 231–248.

26 Jackson, Bailey, and Foucault Welles, *#Hashtag Activism*, p. xxvii.

27 Ibid.

28 Reed, *Digitized Lives*, p. 129.

29 Campos, Ricardo, José Alberto Simões, and Inês Pereira. "Digital media, youth practices and representations of recent activism in Portugal." *Communications* 43, no. 4 (2018): 489–507.

30 Eslen-Ziya, Hande. "Social media and Turkish feminism: New resources for social activism." *Feminist Media Studies* 13, no. 5 (2013): 860–870.

31 Clark-Parsons, Rosemary. ""I see you, I believe you, I stand with you":# MeToo and the performance of networked feminist visibility." *Feminist Media Studies* 21, no. 3 (2021): 362–380.

32 Shifman, *Memes in Digital Culture*, p. 121.

33 Ibid., pp. 4–6.

34 Fadnis, Deepa. "Feminist activists protest tax on sanitary pads: Attempts to normalize conversations about menstruation in India using hashtag activism." *Feminist Media Studies* 17, no. 6 (2017): 1111–1114.

35 Reed, *Digitized Lives*, p. 131.

36 Jenkins, Ford, and Green, *Spreadable Media*, p. 191.

37 Nahon, Karine, and Jeff Hemsley. 2013. *Going Viral*. Malden, MA: Polity Press, pp. 1–3.

38 Jenkins, "Youth voice, media, and political engagement," pp. 43–44.

39 Obar, Jonathan A. "Canadian advocacy 2.0: an analysis of social media adoption and perceived affordances by advocacy groups looking to advance activism in Canada." *Canadian Journal of Communication* 39, no. 2 (2014): 211–233.

40 Candón-Mena, José, and David Montero Sánchez. "From cyber-activism to technopolitics: A Critical take on historical periods and orientations in the use of digital technology by social movements." *International Journal of Communication* 15 (2021): 2921–2941.

41 Tufekci, *Twitter and Tear Gas*, pp. 212–214.
42 Uwalaka, Temple, and Jerry Watkins. "Social media as the fifth estate in Nigeria: An analysis of the 2012 Occupy Nigeria Protest." *African Journalism Studies* 39, no. 4 (2018): 22.
43 Lev-On, Azi. "The igniter and the megaphone: Perceptions of Facebook's role in activism." *Convergence* 26, no. 3 (2020): 577–592.
44 Van Leeckwyck, Robin, Pieter Maeseele, Maud Peeters, and David Domingo. "Indymedia in Belgium: The delicate balance between media activism and political activism." *Media, Culture & Society* 42, no. 6 (2020): 1031–1038.
45 Lee, Ashley. "Invisible networked publics and hidden contention: Youth activism and social media tactics under repression." *New Media & Society* 20, no. 11 (2018): 4095–4115.
46 Martini, Michele. "Online distant witnessing and live-streaming activism: Emerging differences in the activation of networked publics." *New Media & Society* 20, no. 11 (2018): 4035–4055.
47 Thorburn, Elise Danielle. "Social media, subjectivity, and surveillance: Moving on from Occupy, the rise of live streaming video." *Communication and Critical/Cultural Studies* 11, no. 1 (2014): 52–63.
48 Hermida, Alberto, and Víctor Hernández-Santaolalla. "Twitter and video activism as tools for counter-surveillance: The case of social protests in Spain." *Information, Communication & Society* 21, no. 3 (2018): 416–433.
49 Kuo, Rachel. "Racial justice activist hashtags: Counterpublics and discourse circulation." *New Media & Society* 20, no. 2 (2018): 495–514.
50 Mann, Benjamin W. "Rhetoric of online disability activism: #Cripthevote and civic participation." *Communication Culture & Critique* 11, no. 4 (2018): 604–621.
51 Gonzalez, Victoria. "Embodiment in activist images: Addressing the role of the body in digital activism." *Media, Culture & Society* 44, no. 2 (2022): 263.
52 Lim, Merlyna. "Framing Bouazizi: 'White lies,' hybrid network, and collective/connective action in the 2010–11 Tunisian Uprising." *Journalism* 14, no. 7 (2013): 921–941.
53 Ibid., pp. 921–941.
54 Pakanati, Rajdeep, and Jeannine E. Relly. "Deepening democracy through a social movement: Networks, information rights, and online and offline activism." *International Journal of Communication* 14 (2020): 4760–4780.
55 Dumitrica, Delia, and Mylynn Felt. "Mediated grassroots collective action: Negotiating barriers of digital activism." *Information, Communication & Society* 23, no. 13 (2020): 1821–1837.
56 Gerbaudo, Paolo. "Social media teams as digital vanguards: The question of leadership in the management of key Facebook and Twitter accounts of Occupy Wall Street, Indignados and UK Uncut." *Information, Communication & Society* 20, no. 2 (2017): 185–202.
57 Azer, Evronia, G. Harindranath, and Yingqin Zheng. "Revisiting leadership in information and communication technology (ICT)-enabled activism: A study of Egypt's grassroots human rights groups." *New Media & Society* 21, no. 5 (2019): 1141–1169.
58 Dencik, Lina, and Peter Wilkin. "Digital activism and the political culture of trade unionism." *Information, Communication & Society* 23, no. 12 (2020): 1728–1737.
59 Tufekci, *Twitter and Tear Gas*, pp. 83–85.

60 Valenzuela, Sebastián, Arturo Arriagada, and Andrés Scherman. "The social media basis of youth protest behavior: The case of Chile." *Journal of Communication* 62, no. 2 (2012): 299–314.

61 Ibid., pp. 299–314.

62 Treré, Emiliano. "Reclaiming, proclaiming, and maintaining collective identity in the #Yosoy132 movement in Mexico: An examination of digital frontstage and backstage activism through social media and instant messaging platforms." *Information, Communication & Society* 18, no. 8 (2015): 901–915.

63 Raynauld, Vincent, Emmanuelle Richez, and Katie Boudreau Morris. "Canada is #IdleNoMore: Exploring dynamics of indigenous political and civic protest in the Twitterverse." *Information, Communication & Society* 21, no. 4 (2018): 626–642.

64 Ibid.

65 Navarro, Celina, and Òscar Coromina. "Discussion and mediation of social outrage on Twitter: The reaction to the judicial sentence of 'La Manada.'" *Communication & Society* 33, no. 1 (2020): 93–106.

66 Bernal-Triviño, Ana, and Sandra Sanz-Martos. "Las Periodistas Paramos in Spain: Professional, feminist internet activism." *European Journal of Communication* 35, no. 4 (2020): 325–338.

67 Ibid., p. 328.

68 Choi, Sujin, and Han Woo Park. "An exploratory approach to a Twitter-based community centered on a political goal in South Korea: Who organized it, what they shared, and how they acted." *New Media & Society* 16, no. 1 (2014): 129–148.

69 Ibid., p. 129.

70 Chen, Hsuan-Ting, Michael Chan, and Francis L.F. Lee. "Social media use and democratic engagement: A comparative study of Hong Kong, Taiwan, and China." *Chinese Journal of Communication* 9, no. 4 (2016): 348–366.

71 Tufekci, *Twitter and Tear Gas*, p. 103.

72 Chan, Michael. "Media use and the social identity model of collective action: Examining the roles of online alternative news and social media news." *Journalism & Mass Communication Quarterly* 94, no. 3 (2017): 663–681.

73 Ibid." p. 663.

74 Bastos, Marco T., Dan Mercea, and Arthur Charpentier. "Tents, tweets, and events: The interplay between ongoing protests and social media." *Journal of Communication* 65, no. 2 (2015): 320–350.

75 Esfandiari, Maryam, Bohdan Fridrich, and Junxi Yao. "Visual content of twitter during the 2018 protests in Iran: Analysis of its role and function." *Global Media and Communication* 17, no. 2 (2021): 213–230.

76 McIlwain, *Black Software*, p. 254.

77 Jackson, Sarah J., and Brooke Foucault Welles. "# Ferguson is everywhere: Initiators in emerging counterpublic networks." *Information, Communication & Society* 19, no. 3 (2016): 397–418.

78 Mislán, Cristina, and Sara Shaban. "'To Ferguson, love Palestine': Mediating life under occupation." *Communication and Critical/Cultural Studies* 16, no. 1 (2019): 43–60.

79 Lefebvre and Armstrong, "Grievance-based social movement mobilization in the #Ferguson Twitter storm," p. 3.

80 McIlwain, *Black Software*, p. 254.

81 Ibid.

82 Snow, David, Robert Benford, Holly McCammon, Lyndi Hewitt, and Scott Fitzgerald. "The emergence, development, and future of the framing perspective: 25+ years since frame alignment." *Mobilization: An International Quarterly* 19, no. 1 (2014): 23–46.

83 Daellenbach, Kate, and Joy Parkinson. "A useful shift in our perspective: Integrating social movement framing into social marketing." *Journal of Social Marketing* 7, no. 2 (2017): 188–204.

84 Zirin, Dave. "Kyle Korver challenges every white athlete to listen and act." *The Nation*, April 9, 2019. https://www.thenation.com/article/archive/kyle -korver-white-privilege-racism-nba/.

85 Badenhausen, Kurt. "Social media's most valuable athletes: Ronaldo, McGregor and LeBron score big." *Forbes*, August 3, 2019. https://www .forbes.com/sites/kurtbadenhausen/2019/08/03/social-medias-most-valuable -athletes-ronaldo-mcgregor-and-lebron-score/#16eb66be2f98.

86 James, Xandria, and Lombardo, Kayla. "A history of LeBron James's activism." *Sports Illustrated*, January 6, 2016. https://www.si.com/nba/lebron -james-cleveland-cavaliers-social-political-activism.

87 Wagoner, Nick. "Colin Kaepernick to opt out, become free agent." ESPN, March 1, 2017. https://www.espn.com/nfl/story/_/id/18796373/colin-kaeper- nick-san-francisco-49ers-opts-contract

88 Lauletta, Tyler. "Colin Kaepernick has already donated more than $1 million of his NFL Earnings to social justice charities." *Business Insider*, September 5, 2018. https://www.businessinsider.com/colin-kaepernick-donations-social -justice-charities-2018-9.

89 Deitsch, Richard. "Maya Moore is the greatest winner in history of women's basketball – and best may be yet to come." *Sports Illustrated*, December 5, 2017. https://www.si.com/sportsperson/2017/12/05/maya-moore-sports -illustrated-performer-of-the-year.

90 Streeter, Kurt. "W.N.B.A.'s Maya Moore to skip another season to focus on prisoner's case." *New York Times*, January 22, 2020. https://www.nytimes .com/2020/01/22/sports/basketball/maya-moore-jonathan-irons.html.

91 Stelloh, Tim, and Blayne Alexander. "Judge overturns convictions in case championed by WNBA star Maya Moore." NBC News, March 9, 2020. https://www.nbcnews.com/news/us-news/judge-overturns-convictions-case -championed-wnba-star-maya-moore-n1153736.

92 Ibid.

93 Frederick, Evan L., Ann Pegorano, and Jimmy Sanderson. "Divided and united: Perceptions of athlete activism at the ESPYS." *Sport in Society*, 12 (2018): 1919–1936.

94 Barone, Michael J., Anthony D. Miyazaki, and Kimberly A. Taylor. "The influence of cause-related marketing on consumer choice: Does one good turn deserve another?" *Journal of the Academy of Marketing Science* 28, no. 2 (2000): 248–262.

95 Kotler, Philip, and Christian Sarkar. "Finally, brand activism!" *Marketing Journal*, January 9, 2017. https://www.marketingjournal.org/finally-brand -activism-philip-kotler-and-christian-sarkar/.

96 Manfredi-Sánchez, Juan Luis. "Brand activism." *Communication & Society*, 32 no. 4 (2019): 343–359.

97 Draper, Kevin, and Ken Belson. "Colin Kaepernick's Nike campaign keeps N.F.L. anthem kneeling in spotlight." *New York Times*, September 3, 2018. https://www.nytimes.com/2018/09/03/sports/kaepernick-nike.html.

98 Sangha, Barry. "Just buy it: A critical analysis of Nike's 'Dream Crazy' advertisement campaign." *The Startup*, December 9, 2019. https://medium .com/swlh/just-buy-it-acritical-analysis-of-nikes-dream-crazy-advertisement -campaign-169190f14a89.

99 Ibid.

100 Monllos, Kristina. "Pepsi's tone-deaf Kendall Jenner ad co-opting the resistance is getting clobbered in social." *Ad Week*, April 5, 2017. https://www .adweek.com/brand-marketing/pepsis-tone-deaf-kendall-jenner-ad-co-opt-ing-the-resistance-is-getting-clobbered-in-social/.

101 Suarez, Maribel, and Russell Belk. "Cultural resonance of global brands in Brazilian social movements." *International Marketing Review* 34, no. 4 (2017): 480–497.

102 Manfredi-Sánchez, "Brand activism," p. 346.

103 Lee, Shin Haeng, and Tae Yun Lim. "Connective action and affective language: Computational text analysis of Facebook comments on social movements in South Korea." *International Journal of Communication* 13 (2019): 20.

104 Ibid., p. 20.

105 Clark, Rosemary. "'Hope in a hashtag': The discursive activism of# WhyIStayed." *Feminist Media Studies* 16, no. 5 (2016): 788–804.

106 Dejmanee, Tisha, Zulfia Zaher, R. Samantha, and Michael J. Papa. "#MeToo; #HimToo: Popular feminism and hashtag activism in the Kavanaugh hearings." *International Journal of Communication* 14 (2020): 3946–3963.

107 Lee, Francis L.F., Michael Chan, and Hsuan-Ting Chen. "Social media and protest attitudes during movement abeyance: A study of Hong Kong university students." *International Journal of Communication* 14 (2020): 20.

108 Ting, Tin-Yuet. "East Asia in action: Everyday networked activism in Hong Kong's Umbrella Movement: Expanding on contemporary practice theory to understand activist digital media usages." *International Journal of Communication* 13 (2019): 20.

109 Soon, Carol, and Hichang Cho. "OMGs! Offline-based movement organizations, online-based movement organizations and network mobilization: A case study of political bloggers in Singapore." *Information, Communication & Society* 17, no. 5 (2014): 537–559.

110 Jenkins, Ford, and Green, *Spreadable Media*, p. 163.

111 Ibid.

112 Jackson, Bailey, and Foucault Welles, *#Hashtag Activism*, pp. 196–197.

113 Tufekci, *Twitter and Tear Gas*, pp. 110–111.

# ADVOCATES FOR ACTION

## Patsy Takemoto Mink

1927–2002
Hometown: Hāmākua Poko, Hawai'i Territory, USA
Movements: Gender equality, racial equality, education, environmentalism
Organizations: Everyman Organization, Americans for Democratic
   Action, The Public Reporter

*Phoebe L. Bogdanoff*

Born in 1927 in Honolulu, Hawai'i, Patsy Mink was a third-generation Japanese-American who faced discrimination throughout her life that later inspired her to fight for equality as a lawyer, state and federal legislator, and advocate in the private sector.[1] Her passion for politics began in high school when she was elected as student body president and continued throughout her years in college. While at the University of Nebraska, USA, she successfully lobbied to end dorm segregation by leading a grassroots campaign to unite students, parents, administrators, employees, alumni, and sponsoring corporations/businesses.[2] After being denied entry to multiple medical schools, she ultimately pursued a law degree from the University of Chicago, Illinois, USA, establishing her as the first Japanese-American woman licensed to practice law in Hawai'i. Because of employment discrimination, Mink established her own private law firm,[3] specializing in criminal and family law.[4]

Mink was a pioneer for women in politics and a strong voice for marginalized communities. Throughout her career, Mink held the title of "first" multiple times, cementing her place in history as a political trailblazer who changed history by captivating and inspiring audiences. In 1965, Mink

DOI: 10.4324/9781003291855-25

became the first woman of color elected to the US House of Representatives after Hawai'i declared statehood, formerly holding positions in the territorial House of Representatives and Senate.[5] She was the first woman of color to serve in the US Congress, and the first Asian-American woman to be elected to Congress.[6] She served 12 terms in the US House of Representatives, from 1965 to 1977, and then again from 1990 until her death in 2002.[7] In 1972, she became the first Asian-American woman to run for president, which she did on an anti-war platform. Throughout her legislative career, she was known for her liberal opinions, specifically in areas like education, employment, housing, poverty, and taxation.[8] Mink was also the co-author of the Title IX Amendment of the Higher Education Act, which prohibits sex discrimination in educational programs and activities that receive federal financial assistance.[9]

She is best-known for co-authoring and advocating for the Title IX Amendment of the Higher Education Act as well as later introducing the Women's Educational Equity Act. After leaving federal positions altogether to work in the private sector and then Honolulu City Council, she returned to the House of Representatives, and when Clarence Thomas was nominated for the Supreme Court, helped organize a public protest against the judicial committee's denial of Anita Hill's testimony.[10] Toward the end of her career, Mink did not end her inspiring political efforts, and instead co-founded the Congressional Asian Pacific American Caucus and co-sponsored the DREAM Act to continue her work in bettering the lives of others.[11]

After her death in 2002, the Title IX Amendment of the Higher Education Act was renamed the Patsy T. Mink Equal Opportunity in Education Act to honor her work in creating the legislation and advocating for the end of discrimination, along with the ongoing legacy she has left for students nationwide.[12] Additionally, President Obama posthumously awarded Mink the Presidential Medal of Freedom in 2014, further positioning her in American history. Moving forward, the Patsy Takemoto Mink Education Fund set up in her honor provides educational funding for low-income women and children, ensuring her life's work will persevere.[13]

Mink faced discrimination throughout her life due to her race and gender, but her experiences inspired her to become an advocate for equality and civil rights.

## Notes

1 Cruz, Tania, and Eric Y. Yamamoto. "A tribute to Patsy Takemoto Mink." *Asian-Pacific Law & Policy Journal* 4, no. 2 (2003): 569–579. https://

scholarspace.manoa.hawaii.edu/server/api/core/bitstreams/5d57364b-a3ff-4f4d-bbae-4f8808336869/content

2 Ibid.

3 "Mink, Patsy Takemoto." US House of Representatives: History, Art & Archives. Accessed November 29, 2022. https://history.house.gov/People/Detail/18329.

4 Leavitt, Judith A. 1985. "Mink, Patsy Takemoto." In *American Women Managers and Administrators: A Selective Biographical Dictionary of Twentieth-century Leaders in Business, Education, and Government.* Westport, CT: Greenwood Press, pp. 183–184.

5 "Mink, Patsy Takemoto." National Women's Hall of Fame. Accessed November 29, 2022. https://www.womenofthehall.org/inductee/patsy-take-moto-mink/.

6 Pineda, Daenerys. "Building our own houses: AAPIs in Congress." (2022). CMC Senior Theses. 3073. https://scholarship.claremont.edu/cmc_theses/3073

7 Korgel, Skyler Allyn. 2018. "*Hoʻomalimali and the succession model of political inheritance in Hawaiʻi: A study of the electoral dominance of Americans of Japanese ancestry in state and congressional politics.*" Ph.D. dissertation.

8 "Mink, Patsy Takemoto." US House of Representatives: History, Art & Archives.

9 Mertens, Richard. "Legacy: Patsy Mink (1927–2002): A tenacious and determined politician." *University of Chicago Magazine* 105, no. 1. (2012): 46–49.

10 "Patsy Mink." National Park Service. Accessed November 29, 2022. https://www.nps.gov/people/patsy-mink.htm.

11 Gutgold, Nichola D. 2017. *Still Paving the Way for Madam President.* Blue Ridge Summit, PA: Lexington Books.

12 Gootman, Elissa. "Patsy Mink, veteran Hawaii congresswoman, dies at 74." *New York Times*, September 30, 2002.

13 Arinaga, Esther K.; Ojiri, Renee E. (Summer 2003). A Tribute to Patsy Takemoto Mink. *Asian-Pacific Law & Policy Journal.* William S. Richardson School of Law. https://scholarspace.manoa.hawaii.edu/server/api/core/bitstreams/5d57364b-a3ff-4f4d-bbae-4f8808336869/content

# 11

# DOES ONLINE ACTIVISM IMPACT OFFLINE IMPACT?

## A Cultural Examination of Slacktivism, "Popcorn Activism," Power, and Fragility

*Monica L. Ponder, Yewande O. Addie, Ajia I. Meux, Natalie T.J. Tindall, and Britney Gulledge*

### Introduction

"Raising awareness is a critical part of social activism, but does it translate to real change?" This question was presented to us when we were asked to write this chapter. The original conceptualization of this section was to focus on the limits of **hashtag activism**, also commonly referred to as **slacktivism** and clicktivism,[1] yet these issues extend beyond the functional practice of hashtag posting. Extending this definitional frame, our chapter examines the power dynamics of online activism and the fragility of social and community cultural wealth within the scope of online activism. We change the frame to address these questions: Who defines who is an activist and what is activism; and who gets to decide what impacts and strategies are relevant and effective? We embark on this chapter as five US-based Black women scholars with a myriad of life experiences and connections to both online and offline community activism, and the examples within this chapter stem from online activism within the Black diaspora.

### Online Presence as the Minimal Gateway to Activism: The Public Relations Paradox

To start, it is important to distinguish between two common audience frames in this area: (1) social movements and activist groups that use the internet as a means, among many, to disseminate content, and (2) activists and social movements that operate exclusively online. What Loader[2] considered as "online social movements" is *de rigeur* for all social movements;

DOI: 10.4324/9781003291855-26

they have adopted and use information and communication technologies, such as multimedia, telecommunications, and the World Wide Web. However, across the literature, social movements that take place exclusively online are also referred to formally as "online" social movements.[3] Hence, digital media is critical for any organization operating in the 21st century. In the same way that corporations and nonprofits must have an online presence, social movements and activist struggles of all creeds have staked their claims to online real estate. As Freelon, Marwick, and Kreiss noted, "digital media offer unprecedented tools for activists around the world to help realize their sociopolitical visions." [4]

Every tactic we have in the arsenal of strategic communication is neutral, and progressive and regressive activists use these tactics to organize, create groundswell, generate goodwill, build communities, and develop spaces of belonging for those who identify with and believe in the movement's goals. They have websites, use social media, launch chatbots, and send email newsletters. Actors on every side of the political spectrum have their own unique methods for reaching and building audiences, including deploying hashtag activism, manipulating social media algorithms, using bots (conservative), and creating their own media ecosystems and channels.[5] With this baseline understanding, how can scholars differentiate between the aforementioned audience frames? How are we to discern the sole online activist from the organization that occasionally (or routinely) advocates online?

Public relations has been accused of possessing an intellectual myopia that has "a systemic nearsightedness regarding alternative perspectives."[6] Within the public relations context, activism has been given short shrift in the quest for corporatist approval. A new wave of scholars are recasting activism; however, lingering discourse regarding activist strategies as outside the "organization" (or corporation) is still the norm. Part of the reason why is how we define public relations. Ciszek pointed out that "public relations – one area of strategic ˇ communication – is sometimes a contested and controversial practice with multiple definitions informed by diverse assumptions, values, and worldviews."[7] If one is using one of the common conceptualizations of public relations, the primary concern is about relationship-building and maintenance and organizations. If one is approaching activism through the prism of the Excellence Theory, there is an assumption that all parties in the agora of public debate are equal actors with equal fervor and power and that there is a win–win zone. Also, as Dozier and Lauzen countered in their redress of this core public relations theory, there is a need to decouple the theory from its long and explicit relationship with organizational power and "preoccupation" with the professionalization of the function.[8] Thus, this limited conceptualization of practice can itself be an implicit driver of inequitable approaches in engaging publics.

Thinking beyond that boundary, the work of activism in online and offline spaces requires the use of another definition and approach. This is a necessary step before scholars can begin to more accurately weigh the merits of online activism's impact, real-world effectiveness, or cultural implications. Activists and social movements using social media are not engaging in the same ways as corporations. The use of hashtags and other strategies allow for amplification and momentum. Also, these movements have unequal, asymmetrical relationships with government, media, and other institutions.

### Delineating Activism, Slacktivism, and "Popcorn Activism"

The flattening of online activism and slacktivism into a shallow enterprise serves the advances of some elite commentators. In a study of how social media changed social movements, networks, and action through the lens of the Arab Spring protests, Zeynep Tufekci chides those elite observers who see online engagement as frivolity due to their limited understanding of digital tools and realities,[9] and she calls out the fallacy of "digital dualism." Under the idea of digital dualism, the internet is something happening in a space bifurcated from real life; the online is seen as less real and less impactful than the same thing happening in real life. An example of this is how slacktivism has been defined by multiple authors:

- "feel-good online activism with little meaningful social or political impact"[10]
- "low-risk, low-cost activity via social media whose purpose is to raise awareness, produce change, or grant satisfaction to the person engaged in the activity"[11]
- "feel-good online activism that has zero political or social impact"[12]

From this assemblage, slacktivism is a pejorative term with its only goals being clicks, social loafing, and eudemonic feelings. However, slacktivism replete with hypocrisy and irony occurs in the real-life spaces we occupy. Mayors of multiple cities were asking for Black Lives Matter murals to be painted in their cities while presiding over city budgets that increased police budgets or scraped together new funds for jails. Corporate slacktivism happens at the start of every Pride month, when logos are changed to rainbow yet substantive changes in corporate culture are nil. At the start of Russia's aggressive invasion of Ukraine, people flew the Ukrainian blue-and-yellow flags and companies changed their logos to blue and yellow in

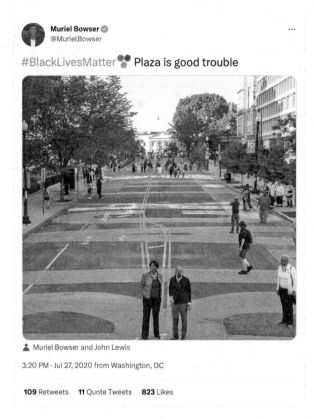

Muriel Bowser ✓
@MurielBowser
...

#BlackLivesMatter ✊🏿 Plaza is good trouble

👤 Muriel Bowser and John Lewis

3:20 PM · Jul 27, 2020 from Washington, DC

**109** Retweets   **11** Quote Tweets   **823** Likes

FIGURE 11.1   During the 2020 protests, Mayor Muriel Bowser of Washington, DC commissioned this installation along a two-block area of 16th Street NW in Downtown, DC. It features "Black Lives Matter" in 50-foot-tall letters, in yellow and all caps, as well as the flag of the district. She posted this photo to her Twitter feed (@MurielBowser) on July 22, 2020 of her and Rep. John Lewis in front of the installation twitter.com/@MurielBowser

a show of support. In sum, slacktivism or "easy-to-engage-in effort that makes little difference in the world"[13] and "having done something good for society without actively engaging in politics, protest, or civil disobedience, or spending or raising money"[14] happen across all spaces where human exist, interact, and communicate.

Slacktivists are a pseudo-public, and are related to two ideas within the construction of publics: instant publics and hot-issue publics. According to Park and Rim, instant publics are reactive publics that are responding to "a type of public inflammatory data, findings, events, or reporting, whether true or constructed falsely, which motivates them to be aware of a problem immediately and participate actively in solving it."[15] Within public relations, the term "hot-issue public" has been used to classify quickly engaged and aware publics that flare out when the news cycle shifts or attention dwindles.[16] Grunig defined a hot-issue public as "active only on a single problem that involves nearly everyone in the population and that has received extensive media coverage,"[17] and scholars have continued to investigate how hot-issue publics form in the social media environment and call for the continued study of the sub-partitions within hot-issue publics.[18] Kim found that hot-issue publics contain multiple groups with differing interests, varying political knowledge, and assorted levels of political actions.[19] Chen et al. concluded that the uptick and intensity of media coverage exacerbated individuals' problem recognition of an issue.[20] A related concept comes from African political studies, Mottiar described "popcorn protest" as "popping up, bursting, then rapidly diminishing in strength" during the South African delivery protests.[21] Bond and Mottair provide further detail about this type of high-level protest, noting that it has a "tendency to flare up and settle down immediately; indeed, while 'up in the air,' protesters were often subject to the prevailing winds."[22] With both hot-issue publics and popcorn protests, incredible heat (attention) is drawn to a problem. Hot-issue publics communicate actively and through the mechanisms of slacktivism about this issue until the issue fades. The public maintain an awareness, but lack the formation and structure to build continuous momentum. Similarly, within its theoretical exploration, popcorn activism has brought forth short-term change due to the lack of linkages between protests and activist groups and a void of strategic cohesiveness. As demonstrated in the South African protest example, **popcorn activism** – the quick-to-react but slow-to-sustain continuum of activism – occurs both offline and online.

### From Popcorn Activism to Sustaining Social Movements

Sustained change will always require action on various levels by different groups in a number of spaces. Sporadic slacktivist efforts in conjunction with unrelenting activist labor and commitment are necessary for any change to happen. When operating synergistically in its best forms, slacktivism brings the catalyst spark that can fuel long-term illumination for social change. Across disciplines, there are various conceptual models that explain scaffolded levels of engagement and impact. In public health, the social ecological model offers five spheres of influence – intrapersonal, interpersonal, institutional, community, and public policy

– in which practitioners can effectuate positive changes in population health.[23] Rogers describes the way innovative ideas and technologies trickle down from innovators and early adopters to laggards among the critical mass.[24] In their much-lauded text, *Groundswell*, Li, Bernoff, and Groot[25] use their practitioner expertise in research and strategic business leadership to propose the value of businesses actively engaging consumers through social communication technologies. Within this work, Li and others developed a typology of social media personas referred to as the Social Technographics Ladder that details a range of engagement activities associated with each consumer group – Creators, Conversationalists, Critics, Collectors, Joiners, Spectators, and Inactives. These are all examples that support a significant point: digital activism is one space that operates in tandem with other forms of social action. These efforts increase communication visibility and message and network transparency, and aggregate knowledge on a topic or issue.[26] They also present valuable "performative expressions of a digital culture practice that articulates online participatory politics as a playful yet serious intervention in the public sphere."[27]

Activist communicators are in alignment with Edwards' definition of public relations: "the flow of purposive communication produced on behalf of individuals, formally constituted and informally constituted groups, through their continuous trans-actions with other social entities."[28] However, given the current online environment with content farms and bots, that definition may need revision. Further, the use of the paid, earned, social, and owned channels and tools does not equate to slacktivism. Rather, activists are strategic communicators, and low-stakes activism (clicktivism or slacktivism) includes tools that can be used to engage. Author and activist Adrienne Maree Brown best articulates the need for online activism and digital outreach: "It is our right and responsibility to write ourselves into the future."[29] The work done in online spaces provides a space for connection and distillation as well as creating a digital archive that cements the history of actions and movements. Further, this work allows communities to visibly recount their lived experiences and perspectives, thereby becoming content producers, and contribute to the larger mass-mediated landscape.

Stories of sharing food through gardens in enslaved quarters[30] and offering health clinics as part of the Black Panther Survival Programs[31] are examples of survival and social movements that needed to be documented through African-American history. These types of contributions are also seen in a more contemporary context when mutual aid societies have assisted people after natural disasters, including Hurricane Katrina.

It is through the narratives, stories, and documentation that these historical movements can inform new contemporary needs.[32]

Social movement-building is often branded and advanced by both collective action and compelling storytelling accounts.[33] We can look at many historical examples of movements that were thematically branded in similar ways. For example, published 19th-century slave narratives helped elevate the public's social consciousness around abolition. Philosophies around nonviolent civil rights movements were driven by the story of charismatic leaders like Nelson Mandela and Dr. Martin Luther King Jr. Within those respective eras, publics often learned of these causes through grassroots techniques or traditional mass media. However, in the present landscape, information consumption is often fractured, personalized according to interests, and occurring via information and communication technologies,[34] which means some of the contemporary work of social activism tends to now be amplified through storied accounts in online communities. Critical story-building and live or semi-real-time discussion of social issues on social networking sites are indexed together through unique hashtags. This simple act creates topical communities by inviting fairly democratized dialogue between otherwise very dispersed groups, including issue experts, thought leaders, and lay audiences. Issue awareness can be lifted further through celebrity and influencer engagement, along with algorithmic trending.[35]

## Culture, Communication, and Online Activism: Connecting the Diaspora

Online activism skews toward historically underrepresented and unheard voices, and that can create more damage and disruption in the media ecosystem and within the social movement. Marginalized groups enjoy more visibility in the heavily segmented online activist culture, drawing attention to issues that have been excluded from public debate. They can find each other more easily, coalesce and amplify each other's voices via @ replies, hashtagging, sharing, and retweeting as a mechanism to amplify individual voices. Though it is true that the shift from traditional activist methods to digital activism has created an opportunity for everyone to participate despite place and space, the fragmentation that comes from co-option of online discourse is, indeed, a challenge for those who wish to engage. These "counterpublics" – as Habermas[36] initially conceived to explain the unique sites and methods that members of marginalized citizens use to produce non-dominant forms of knowledge – now reflect mainstream sources that can use similar tactics to delegitimize counter-movements to realign them with dominant narratives that can undermine the legitimacy of social movements.[37]

Hashtag activism detractors who discredit online movement work by dismissively labeling it as slacktivism or clicktivism undermine the barriers marginalized groups experience in taking up traditionally unsupported causes. It is important to note that continental African and Black American-based digital activism run in parallel, just as the US Civil Rights and African independence movements did, evoking an unintentional and metaphorical diasporic call and response to matters of injustice. Hashtag movements like the Arab Spring and #BringBackOurGirls (#BBOG) occur alongside early hashtag activism from groups like #BlackLivesMatter, a liberation-oriented group that set out to amplify the perpetrators of discriminatory, racially motivated violence against Blacks through the strategic virality of images and recorded interactions. In both contexts, early movement action also functioned in a decentralized, leaderless manner, which makes sense considering the historical precedence of violent retaliation and death perpetrated against 20th-century Black movement leaders globally.

### Cases in Digital Activism across the Black Diaspora

Arguments that disregard the reality of digital dualism and reduce this type of engagement to simple "slacktivism" fail to consider how particularly valuable the approach can be in countries outside the Western gaze. This is especially true in African countries, where national news topics from the Global South remain systematically and scarcely reported or deeply biased in international news coverage,[38] are published in underdeveloped traditional mediums that are heavily suppressed, distorted and monitored by hierarchical authoritative regimes,[39] and are constructed by both professional and citizen journalists that do not have the luxury of public free speech without the potential threat of violence.[40]

With increased cellphone penetration across the African continent,[41] online activism does more to draw in actors that may not ordinarily be able to participate in traditional civic engagement. This includes citizens in countries with cultures plagued with the abovementioned qualities or others in environments that remain challenged by obstacles linked to personal agency, income, or the ability (physical or mental) to act in person.

The Arab Spring and #BringBackOurGirls social movements are classic examples of this dynamic. The Arab Spring refers to a series of revolutionary North African uprisings that began in the early 2010s and sent shockwaves across the Arab world. Dissatisfaction over intense political corruption, unemployment, and deep authoritarianism reached fever pitch when Tunisian citizen Mohammed Bouaziz set himself on fire as a final

FIGURE 11.2 First Lady Michelle Obama holding a sign with the hashtag #BringBackOurGirls in support of the campaign about the 2014 Chibok kidnapping, posted to the @FLOTUS Twitter account on May 7, 2014.[83]

act of protest. Although there were related protests in the years leading up to this moment, images and recordings of Bouaziz's self-immolation accelerated strategic engagement from activists, triggering organizing actions on Facebook pages and Twitter.[42]

Clearly, internet use was in no way a new convention at the time. However, this digital social movement demonstrates a phenomenon of sorts: documented emergence of political activity (i.e., posting images, video) on social media sites originally intended to revolve around personal profile presentation.[43]

With regard to the Arab Spring:

social media created unprecedented opportunities for the exchange of information outside the control of the dominant and supervised mainstream media of the Arab regimes. Information on the internet, not available in the mainstream media, and coming from alternative sources that otherwise were not heard, enhanced the resources available to actors in social and political struggles.[44]

After nearly 300 Nigerian schoolgirls were abducted by members of ter-
rorist group Boko Haram in April 2014, the hashtag #BringBackOurGirls
became a media phenomenon. Although campaign impacts cannot be
completely attributed to digital activism, the hashtag likely helped topically transition the story from a local Nigerian current event to a global
campaign aimed at appealing to any entity that could secure the girls'
rescue. The prominence of Nigeria's kidnapped schoolgirls online has
become a major case study in African feminism, showcasing the reality
of gender-based violence prevalent on the continent and on the global
justice agenda.[45] Notable advocacy outcomes from the #BBOG campaign are the negotiations that led to the release of over 100 Chibok
girls, more earmarked resources for internally displaced Nigerians, and
renewed interest in economic/educational development investments in
northeastern Nigeria. "Legitimate questions may be raised over whether
the movement … inadvertently prolonged the captivity of the Chibok
girls, (however) it is not inconceivable that the society would have moved
on without #BBOG intervention."[46] Regarding real-world impacts, several members linked to the #BBOG social movement went on to create
actual non-governmental organizations based in the region that support
those internally displaced by Boko Haram:

> At a structural level, the #BBOG has advanced the frontiers of non-
> violent protest in Nigeria through a lawsuit filed in Abuja in 2014.
> #BBOG's victory in the case made the police "backtrack" over the
> cancellation of peaceful protests in Abuja.[47]

It also led to the police issuing a statement of support for more democratic policing.[48] Global perceptions perpetuated by the hashtag about
the government's mishandling of the Chibok girls situation even inspired
shifts in political leadership at the presidential level[49].

#EndSARS is a more contemporary example of an online social move-
ment that is in some ways still emerging, and unique when compared to
its predecessors. First tweeted in 2017, #EndSARS is a digital mass protest against Nigeria's Special Anti-Robbery Squad. The squad was created in the 1990s as a unit in the Nigerian Police Force.[50] Though the
unit was assembled to curb armed robbery and related criminal activity, as implied by the name, scores of similar allegations and abuses of

power were lodged at the unit online using the hashtag. Supporters on Twitter maintain that young people aged 18–35 were the primary targets of SARS' ire, most especially if they appeared to have money, an iPhone, or other valuable goods.[51] According to a 2020 Amnesty International report, between January 2017 and May 2020 there were more than 80 cases of documented abuse.

Beyond confiscating phones during illegal stops and seizures, enacting forced ATM withdrawals, and swindling loved ones out of bail fees (bail in Nigeria is free unless requested otherwise by the courts),[52] the report said:

> detainees in SARS custody have been subjected to a variety of methods of torture, including hanging, mock execution, beating, punching and kicking, burning with cigarettes, waterboarding, near-asphyxiation with plastic bags, forcing detainees to assume stressful bodily positions and sexual violence.[53]

Trending energy around the hashtag was reprised in October 2020 after a young man from Delta State, Nigeria was shot and killed by SARS officers shortly before they made off with his luxury vehicle.[54] Graphic hashtagged images from his murder went viral, triggering a series of protests that forced the government's hand. It agreed to disband SARS and supplant it with another unit called the Special Weapons and Tactics team. Convinced its replacement would simply be SARS by another name, waves of demonstrations continued, with the climax of rising action occurring at Lekki Toll Gate in Lagos. On October 20, 2020, peaceful protestors were attacked by members of the Nigerian Army. Army officers opened fire on crowds hours before the newly instituted curfew. Referred to as the Lekki Toll Gate Massacre (LTGM), the shootings resulted in 48 gunshot casualties, including nine deceased and four declared missing or presumed dead.[55]

Before and after the LTGM, Twitter users included the #EndSARS hashtag while sharing stories about personal experiences with SARS or recollecting experiences from friends and family. Hashtag supporters used it to critique media personalities, celebrities, politicians, musicians, or other influential groups that were not actively speaking out against SARS online.[56] In fact, a sloganized version of this exact phrase surfaced online as a sub-hashtag: #SoroSoke, which is a phrase in the Yoruba language of one of Nigeria's major ethnic groups. In the Twitterverse, #EndSARS #EndSWAT and #SoroSoke were used to mobilize protesters and coordinate in-person action on the ground in Nigeria and in communities throughout the diaspora.[57] In solidarity, protestors turned

**FIGURE 11.3**  #EndSARS protests in Nigeria.[84]

out in droves across Europe, Canada, and the United States.[58] On the ground, corporate and business communities in and outside Nigeria also rallied in support of the campaign, even announcing their efforts on Twitter:

> Among the early supporters of the protests was the financial technology company (Fintech) Flutterwave ... the CEO of Flutterwave, Olugbenga Agboola, announced via his Twitter handle on October 9 that the staff of the firm had raised the sum of N2million internally as support to victims, and had also decided to make the fund open to the public to help raise more for the cause.[59]

Fintech and cryptocurrency companies visibly raised funds and publicly announced contributions on Twitter. Global chains like Dominos Pizza and Coldstone Creamery joined national chains like Chicken Republic in donating food to protestors, who used the campaign hashtag to express gratitude. Even the Twitter platform itself and its CEO, Jack Dorsey, engaged directly with the campaign through retweets and donations: "Twitter created a special emoji (a tight fist embedded with Nigeria's national colors) that appeared anytime a person tweeted with the #EndSARS hashtag[60] (and) ... verified the handles of many leading activists who were championing the #EndSARS cause"[61] in order to clamp down on account holders attempting to impersonate key organizers.[62]

Recent activity has waned since the LTGM, but digital supporters remain protective of the movement. In May 2022, quotes from Trish Lorenz, a White Berlin-based journalist and author mistakenly insinuated that she coined the term "Soro Soke."[63] Outraged at the threat of blatant appropriation, Nigerians and #EndSARS enthusiasts created and circulated a petition titled "Recall 'Soro Soke' from Publication – Author cannot CO-OPT and steal a Nigerian Movement!"[64] Also, as of summer 2022, Nigerian celebrities that were engaged in #EndSARS were leveraging the campaign and their influence to urge young people to register to vote in Nigeria's 2023 presidential election.[65] Historically, violence has been a commonplace political strategy and byproduct of democratic national election processes in Nigeria and across the African continent.[66] This hashtag-to-collective action loop could be perceived as threatening to Nigeria's political elite. It could also shift voter demographics and turnout.

The importance of African digital activism is further underscored by state-sponsored attempts to stifle its production. Ongoing tension between Francophone and Anglophone groups in Cameroon and Nigeria's 2021 Twitter ban are examples of that strategy.[67] Although social movement-building in the digitalscape can empower ordinary people to execute new social acts[68] and develop new organizing tools,[69] it is not without its limitations. The leaderless function of activism on social media exists in a bottom-up structure; it does so to resist the power dynamic rife in traditional systems of governance and control.[70] But in some cases, it can inspire confusion about objectives, mission, and directives. In an African context, the language embedded in the hashtag and subsequent threads is normally culturally tailored and specific to the cause being promoted. #SoroSoke from the #EndSARS campaign is an excellent example of integrating indigeneity in a digital social movement. However, it is specific to the Yoruba of Nigeria, which could have unknowingly stoked problematic responses to perceived ethnocentrism, alienating hundreds of other ethnic groups present in the country. Another continental consideration is that these examples showcase organizing power in urban metropoles, but African "rural populations still experience lower rates of internet connectivity and lack broader participation in the digital economy.[71] The digital divide in Africa undercuts participation of rural populations on online-based platforms."[72]

Hashtagging of global issues can elevate them and put the necessary pressure on lawmakers and leaders in governance. But as topics are adapted by cultural outsiders, cultural nuance can be compromised. For example, in the case of Nigeria's kidnapped schoolgirls, failed rescue attempts and social media critiques emphasized the incompetence of Nigerian governance.[73] Narratives around kidnapped schoolgirls have become politicized to catalyze US foreign policies on terrorism. Through the campaign's hashtag, a binary is perpetuated: the girls themselves are flattened into victimized protagonists, existing in opposition to villains of terrorism in stories that neither group have the power to narrate for the public.[74] Even the associative symbolism between Chibok school-girls and the importance of girlhood education reinforces a paternalis-tic dichotomy between the Global North and South whereby children of the Global South are subject to evaluations of worth via the Western gaze.[75]

In addition to criticism about digital activism proliferating lazy activ-ism and poor real-life results, in more extreme cases hashtags can be co-opted by hostile and oppositional commentators or disrupted by hashtag spamming.[76] Platforms and politically uninformed users are susceptible to being propagandized with misinformation/disinformation that is counter-intuitive to the hashtag.[77]

### Charting a Course beyond "Popcorn Activism"

At the conclusion of this chapter, we realize that we now pose the fol-lowing question to you as the reader: Who wishes to engage in activism with diminishing social capital in real life, and a fragmented and co-opted online activist environment?

Theoretical and practical recommendations are needed when discuss-ing social movements and their social media strategies and activations. Tactics may change due to ever-shifting algorithms, changing popular-ity of social networks, timing, speech crackdowns, or other variables. For example, Madden et al. offered a six-point list of recommendations for conducting culture jamming via social media, and one of those tac-tics was creating a social media army.[78] However, building that army to increase visibility has now become harder. Activist and advocacy groups use social media to coordinate amplification and newsjack conversations by sharing toolkits with prepared statements and comments. A tactic that is used with legislative outreach received backlash online, with charges of copypasta (a term to describe duplicative content with a nod to copy-and-paste functionality) and "coordinated inauthentic behavior." This led to crackdowns from social media companies. In May 2022, Twitter announced new policies to detect and root out what it calls "bad actors," a move that Meta (a.k.a. Facebook and Instagram) had worked on since 2018.[79] These changes have prompted groups to reconsider their digital strategies, becoming less reliant on hashtags and text, and using more art-based items to attract people to their causes and amplify their messages. The propositions we offer are conceptual and not beholden to one network.

## Proposition 1

Slacktivism, popcorn activism, and online (hashtag) activism are three distinct concepts. The universalizing of these concepts into one entity ignores the nuance, power dynamics, and risks involved. To not include these considerations may be neglecting how identity shapes activism commitments and engagements, and may contribute to harms focused on the digital organizing of historically marginalized and/or racialized communities.

## Proposition 2

Social movements must have a presence online and offline. Online action can drive offline action. However, social movements functioning without care and responsibility engage in popcorn activism. Policy change cannot be achieved through communication alone.

## Proposition 3

In digital spaces, social movements must use enclave publics, and outside WEIRD (Western, Educated, Industrialized, Rich, and Democratic) countries and constructs, the online space provides a refuge for diasporic voices. Slacktivism can be a performative action or a call for engagement. However, the lens we are looking through determines what we see. We call for scholars to take a more expansive approach.

## Proposition 4

The opportunity to connect and participate in activist movements is not available to everyone. Scholars and practitioners must apply an equity lens to critiques of activism discourse. Some slacktivism activities are undertaken because people do not know where to start or who to connect with to solve an ever-evolving problem. Popcorn activism and hot-issue publics exist due to heightened media coverage, one's own media consumption, and problem recognition. These popcorn activists are engaged in a heavily mediated situation and have some awareness about the issue; it is possible that they could do more, but choose not to because the issue or problem does not have a sustained effort beyond the initial furor. Also, organizations create stumbling blocks and unintentional barriers that do not allow people to think about these matters or organize. There are levels of engagement regarding activism, problem recognition, and issue involvement. Some people will be amplifiers only. Others may take steps to volunteer and lead. Some can only donate to the cause and support by aligning with the cause. All levels are not equal, but all levels are necessary.

### Proposition 5

Activism cannot be divorced from social capital. At all levels, social capital as well as the factors of community cultural wealth must be considered, built, and nurtured. Social capital, as indicated by Bourdieu, is the value associated with a network that allows those within the network to access the social resources available.[80] Putnam asserts that networked structures and social connectedness are vital in maintaining and sustaining social institutions.[81] He asserts that civic engagement and participation in networked activities create communities that are better for its citizens. Brown and Brown note that formal and informal networks tend to foster trust and feelings of mutual obligation among individuals.[82]

### Reflections

- What does it mean to call someone an "activist"? What characteristics are important?
- Can you identify online campaigns or social movements that have had long-standing cultural impact? Why, or why not?
- Who defines who is an activist or (what is considered) activism? What power dynamics are present in this answer?
- Is activism a privileged action, or one that is accessible to all (including historically racialized and marginalized groups)? Why, or why not?
- Who gets to decide what activism impacts and strategies are relevant and effective?

### Notes

1 Cabrera, Nolan L., Cheryl E. Matias, and Roberto Montoya. "Activism or slacktivism? The potential and pitfalls of social media in contemporary student activism." *Journal of Diversity in Higher Education* 10, no. 4 (2017): 400. Fang, Jenn. "In defense of hashtag activism." *Journal of Critical Scholarship on Higher Education and Student Affairs* 2, no. 1 (2015): 10. Jackson, Sarah J., Moya Bailey, and Brooke Foucault Welles. 2020. *# HashtagActivism: Networks of Race and Gender Justice.* Cambridge, MA: MIT Press.
2 Loader, Brian. "Social movements online." 2003. In K. Christensen and D. Levinson (eds.), *Encyclopedia of Community: From the Village to the Virtual World.* Washington, DC: Sage, pp. 1319–1320.

3  Hara, Noriko, and Bi-Yun Huang. "Online social movements." *Annual Review of Information Science & Technology* 45 (2011): 489–522.
4  Freelon, Deen, Alice Marwick and Daniel Kreiss. "False equivalencies: Online activism from left to right." *Science* 369, no. 6508 (2020): 1197–1201.
5  Ibid., p. 2.
6  Dozier, David M., and Martha M. Lauzen. "Liberating the intellectual domain from the practice: Public relations, activism, and the role of the scholar." *Journal of Public Relations Research* 12, no. 1 (2000): 3–22.
7  Ciszek, Erica L. "Activist strategic communication for social change: A transnational case study of lesbian, gay, bisexual, and transgender activism." *Journal of Communication* 67, no. 5 (2017): 702–718.
8  Dozier and Lauzen, "Liberating the intellectual domain from the practice."
9  Tufekci, Zeynep. 2017. *Twitter and Tear Gas: The Power and Fragility of Networked Protest.* New Haven, CT: Yale University Press.
10  Kristofferson, Kirk, Katherine White, and John Peloza. "The nature of slacktivism: How the social observability of an initial act of token support affects subsequent prosocial action." *Journal of Consumer Research* 40, no. 6 (2014): 1149–1166.
11  Rotman, Dana, Sarah Vieweg, Sarita Yardi, Ed Chi, Jenny Preece, Ben Shneiderman, Peter Pirolli, and Tom Glaisyer. 2011. "From slacktivism to activism: participatory culture in the age of social media." In *CHI'11 Extended Abstracts on Human Factors in Computing Systems.* New York: Association for Computing Machinery, pp. 819–822.
12  Skoric, Marko M. "What is slack about slacktivism?" *Methodological and Conceptual Issues in Cyber Activism Research* 77, no. 7 (2012): 7–92.
13  Vie, Stephanie. "In Defense of 'slacktivism': The human rights campaign facebook logo as digital activism," *First Monday* 19, no. 4 (March 30, 2014), accessed May 9, 2023, https://doi.org/10.5210/fm.v19i4.4961.
14  Neumayer, Christina, and Judith Schoßböck. "Political lurkers? Young people in Austria and their political life worlds online," 2011. In Peter Parycek, Manuel J. Kripp, and Noella Edelmann (eds.), *CeDEM11: Proceedings of the International Conference for E-democracy and Open Government, 5-6 May 2011, Danube University Krems, Austria.* Krems: Donau-Universität, pp. 131, accessed May 9, 2023, https://pure.itu.dk/en/publications/political-lurkers-young-people-in-austria-and-their-political-lif. details.
15  Park, Keonyoung, and Hyejoon Rim. "'Click first!': the effects of instant activism via a hoax on social media." *Social Media + Society* 6, no. 2 (2020): 1–13.
16  Aldoory, Linda, and James E. Grunig. "The rise and fall of hot-issue publics: Relationships that develop from media coverage of events and crises." *International Journal of Strategic Communication* 6, no. 1 (2012): 93–108.
17  Grunig, James E. "A situational theory of publics: Conceptual history, recent challenges and new research." *Public Relations Research: An International Perspective* 3 (1997): 48.
18  Madden, Stephanie. "Alerting a campus community: Emergency notification from a public's perspective: alerting a campus community." *Journal of Contingencies and Crisis Management* 23, no. 4 (2015): 184–92.
19  Kim, Young Mie. "The shifting sands of citizenship: Toward a model of the citizenry in life politics." *Annals of the American Academy of Political and Social Science* 644, no. 1 (2012): 147–158.
20  Chen, Yi-Ru Regina, et al. "Identifying active hot-issue communicators and subgroup identifiers: Examining the situational theory of problem solving." *Journalism & Mass Communication Quarterly* 94, no. 1 (2017): 124–47.

21 Mottiar, Shauna. "From 'popcorn' to 'Occupy': Protest in Durban, South Africa." *Development and Change* 44, no. 3 (2013): 603–619. Biekart, Kees, and Alan Fowler. "Transforming activisms 2010+: Exploring ways and waves." *Development and Change* 44, no. 3 (2013): 527–546.

22 Mottiar, Shauna, and Patrick Bond. "The politics of discontent and social protest in Durban." *Politikon* 39, no. 3 (2012): 309–330.

23 Bronfenbrenner, Urie. 1979. *The Ecology of Human Development: Experiments by Nature and Design.* Cambridge, MA: Harvard University Press, 1979. McLeroy, Kenneth R., Daniel Bibeau, Allan Steckler, and Karen Glanz. "An ecological perspective on health promotion programs." *Health Education Quarterly* 15, no. 4 (1988): 351–377.

24 Rogers, Everett. 1962. *Diffusion of Innovations.* New York: Free Press of Glencoe. Moore, Geoffrey A. 1999. *Crossing the Chasm: Marketing and Selling Disruptive Products to Mainstream Customers.* New York, NY: Collins Business Essentials, accessed May 9, 2023.

25 Li, Charlene, and Bernoff, Josh. 2011. *Groundswell: Winning in a World Transformed by Social Technologies.* updated and expanded ed. Boston, Mass.: Harvard Business, accessed May 9, 2023.

26 Leonardi, Paul M. "Social media, knowledge sharing, and innovation: Toward a theory of communication visibility." *Information Systems Research* 25, no. 4 (2014): 796–816.

27 Yuku, James. "The hashtag as archive: Internet memes and Nigeria's social media election," 2018. In Abimbola Adunni Adelakun and Toyin Falola (eds.), *Art, Creativity, and Politics in Africa and the Diaspora.* Cham, Switzerland: Palgrave Macmillan, pp. 217, accessed May 9, 2023, https://link.springer.com /book/10.1007/978-3-319-91310-0.

28 Edwards, Lee. "Defining the 'object' of public relations research: A new starting point." *Public Relations Inquiry* 1, no. 1 (2012): 7–30.

29 Adrienne Maree Brown, often styled adrienne maree brown, is a writer, activist, and facilitator. From 2006 to 2010, she was the Executive Director of the Ruckus Society. She also co-founded and directed the United States League of Young Voters.

30 White, Monica M. 2018. *Freedom Farmers: Agricultural Resistance and the Black Freedom Movement.* Chapel Hill, NC: University of North Carolina Press.

31 Bassett, Mary T., "Beyond berets: The Black Panthers as health activists." *American Journal of Public Health* 106, no. 10 (2016): 1741–1743.

32 Robinson, Sue. "We were all there': Remembering America in the anniversary coverage of Hurricane Katrina." *Memory Studies* 2, no. 2 (2009): 235–253.

33 Beraldo, Davide. "Movements as multiplicities and contentious branding: Lessons from the digital exploration of #Occupy and #Anonymous." *Information, Communication & Society* 25, no. 8 (2020): 1–17.

34 Lee, Eun-Ju, and Edson C. Tandoc Jr. "When news meets the audience: How audience feedback online affects news production and consumption." *Human Communication Research* 43, no. 4 (2017): 436–449.

35 Dobrin, D. "The hashtag in digital activism: A cultural revolution." *Journal of Cultural Analysis and Social Change* 5, no. 1 (2020): 1–14.

36 Habermas, Jürgen. 1989. *Jürgen Habermas on Society and Politics: A Reader.* Boston, MA: Beacon Press.

37 Jackson, Bailey, and Foucault Welles, *# HashtagActivism.*

38 Addie, Yewande O. "African story time: An exploratory study of narrative as a reporting technique in US news coverage of Nigeria's missing girls." *Journal*

of *Public Interest Communications* 3, no. 2 (2019): 53–63. Baum, Matthew A., and Yuri M. Zhukov. "Filtering revolution: Reporting bias in international newspaper coverage of the Libyan civil war." *Journal of Peace Research* 52, no. 3 (2015): 384–400. Dietrich, Nick, and Kristine Eck. "Known unknowns: Media bias in the reporting of political violence." *International Interactions* 46, no. 6 (2020): 1043–1060.

39 Ingraham, Lindsey. "Media suppression in Africa and the Balkans: How economic distribution impacts freedom of the press on an international level." *INSPIRE Student Research and Engagement Conference* (2022), p.69. Jatula, Victor. "Media and underdevelopment in Anglophone west Africa." *African Research Review* 13, no. 2 (April 16,2019): 13, accessed May 9, 2023, https://doi.org/10.4314/afrrev.v13i2.2.

40 Alade, Moyosore Omowonuola, and Bernice Oluwalanu Sanusi. 2022. "Endangered voices: Nigerian journalists' safety amid the COVID-19 pandemic." In Carol Azungi Dralega and Angella Napakol (eds.), *Health Crises and Media Discourses in Sub-Saharan Africa.* New York: Springer, pp. 109–126. Hamada, Basyouni Ibrahim. "Determinants of journalists' autonomy and safety: Evidence from the Worlds of Journalism study." *Journalism Practice* (2021): 1–21. Mutsvairo, Bruce, and Susana Salgado. "Is citizen journalism dead? An examination of recent developments in the field." *Journalism* 23, no. 2 (2022): 354–371.

41 Aker, Jenny C., and Isaac M. Mbiti. "Mobile phones and economic development in Africa." *Journal of Economic Perspectives* 24, no. 3 (2010): 207–232.

42 Frangonikolopoulos, Christos A., and Ioannis Chapsos. "Explaining the role and the impact of the social media in the Arab Spring." *Global Media Journal: Mediterranean Edition* 7, no. 2 (2012): 10–20. Stepanova, Ekaterina. "The role of information communication technologies in the 'Arab Spring.'" *Ponars Eurasia* 15, no. 1 (2011): 1–6.

43 Frangonikolopoulos and Chapsos, "Explaining the role and the impact of the social media in the Arab Spring."

44 Ibid.

45 Datiri, Blessing Dachollom. "Online activism against gender-based violence: How African feminism is using Twitter for progress." *Debats: Revista de cultura, poder i societat* 5 (2020): 271–286.

46 Oriola, Temitope B. "Framing and movement outcomes: The# BringBackOurGirls movement." *Third World Quarterly* 42, no. 4 (2021): 641–660, at p.655.

47 Ibid., p. 656.

48 Okakwu, Vanessa. "After public condemnation, Nigeria Police backtrack, pledge to allow peaceful protests in Abuja." *Premium Times*, September 10, 2016. http://www.premiumtimesng.com/news/headlines/210179-public-condemnation-nigeria-police-backtrack-pledge-allow-peaceful-protests-abuja.html, para. 2

49 Temitope, "Framing and movement outcomes, p. 642.

50 Uwazuruike, Allwell Raphael. "#EndSARS: The movement against police brutality in Nigeria." *Harvard Human Rights Journal* 35 (2020): 1–3.

51 Abimbade, Oluwadara, Philip Olayoku, and Danielle Herro. "Millennial activism within Nigerian Twitterscape: From mobilization to social action of #ENDSARS protest." *Social Sciences & Humanities Open* 6, no. 1 (2022): 100222.

52 Dambo, Tamar Haruna, Metin Ersoy, Ahmad Muhammad Auwal, Victor Oluwafemi Olorunsola, Ayodeji Olonode, Abdulgaffar Olawale Arikewuyo,

and Ayodele Joseph. "Nigeria's# EndSARS movement and its implication on online protests in Africa's most populous country." *Journal of Public Affairs* 22, no. 3 (2020): e2583, at p. 10.

53 Okanga, Okanga Ogbu. "A law and politics contextualization of corporate activism in Nigeria's 2020 anti-police brutality campaign." *SN Social Sciences* 2, no. 3 (2022): 1–28, at p.3

54 Abimbade, Olayoku, and Herro, "Millennial activism within Nigerian Twitterscape.

55 Okanga, "A law and politics contextualization of corporate activism in Nigeria's 2020 anti-police brutality campaign," p. 6.

56 Asemah, Ezekiel S., Ransom Acheme, and Ijeoma Taiwo. 2022. "An evaluative study of select Nigerian celebrities' views of spiral of silence effect and social media during the 2020 #EndSars protests in Nigeria." In E. S. Asemah, D. O. Ekhareafo, and T. Santas (eds.), *Discourses on Communication and Media Studies in Contemporary Society*, pp. 210, accessed May 9, 2023, https://professorezekielasemah.com/wp-content/uploads/2022/04/Ezekiel-5 -Final-Corrections-Discourses-on-Com-1.pdf.

57 Abimbade, Olayoku, and Herro, "Millennial activism within Nigerian Twitterscape."

58 Iwuoha, Victor Chidubem, and Ernest Toochi Aniche. "Protests and blood on the streets: Repressive state, police brutality and #EndSARS protest in Nigeria." *Security Journal* 35 (2021): 1–23, at p. 19.

59 Okanga, "A law and politics contextualization of corporate activism in Nigeria's 2020 anti-police brutality campaign," p. 17.

60 Augoye, J. "EndSARS: Twitter creates special emoji in solidarity with protesters." *Premium Times* (blog), entry posted October 16, 2020, accessed May 9, 2023, https://www.premiumtimesng.com/news/top-news/421190-endsars-twitter-creates-special-emoji-in-solidarity-with-protests.html?tztc=1.

61 Ibid, p. 71.

62 Okanga, "A law and politics contextualization of corporate activism in Nigeria's 2020 anti-police brutality campaign," p. 9.

63 Akintade, Adefemola. "Trish Lorenz did not name #EndSARS protesters 'Soro-Soke'; it was an error: Cambridge University." *People's Gazette*, May 31, 2022. https://gazettengr.com/trish-lorenz-did-not-name-endsars-protesters-soro-soke-it-was-an-error-cambridge-university/.

64 OLÁOLÚWA ÒNÍ, "Understanding the Failure of Police Reform in Nigeria: A Case for Legal History Through Literature." 2022, master's thesis: York University, accessed May 9, 2023, https://yorkspace.library.yorku.ca/xmlui/ bitstream/handle/10315/40576/Oni_Olaoluwa_F_2022_LLM.pdf.

65 Obioha, Vanessa, and Iyke Bede. "How #EndSARS and Celebrities Will Possibly Influence the 2023 Elections." *This Day*, June 10, 2022. https://www .thisdaylive.com/index.php/2022/06/10/how-endsars-and-celebrities-will -possibly-influence-the-2023-elections/.

66 Goldsmith, Arthur A. "Electoral violence in Africa revisited." *Terrorism and Political Violence* 27, no. 5 (2015): 818–837.

67 Endong, Floribert Patrick C. "Internet blackouts in Africa: A critical examination, with reference to Cameroon and Nigeria." *Digital Policy Studies* 1, no. 1 (2022): 39–51.

68 McGarty, Craig, Emma F. Thomas, Girish Lala, Laura G.E. Smith, and Ana-Maria Bliuc. "New technologies, new identities, and the growth of mass opposition in the Arab Spring." *Political Psychology* 35, no. 6 (2014): 725–740.

69 Dessewffy, Tibor, and Zsofia Nagy. "Born in Facebook: The refugee crisis and grassroots connective action in Hungary." *International Journal of Communication* 10 (2016): 23.

70 Dambo et al., "Nigeria's# EndSARS movement and its implication on online protests in Africa's most populous country."

71 Alzouma, Gado. "Myths of digital technology in Africa: Leapfrogging development?." *Global Media and Communication* 1, no. 3 (2005): 339–356.

72 Sebeelo, Tebogo B. "Hashtag activism, politics and resistance in Africa: Examining #ThisFlag and #RhodesMustFall online movements." *Insight on Africa* 13, no. 1 (2021): 95–109, at p. 96.

73 Ofori-Parku, Sylvester Senyo, and Derek Moscato. "Hashtag activism as a form of political action: A qualitative analysis of the# BringBackOurGirls Campaign in Nigerian, UK, and US press." *International Journal of Communication* 12, no. 23 (2018): 2488–2489.

74 Addie, "African Story Time." Maxfield, Mary. "History retweeting itself: imperial feminist appropriations of 'Bring Back Our Girls.'" *Feminist Media Studies* 16, no. 5 (2016): 886–900.

75 Berents, Helen. "Hashtagging girlhood: #IAmMalala, #BringBackOurGirls and gendering representations of global politics." *International Feminist Journal of Politics* 18, no. 4 (2016): 513–527, at p. 525.

76 Greenfield, Rebecca. "Twitter is torturing social media nerds with hashtag spam." *The Atlantic*, May 3, 2012. https://www.theatlantic.com/technology/archive/2012/05/twitter-torturing-social-media-nerds-hashtag-spam/328581/.

77 Endong, Floribert Patrick C. "The 'dark side' of African digital diplomacy: The response of Cameroon and Nigeria to separatists' online propaganda." *South African Journal of International Affairs* 28, no. 3 (2021): 449–469. Sebeelo, "Hashtag activism, politics and resistance in Africa."

78 Madden, Stephanie, Melissa Janoske, Rowena Briones Winkler, and Zach Harpole. "Who loves consent? Social media and the culture jamming of Victoria's Secret." *Public Relations Inquiry* 7, no. 2 (2018): 171–186.

79 Adler, Maxwell. "Twitter plans aggressive pitch to calm advertisers amid musk deal." Bloomberg, May 4, 2022, https://www.bloomberg.com/news/articles/2022-05-04/twitter-plans-spectacle-to-calm-advertisers-amid-musk-deal.

80 Bourdieu, Pierre. "The social space and the genesis of groups." *Social Science Information* 24, no. 2 (1985): 195–220.

81 Putnam, Robert D. "Tuning in, tuning out: The strange disappearance of social capital in America." *PS: Political Science & Politics* 28, no. 4 (1995): 664–683.

82 Brown, R. Khari, and Ronald E. Brown. "Faith and works: Church-based social capital resources and African American political activism." *Social Forces* 82, no. 2 (2003): 617–641.

83 https://upload.wikimedia.org/wikipedia/commons/f/f3/Michelle-obama-bringbackourgirls.jpg

84 https://upload.wikimedia.org/wikipedia/commons/d/d5/Salako_Ayoola_Portraits_-CLS01705.jpg

# ADVOCATES FOR ACTION

## Corazon Aquino

1933–2009
Hometown: Paniqui, the Philippines
Movements: Democracy
Organizations: People Power Revolution

*Allison De Young and Elizabeth Wilson*

Corazon Aquino was the first female president of the Philippines, serving from 1986 to 1992. She was a key figure in the People Power Revolution which toppled the authoritarian regime of Ferdinand Marcos, and is widely admired for her efforts to restore democracy and human rights in the Philippines.[1] Aquino was born into a prominent political family, and was known for her humility and her commitment to social justice.

Born as the sixth out of eight children, Aquino grew up financially stable and in a religious household. Her family owned a sugar plantation, making them one of the richest families in the area, which allowed her to attend high school and college in the United States. It was during her studies at the College of Mount St. Vincent in New York City that she met her husband, Benigno S. Aquino Jr., who became a prominent political figure and was elected the youngest governor of the Philippines ever.[2] Ninoy became known for opposing then President Ferdinand Marcos' political views and attempted to run against him. After running once, being imprisoned, and then running again, Benigno was eventually assassinated, leaving behind Corazon and their children.[3]

DOI: 10.4324/9781003291855-27

Upon her husband's death, Corazon kept his fight going by joining the People Power Revolution, an anti-Marcos political campaign, and participated in peaceful and nonviolent demonstrations against the regime.[4] Eventually, she took it a step further and ran against Marcos for the presidency. After being the projected winner in a close race, Corazon lost, but believed she was cheated like her husband had been before. Corazon and Philippine citizens throughout the country protested intensely, but made sure to keep it peaceful so as not to cause any harm.[5] Finally, in 1986, Marcos retreated to the United States in exile and Corazon was sworn in as president.[6] During her term, she focused on restoring the constitution, initiating a variety of legal reforms, and making the government more democratic compared to the rule of Marcos.[7] After her presidency ended in 1992, she continued to speak out, and focused on homelessness and violence in the Philippines.

Throughout her time in the political spotlight, Corazon received numerous awards, honors, recognitions, and accolades for her work. Some of her honors in 1986 included being named *Time*'s Woman of the Year, receiving the Eleanor Roosevelt Human Rights Award, the United Nations Silver Medal, and many more.[8] Her tenacity and ambition inspired her son, Benigno "Noynoy" Aquino, to enter politics. He successfully ran for Senate in 2007 and was elected President of the Philippines in 2009.[9] Corazon eventually died from cancer in 2009. She is remembered as a symbol of hope and change in the Philippines, and her legacy continues to inspire people around the world.

## Notes

1  Mendoza, Diana J., and Maria Elissa Jayme Lao. 2017. "Corazon Aquino: The reluctant first female President of the Philippines." In Verónica Montecinos (ed.), *Women Presidents and Prime Ministers in Post-Transition Democracies.* London: Palgrave Macmillan, pp. 205–219.
2  Alexander, Kerri Lee. "Corazon Aquino." National Women's History Museum. 2019. www.womenshistory.org/education-resources/biographies/corazon-aquino.
3  Fontaine, Roger W. "The Philippines: after Aquino." *Asian Affairs: An American Review* 19, no. 3 (1992): 170–190.
4  Alexander, "Corazon Aquino."
5  Iowa State University. "Corazon Aquino." Accessed November 15, 2022. https://awpc.cattcenter.iastate.edu/directory/corazon-aquino/.
6  Alexander, "Corazon Aquino."
7  Iowa State University. "Corazon Aquino."
8  Helen James. The Australian Demographic and Social Research Institute CASS, ANU "The Legacy of Corazon Aquino: Aspirations for a more Robust Democratic Polity." (2010) https://www.researchgate.net/profile/Helen-James-5/publication/266590392_Title_of_Paper_The_Legacy_of_Corazon

_Aquino_Aspirations_for_a_more_Robust_Democratic_Polity/links/555
d2c1c08ae8c0cab2a80b5/Title-of-Paper-The-Legacy-of-Corazon-Aquino
-Aspirations-for-a-more-Robust-Democratic-Polity.pdf.
9 Teehankee, Julio Cabral, and Yuko Kasuya. "The 2019 midterm elections in
the Philippines: Party system pathologies and Duterte's populist mobilization." *Asian Journal of Comparative Politics* 5, no. 1 (2020): 69–81.

# 12

# RECLAIMING WHOLENESS

## The Future and Hope of Digital and Social Activism

*Candace Parrish, Candice L. Edrington, and LaShonda L. Eaddy*

## Introduction

According to Gerbaudo and Treré,[1] social operations help social movements define their sense of self collectively and identify what they stand for. Social media platforms such as Facebook, Instagram, and Twitter are pervasive in Web communication and are integral to collective identity construction. Social and digital media activism (SDMA) has become prevalent throughout the world, and has become a catalyst for awareness across populations and a motivator of behavioral changes. Although social movements are not new, the addition of social and digital media (SDM) has allowed groups to "rally the troops" for their causes and evoke meaningful and enduring change. This chapter highlights the history of activism, its intersectionality among marginalized groups, and the various ways it is enacted. It also chronicles the rise of social and digital media, and their contributions to activist movements. The chapter shares contemporary case studies to demonstrate how SDMA has accomplished victories when combined with tried-and-true strategic planning best practices, also alluding to the future of SDMA.

## Literature Review

In highlighting future directions for SDMA, it is imperative that we review the history of activism to draw parallels of the foundational functions of advocacy, regardless of medium. In this literature review, we will also detail how social and digital media have enhanced potential reach in

DOI: 10.4324/9781003291855-28

activism and changed the landscape of communication from local and/or national communities to more globalized communities.

## History of Activism

**Activism** – acting on behalf of a person, group, or organization as they relate to social, political, and cultural issues through various forms such as demonstrations, campaigning, petitioning, etc. – and **advocacy** – speaking out on behalf of a person, group, or organization as they relate to social, political, and cultural issues – have been a part of the human experience for centuries. It seems, for every governing body or regime, regardless of location and time, there are counter-movements that are created to shift power and resources. These movements are often created in an attempt to advocate for access, equal rights, and/or freedom. Activism has proven to be a global means of advocacy, whether its subject be race, social class, and/or gender and sexuality.

### Racial Activism

American history has no shortage of racial activism and advocacy. During the 1800s, there were many movements and rebellions among slaves and free African-Americans for the movement toward freedom and equal rights.[2] Harriet Tubman worked throughout the mid-1800s to free roughly 70 slaves through a process coined "the Underground Railroad."[3] As dangerous as the process to secretly transport slaves to free lands was, the prospect of freedom and protection from subjugation was a far greater incentive. Tubman was not alone: there were also rebellions in South Hampton County, Virginia and New York City, where enslaved African-Americans silently plotted revolts to fight for their freedom, or at least create an opportunity to escape.[4]

In the 1900s, these movements continued as former slaves and descendants of slaves fought for equal rights. In the 1950s and 1960s, there were various groups and movements that were spawned as a result of unfair and unequal treatment African-Americans received in the United States. Organizations like the National Association for the Advancement of Colored People, Student Nonviolent Coordinating Committee, and the Freedom Fighters held marches, protests, and community organization events to help unify African-American communities toward equality advocacy.[5] Monumental leaders like Malcolm X and Dr. Martin Luther King, Jr. both utilized their religious networks to engage in protest and negotiation with political leaders to contribute to the advancement of persons of color.[6] Unfortunately for these two leaders, whether they believed in violence as a means of protection or nonviolence, they were both assassinated for their preaching and actions toward equality for African-Americans. Circumstances like these denote the danger for minority communities in standing up for justice in America – even protesting and advocating in nonviolent ways can wind up in violence for minority activists and organizers.

## Gender and Sexuality Activism

Gender equality has also been a pivotal pillar of activists both nationally and internationally. In the early 1900s, women in the United States began to organize and agree on strategies to advance access and opportunities for work and wellbeing.[7] These early initiatives snowballed over the years and became prominent movements that paralleled the civil rights movements for African-Americans from the 1950s and beyond. Feminist organizers and leaders created the feminist movement in the late 1840s to define a body of work and action centered on the advancement, safety, and equality for women.[8] Feminist efforts include, but are not limited to, equal pay, equal job opportunities, and equal access to social rights – like voting.[9]

Advocacy for sexuality has been an emerging genre of activism globally as freedom of sexual preference and identity gain space in society. Prominent movements from the 1980s and beyond have advocated for equal marriage rights and more for gay and lesbian US citizens.[10] In addition to rights, activism has been enacted to counter social stigmas and discrimination of various members of the lesbian, gay, bisexual, transgender, queer/questioning, intersex, asexual, and more (LGBTQIA+) communities.[11]

## Social and Health-Centered Activism

Movements to protect and uplift various social classes within society have also been prominent in American history. From social class to health, activations are employed as strategies to protect members of our society who need the most, but are often overlooked. Disability rights movements gained more traction in the 1970s and 1980s, and have now advanced part of our daily protocols for protections in various aspects of society.[12] Buildings are required to have some sort of ease of access for those in wheelchairs, and workplace processes by law have to implement varied ways of working for inclusiveness of disabled persons.[13]

In the United States, the democratic capitalist societal structure unfortunately allows for many to succumb to low wages, loss of work, and even homelessness. Therefore, there have been many movements and initiatives that have focused on the lower classes of society – from nonprofit to governmental. For instance, the Food Stamp Act of 1964 was enacted into law years after the Great Depression had taken its toll in creating a large population that suffered from poverty and famine.[14] Currently, there are organizations that help combat homelessness and food disparities – all resulting from grassroots efforts to raise awareness about society hardships that were turned into nonprofit organizations to gain more effective ways of governing and disbursing help and resources.[15]

## Intersectionality

Coincidentally, there are often intersections between multiple areas, or facets, of categories within society. For instance, African-Americans and other minorities are likely to be marginalized and/or the unfortunate victims of poverty, loss of jobs, and low wages due to racism.[16] Racism is structural, and much of American history was built on racism. Therefore, minorities are often discriminated against and not afforded opportunities to help secure a modest lifestyle, often having to work harder than members of the majority, and resulting in health and financial issues that create cycles of struggle and strife.[17]

Likewise, transgender women can also bear the burden of enduring multiple discriminatory acts, in that: (1) gender and sexuality acceptance is a relatively new area of activism and (2) their new declaration as a woman makes them susceptible to patriarchal societal stigmas.[18] Activism offers endless possibilities for intersectionality. In fact, many organizations' advocacy spans various areas of activism due to intersectionality. According to the Center for Intersectional Justice,[19] intersectionality is defined as "ways in which systems of inequality based on gender, race, ethnicity, sexual orientation, gender identity, disability, class and other forms of discrimination 'intersect' to create unique dynamics and effects." For instance, a transgender student who is Latinx at a predominantly White institution most likely experiences life on campus at the intersection of being a minority by race and gender. These two identifiers intersect to create a unique scenario for lived experiences in various social settings.

## Activism Styles – Demonstrations and/or Mediated

This discussion should also highlight the historical ways activism and protests have been implemented considering the various mechanisms by which areas of activism can emerge. Depending on the nature of what was at stake, some forms of activism tended to be enacted in an underground word-of-mouth manner – like Harriet Tubman's Underground Railroad plan. Activations like these often led to violent repercussions and were not publicized because such activity was illegal and could result in death, harsh physical abuse, and/or further enslavement.[20] Contrarily, other forms of activism have benefited from larger crowds and amplified voices and may be enacted in public spaces – much like the Civil Rights protests of the 1960s, where marches and sit-ins were captured via photos and films for people around the world to see.[21]

This chapter highlights two styles of activation which many forms fall under – demonstrations and mediated activism. **Demonstrations** are physical gestures or performances that can be secretive or publicized – ranging from marches and protests to secret meetings and/or escape routes. **Mediated activism** is non-physical, but exists in the form of social campaigns via advertising, radio, television, and social/digital media.

There are many opportunities for these to be used separately and in tandem. A nonprofit may choose to conduct a corporate-style activism campaign by raising funds and awareness for a particular societal issue via mediated strategies only, while a grassroots organization may choose to communicate about a march or protest by using mediated activism methods that lead people to join a demonstration. In the history of activism, the two forms have been used in various ways to solve issues and combat injustice.

### Rise of Social and Digital Media

The creation of online platforms for social and community use in the mid- to late 2000s created an uptick in social and digital media use. Platforms like Myspace, Facebook, and eventually Twitter made local, national, and international conversation accessible to millions with a few keystrokes.[22] There are a multitude of community interactions that happen in daily life, including good, bad, moral, immoral, and violent exchanges. In the age of digital and social mediated communication, these same interactions are present online in varying degrees. It is just as easy to tell someone to have a wonderful day as it is to spew verbal abuse online because many feel their identity is protected by a digital wall. Likewise, SDM makes it easy for people to create new identities, allowing them to cast an online role they wish to live in real life.

Beyond the myriad ways people use SDM to extend their daily interactions and communication into the digital verse, many have also used the platforms to spread information on various subjects.[23] Online advocating and activism lie in this field of information sharing.

### Activism as a Social Mediated Tool

Activism has found a lofty home on SDM platforms as the process of community-building is a key aspect of social media use.[24] People building activism campaigns or spreading information have experienced great success with implementing activism strategies online that can inform those who would otherwise not receive the information. The opportunity for people to reshare a message or form of content with a few clicks supersedes the physicality of "word of mouth" because unlike traditional word of mouth strategies, resharing can be done in seconds without having a conversation with another individual.

### National

Perhaps a wonderful aspect of activism dwelling on SDM platforms is that people can reach like-minded communities and circles beyond their neighborhoods, cities, and states. Such campaigns include the one for Cyntoia Brown, who was pardoned by the Governor of Tennessee after spending years in jail for murdering someone during self-defense during an assault.[25] Organizers created a social media campaign that was equipped with information, education, and calls to action. Social media viewers could read the story about Cyntoia, share it, and perform the short steps of emailing the governor (with a pre-composed email) all in a matter of minutes. The campaign was shared so much that it eventually caught the attention of celebrities and national political leaders, eventually leading to the governor pardoning Cyntoia – a feat that would probably not have happened if a social mediated campaign was not enacted to (1) spread the work online and (2) get folks to share and follow the ready-made steps for activation.

### Global

There have been many instances where SDM have created a communication bridge, connecting people on opposite sides of the globe who would otherwise never connect outside of visiting an international location with the chance to converse with others via SDM on their phones and computers. Michael Brown was killed by a police officer, and his body was left in the street for hours after he died.[26] When protests for Michael Brown began in 2015, the situation became politically charged and physically confrontational as the National Guard was called in to inflict violence on protestors and diminish activism efforts. Public outcry against this act was exemplified via marching and rioting in Ferguson, Missouri, where the incident took place.[27] During the demonstrations, the authorities launched tear gas and chemicals into the crowd to disperse it. On Twitter, people in the Middle East, who often were subjected to brutal authoritative force via tear gas, communicated to people in Missouri how to withstand tear gas in efforts to continue protesting.[28] This was a historical moment in the use of SDM for activism because it was one of the first instances of citizens on different continents having the ability to share activism strategies and overall comradery nearly instantaneously.

## Slacktivism and Clicktivism

In the rise of social and digital activism, there have been several counter-arguments that have questioned the true commitment of those practicing activism online. The terms **slacktivism** and **clicktivism** surfaced to define Millennials who were emotionally connected to various topics of activism but rarely did more for those movements beyond liking or sharing posts and videos. Although simple, these types of passive engagement have been flagged as critically negative to the growth of actual actions taken toward any sort of injustice resolution. The Millennial and Gen Z generations have been criticized for their slacktivist and clicktivist habits in enacting social justice by simply liking or sharing a post about social injustice.[29] However, as we know today, activism is not just about something you do, it is also about impacting and changing your understanding and mindset on a particular subject/occurrence. Thus, passive engagement with online information might seem minimal, but over time it might have a great impact on how a person carries their daily life in their real-world settings. Further, a lot of information being shared online is educational and can provide clear steps for people to take when they witness various injustices – potentially combating the digital bystander effect.

## Digital Bystander Effect

In real life, there are daily examples of bystanders who passively watch and take no action during situations that range from mild to dire. The same happens in digital spaces. When social media users witness cyber-bullying, many admit to watching and doing nothing because they either (1) feel like someone else is going to step in, (2) don't know what to say or do to create change, and/or (3) feel worried that if they step in they will be penalized for their actions.[30] Many instances of people feeling like bystanders online can be combated by the creation of increased options in those spaces. For instance, many social media platforms have the opportunity to report negative content or interactions for review by that platform. Although there are critical arguments made about the review of those reports, these options have increased the feeling of empowerment for some online users to take some steps for action.[31]

*Hope and Vision in Activism*

A key component in the increasing efforts to continue activism is hope. Hope, an intangible element, is so important to both corralling a group of people toward actions of change and also toward building systems/platforms/technology that can one day increase the efficiency of mobilization. For many, having hope for change inspires the vision that in turn guides the strategy acting against injustice. There are many instances where messaging around hope for better times has been used to keep groups of people motivated to continue their journey, from Harriet Tubman during slavery to Martin Luther King Jr. during the Civil Rights era of the 1960s. In today's times, the use of hope is pivotal to combating deflation of morale during digital activations. Inspirational messages, videos, and images are shared globally to inspire gratitude for national and international efforts in creating change. Hope and vision in SDMA will remain a critical component of the recipe for success in social justice even during future digital appropriations of activations.

## Notable Cases of Social and Digital Media Activism

In the last decade, there have been several notable cases of SDMA efforts. These efforts have educated, mobilized, and inspired people to take various actions toward change – whether digital or physical action steps. In this chapter, we will highlight and examine three cases for their impact and contribution to the current state of SDMA.

*From #MeToo to #TimesUp*

In 2006, women's advocate Tarana Burke coined the phrase "Me Too" on Myspace.[32] Its purpose was to empower women who had experienced sexual assault, harassment, and/or violence by showing them that they were not alone in their experience and journey to healing. It wasn't until October of 2017 that the #MeToo hashtag materialized after actress Alyssa Milano used it on Twitter asking her followers to respond "me too" if they'd been sexually harassed or assaulted. Her tweet came after famed Hollywood director Harvey Weinstein was accused of sexually assaulting women in the entertainment industry. Unaware of the beginnings of the phrase, Milano was an unsuspected catalyst to a movement that had been brewing for over a decade. After her tweet, millions of social media users began to use the hashtag on both Twitter and Facebook, causing it to explode and trend in over 85 countries. In the days to come, the concept of "me too" transcended beyond the entertainment industry to include politicians, athletes, and fashion designers. One month later, hundreds of people participated in the "Me Too Survivors" march down Hollywood Boulevard.

#MeToo materialized into a hashtag movement with hopes of empowering women who had experienced sexual assault, harassment, and/or violence. This hashtag generated a path for other gender equality hashtag movements such as #TimesUp. Initially created to bring awareness and build community, these two hashtag movements were widely successful in the United States. The #MeToo movement prompted conversations that broke the silence and stigma on issues of sexual assault, violence, and harassment which led to unprecedented tangible impacts and outcomes globally such as legal action, legislative reform, and amplification of these issues.

Legal action was taken in countries such as South Korea, Sweden, and Egypt. In South Korea, the movement's impacts were felt when a lawyer accused her former boss of sexual misconduct during an interview.[33] Her courageousness created space for others to come forward, resulting in resignations and prison sentences. In Sweden, artist Jean-Claude Arnault's 2018 Nobel Prize in literature was canceled after he was accused of sexual assault by over 18 women. He was later found guilty of rape and sentenced to prison. In Egypt, a woman used video footage of her fighting off her attacker as evidence to win her sexual harassment case. Legislative reform in other countries has also brought victories for the movement. France passed a bill on sexual harassment, China proposed workplace protections, Spain's government vowed to change its penal codes, and the Australian and UK parliaments created and passed codes of conduct for their members. Although legal action has not been the outcome of all #MeToo global efforts, women have still been empowered to amplify these issues on social media in places such as Senegal, Central Asia, Nigeria, and India. It is evident that social and digital media also aided in the global success of #MeToo.

Initially created to bring awareness and build community, the #MeToo movement prompted a global conversation that broke the silence on issues of sexual assault, violence, and harassment. In addition to generating much-needed conversation, this movement also helped to bring legal punishments for some of the accused offenders, prompted several states to ban nondisclosure agreements, and created the Time's Up Legal Defense Fund.

Deriving from the #MeToo movement, the #TimesUp movement provided an action-oriented sequel to the overall women's empowerment momentum. Initiated by over 300 celebrity women, the purpose of #TimesUp was to move beyond conversation and produce tangible change. This movement extended beyond sexual assault and harassment to include issues of workplace equity for women and people of color. A main point of change hoped for from this movement was legislation and policy change. To accomplish this, the Time's Up Legal Defense Fund was created as a source of financial support for women and men to fight sexual harassment and assault in the workplace regardless of their job titles. In just two months, the fund raised over US $24 million becoming one of the most successful fundraisers on GoFundMe to date. Moreover, celebrities advocating for the #TimesUp movement dressed in all black and invited lesser-known activists as their guests to the 75th annual Golden Globes award ceremony. During the ceremony, they used the hashtag #WhyWeWearBlack in addition to #TimesUp to post pictures of them and their guests on social media, and to discuss the advocacy efforts of the movement. Together, these two movements show how social and digital media was and can be used to raise awareness, build community, and promote action through increasing visibility, connecting conversations, and using agenda-building strategies.

## March for Our Lives and youth-centered activism

The March for Our Lives (MFOL) movement is arguably one of the greatest examples of youth-centered activism in the 21st century. Created after the mass shooting at Marjory Stoneman Douglas High School in Parkland, Florida that took the lives of 17 and injured 14, this movement initially advocated for stronger gun laws and background checks. Just hours after the shooting and even during it, several students who survived the massacre used their own social media accounts and traditional news outlets to bring awareness to the need for stronger gun laws. Days after the shooting, these same students met to strategize how to leverage social media to advance their efforts. This meeting resulted in a mega-protest in Washington, DC that gained hundreds of thousands of participants, hundreds of smaller protests around the country, and expanded the movement efforts to include youth voter registration drives.

The makings of this movement actually began while the shooting was still in progress. Inside the school, one student, David Hogg, recorded himself urging others to take a stance on gun laws and policies for the lives of children.[34] Once the school was cleared, Hogg found a news truck and gave his first interview to further his plea. Concurrently, other students used their personal social media platforms (Facebook, Instagram, and Twitter) to advocate for the same issue through the use of personal reflection and hashtag creation. These students were joined by others in the coming days to strategize a plan forward.

This plan included creating an official website to articulate the movement's agenda, creating social media accounts for the student leaders who didn't already have one, creating memes and other social media content to address the National Rifle Association and politicians that supported the organization, and staging the largest youth-centered protest ever in Washington, DC. In addition to their knowledge and usage of social media, the leaders of the MFOL movement took an inventory of the political environment and capitalized on it to advance their agenda. For example, they understood the younger generation's voting power, and decided to expand their causes to include voter registration. They embarked on the "Road to Change" voter registration bus tours to encourage youth to register to vote.

Furthermore, MFOL co-hosted a gun safety forum in 2020 with Giffords, a gun reform advocacy group, considering that gun violence was a leading issue for the presidential candidates at the time. MFOL leaders included other tactics such as online petitions and the creation of a "Peace Plan" outlining a more transformative gun control policy. The MFOL movement is not only an example of using social and digital media to bring awareness to the movement's agenda, but also of how to use strategy to go beyond awareness. These students moved beyond social and activated thousands of others in the movement through strategy meetings, brainstorming sessions, and connecting with larger organizations.[35]


## Black Lives Matter and Its Resurgence

The Black Lives Matter (BLM) movement may be one of the most recent and notable cases of race-related social and digital media activism. Making its first official appearance on social media in 2013, this movement has been likened to the 1960s Civil Rights movement, advocating for the racial justices of African-Americans. In the case of the Black Lives Matter movement in particular, activists advocated for justice against state-sanctioned brutality experienced by African-Americans. The resurgence of the Black Lives Matter movement in the summer of 2020, however, was strikingly different from its beginnings on Facebook and Twitter after the shooting deaths of Trayvon Martin and Michael Brown, respectively. In both instances, social and digital platforms were used as the means to circulate context related to the shootings, images of the victims, and pertinent mobilization information for protestors and other activists. While the deaths of Ahmaud Arbery, Breonna Taylor, and George Floyd initiated the same activation from activists (circulating context, images, and mobilization information), they also stimulated global outcry, corporate attention, and other niche campaigns.

Although the deaths of Arbery in February and Taylor in March gained media attention, neither compared to the global coverage of Floyd's death just a few months later, in May 2020. This could partially be attributed to the lack of video evidence (at the time) of the previous murders. Yet it could also be attributed to the strategic leverage of the COVID-19 health crisis. During this time, global citizens were mandated to quarantine indoors out of extreme caution about the highly contagious coronavirus. Everyone was tuned in to the news and social media platforms for the latest pandemic updates on the strength of mandate orders. Those who otherwise might not have considered the racial injustices experienced by African-Americans in the United States were alerted to these realities as news of Floyd's murder was circulating concurrently with health notifications. The undeniable imagery of Floyd being held down for 8 minutes and 46 seconds with a knee to his neck sparked global outrage.

Citizens from all over the world participated in marches and protests in honor of Floyd, with estimates of 15–26 million participants, propelling BLM to the largest movement in US history to date. In addition to global outcry, corporations began to take a stance on racial issues. Dissimilar to other contentious issues in the past, there was a huge increase in **corporate social advocacy**. Corporations did not shy away from showing their support for racial equality, Black lives, and BLM. Netflix and Facebook, for example, expressed their support through statements, financial donations, and other initiatives. Netflix set in motion a "Black Lives Matter Collection" for Black storytellers, later categorized as "Black Stories," on its streaming platform, while Facebook, another major corporation, donated $10 million to organizations supporting and campaigning for racial justice.

Finally, the resurgence of BLM demonstrates noteworthy differences due to the multiple campaigns that unfolded as a result. Hashtag campaigns such as #BlackOutTuesday, #IAmABlackMan, and #ShareTheMicNow generated segmented conversations of the larger BLM movement. #BlackOutTuesday was an initiative commenced by the music industry with the sole purpose of halting business operations. On June 2, 2020, black squares appeared on Instagram as a statement of solidarity for BLM and #BlackOutTuesday. Although well intended, the campaign was deemed performative and a distraction as the #BlackOutTuesday hashtag was used in the same conversations as #BlackLivesMatter. This prevented essential movement information from circulating.

However, many businesses halted their operations for the day, stating that they had given their employees the day off to reflect and participate in social justice initiatives. #IAmABlackMan was another hashtag campaign that catalyzed race-related conversations. This initiative challenged Black men to post pictures of themselves with a caption aimed at highlighting the positives of Black men. Its purpose was to counter the negative and stereotypical narratives of African-American men that typically circulate throughout the media. Images of Black men in all of their "Black boy joy" circulated on social media platforms such as Facebook, Instagram, and Twitter in an effort to uplift Black men after Floyd's murder.

Lastly, #ShareTheMicNow was a hashtag campaign on Instagram with the sole purpose of amplifying the voices of Black women. White women celebrities and influencers relinquished control of their social media pages to Black women activists and influencers with smaller followings. Through this initiative, Black women used digital storytelling to share their experiences, provide resources, and educate others about allyship and anti-racism. All of these niche initiatives that were expounded through the BLM resurgence helped to generate meaningful and timely conversations that had otherwise gone unheard.

## Future of Social and Digital Media Activism

In normal societal progression, with new technology comes new and enhanced daily communication practices. Technology is certainly enhancing the world of activism and social justice – as we can see with current social mediated practices. Beyond social media, there are new and emerging media that are finding new ways of enhancing activism in social and digital media.

### Technology and Activism

Increased uses for technology in activism have allowed citizen-level participation in more effective strategies for activation. Placing social justice in the hands of many in society can be an effective way to balance power between citizens and government entities. For instance, phone camera technologies have improved such that that citizens can not only film corrupt and violent behaviors by law enforcement officers, but also now have the capability to stream live video footage via social media to give national and international audiences firsthand views of various injustices, making what would usually be an unbelievable headline a clear visual that can be confirmed by all witnessing. George Floyd was a prominent case in point.

The videotaping of his death was captured in real time, and folks around the world were able to witness and replay the violent act for themselves – causing international uproar surrounding racism and violent acts against Black, indigenous, and people of color globally.

Additionally, as the world of social interaction online advances, we have new forms of digital media that enhance our reality and even immerse us in fully digital realities. These mixed arrays of media are often clustered in a group as mixed reality; however, the two most prominent forms of immersive media are augmented reality and virtual reality. Together and separately, they both offer a new frontier for the world of activism and social justice in digital spaces.

### Augmented Reality

Augmented reality (AR) is most notably used on social media platforms like Instagram, Snapchat, and TikTok in the form of filters. AR filters offer more than just an enhancement in color, they also feature graphic and stylized images that augment our reality. For instance, you can have bunny ears, a hat, and a scarf, or look like a creature from a Disney movie all by using an AR filter created by developers for various social media platforms. These filters used to be exclusive to larger companies with access to resources. However, now anyone with software like Spark AR can create their own AR filter for social media. AR filters can also be used for spreading messages about social justice causes on social media platforms. After the murders of Ahmad Arbury, Briana Taylor, and George Floyd, AR filters like the "Say Their Names" filter were accessible on Instagram. The filter would transparently overlay on anyone's face and display a plethora of Black, Indigenous people of color (BIPOC) names who were murdered in racially motivated incidences.

Additionally, AR can be used in more flatform ways, like for scanning quick response (QR) codes. QR codes are usually a cluster of shapes within a square that, when scanned by a phone's camera, can produce a website and/or app redirection link. Although not as sophisticated as AR filters, QR codes still have the opportunity to be used for SDMA. Jill Collen Jefferson, founder of the Julian Legal Civil Rights and Human Right law firm, has stated that QR codes will be featured in a larger plan to help citizens scan codes that will be placed throughout areas where racism and police brutality are most prevalent to help citizens there have access to a quick way of reporting an incident.[36] People who witness an injustice can film what has happened, scan a nearby QR code, and upload the video directly to an app for reporting and legal advice. Opportunities for use of technological advancements in SDMA practices increase chances for community-driven change and influence. The use of AR can empower members of any community or group to act as opportunities to spread information through filters or QR codes are right at their fingertips.

## Virtual Reality

A world of virtual reality (VR) technology exists alongside current AR technological progressions. In the past ten years alone, VR has progressed from a pretty inaccessible form of hardware to being as accessible as a gaming system. Larger SDM companies like Facebook and Google have played a huge role in the progression of access to VR headsets and software. In 2017, Facebook launched its first VR headset, the Oculus.[37] Since then, there have been several variations, and the latest version cost less than most gaming systems, making it largely accessible to many across the United States. Additionally, the Oculus can connect to each person's Facebook account helping to infuse the digital media technology right into everyday social media use.[38]

The importance of the progression of VR and the fact that more people can use it on a daily basis will have a huge effect on the future of SDMA. In recent years, VR has been called an empathy machine because of its ability to not only share visual content, but immerse a user in a virtual situation, giving them much more of a realistic view of any presented scenario.[39] Today, there are many apps and 360-degree videos (videos that provide a complete and surrounding view of virtual scenes) that have been created to show users what it might be like to experience a day in the life in economically disadvantaged parts of the world or what it might be like to move about life as a member of a different racial/ethnic group. In one video, there is a reenactment of an African-American male being pulled over by a police officer during a traffic stop.[40] The video helps to display all of the different aspects of what can happen, in terms of discrimination when African-Americans get pulled over. Another effective VR video follows the experience of a young African British girl with autism.[41] It shows the viewer a 360-degree view of what she sees and hears during a simulation of a party, and allows the viewer to experience the emotion of her actions through each scene – giving a much more empathy-led understanding of autism. For non-BIPOC experiencing these, it can provide a more realistic experience of witnessing various forms of systemic racism that impact feelings and emotions much more than a news video or article headline.

The opportunities AR and VR have to (1) be accessible forms of cellular and household technology and (2) provide emotion-impacting immersive experiences have a great chance of progressing the future of SDMA. It means that users can share immersive experiences that work to challenge and change people's perceptions of negative societal occurrences. Additionally, these advanced and varied ways of using accessible technology may provide more empowerment for users to take action (even if only a few clicks on a device) to limit the number of bystanders who feel powerless while witnessing social injustices in digital spaces.

## Social and Digital Media Activism Best Practices

### Best Practice – Lean on History

When building future SDMA practices, it will be important for practitioners, citizens, and researchers to learn about and lean on what incidents and actions have taken place in the past. Activism is still a social approach to achieving change that is human-centered, regardless of whether the process of implementation takes place physically or digitally. Therefore, it will be pivotal for future SDMA approaches to build upon past activism to create a more solid foundation for successful digital efforts. For instance, in the 1960s Civil Rights era, effective protest organization was largely done via word of mouth. Even though technological advancements exist, we are still communicating via spreading messages to one another in digital spaces. So it will be important for SDMA organizers to envision word-of-mouth practices which are effective in mobilizing national and international communities toward an effort and can be translated into future digital forms of activism.

### Best Practice – Create Effective Strategies

It is common to think that activist efforts using social and digital media happen overnight or suddenly. However, these efforts are similar to traditional (historic) activist efforts, in that they are strategic. Effective social and digital media activist efforts have been strategized and follow a plan of action that attempts to move beyond the digital. Examples of utilizing strategy in SDMA are the use of hashtags and immersive technology.

### Hashtags

Using hashtags on social media are a great way to connect and archive conversations and to increase visibility of vital social movement information. They are a great way for SDMA organizers to house specific movements in accessible categories for users to find on various digital platforms.

*Immersive Technology*

The use of immersive technology like AR and VR can have a great effect on inciting change in viewpoints and perceptions. This could be a pivotal opportunity within SDMA that helps to increase empathy and even action based-upon the ability of immersive technology to potentially impact emotions.

### Best Practice – Advancing Cultural Systems within Technology

In the future of SDMA practices, it is going to be especially important to uproot old practices and create new ones that are not impacted by systematic racism. Otherwise, those old racially inequitable practices will get woven into the foundations of the new technology we use. There will be an extreme need for more diversity in the creation of technology used for SDMA to avoid one-sided approaches to activism that are inherently designed to oppress minorities. Such instances can be seen even in the design of the VR headsets. The straps to secure the headsets were predominantly designed by persons with short hair, thus there is no consideration for persons with longer hair who have to adjust their hair into a low bun in order to wear the technology. Similar occurrences can happen with technology if certain considerations about accessibility and economic status are not included into the foundation of new technologies.

## Conclusion

SDM have had a great impact on the way citizens, practitioners, and researchers enact and view activism approaches. Social media has created opportunities for global communities to connect and unite to effect change across the world. New emerging media like AR and VR are helping to change perceptions and viewpoints toward social justice that could otherwise be complicated to achieve through discourse and online coverage. Our global societal efforts to advance various injustices – from race to gender and sexuality – have come on in tremendous leaps and bounds from the 1960s to now. There will always be challenges to increasing efforts to fight social justice; however, technology has allowed so much opportunity and headway for activists of all kinds to create activations and mobilize communities toward action. The future of SDMA is considerably bright as long as the past can be continually reviewed and regarded in the creation of future practices. Citizens, practitioners, and researchers can use this body of research as an overview to expound upon within future discourse and movement-building around activism and social justice.

## Reflections

This chapter illuminates activism's progression from historical movements like the Civil Rights movement to contemporary ones like MFOL. Strategic planning and implementation have proven to be invaluable, whether through grassroots initiatives, corporate social advocacy, or other forms of enactment. SDMA is perhaps an answer to injustices and strife that historically marginalized populations have faced and continue to endure. It is evident that SDMA combines much of the solid strategy of historical activism with the benefits of social media virality, creating lasting awareness and behavioral changes that transcend online boundaries into the physical space, ultimately in hopes of reclaiming wholeness. Wholeness is this space can and will look like a multitude of actions, movements, and scenarios. There is always the presence of negativity whenever a great opportunity emerges. However, with the power of SDMA, social movements have the opportunity to be stronger and more widespread. For the future of SDMA, the concept of wholeness invites a whole world of possibilities for unity.

To aid in the digestion of this chapter, we provide a few questions to reflect upon as each reader explores how they have witnessed or engaged in activism online and/or are inspired to make future plans toward positive digital activism:

- In your opinion, how have historical movements, like the Civil Rights movement, paved the way for current SDMA movements?
- In terms of intersectionality, what are the intersections in your life that provide you with advantages and/or disadvantages? Do you perceive these intersections as positive or negative?
- When you think about the future of SDMA, what ways do you think technology can be used to improve online activism?
- How, if at all, do you plan to practice activism and/or social justice in your daily digital life? This could be anything from reporting cyberbullying to planning a digital-led activism event or group.

## Notes

1 Gerbaudo, P., and E. Treré. "In search of the 'we' of social media activism: Introduction to the special issue on social media and protest identities." *Information, Communication and Society* 18, no. 8 (2015): 865–871.
2 Masur, Kate. "Decades before the Civil War, Black activists organized for racial equality." *Smithsonian Magazine*, March 24, 2021. https://www.smithsonianmag.com/history/decades-civil-war-black-activists-organized-racial-equality-180977321/.
3 Errick, Jennifer. "5 facts you might not know about Harriet Tubman." National Parks Conservation Association, February 8, 2022. https://www.npca.org/articles/2314-5-facts-you-might-not-know-about-harriet-tubman.

4  Gates, Jr., Henry Louis. "Did African-American slaves rebel?" PBS. Accessed December 16, 2022. https://www.pbs.org/wnet/african-americans-many-rivers-to-cross/history/did-african-american-slaves-rebel/.

5  Janken, Kenneth R. "The Civil Rights movement: 1919–1960s." Freedom's Story. Accessed December 16, 2022. http://nationalhumanitiescenter.org/tserve/freedom/1917beyond/essays/crm.htm#:~:text=National%20Association%20for%20the%20Advancement,Nonviolent%20Coordinating%20Committee%20(SNCC).

6  Maranzani, Barbara. "Martin Luther King Jr. and Malcolm X only met once." Biography, January 19, 2021. https://www.biography.com/news/martin-luther-king-jr-malcolm-x-meeting.

7  "Women's suffrage." History, March 28, 2023. https://www.history.com/topics/womens-history/the-fight-for-womens-suffrage.

8  Rampton, Martha. "Four waves of feminism." Pacific University Oregon October 25, 2015. https://www.pacificu.edu/magazine/four-waves-feminism.

9  "Women's rights," ACLU. Accessed December 16, 2022. https://www.aclu.org/issues/womens-rights.

10 Mahre, Rachel. "LGBT issues in the 1980s: Building coalitions and consensus in Seattle." City of Seattle. Accessed December 16, 2022. https://www.seattle.gov/cityarchives/exhibits-and-education/digital-document-libraries/lgbt-issues-in-the-1980s.

11 Mallenbaum, Carly, Jane Ackermann, and Becky Murray. "The history of queer stigma – and how it affects the community's mental health today." theSkimm, February 24, 2022. https://www.theskimm.com/pride/history-gay-lgbtq-queer-stigma-mental-health.

12 ADL Education. "A brief history of the Disability Rights Movement." ADL, May 3, 2022. https://www.adl.org/resources/backgrounder/brief-history-disability-rights-movement?gclid=CjwKCAiAy_CcBhBeEiwAcoMRHNHV_6nPZudnQo6eU-GDKMryAvtAfPM9grMfgXLN5Vik38DsuPxiBRoCHzwQAvD_BwE.

13 "ADA standards for accessible design." American Disabilities Association. Accessed December 16, 2022. https://www.ada.gov/law-and-regs/design-standards/.

14 "A short history of SNAP." US Department of Agriculture, September 11, 2018. https://www.fns.usda.gov/snap/short-history-snap#:~:text=Among%20the%20official%20purposes%20of,enact%20the%20regulations%20into%20law.

15 Moore, Brett. "10 charities that fight hunger worldwide." The Spruce Eats, July 22, 2021. https://www.thespruceeats.com/charities-that-fight-hunger-1666012.

16 Pine, Adam. "Food system activism and the housing crisis." Journal of Agriculture, Food Systems, and Community Development 11, no. 3 (2022): 13–17.

17 Kleven, Thomas. "Systemic classism, systemic racism: Are social and racial justice achievable in the United States?" Connecticut Public Interest Law Journal 8, no. 2 (2009): 37–83.

18 White Hughto, Jaclyn M., Sari L. Reisner, and John E. Pachankis. "Transgender stigma and health: A critical review of stigma determinants, mechanisms, and interventions." Social Science and Medicine 147 (2015): 222–231.

19 "What is intersectionality?" Center for Intersectional Justice. Accessed December 16, 2022. https://www.intersectionaljustice.org/what-is-intersectionality.

20 "The Underground Railroad." *National Geographic*, May 20, 2022. https:// education.nationalgeographic.org/resource/underground-railroad.
21 Jackson, Ashawnta. "How civil rights groups used photography for change." JSTOR Daily, February 1, 2021. https://daily.jstor.org/how-civil-rights-groups -used-photography-for-change/.
22 Samur, Alexandra. "The history of social media: 29+ key moments." *Hootsuite Blog*, November 22, 2018. https://blog.hootsuite.com/history -social-media/.
23 Riddle, Jason. "All too easy: Spreading information through social media." University of Arkansas Little Rock, March 1, 2017. https://ualr.edu/social- change/2017/03/01/blog-riddle-social-media/.
24 Hu, Jane. "The second act of social-media activism." *The New Yorker*, August 3, 2020. https://www.newyorker.com/culture/cultural-comment/the-second -act-of-social-media-activism.
25 Di Sabatino, Alyssa. "Cyntoia Brown's case shows how internet activism can pay off." *The Cord*, January 16, 2019. https://thecord.ca/cyntoia-browns-case -shows-how-internet-activism-can-pay-off/.
26 Bosman, Julie, and Joseph Goldstein. "Timeline for a body: 4 hours in the middle of a Ferguson street." *New York Times*, August 23, 2014. https://www .nytimes.com/2014/08/24/us/michael-brown-a-bodys-timeline-4-hours-on-a -ferguson-street.html.
27 "Timeline of events in shooting of Michael Brown in Ferguson." Associated Press, August 8, 2019. https://apnews.com/article/shootings-police-us-news-st -louis-michael-brown-9aa32033692547699a3b61da8fd1fc62.
28 Mackey, Robert. "Advice for Ferguson's protesters from the Middle East." *New York Times*, August 14, 2014. https://www.nytimes.com/2014/08/15/ world/middleeast/advice-for-fergusons-protesters-from-the-middle-east.html.
29 Dookhoo, Sasha, and Melissa Dodd. "Slacktivists or activists? Millennial motivations and behaviors for engagement in activism." *Public Relations Journal* 13, no. 1 (2019). https://instituteforpr.org/slacktivists-or-activists -millennial-motivations-and-behaviors-for-engagement-in-activism/.
30 Parrish, Candace, et al. 2022. "You can start a movement with a hashtag: An exploration of student-led social media activism." In Lisa M. Cuklanz (ed.), *Gender Violence, Social Media, and Online Environments: When the Virtual Becomes Real*. London: Routledge, pp. 170–191..
31 "Social media tools to help stop cyberbullying." HughesNet. December 16, 2022. https://www.hughesnet.com/blog/social-media-tools-help-stop -cyberbullying.
32 Ohlheiser, Abby. "The woman behind 'Me Too' knew the power of the phrase when she created it – 10 Years ago." *Washington Post*, October 26, 2021. https://www.washingtonpost.com/news/the-intersect/wp/2017/10/19/the -woman-behind-me-too-knew-the-power-of-the-phrase-when-she-created-it -10-years-ago/.
33 Stone, Meighan, and Rachel Vogelstein. "Celebrating #MeToo's global impact." *Foreign Policy*, March 7, 2019. https://foreignpolicy.com/2019/03 /07/metooglobalimpactinternationalwomens-day/.
34 "The March for Our Lives activists showed us how to find meaning in trag- edy." *Smithsonian Magazine*, December 1, 2018. https://www.smithsonian- mag.com/innovation/march-for-our-lives-student-activists-showed-meaning -tragedy-180970717/.
35 Edrington, Candice L. "Social movements and identification: An examination of how Black Lives Matter and March for Our Lives use identification strategies

on Twitter to build relationships." *Journalism & Mass Communication Quarterly* 99, no. 3 (2022): 643–659.

36 Collen Jefferson, Jill. "The future of civil rights," Julian Legal Civil Rights and Human Rights. Accessed December 16, 2022. https://www.julianlegal.com/about.

37 Morby, Alice. "Facebook launches virtual-reality headset that can be used without other devices." *Dezeen*, October 13, 2017. https://www.dezeen.com/2017/10/13/facebook-oculus-go-virtual-reality-vr-headset-technology/.

38 McAllistor, Matt. "15 things you can do with your Oculus Quest VR headset." *Adoroma*, June 10, 2022. https://www.adorama.com/alc/to-do-oculus-quest-vr-headset/.

39 Wang, Shanshan, Candace Parrish, and James Castonguay. 2022. "Virtual reality, empathy, solidarity." In Belinha S. De Abreu (ed.), *Media Literacy, Equity, and Justice*. New York: Routledge, pp. 229–234.

40 "The Messy Truth VR experience." *The Messy Truth*. Accessed December 16, 2022. https://www.messytruth.com/vr.

41 The Guardian. "The Party: A virtual experience of autism – 360 film." YouTube video, 07:21, October 17, 2017. https://www.youtube.com/watch?v=OtwOz1GVkDg&list=PLMyQHHP63gpfjTxmXhOPPOS8Ech00caIW&index=3.

# ADVOCATES FOR ACTION

## Wilma Pearl Mankiller

1945–2010
Hometown: Tahlequah, Oklahoma, USA
Movement: Indigenous peoples' rights
Organizations: Native American Youth Center, Oakland, USA
*Allison Schuster, Claire Zoller, and Allison De Young*

Wilma Pearl Mankiller was an admired Cherokee woman who spent her life fighting for the rights of Indigenous peoples. "As the Cherokee Nation's first female chief, she transformed the Nation-to-Nation relationship between the Cherokee Nation and the Federal Government and served as an inspiration to women in Indian Country and across America," said former President Barack Obama of the fearless activist.[1] As the first woman elected as chief of any major Native tribe, she tirelessly advocated for improved education, healthcare, and housing services for her community.[2] Inspired by the Indigenous peoples' takeover of Alcatraz in 1969, Mankiller strived to empower Indigenous communities as Director of Oakland's Native American Youth Center. She understood the importance of education and pride in social movements, and thus prioritized the restoration of pride in Indigenous heritage for the youth.[3]

In 1977, Mankiller founded the Community Development Department for the Cherokee Nation, which strived to increase Indigenous access to water and housing.[4] Utilizing effective persuasive and engaging communication styles, Mankiller was so successful in her projects that she was named Deputy Principal Chief and, soon after, Principal Chief of the Cherokee Nation in 1985. As a result of her significant achievements

DOI: 10.4324/9781003291855-29

during her life, Mankiller was recognized as the *Ms.* Magazine Woman of the Year in 1987. Just six years later, she was inducted into the National Women's Hall of Fame, followed shortly by receiving the honored Presidential Medal of Freedom from President Bill Clinton.[5] In 2010, Mankiller passed away at age 64 from cancer. Gloria Steinem, a fellow women's rights activist and a personal friend, spoke of her legacy, saying "ancient traditions call for setting signal fires to light the way home for a great one; fires were lit in 23 countries after Wilma's death. The millions she touched will continue her work."[6]

## Notes

1 Brando, Elizabeth. n.d. "Biography: Wilma Mankiller." National Women's History Museum. Accessed December 29, 2022. https://www.womenshistory.org/education-resources/biographies/wilma-mankiller.
2 "Four Native women leaders you should know about." n.d. Vision Maker Media. Accessed December 29, 2022. https://visionmakermedia.org/four-native-women-leaders.
3 Carpenter Jr, R. R. (2005). *The time of the butterfly: Native American women's autobiography in the twentieth century.* The University of Utah.
4 Mankiller, Wilma. "Rebuilding the Cherokee nation." Speech given at Sweet Briar College, Sweet Briar, VA (1993). https://awpc.cattcenter.iastate.edu/2017/03/21/rebuilding-the-cherokee-nation-april-2-1993/
5 Shioshvili, Tamar. "American women making breakthrough in the arenas of politics and government." *Journal in Humanities* 10, no. 1 (2021): 64–68.
6 Stogsdill, Sheila. "Gloria Steinem reflects on friendship with Wilma Mankiller." *The Oklahoman*, April 8, 2010. https://www.oklahoman.com/story/news/politics/2010/04/08/gloria-steinem-reflects-on-friendship-with-wilma-mankiller/61264327007/

# GLOSSARY

**Activism:** The policy or action of using vigorous campaigning to bring about political or social change.

**Activist:** A person or organization that campaigns to bring about political or social change.

**Advocacy:** Speaking out on behalf of a person, group, or organization as it relates to social, political, and cultural issues.

**Agenda Melding:** The theory which allows scholars to analyze how media users find and use blended forms of information from various platforms

**Agenda-Setting Theory:** A theory that explains that media has a large influence on audiences by choosing which stories to make prominent.

**Algorithmic Resistance:** Media users' resistance to algorithmic power – that is, the control behind the algorithm.

**Arab Spring:** A series of protests and activities that took place in North Africa and the Middle East beginning in 2010–2011.

**Argument:** A claim warranted by some data or evidence. Also the process of two or more people reasoning together by exchanging claims and evidence.

**Assumption:** An idea or belief about what is true that has been accepted without evidence, or with limited evidence.

**Augmented Reality (AR):** A form of digital media technology that lays over our view of reality to enhance or alter visuals in real-world or digital spaces.

**Belonging:** One's sense of attachment to a group, a basic human need.

**Bias:** Interpersonal dimensions of systemic oppression like racism, (cis) sexism, homophobia, ableism, and so on that are usually enacted unconsciously

**Clicktivism:** Supporting a political or social cause via the internet by means such as social media or online petitions, typically characterized as involving little effort or commitment.

**Collective Action (CA):** Action taken together by a group of people whose goal is to enhance their conditions and achieve a common objective.

**Collective Identity:** The shared definition of a group that derives from its members' common interests, experiences, and solidarities.

**Computational Social Science:** An emerging field that integrates social science theories and research methods with data science/computational methods.

**Corporate Social Advocacy (CSA):** An organization making a public statement or taking a public stance on social-political issues.

**Counterpublic/Subaltern Counterpublic:** A discursive community consisting of marginalized people that develops in parallel to the dominant, hegemonic, public sphere.

**Demagoguery:** A communicative culture that restricts public discourse to three stages – group identity, need, and punishing the outgroup – thus making policy argumentation challenging

**Democracy:** When citizens of a country take an active role in managing their country by electing representatives.

**Demonstration:** A physical gesture or performance that can be secretive or publicized, ranging from marches and protests to secret meetings and/or escape routes.

**Digital Immigrant:** Someone who lived their formative years before the widespread use of technology and the internet.

**Digital Native:** Someone who has grown up only knowing technology and the internet.

**Digital Press Room:** A Web page featuring materials like press releases and company news, meant for the press.

**Digital Repression:** Targeting of online voices of dissent which include these three areas: online activists suffering from traditional repressive actions, digital tools used to oppress protests in traditional ways, and digital tools used to suppress activists in innovative ways.

**Disinformation:** False information which is intended to mislead, especially propaganda issued by a government organization to a rival power or the media.

**Epistemology:** Investigation of what distinguishes justified belief from opinion.

**Exposure:** The frequency and time frame of content's appearance on a media platform.

**Femicide or _Feminicidio_:** A term centralizing the experiences of Mexican (and also Latin American) women to include killing of women based on their gender.

**Framing Theory:** A theory that suggests that how something is presented to the audience, called "the frame," influences the choices people make about how to process the information. Related to the ability of news media to influence people's attitudes and behaviors by subtle changes to how they report on an issue.

**Gatekeeper**: A person or organization that controls access to the media and decides if a story or news item will be published, posted, or aired on a TV or radio station.

**Global Communication**: Communication which transcends international borders, often through social media.

**Global Village**: Marshall McLuhan's term that describes the phenomenon of the entire world becoming more interconnected as the result of global media technologies.

Iranian **Green Movement or Green Wave of Iran**: A social movement that broke out in 2009 after Iranian leader Mahmoud Ahmadinejad declared victory over challenger Mir Hossein Moussavi.

**Group Cohesion**: The solidarity of a group, evident by how closely members are linked to the group as a whole.

**Group Theories**: Theories of how people feel (affect), act (behavior), and think (cognition) in group settings, and how people are influenced by each other in social situations. Broadly divided into intergroup theories and intragroup process theories, addressing topics such as prejudice and stereotypes, social identities, and organizations.

**Hashtag**: A word or phrase preceded by a hash sign (#), used on social media sites and applications, especially Twitter, to identify digital content on a specific topic.

**Hashtag Activism**: The use of Twitter's hashtags for internet activism.Heteronormity: A social phenomenon that propagates the idea that heterosexuality is superior.

**Horrorism**: A focus on the suffering and powerlessness of victims and senseless violence against them.

**Mainstream Media**: Media (not social media platforms) consisting of newspapers, magazines, television, and radio outlets.

**Media Ecology**: A theory about the study of media, technology, and communication and how they affect human environments. Theoretical concepts were proposed by Marshall McLuhan in 1964, while the term media "ecology" was first formally introduced by Neil Postman in 1968.

**Mediated Activism**: A form of activism that is non-physical, but exists in the form of social campaigns via advertising, radio, television, and social/digital media.

**Mediated Mobilization**: Social movements and community organizing facilitated through the use of social media tools.

**Meta (Facebook)**: A social media platform founded in 2004 that allows users to connect with others.

**Minority Influence**: The process by which minority members of a group change the norm of majority members and introduce a new norm.

**Misinformation**: False or inaccurate information, especially that which is deliberately intended to deceive.

**Mobilizing:** A process by which inspirational leaders or other persuaders can encourage a large number of people to join a movement or engage in a particular movement action.

**Myspace:** Launched in 2003, the first social network to reach a global audience. It has had a significant influence on technology, pop culture, and music.

**Narrative:** The different ways media can tell a story.

**Netroots Activism:** A term coined in 2002 by Jerome Armstrong to describe political activism organized through blogs and other online media, including wikis and social network services.

**Networked Social Movement:** A type of networked politics, characterized as the decentralized or leaderless organization of various parties in a social movement.

**News Values:** Criteria that influence the selection and presentation of events as published news.

**Newsgathering:** The process of researching news items for publication.

**Noise:** Anything that imposes a block between a message source and an intended target audience.

**Occupy Wall Street:** A series of protests in defiance of economic inequality which started in New York City in 2011 and spread around the globe

**Online Social Movements:** Organized efforts to push for a particular goal through the use of new communications and information technologies, such as the internet.

**Oppression:** The social act of placing severe restrictions on an individual, group, or institution.

**Organizing:** A practice aimed at helping people create the social movements and political organizations necessary to wage campaigns and win power.

**Other:** A term describing the labeling of a person as a subaltern native, belonging to a socially subordinate category of the Other.

**Outcome:** A measure of the effect of communication or other actions on the target audience.

**Outputs:** Actions rather than changes resulting from those actions.

**Persuasion:** A process in which communication artifacts attempt to evoke change among an audience

**Place Attachment:** A theory that extends belonging to characterize people's bonding to a place or a community through their ABC: affect (A), behavior (B), and cognition (C). Also referred to as psychological place attachment.

**Popcorn Activism:** Quick-to-react but slow-to-sustain activist efforts, often occurring when an issue is "hot" in the media and falters because the efforts are not coordinated or organized.

**Public Opinion:** Collective opinion on a specific topic relevant to a society. People's views on matters affecting them.

**Publicity Stunt:** A planned event designed to attract the public's attention, often through media coverage, to the event's organizers or their cause.

**Rhetoric:**   A collective art of determining problems within and solutions for specific historical, social, and political situations.

**Self-Publishing:**   Publication of media by its author without the involvement of an established publisher.

**Sentiment:**   Feelings (attitudes, beliefs, emotions) expressed about a topic or event, most often through social media communication.

**Slacktivism:**   The practice of supporting a political or social cause by means such as social media or online petitions, characterized as involving very little effort or commitment.

**Social Algorithm:**   A method used by social media platforms to sift through all the content that gets posted every day to decide what posts are publicized and what posts are buried.

**Social Movement:**   A loosely organized effort by a large group of people to achieve a particular goal, typically a social or political one.

**Social Movement Coalition:**   Distinct activist organizations pooling resources and working together toward a common goal.

**Solidarity:**   Unity or agreement of feeling or action, especially among individuals with a common interest; mutual support within a group.

**Stakeholder:**   People or organizations that have a "stake" in a company, organization, or social movement. They may include activists, protestors, supporters, employees, voters, and more. A stakeholder may also be an individual or organization that opposes a cause, as they too have a stake in it.

**State Repression:**   Actions of key institutions related to suppressing contention. It includes both national and local state coercive authorities such as militaries and law enforcement, and bureaucracies such as tax authorities.

**Status Quo:**   The existing situation, especially regarding social or political issues.

**Stigma:**   A socially created conceptualization of an individual or group of individuals that deems the person or group "other" based on the possession of some shared attribute considered undesirable

**Tabloid:**   A small-format newspaper dominated by headlines, photographs, and sensational stories.

**Theory of Change:**   A method used in planning, participation, adaptive management, and evaluation used by organizations, companies, and individuals to promote social change.

**Transnational Alternative Public Spheres:**   Transnationally mediated counter public spaces in which geographically disparate individuals, communities, and organizations come together through similarly aligned networked counter publics.

**Twitter:**   A free social networking site where users broadcast short posts known as tweets. These tweets can contain text, videos, photos, or links.

**Virtual Reality (VR):**   Digital hardware and software that provide an immersive view and experience through virtual and interactive settings.

**Visual Narrative:**   Sometimes referred to as visual storytelling, a story told primarily through the use of visual media. The story may be told using still photography, illustration, or video, and can be enhanced with graphics, music, voice, and other audio.

**Xenophobia:**   An extreme and illogical fear of foreigners and their beliefs or practices.

# INDEX

Printed in the United States
by Baker & Taylor Publisher Services